A Guide to Conclusive Proofs FOR THE *Principles of Belief*

CENTER FOR MUSLIM CONTRIBUTION TO CIVILIZATION

The Center for Muslim Contribution to Civilization, a non-government, non-profit making cultural organization, strives to lead Muslims and non-Muslims alike to a better understanding of the Muslim contribution to civilization and to a better knowledge of Islam.

Located in Doha, State of Qatar, the Center has the warm support of its patron, the Emir of Qatar, H.H. Sheikh Hamad Bin Khalifa Al-Thani. Presenting accurate translations of some of the best known works of the most eminent Muslim savants, spanning the 800 years of the classical period of Islamic civilization (*c*. 620 AD to *c*. 1500 AD), since its establishment in 1983 the Center has produced nine volumes covering five major works in different fields of knowledge.

For further information on the work of the Center, all correspondence should be directed to

The General Supervisor
Center for Muslim Contribution to Civilization
P.O. Box 327
Doha
State of Qatar
Arabian Gulf

The Center for Muslim Contribution to Civilization

A Guide to Conclusive Proofs FOR THE *Principles of Belief*

Kitāb al-irshād ilā qawāṭiʿ al-adilla fī uṣūl al-iʿtiqād

Imām al-Ḥaramayn al-Juwaynī

Translated by Dr Paul E. Walker

Reviewed by Dr Muhammad S. Eissa

Garnet
PUBLISHING

A GUIDE TO CONCLUSIVE PROOFS FOR THE PRINCIPLES OF BELIEF

Published by
Garnet Publishing Limited
8 Southern Court
South Street
Reading
RG1 4QS
UK

First Edition

ISBN 1 85964 157 1

British Library Cataloguing-in-Publication Data
A catalogue record for this book is available from the British Library

Jacket design by David Rose
Typeset by Samantha Barden

Printed in Lebanon

Contents

Foreword xi
About this Series xiii
Center for Muslim Contribution to Civilization: Board of Trustees xv
Center for Muslim Contribution to Civilization: Board xvi
Translator's Preface xvii
Introduction xix

A Guide to Conclusive Proofs for the Principles of Belief

Author's Preface 1
Section: On the Character of Reason 3
Chapters
On the opposition of reasoning to knowledge, ignorance and doubt 4
Sound reasoning and false reasoning 5
On proofs 5
Reasoning is a requirement of the law 5

Section: The True Nature of Knowledge 8
Chapters
Knowledge is both eternal and temporally produced 9
Kinds of knowledge and their contraries 9
Intellect is necessary knowledge 9

Section: The Doctrine of the World's Contingency 11
Chapter
On the proof that the eternal cannot possibly be non-existent 13

Section: A Statement Affirming the Knowledge of the Maker 17

Section: A Statement of What Attributes God Requires 19
Chapters
The proof of the Exalted Creator's eternity 20
God, the Exalted, subsists by Himself 21
One attribute of God is utter difference from the temporally produced 21
On the mutually similar and dissimilar 22
Concerning what cannot be attributed to God 24
That God is not a body, in contrast to the doctrine of the Karrāmiyya 26
That God does not accept accidents 27

Proving the impossibility that the Exalted Lord is a substance (some notes for a refutation of the Christians) 28

Section: The Knowledge of God's Absolute Oneness **31**

Section: Affirming Knowledge of Qualifying Attributes **36**

Chapters

That the Maker of the world is purposeful 37

The Exalted Creator is all-hearing and all-seeing 42

It cannot be said of the Creator, the Exalted, that He can taste and smell and so forth 45

The Lord is perpetual and of continuous existence 45

Section: A Statement Affirming Knowledge of the Attributes **46**

Chapters

On affirming the modes and refuting those who deny them 46

The causation of the necessary and the refutation of those who reject it 48

The will of God is eternal 54

The opinion of Jahm that affirms temporally contingent items of knowledge 55

God speaks, commands and prohibits 56

On the real nature of speech and its definition and meaning 58

The Muʿtazilites deny interior speech 59

That the speaker is the one in whom speech occurs 61

Some doubts of the adversaries 66

That the speech of God is eternal according to the literalists 71

Our creed concerning recitation 72

Our creed concerning what is recited 73

The Exalted God's word does not inhere in copies of the Qurʾān 73

The speech of God is heard 73

The meaning of the revealing of the Exalted God's speech 74

The speech of the Exalted God is one 75

The attributes are not distinct from the essence 75

What we say about the attribute of perpetuity 76

Section: A Statement of the Meaning in the Names of God, the Exalted **78**

Chapters

What should be said about the designation and the name 78

The law and the names of God 79

The meanings of the names of God 79

The two hands, the two eyes, and the face 86

Section: A Statement of What is Possible for God **92**

Section: Proof that the Vision of God is Possible **93**

Chapters
Affirming perception 93
The perceptions are five 96
Every existent may be seen 96
The obstacles to perception 97
The vision of God, the Exalted 97
The vision of the Exalted God will take place in paradise 100
The difference between the vision and smell, feeling, and taste 102

Section: A Statement about the Creation of Acts **103**

Chapters
That the human is not a creator 103
The distinction between the claim upon the servant with respect to his colours and his body versus the claim upon him with respect to his acts 111
On the application of the contingent power to what it empowers 114
On being guided, in error, under seal and stamp 115

Section: The Doctrine of Capacity and Its Characteristic Property **118**

Chapters
The contingent power does not persist 119
Once more on the contingent power 120
The contingent being in the state of coming to be is subject to the power of God, the Exalted 120
What is subject to the contingent power is a single thing 122
On obligating what cannot be done 123
The power over colours, tastes and the like 125
The power of God, the Exalted, to do what will not come to pass 125
Those things that comprise the refutation of the upholders of the doctrine of production 126
Concerning forces and intellects 128
On willing things that come to exist 129
Various arguments of the Muʿtazilites 136
On grace and abandonment 139
On censuring the Proponents of *Qadar* 140

Section: The Doctrine of Justice and Injustice **141**

Chapters
Preliminary points and the issues 141
The good and the bad 141

That neither humans nor God are subject to the obligations of reason 147
On suffering and its characteristics 149
On compensations 152
Again on compensation 152

Section: The Doctrine of the Good and the Best **157**
Chapter
The doctrine of grace 164

Section: A Statement in Proof of the Prophetic Missions **165**
Chapters
On proving the possibility of prophetic missions 165
On prophetic miracles and their conditions 167
On the affirmation of saintly marvels and on distinguishing them from prophetic miracles 172
Sorcery and what is connected with it 175

Section: A Statement of the Way in Which a Miracle Proves the Veracity of the Prophet, God Bless Him and Keep Him **177**
Chapters
That there is no proof of the veracity of the Prophet other than the miracle 180
The impossibility of God lying is a condition in the miracle's proof 180

Section: The Doctrine about Proving the Prophecy of Our Prophet Muḥammad, God Bless Him and Keep Him **184**
Chapters
On abrogation 184
On the miracles of Muḥammad, God bless him and keep him 187
On the various ways the Qurʾān is inimitable 189
The miraculous signs of the apostle, God bless him and keep him, other than the Qurʾān 191

Section: The General Characteristics of the Prophets **193**
Chapters
The doctrine of the prophets' characteristics in general, the blessings of God be upon them all 193
On the impeccability of the prophets 193

Section: The Doctrine Concerning the Evidence from Tradition **195**

Section: On Time Limits **197**

Section: On Subsistence **199**

Section: On Prices **201**

Section: On Commanding the Good and Prohibiting the Reprehensible **202**

Section: On Resurrection **204**

Section: On Various Characteristics of the Afterlife as Stipulated in Tradition **206**

Chapters
On the soul and its significance 207
On paradise and hellfire 207
On the bridge (and the balance, the pool and the pages) 208

Section: On Reward and Punishment, the Spoiling of Human Acts, and the Refutation of the Muʿtazilites, the Khawārij, and the Murjiʾa on the Promise and the Threat **209**

Chapters
On eternal reward 210
On the spoiling of good deeds and the threat 211
A grave sin ruins the reward for acts of obedience according to the Muʿtazilites 213
On the difference between venial and grave sins 214
On those who die while persevering in an act of disobedience 215
On intercession 215

Section: On Names and Characteristics **217**

Chapters
On the meaning of faith 217
The increase of faith and its diminution 218

Section: On Repentance **220**

Chapters
On the acceptance of contrition 221
The necessity of contrition 221
On contrition for some sins but not others 222
On the renewal of repentance 223
Is the new found faith in an unbeliever contrition? 224
On the contrition of a person who reverts to sin 224

Section: The Doctrine of the Imamate **225**

Section: On the Various Categories of Reports in the Tradition 226

Section: On the Denial of Succession to the Imamate by Designation and the Affirmation of Election 231

Section: On Election, Its Characteristics, and How the Imamate is to be Invested 234

Chapters

On investing the imamate in two individuals 234

On deposing the imam 234

On the qualifications for the imamate 235

Section: Our Doctrine Affirms the Imamate of Abū Bakr, ʿUmar, ʿUthmān, and ʿAlī, May God be Pleased with Them All 236

Chapters

On the imamate of the less qualified and the relative superiority of the Companions 237

On the unjust killing of ʿUthmān 238

On the calumny of the Companions 238

On the rule regarding waging war against ʿAlī 239

Bibliography 241

Index 243

Appendix 249

In the Name of God, the Beneficent, the Merciful

FOREWORD

THE interrelationship and interaction of human cultures and civilisations has made the contributions of each the common heritage of men in all ages and all places. Early Muslim scholars were able to communicate with their Western counterparts through contacts made during the Crusades; at Muslim universities and centres of learning in Muslim Spain (al-Andalus, or Andalusia) and Sicily to which many European students went for education; and at the universities and centres of learning in Europe itself (such as Salerno, Padua, Montpellier, Paris, and Oxford), where Islamic works were taught in Latin translations. Among the Muslim scholars well-known in the centres of learning throughout the world were al-Rāzī (Rhazes), Ibn Sīnā (Avicenna), Ibn Rushd (Averroes), al Khwārizmī and Ibn Khaldūn. Muslim scholars such as these and others produced original works in many fields. Many of them possessed encyclopaedic knowledge and distinguished themselves in many disparate fields of knowledge.

In view of this, the Center for Muslim Contribution to Civilization was established in order to acquaint non-Muslims with the contributions Islam has given to human civilisation as a whole. The Great Books of Islamic Civilization Project attempts to cover the first 800 years of Islam, or what may be called Islam's Classical Period. This project aims at making available in English a wide selection of works representative of Islamic civilisation in all its diversity. It is made up of translations of original Arabic works that were produced in the formative centuries of Islam, and is meant to serve the needs of a potentially large readership. Not only the specialist and scholar, but the non-specialist with an interest in Islam and its cultural heritage will be able to benefit from the series. Together, the works should serve as a rich source for the study of the early periods of Islamic thought.

In selecting the books for the series, the Center took into account all major areas of Islamic intellectual pursuit that could be represented. Thus the series includes works not only on better-known subjects such as law, theology, jurisprudence, history and politics, but also on subjects such as literature, medicine, astronomy, optics and geography. The specific criteria, used to select individual books, were these: that a book should give a faithful and comprehensive account of its field; and that it should be an authoritative source. The reader thus has at his disposal virtually a whole library of informative and enlightening works.

Each book in the series has been translated by a qualified scholar and reviewed by another expert. While the style of one translation will naturally differ from another, the translators have endeavoured, to the extent it was possible, to make the works accessible to the common reader. As a rule, the use of footnotes has been kept to a minimum, though a more extensive use of them was necessitated in some cases.

This series is presented in the hope that it will contribute to a greater understanding in the West of the cultural and intellectual heritage of Islam and will therefore provide an important means towards greater understanding of today's world.

May God Help Us!

Muhammad bin Hamad Al-Thani
Chairman of the Board of Trustees

About this Series

This series of Arabic works, made available in English translation, represents an outstanding selection of important Islamic studies in a variety of fields of knowledge. The works selected for inclusion in this series meet specific criteria. They are recognized by Muslim scholars as being early and important in their fields, as works whose importance is broadly recognized by international scholars, and as having had a genuinely significant impact on the development of human culture.

Readers will therefore see that this series includes a variety of works in the purely Islamic sciences, such as Qurʾān, *ḥadīth*, theology, prophetic traditions (*sunna*), and jurisprudence (*fiqh*). Also represented will be books by Muslim scientists on medicine, astronomy, geography, physics, chemistry, horticulture, and other fields.

The work of translating these texts has been entrusted to a group of professors in the Islamic and Western worlds who are recognized authorities in their fields. It has been deemed appropriate, in order to ensure accuracy and fluency, that two persons, one with Arabic as his mother tongue and another with English as his mother tongue, should participate together in the translation and revision of each text.

This series is distinguished from other similar intercultural projects by its distinctive objectives and methodology. These works will fill a genuine gap in the library of human thought. They will prove extremely useful to all those with an interest in Islamic culture, its interaction with Western thought, and its impact on culture throughout the world. They will, it is hoped, fulfil an important rôle in enhancing world understanding at a time when there is such evident and urgent need for the development of peaceful coexistence.

This series is published by the Center for Muslim Contribution to Civilization, which serves as a research centre under the patronage of H.H. Sheikh Hamad bin Khalifa al-Thani, Amir of Qatar. It is directed by a Board of Trustees chaired by H.E. Sheikh Muhammad bin Hamad al-Thani, the former Minister of Education of Qatar. The Board is comprised of a group of prominent scholars. These include H.E. Dr Abul-Wafa al-Taftazani*, Deputy Rector of Cairo University, and Dr Yusuf al-Qaradhawi, Director of the Sira and Sunna Research Center. At its inception the Center was directed by the late Dr Muhammad Ibrahim Kazim, former Rector of Qatar University, who established its initial objectives.

The Center was until recently directed by Dr Kamal Nagi, the Foreign Cultural Relations Advisor of the Ministry of Education of Qatar. He was assisted by a Board comprising a number of academicians of Qatar University, in addition to

* Died 1994, may Allāh have mercy on him.

a consultative committee chaired by Dr Ezzeddin Ibrahim, former Rector of the University of the United Arab Emirates. A further committee acting on behalf of the Center has been the prominent university professors who act under the chairmanship of Dr Raji Rammuny, Professor of Arabic at the University of Michigan. This committee is charged with making known, in Europe and in America, the books selected for translation, and in selecting and enlisting properly qualified university professors, orientalists and students of Islamic studies to undertake the work of translation and revision, as well as overseeing the publication process.

CENTER FOR MUSLIM CONTRIBUTION TO CIVILIZATION

Board of Trustees

H.E. Sheikh Muhammad bin Hamad al-Thani
Chairman

Members

1. H.Eminence Sheikh al-Azhar, Cairo, Arab Republic of Egypt.
2. Director-General of the Islamic Educational, Scientific and Cultural Organization (ISESCO).
3. Director-General of the Arab League Educational, Cultural and Scientific Organization (ALECSO).
4. H.E. the Minister of Education, State of Qatar.
5. H.E. the Minister of Education, Kuwait.
6. H.E. the Minister of Education, Oman.
7. H.E. the Secretary-General of the Muslim World Association, Saudi Arabia.
8. H.E. Dr Ezzeddin Ibrahim, Cultural Advisor to H.H. the President of the U.A.E.
9. Professor Yusuf al-Qaradawi, Director, Sira and Sunna Research Centre, University of Qatar.
10. Chairman, Arab Historians Union.
11. Professor Cesar Adib Majul, Professor at the American Universities.

Following are the names of the late prominent Muslim figures who (may Allāh have mercy upon them) passed away after they had taken vital roles in the preliminary discussions of the Center's goals, work plan and activities. They are:

1. Dr Kamal Naji, former General Supervisor, Center for Muslim Contribution to Civilization, Qatar (7 October 1997).
2. Sheikh Jad al-Haq Ali Jad al-Haq, Sheikh al-Azhar, Cairo, Arab Republic of Egypt.
3. Dr Muhammad Ibrahim Kazim, former Rector, University of Qatar.
4. Sheikh Abdullah bin Ibrahim al-Ansari, former Chairman, Department for the Revival of Islamic Cultural Heritage, State of Qatar.
5. Muhammad al-Fasi, former Honorary Chairman, Islamic University Rabat, Kingdom of Morocco.
6. Dr Abul-Wafa al-Taftazani, former Deputy Rector, University of Cairo, Arab Republic of Egypt.
7. Senator Mamimatal Tamano, former member of the Philippino Congress and Muslim leader in the Philippines.

CENTER FOR MUSLIM CONTRIBUTION TO CIVILIZATION

Board

H.E. Sheikh Muhammad bin Hamad al-Thani
Chairman of the Board of Trustees

Professor Osman Sid-Ahmad Ismail al-Bili
General Supervisor, Professor of Middle Eastern and Islamic History, University of Qatar

Members

1. H.E. Professor Muhammad Abdul–Rahim Kafud, Minister of Education and Higher Education, State of Qatar.
2. Professor Ibrahim Saleh al-Nuaimi, former Rector, University of Qatar.
3. Professor Yusuf al-Qaradawi, Director, Sira and Sunna Research Centre, University of Qatar.
4. Professor Husam al-Khateeb, Professor of Arabic, University of Qatar.
5. H.E. Dr Hasan al-Nima, Ambassador, State of Qatar.
6. Dr Hasan al-Ansari, Amiri Diwan, State of Qatar.
7. Dr Ahmad Muhammad Ubaidan (Treasurer) Observer, Advisory Council and Director-General, Trans-Orient Establishment (Doha, Qatar).

Center's Advisors

H.E. Dr Ezzeddin Ibrahim
Cultural Advisor to H.H. the President of the U.A.E.

Professor Raji Mahmoud Rammuny
Director of the Center's Translation Committee in the U.S.A.
Professor of Arabic Studies, Department of Near Eastern Studies,
University of Michigan, U.S.A.

Translator's Preface

When I first accepted a commission from the Center for Muslim Contribution to Civilization to undertake a translation of al-Juwaynī's *al-Irshād*, I looked upon this project as a worthy exercise offering me a valuable personal experience. I had no doubt at all about the enormous importance of the book as a classic of Islamic theology. Mastering al-Juwaynī's thought, no matter how difficult and complex, could not but significantly improve the state of my soul, I reasoned. Secretly, however, I confidently expected that my first step would be to comb the library for the many articles and studies about al-Juwaynī. They would teach me everything I needed to know. Surely, I told myself, other translations in English of at least parts of this work had to exist. But, once launched on the project, I quickly discovered that I had been dead wrong. There are few, if any, studies of al-Juwaynī; the scholarly literature about him or his works is woefully thin, especially in English. Coming to grasp the thought and understand the language of this great classical master would not be easy. I faced a daunting prospect indeed.

This project had originally been given to Professor Victor Danner of the University of Indiana (in the USA). He was to have Professor Salih J. Altoma, his colleague at the same university, as his reviewer. Unfortunately, Professor Danner did not live to complete the translation he had begun. When I subsequently assumed the role of translator, I received a copy of some two dozen pages that he had finished. I cannot say if he had done more. With only that much in hand, I decided to begin afresh since in that way I could control the text as I saw fit, style being in part a personal matter. Therefore, despite recognizing Professor Danner's efforts, the present translation does not reflect what he might previously have done.

At the start of my own attempt to translate the *Irshād*, Professor Altoma agreed that he would continue to act as reviewer. However, when at last I reached a point where I could send him the first draft of the translation, he was already committed to other projects and did not have sufficient time for this one. Luckily, after Professor Altoma withdrew, we were able to convince Professor Mohammad S. Eissa, now of the University of Michigan (USA), and a friend and colleague, to take over as reviewer. His help and advice have been most useful.

For the understanding of al-Juwaynī's theology, I consulted Professor Richard M. Frank, another old friend. Professor Frank is quite possibly the most knowledgeable scholar now active in the field of *kalām* studies. Of those who write in English, he is certainly the leading expert. Unfortunately, despite the value of Professor Frank's learning and his advice when I could find a suitable opportunity to discuss al-Juwaynī with him, it proved difficult to make the best use of him. One would need to have him on call at all times, and that I could not quite arrange. And he certainly cannot be blamed for my failings.

As the success or failure of a translation depends largely on how the final product reads irrespective of its original, at a late stage I sought a reader who could judge the final English text. Here I must express my sincerest thanks to Bruce Craig, the bibliographer of the University of Chicago Middle East collection, who kindly read a draft of the entire work and suggested corrections to the text in many places.

Finally, I wish to recognize and thank Professor Raji Rammuny, who, acting for the Center, brought this project to me when we were colleagues in the Department of Near Eastern Studies at the University of Michigan. It is he who has kept it on track ever since.

Paul E. Walker
University of Chicago
USA

Introduction

Islamic theology in its classical phase involved a science of great intellectual sophistication and complexity, but it was both then and now poorly understood and little appreciated outside of its own circle of experts. Accordingly, modern investigations by scholars of Islam often fail to take account of the rich content in the thought and writings of the theologians, preferring instead to study, for example, Qurʾānic exegesis, *ḥadīth*, law, history, or even philosophy rather than this arcane subject. To be sure, the difficulty of the material and the narrow strictures necessary in theological discourse readily prevent a casual interest in it. There has long existed, moreover, within Islam itself, a palpable hostility towards any attempt to explain rationally what should and should not be the accepted doctrine about God. Many Muslims would rather not subject their religion to the debates of contending specialists in theological arguments. But that is true in almost any religion. The abstraction rules of theology seem forbidding and foreign to ordinary piety and devotion, all the more so if the result of the deliberations by skilled theoreticians are later imposed on the rest or where conflict and enmity subsequently envelop the community of believers because of it. Nevertheless, partly because of previous disagreements, theology in the Islamic world eventually assumed a highly significant place among its most competent practitioners. Over several centuries it became ever more exact, achieving at its best an elegant refinement in technical expression and an extraordinary sophistication in its solutions for the most intractable problems.

Near the summit of this long development stands the author of the present work, Abu'l-Maʿālī ʿAbd al-Malik b. Muḥammad al-Juwaynī (419/1028–478/1085), who was (and still is) commonly known as the Imām al-Ḥaramayn, "the leading master of the two holy cities" – Mecca and Madina. He was a consummate theologian of towering influence in his own time and thereafter. Enormously gifted with a prodigious intellect, his contributions in the field of law and legal theory were possibly of even greater importance than those in theology. Besides these two areas he was noted for his literary talent, especially in the writing and delivery of his sermons.[1] The one slight reservation in regard to his reputation and success, if it can be cited as such, is that he happened to produce a student who surpassed him in nearly every regard and who thus took away some of the esteem and attention he might otherwise have attracted. But that one student was Abū Ḥāmid Muḥammad al-Ghazzālī (450/1058–505/1111), quite possibly the most eminent theologian ever to appear in the Islamic world. That the famous al-Ghazzālī was in some sense the product of al-Juwaynī's teaching and instruction certainly accrues immense credit to the teacher but the

1 In fact, a book of his sermons, *dīwān khuṭabihi*, once existed according to al-Subkī.

overwhelming achievements of the pupil in this case tended to diminish those of his mentor.

None the less, it is not hard to find impressive testimonials to al-Juwaynī's own accomplishments and to the continued importance of his works. One striking example occurs in the famous "Introduction" (the *Muqaddima*) to history by ʿAbd al-Raḥmān Ibn Khaldūn (732/1332–808/1406). Writing a general assessment of various kinds of knowledge and the sciences, Ibn Khaldūn looked back from the vantage point of almost eight full centuries of Islamic scholarship. Given his own impressive academic credentials, his judgment assumes major importance. Towards the subject of theology as a whole he was not, however, enthusiastic and he regarded it as having outlived its usefulness long before his time. Nevertheless, he knew and could evaluate the contributions of the various schools and theologians of the distant past. In his view Islamic theology had gone through two major phases: an earlier one during which the discipline of theology existed quite separately from that of philosophy, and a later one in which these two sciences were mixed together and thereafter became mutually indistinct and thus confused. The latter trend began with al-Ghazzālī. Ibn Khaldūn, none the less, admits that the work of al-Ghazzālī is necessary in order adequately to refute the Philosophers in Islam (al-Fārābī, Ibn Sīnā, and Ibn Rushd), but the approach that most approximates that of the early Muslims, who are, according to him, the ones that ought to be emulated, closely adheres to the older methods in the earlier phase. He then states quite clearly, "The basic work of this kind is the *Kitāb al-irshād*"[2] of the leading Ashʿarite master the Imām al-Ḥaramayn Abu'l-Maʿālī." The people, he adds, adopted the *Irshād* and its author as their guide in matters of belief.[3]

It is this very work that follows here and therefore Ibn Khaldūn's ringing endorsement of it holds special importance. His testimony, moreover, indicates that, despite the outstanding contributions of al-Ghazzālī, the works of his teacher never ceased to be studied, appreciated and emulated. They, particularly the *Irshād*, continued to have an essential place; in classical Islamic theology, as Ibn Khaldūn indicates, this one book had become its basic text and, more than three centuries after it was written, remained a fundamental guide to the principles of Islamic belief.

al-Juwaynī's life and career

The author of the *Irshād* was born in the year 419/1028 in the village of Bushtaniqān on the outskirts of Naysābūr, the major city in the Iranian province of Khurasan.[4] This region was then a flourishing centre of commerce and trade;

2 *Muqaddima*, ed. Quatremere, III, 43, Rosenthal trans., III, 53–54 (See Bibliography, page 239).

3 *Muqaddima*, ed. Quatremere, III, 40–41, Rosenthal trans., III, 51.

4 The primary sources for the life of al-Juwaynī include entries in a number of later biographical dictionaries most notably Ibn Khallikān's *Wafayāt al-aʿyān*, al-Subkī's *Ṭabaqāt al-shāfiʿiyya*

its élite included a large number of highly educated scholars who, together, formed a patrician upper class that was marked by its learning and devotion to the study of Islamic sciences. Al-Juwaynī himself was the son of a prominent master of Islamic law, a pillar of the local Shāfiʿī community, Abū Muḥammad ʿAbdallāh b. Yūsuf al-Juwaynī. The father was quite well known.[5] Born in the district of Juwayn the western most region of Khurasan, he had studied law in both Marv and Naysābūr, before taking up a teaching responsibility in the latter city in 407/1016. The elder al-Juwaynī's brother Abu'l-Ḥasan ʿAlī al-Juwaynī (d. 463/1071) was a noted Sufi who travelled extensively prior to settling likewise in Naysābūr where he taught *ḥadīth*.

The younger al-Juwaynī thus did not need to venture far afield for his education. Not only was his own father one of the more important of the local scholars and authorities, especially in law, but Naysābūr where he grew up was then a major educational centre that attracted others to study there. By the time his father died in 438/1047, the son, who was then not yet twenty, could boast of such learning, primarily gleaned from his father, that he had little difficulty in taking up the latter's teaching responsibilities. Although such a feat almost seems standard in the biographies of major Islamic scholars of the period, in al-Juwaynī's case it must have been amply justified as evidenced by the precocious erudition he was to display throughout his later life. He was, moreover, noted for his stubborn insistence on rethinking for himself all arguments and issues that he encountered in the books he studied, including those written by his own father. In no sense was he ever guilty of accepting to follow blindly the doctrines he inherited from those who went before him, a fact duly recorded by later biographers, some of whom at times regarded this trait negatively, since it implied that al-Juwaynī thus continually exercised his own independent judgment when he should have adhered to accepted doctrine.

At some point over the next few years al-Juwaynī studied Ashʿarite theology in Bayhaq – another of the cities in the region – with Abu'l-Qāsim ʿAbd al-Jabbār al-Iskāf al-Isfarāyīnī (d. 452/1060), the leading theologian of this school in all of Khurasan. Abu'l-Qāsim in turn had studied with Abū Isḥāq Ibrāhīm al-Isfarāyīnī (d. 418/1027), who with Abū Bakr Muḥammad Ibn Fūrak (d. 406/1015), was the leading exponent of Ashʿarite theology in Naysābūr at the turn of the fourth/eleventh century. Both masters had studied earlier in Baghdad with Abu'l-Ḥasan al-Bāhilī at a time when the famous qadi and Ashʿarite theologian Abū Bakr Muḥammad al-Bāqillānī (d. 403/1013) was also there. Al-Bāhilī was himself a disciple directly of the founder of the school Abu'l-Ḥasan ʿAlī b. Ismāʿīl al-Ashʿarī (d. 324/936). These links in the transmission of Ashʿarite teachings were important not only to ensure orthodoxy within the school but to

---

al-kubrā, Ibn ʿAsākir's *Tabyīn kadhib al-muftarī*, and al-Dhahabī's *Taʾrīkh al-islām*, but there are others as well.

5 See, for example, the biographical entry for him in Ibn Khallikān's *Wafayāt*.

establish the pedigree of authority in it as well. These are the very masters that al-Juwaynī himself cites throughout the *Irshād*, generally with praise even when he disagrees in some way with a doctrine they had expressed.

In the cities of Khurasan the affinity between membership in the school of theology founded by al-Ashʿarī was most often linked to an adherence to the Shāfiʿī *madhhab* in law. But this connection was neither necessary nor without exception. Al-Bāqillānī had been a Mālikī in law even while espousing an Ashʿarīte theology. There were, moreover, many Shāfiʿīs who expressed little active interest in theology and therefore to be identified with one legal school did not automatically determine one's theological preferences. Still, at the time, the main rivals of the Shāfiʿīs in the region were the Ḥanafīs, followers of the legal tradition handed down from Abū Ḥanīfa and his disciples. Furthermore, a significant number of these same Ḥanafīs advocated a theology based on the principles of the Muʿtazilites, a theological tendency at odds with that of the Ashʿarites. Although, again, the connection between legal *madhhab* and theology in this case was not automatic, it was common enough.

Normally the rivalry between the Ḥanafīs and the Shāfiʿīs extended no further than an intense competition for key positions and influence. Still the great patrician families tended to be one or the other, and those who were Ḥanafī did not intermarry with the Shāfiʿīs. And frequently enough the two sides were pushed by some aggravation into open hostility, their legal disagreements in such cases often having been made worse by conflicts over theological doctrine.

Al-Juwaynī was a key member of both the Shāfiʿī community and a leader of the Ashʿarites. He was also by birth and lineage a representative of the privileged élite. Thus, after he had succeeded his father, despite his youth, he occupied a key position in Naysābūr. His prominence and importance made him an obvious target in these periodic disputes.

Around the year 445/1053 or early 446/1054 the level of antagonism and hostility rose to a new intensity and led to an unprecedented crisis. The exact cause of the trouble that ensued is difficult to discern.[6] Later historians and biographers, particularly those writing about the Shāfiʿīs, who were to suffer most, blame the incident on the *wazir* of the Saljuq sultan Ṭughril Beg. This man, ʿAmīd al-Mulk al-Kundurī, is said to have been a fanatic Ḥanafī with a pronounced anti-Ashʿarite bias. Once he was made *wazir* by the sultan and delegated appropriate power to act, he commanded that the Ashʿarites be condemned and forbidden to teach their doctrine. In line with this policy he ordered four of the leading Ashʿarite-Shāfiʿīs in Naysābūr arrested, among them al-Juwaynī.

6 The two basic studies of this event are Richard Bulliet's *The Patricians of Nishapur* (Cambridge, MN, Harvard University Press, 1972), a highly readable analysis of the élite families and the social structure of Naysābūr, including the Juwaynīs, and Heinz Halm's article "Der Wesir Al-Kundurī und die Fitna von Nīṣāpūr" (*Die Welt des Orients* 6 [1970-71], 205–33), perhaps the most comprehensive account of the sources and the information available in them.

There are, however, a number of difficulties with this version of events. Al-Kundurī had once been a protégé of the head of the Shāfiʿīs who had, in fact, played an essential part in bringing the younger man to the attention of the sultan. Moreover, it does not appear likely that al-Kundurī had attained the power to do what he is accused of doing by the year when this crisis erupted. More likely the whole affair grew out of some local conflict and thereafter ran out of control, eventually enmeshing the sultan's retinue, members of which (quite possibly including al-Kundurī) then tried to suppress the Ashʿarite party as a way of reducing the influence of the Shāfiʿīs. All along, the real aim of the general policy of the Saljuq court was to oppose the spread of the Shīʿites – a matter not linked to detaining the Ashʿarites in any way that is at all obvious. Many of the Shīʿites were in fact Muʿtazilite in their theology; the Ashʿarites were simply not connected to them.

The order for arrest named four men: Abu'l-Qāsim al-Qushayrī, Abu'l-Faḍl Aḥmad al-Furātī, al-Juwaynī and Abū Sahl Muḥammad, the son of Imām al-Muwaffaq, the previous head of the Shāfiʿīs, who had once been the patron of al-Kundurī, as mentioned above. The son, Abū Sahl Muḥammad, had assumed the position of his father upon the latter's death in 440/1048, even though he was then only seventeen years old. At the time of the order for his arrest, al-Juwaynī was only twenty-six or twenty-seven and Abū Sahl was barely twenty-two or twenty-three, yet both were already the leaders of their party in the city.

Of the four the first two were caught and imprisoned. Apparently having anticipated the order and preferring to go into exile, al-Juwaynī managed to escape. Abū Sahl went underground intent on putting up a fight. Subsequently, he managed to raise an armed force and to commence hostilities within the city in an attempt to win the release of his Ashʿarite comrades. The battle proved indecisive and ended with all agreeing to cease the fighting. The imprisoned men were released but most of the Ashʿarites, faced with the reality of overwhelming local hostility and lacking sufficient support, accepted exile.

As with the chronology of the onset of the campaign against the Ashʿarites, the movements of the various exiles are not clear in the sources. It appears that al-Juwaynī and some of the others proceeded first to the military headquarters of the Sultan Ṭughril, hoping perhaps to plead their case directly and thus regain their lost positions in Naysābūr. As the Saljuq sultan and his entourage were constantly on the move, there was no fixed capital for his empire. In the latter half of the year 447/1055, he finally made his first appearance in Baghdad. Evidently, many of the Ashʿarites from Khurasan accompanied him and his army and court there. Al-Juwaynī is said to have visited Baghdad at about this same time. As usual the report notes how he impressed the scholars resident there whom he met in and about the city. But if the Ashʿarites harboured any real hope of having the anti-Ashʿarite measures rescinded, it did not happen and a considerable party of them moved on from Baghdad to take up residence in the holy cities of the Hijaz.

An extended stay living in the vicinity of the major shrines of Islam in Mecca and Madina is regarded as an especially meritorious act. More than a pilgrimage, it comprises a special claim of piety. Thus for al-Juwaynī to adopt Mecca and Madina as his interim home is entirely understandable. While there he both taught and issued legal opinions, thereby earning the title by which he was known for the rest of his life, the Imām of the Ḥaramayn, the two holy cities. His stay was, moreover, not short; he remained in the Hijaz four years, long enough to fix this fact forever in his biography.

As with the beginning of the exile, its termination occurred at a date that is hard to determine with certainty. Eventually the ban was lifted, although, on the theory that al-Kundurī was its main instigator, it is normal to presume that its end did not come until after Ṭughril Beg had died and his successor Alp Arslan arrested and executed al-Kundurī, both events taking place in 455/1063. However, there are problems with this chronology. Naysābūr, the source of the troubles, fell, according to the Saljuq family arrangement for dividing the territories they had conquered, under the control of Ṭughril's brother Chaghrī Beg. On his own Chaghrī expressed little interest in or enthusiasm for interfering in its affairs. But in 450/1058, he turned over the governing of Naysābūr to his son Alp Arslan, although he himself remained ruler of the east until his death in 452/1060. Having been granted a free hand, Alp Arslan introduced a change in policy. That policy was largely determined by his own chief advisor and *wazir*, the famous Niẓām al-Mulk, an ardent Shāfiʿī, bent upon cultivating and spreading the teaching of Shāfiʿī law. To that end he personally founded a series of colleges, known after him as the Niẓāmiyya *madrasa*s, the first of which was built in Naysābūr about this time. Thus prior to the demise of al-Kundurī and his master Ṭughril Beg, Alp Arslan and Niẓām al-Mulk had begun to rule Naysābūr and to instigate the changes that were to restore the Shāfiʿīs and Ashʿarites to their former prominence.

It is, however, difficult to be more precise as to the exact date which is, none the less, critical in terms of al-Juwaynī's return. As his fame spread, his status at home increased enormously. Exile, especially in the Ḥaramayn, added to his lustre. Accordingly, when Niẓām al-Mulk made his plan for the Niẓāmiyya, he specified that al-Juwaynī should hold the first chair in it. Subsequently, al-Juwaynī was to direct the affairs of this *madrasa* until his own death in 478/1085 and later authorities commonly reported that his tenure lasted as long as thirty years. But it cannot have added up to thirty years. More likely his return to Naysābūr and taking his position in the newly created *madrasa* occurred about 451/1060. Throughout most of the previous year, Baghdad was in the hands of a Shīʿite force under al-Basāsīrī and the Saljuqs were temporarily in disarray, Ṭughril having lost control over the city at the time. The Saljuq sultan re-established his authority there at the end of 451/January 1060 and the Abbasid caliph, who had been ousted, was then restored to his office. Al-Juwaynī, who was now the beneficiary of Alp Arslan's protection, may well have chosen this moment for his reappearance in Khurasan. If he commenced his teaching in the Niẓāmiyya in 451 or 452, at the time of his death he had occupied that position some twenty-six or twenty-seven years, enough for the later writers to round it up to the convenient figure of thirty.

At the time of his return, al-Juwaynī was still barely more than thirty years old but over the ensuing decades he remained in Naysābūr. In addition to his teaching, he accepted the post of preacher (*khaṭīb*) in the newly built al-Manīʿī Mosque in 456/1064. Later that same year, Abū Sahl Muḥammad, the head of the Shāfiʿīs and former fellow exile, died whereupon his duties passed also to al-Juwaynī. It is quite likely that most of his writings belong to this period. Certainly it was an era that saw a multitude of students gathering to learn from him; in typical fashion it is reported that when he lectured he was surrounded by three hundred students. At the end (in 478/1085) he fell gravely ill, and was taken to his birthplace, Bushtaniqān, reputed for its clean, healthy air and water. But he did not recover and on news of his death, massive displays of mourning broke out in Naysābūr. The pulpit from which he had preached was destroyed and his students did likewise to their pens and inkstands – actions which, by their very exceptional nature, indicated the spontaneous emotion that had caused them. The Imām al-Ḥaramayn was first buried in his own house and then later moved next to his father in the cemetery of al-Ḥusayn b. Muʿādh.

al-Juwaynī's writings

The surviving writings of the Imām al-Ḥaramayn are reasonably numerous, as might be expected from his prominence and general high regard as both an expert in Islamic legal theory and in theology. In the former subject the most famous is his *al-Burhān fī uṣūl al-fiqh*[7] (*The Proof in Regard to the Principles of Religious Law*). As added testimony to al-Juwaynī's refusal simply to copy and relate what others had said before him, this work is both distinctly rational and also extremely complex, so much so that the later biographer al-Subkī called it the "puzzle of the community" ("*lughz al-umma*"). But this judgment is, in part, a testimonial to its originality; in writing it he had not, as al-Subkī also noted, followed any one else.[8] Al-Juwaynī wrote other books and treatises in the field of law, among them an abridgment of the subject[9] and also what one authority describes as the shortest work on the legal theory ever undertaken, al-Juwaynī's *Waraqāt*,[10] upon which, however, many later authors added their own commentaries and even commentaries on these commentaries.[11]

---

7 Edited by ʿAbd al-ʿAẓīm Dīb, 2 vols., Cairo, 1979; printed again in Beirut, 1997.

8 This man is Tāj al-Dīn Abu Naṣr al-Subkī (d. 769/1368), the famous scholar and promoter of the Shāfiʿīs who were also Ashʿarites. See his *Ṭabaqāt*, V, 192.

9 *Kitāb al-talkhīṣ fī uṣūl al-fiqh*, Beirut, 1996.

10 Professor Wael Hallaq notes that it has only 1,600 words in total.

11 Published alone (that is without any of these commentaries), Cairo, Dār al-Turāth, 1977.

Several other works of al-Juwaynī deserve mention here: his *Ghiyāth al-umam fī iltiyāth al-ẓulam*[12] on the imamate, and *al-Kāfiya fi'l-jadal*[13] on legal reasoning. Yet another is his *Mughīth al-khalq fī tarjīḥ al-qawl al-ḥaqq*[14] on the principles (*uṣūl*) of law, and one more is his *Nihāyat al-maṭlab fī dirāyat al-madhhab* on law proper. In the field of apologetics and religious polemic, al-Juwaynī is represented by his *al-Durra al-muḍiya fīmā waqaʿa fīhi al-khilāf bayna al-Shāfiʿiyya wa'l-Ḥanafiyya*,[15] and *Sifāʾ al-ghalīl fī bayān mā waqaʿa fi'l-Tawra wa'l-Injīl min al-tabdīl*.[16]

Strictly in the slightly narrower area of theology as such, al-Juwaynī first set out to write a comprehensive compendium of the subject which he called *al-Shāmil fī uṣūl al-dīn* (*The Complete Book of the Principles of Religion*). In this case the term *uṣūl al-dīn* is the general equivalent of theology in the broadest sense. What survives of the *Shāmil*, which is not all of it, indicates that it was a substantial, multi-volume work – the most complete edition now runs to over seven hundred pages.[17] At several points in his *Irshād* the author refers his reader to the *Shāmil* for additional details and a more elaborate discussion of a given point. Early in the *Irshād* he appears to mean by these references a part of the *Shāmil* already finished. Towards the end, however, he mentions something in it he has not yet completed and perhaps is still in the process of writing. At the outset he also complains about his fears that the major compendiums are too difficult and forbidding to attract ordinary students and he says that this is precisely why he had decided to compose the *Irshād* as an intermediate manual, less overwhelming than the *Shāmil* but not entirely devoid of proofs and argumentation, as would be the case in a simple statement of creed. For al-Juwaynī himself, the latter – a basic statement of creed and not more – is his *al-ʿAqīda al-niẓāmiyya*,[18] a short outline of the creed of orthodox Muslims. In this field he also wrote *Lumaʿ al-adilla fī qawāʾid ʿaqāʾid ahl al-sunna wa'l-jamāʿa*.[19]

In regard to the *Shāmil*, the testimony of the *Irshād* appears to show that al-Juwaynī interrupted his work on that project in order to write the latter and that only later did he return to the larger effort.[20]

---

12 Also called *al-Ghiyāthī*, it was named for the *wazir* Ghiyāth al-Dīn Niẓām al-Mulk. It has been edited by F. ʿAbd al-Munʿin and M. Ḥilmī, Alexandria, 1979; ʿAbd al-ʿAẓīm Dīb, Cairo, 1981.

13 Edited by Fawqiya Ḥusayn Maḥmūd, Cairo, 1979.

14 Cairo, al-Maṭbaʿa al-Miṣriyya, 1934.

15 Qatar, ʿAbd Allāh b. Ibrāhīm al-ʿAnṣarī, 1986.

16 First published by Michel Allard in his *Textes apologétiques de Guwaini*, Beirut, 1968 and later in Cairo, 1979.

17 Edited by ʿAlī Sāmī al-Nashshār, Alexandria, 1969.

18 Edited by Muḥammad al-Kawtharī, Cairo, 1948.

19 Edited by Fawqiya Ḥusayn Maḥmūd, Cairo, 1965; also published by Allard in the work just cited.

20 A full account of the works of al-Juwaynī must await additional research. For an example of what is known and a complete list of all twenty-seven titles presently attributed to him, see Fawqiya Ḥusayn Maḥmūd's introduction to her edition of *Lumaʿ al-adilla*, pp. 42–49.

al-Juwaynī and Islamic theology

Here and throughout this volume the English word "theology" is a direct translation of the Arabic term "*kalām*", which means "speech", "speaking" or "expression". How *kalām* came to be the technical term for theology in the Islamic context is not well understood. Nevertheless, it served formally as the designation of a whole field of study and the phrase *ʿilm al-kalām* ("the science of speaking") indicates a science, the science of theology, in its own right.

Both medieval Islamic discussions of this term and modern attempts to translate it reveal the uncertainty about its connection to theology in general. Western scholars tend to insist on adding various qualifying adjectives when they render *kalām*. Thus, although in an Islamic text it appears as the single term *kalām*, in translation it often comes out as "speculative theology" or "dialectical theology" as if somehow it bears a slightly peculiar connotation not given by the word "theology" in isolation.

However, any notion that Islamic theology was intended as a speculative venture ought to be readily dispelled and would likely be on reading a treatise such as al-Juwaynī's *Irshād*, itself regarded as a classic of work in this very field. Al-Juwaynī quite obviously did not engage in speculation in matters involving religious doctrine, especially those that refer to God. God is not a subject for human speculation in any sense. In fact, according to al-Juwaynī, the principles of belief rest ultimately on a foundation based on convincing proofs, proofs quite soundly demonstrated and anchored in revelation. What is speculative in Islamic theology is inevitably the fantasies of those who deviate from this exacting standard. Therefore speculative theology did not and does not exist in orthodox Islam but rather finds a place only among the heretics, the sceptics and the misguided. To put this point in a more neutral way, speculation about God and His attributes or commandments is something an opponent does and is not a part of an orthodox theology or the work of a credible theologian.

In Arabic, the scholar who engages in the study of theological principles was called a *mutakallim*, a practitioner or student of *kalām*, here a "theologian". For the earliest theologians in Islam the tools of argumentation and debate involved a heavy use of, and reliance on, dialectic. By general agreement the proper application of syllogistic logic was either unknown or seldom applied. Hence Philosophers (al-Falāsifa) such as al-Fārābī and Ibn Rushd could claim that theology (*kalām*) was less sophisticated in its logical rigour and was therefore intellectually inferior to demonstrative philosophy. Even setting this adverse judgment aside, the *ʿilm al-kalām* followed historically a dialectical course of development. It often appears as though new refinements in theological doctrine arose as a direct result of having to counter some perceived deviation and heresy. Critics of the work of the theologians asserted that it was useful and had a valid place in Islam only to defend orthodoxy against its enemies or those who wanted to introduce innovations to the original teaching of the Prophet and the revelation.

The concept that Islamic theology serves solely as a tool of apologetics is also wrong as can be observed from the works of al-Juwaynī. It is true that he explains his doctrine often by reference to an opponent who mistakenly advocated an erroneous method or principle. But his real purpose is to set out the elements that constitute a sure proof of orthodox principles in regard to religious belief. His ongoing refutation of the opponent is a device towards that end; it is not the end in itself.

Al-Juwaynī called this work *A Guide to Conclusive Proofs for the Principles of Belief* and that is its ultimate purpose. He seeks to lay out the way to prove with the greatest certainty possible what a Muslim should and should not believe. Its primary subject and reference is God. At one point in the text al-Juwaynī indicates that theology divides into three subsections: what must be said about God; what must not be said about God; and what is possible in respect to God. All three therefore concern how to speak about God. Accordingly, following him then, *kalām* in this sense means speaking about God, or possibly "expressing" the doctrines that concern God. Far from being speculative or dialectical, al-Juwaynī intends a true theology: a reasoned exposition of orthodox Islamic doctrine about all matters having to do with God.

It is noteworthy that in this work al-Juwaynī did not feel it necessary to defend the science of theology or his own attempt to write about it, as had, by contrast, the founder of Ashʿarism who wrote a special treatise to uphold the correctness and acceptability of *kalām*.[21] In contrast to the study of law and legal theory, theological doctrine had few direct consequences for the ordinary daily lives of Muslims. Many of them felt uneasy with abstractions they could not understand and they preferred to avoid the subject altogether. Hostility to the theologians could therefore come from groups like the Philosophers as well as, even more significantly, conservative Muslim authorities adverse to the very discourse of theological argumentation.[22]

Al-Juwaynī's main opponents, however, were not those opposed to theology as such but the Muʿtazilites who, prior to his time, had been the strongest advocates of it, especially of the role of reason as a fundamental principle in determining theological doctrine. Al-Ashʿarī himself had once belonged to this group but later split with them and developed an opposing doctrine that subsequently became Ashʿarism itself. Quite apart from any local Naysābūri conflict between the Ḥanafī-Muʿtazilīs and the Shāfiʿī-Ashʿarīs, which certainly affected al-Juwaynī's life in several ways, in terms strictly of theology, the

---

21 al-Ashʿarī's *Risālat istiḥsān al-khawḍ fī ʿilm al-kalām* (*A Vindication of the Science of Kalām*), ed. with English translation by Richard J. McCarthy in *The Theology of Al-Ashʿarī* (Beirut, 1953), pp. 117–34 (Eng.), pp. 85–97 (Arabic).

22 There were a number of treatises written to condemn the study of *kalām*, most of them by Ḥanbalīs. See, for example, Ibn Qudāma's *Taḥrīm al-naẓar fī kutub ahl al-kalām*, translated by George Makdisi as *Censure of Speculative Theology* (London, 1962).

Muʿtazilīs claimed a position that both threatened his and yet was rationally sophisticated to a degree not easily refuted. Almost every proof or point of principle that al-Juwaynī needed to establish had earlier been the subject of Muʿtazilite interest. Their approach was certainly different from his and that of the Ashʿarites in many ways but it was close enough to confuse an untrained observer. Al-Juwaynī's teachings are often quite similar to the doctrine of the Muʿtazilites, not infrequently remarkably so. For those that differ, moreover, the implications and consequences of the doctrine of each side often revolve about the most subtle of arguments. In the *Irshād* al-Juwaynī frequently seems to make fun of the Muʿtazilites, but he knew how serious they had been and to what extent they had insinuated their teachings into Islamic thought, even that of himself.

The Muʿtazilites themselves were not a well organized movement but rather a dispersed collection of thinkers largely stemming from two somewhat distinct periods prior to al-Juwaynī. What are called the earlier Muʿtazilites come mainly from the third/ninth century or slightly earlier and include many of the founding generation. No single individual best typifies this group since, even on fundamental issues, there was considerable disagreement among them. Nevertheless, they and later Muʿtazilites speak about five basic principles as if these defined their movement as a whole. These are as follows:

1. A rigorous upholding of God's absolute oneness by denying and rejecting any qualification that would compromise this unity or recognize in it some form of duality.
2. A specification that God is just and can and will do nothing unjust or evil.
3. An affirmation of the reality of God's promise and His threat, and that He will necessarily fulfil both in regard to His human subjects.
4. A declaration that a Muslim who has committed a grave sin and who has not yet repented is neither a believer nor an unbeliever but rather in between; a reprobate or malefactor.
5. An assertion that it is the duty of all Muslims to ensure the good and prevent the unacceptable.

Parts of this programme hardly serve to distinguish the Muʿtazilites from most other Muslims and the reason for having to declare that all five of these principles were required lost its force in later times. The first two are, in fact, ultimately what continued to separate them from other theological schools.

The second phase of the Muʿtazilites belongs to the late third, fourth and fifth (tenth and eleventh) centuries. Here the scattered tendencies of the school coalesced around two groups: the Baṣrans and the Baghdadīs. However, these names indicated not the residence of the theologians involved but an affinity of a theoretical nature. Many of either side, such as Abu'l-Qāsim al-Balkhī al-Kaʿbī (d. 319/931), the leader of the "Baghdadī" group, and the two al-Jubbāʾīs, the father Abū ʿAlī (d. 303/913) and the son Abū Hāshim (d. 321/933), who represent the "Baṣran" side, lived elsewhere, al-Balkhī in Khurasan and the al-Jubbāʾīs in Khūzistān. It is from the Baṣran tendency that Abu'l-Ḥasan al-Ashʿarī himself separated when he turned against the Muʿtazilites and began to formulate his own doctrine.

By the time of al-Juwaynī the differences between the Muʿtazilites and the Ashʿarites revolved around a fairly narrow set of dogmas, which his *Irshād* takes as a major problem. This work is, in fact, an important piece of evidence for the attitudes of both sides. It should be observed here, none the less, that an old view in modern scholarship that the Muʿtazilites were exclusively the party of rationality and reason simply does not hold. Reason is a basic source for Muʿtazilite doctrine but a close inspection of the ways in which they apply reason and reasoning against its use by al-Juwaynī leave little or no distinction for them in opposition to him. He was surely as rational in his arguments as they, and reason occupied a fundamental role in his theology as can be readily observed in the early chapters of the *Irshād*, which have reason, reasoning and what constitutes a proof as their theme.

The primary area of serious difference does not concern the first of their principles – that of God's absolute oneness and how to view the attributes of God so as not to qualify Him with duality. In this area al-Juwaynī speaks much as they do, even employing concepts like the attributes of self, and the attributes of qualification and the notion of the modes (*aḥwāl*) as well as atomic physics – all doctrines that were originally Muʿtazilite. His differences with them concern matters involving the transcendence of God and the implication of what the Muʿtazilites had insisted was His necessary justice. Within this lies also his rejection of their notion of the nature of the Qurʾān and the speech of God. The Muʿtazilites held that there exists an abstract universal goodness and likewise a universal standard for badness and evil. Humans instinctively perceive what is good because this universal of goodness exists. The same applies to evil. God, in a way likewise, does what is good and avoids evil because He is subject to it as well. He is, moreover, under the obligation of universal reason. He cannot perform an evil or unjust act. As a corollary He will do to, or for, humans only what is best for them and He will not punish them for acts that were not of their own making. Hence it follows they have been accorded a power to do what is right or what is wrong by their own free choice. When He rewards them for obeying His commandments and punishes them for disobeying, He does so necessarily in accord with what is just. If He had been responsible for their acts, His punishment would be unjust. Accordingly, an evil act in this life inevitably carries with it the threat of a horrible punishment and, barring repentance and its acceptance by God, God will certainly inflict that penalty.

Within this set of doctrines, there are a number of sub-issues. One is that the human must be granted power to perform voluntarily and willfully actions that involve moral choices between opposites, those that can be either good or evil.

Muʿtazilites continued to insist that the human has free will and possesses the power to act as he wants. These voluntary acts are not, according to them, in any sense the acts of God. If they were subject to His power, if He had done them, God could not thereafter hold the human responsible for them.

Against this al-Juwaynī states clearly, in line with Ashʿarite doctrine, that God creates all acts including those of the human. All power belongs to God; it is He who creates everything. Al-Juwaynī asks how God could have created everything up to the moment of giving humans the power to act as they wish and then delegate some aspect of that power to them. Humans are simply not creators. What is the meaning in giving away power and why at some moment and not another? All power is subject to the power of God. Goodness and badness, moreover, have no abstract existence; what is good is what the revealed law declares good, what is bad is what the law deems bad. Everything that God does is good; if He inflicts a punishment for an act undertaken by a human, that is His right and it is not subject to human judgments as to its justice or not. God is not under the obligation of universal reason in any sense. If He wishes He may punish those who obey Him; if He wishes He can reward those who disobey.

Understanding the speech of God is another interesting area of these differences. The Muʿtazilites asserted that speech consists of letters arranged serially and sounds articulated separately. Thus, the speech that comes from God immediately assumes a sequential and hence temporal form. The result of this fact establishes that the Qurʾān, the word of God, as it exists in this realm, was a creation in time; it is not therefore eternal. Al-Juwaynī objects and the main thrust of his opposition to this doctrine concerns the definition of speech; he claims, rather than consisting of discretely articulated sounds or letters arranged linearly, speech actually arises in the soul prior to its being uttered. The utterance merely signifies what exists in the soul. If so, then the speech of God resides in Him where it is eternal, not in the exemplar of it as spoken by the individual Qurʾān reciter or as written out on the page.

In the *Irshād*, al-Juwaynī cites several other figures and groups that are not a part of the Muʿtazilite movement but few of them need be taken seriously except as an example that shows what is false or erroneous, often grossly so. For example, he mentions what he calls the "Esotericists" (al-Bāṭiniyya) who had espoused a radically negative theology. Although he does not say so explicitly, he must be referring to the Ismāʿīlī Shīʿa who, in fact, held a doctrine similar to the one he describes.[23] Another group is the Karrāmiyya who professed a form of anthropomorphism by admitting that God has bodily characteristics. The Karrāmiyya were quite active in Khurasan in al-Juwaynī's time. Others include the Christians whose arguments in support of the trinity al-Juwaynī takes the

23 On this aspect of Ismāʿīlī doctrine, see Paul E. Walker, *Early Philosophical Shiism: The Ismaili Neoplatonism of Abū Yaʿqūb al-Sijistānī*. Cambridge: Cambridge University Press, 1993, chapter 5, pp. 72–80.

trouble to refute. Another is Jahm b. Ṣafwān, whose assertion that God knows items of contingent knowledge in a temporally specific way required, in al-Juwaynī's view, a special refutation. Yet one more example are the Philosophers. He does not mention anyone by name but offers an interesting although brief denial of their doctrines and then remarks as follows:

> One of their strange declarations is for them to reject the convincing proofs given by the theologians by insisting that they are sophisms, that the best of them are merely dialectical, and that none of them consist of demonstrative syllogisms. Yet, . . . they accept, without argumentation, what conforms to nature, despite admitting that it is a matter as obscure as it can be. It might be asked of them: why do you not consider the first existent to be the necessary cause of every other thing? What is it that proves to you the necessity of the first spiritual being and then the necessary causing of what is lower by that spiritual being? Is this not a purely arbitrary judgment lacking merit? This belief yields no more than that.

Clearly al-Juwaynī thought that it was the Philosophers who had failed the standard of rationality, not the theologians. His own pupil al-Ghazzālī was to write a major, perhaps *the* major Islamic, denunciation of the Philosophers in his famous *The Incoherence of the Philosophers* (*Tahāfut al-falāsifa*). Surely teacher and student had discussed this very subject.

The content of the *Irshād*

Al-Juwaynī's general purpose with his *Irshād* is clearly stated in its title. It is a (or *the*) guide – a guidebook – to conclusive proofs for the principles of belief (*Kitāb al-irshād ilā qawāṭiʿ al-adilla fī uṣūl al-iʿtiqād*). Two terms in the title function as keys to what he wants to accomplish: in Arabic *qawāṭiʿ al-adilla* and *uṣūl*, in English "conclusive proofs" and "principles". The word *uṣūl* refers to the roots or foundations upon which all matters of belief and law depend. Another meaning is "sources" but not in a vague sense. Here the sources are primarily the revelation, that is, the Qurʾān and the Sunna, the practice of the Prophet taken by his Companions and his community as normative. Reason is not in itself a source although it is a criterion used to understand these sources and to determine what they indicate about religion and the law. By "conclusive proofs" he means those proofs that have definitive certainty and are in no way subject to doubt or conflicting interpretation. If any issue is validly open to a difference of opinion, or does not carry or yield to incontrovertible proof, it remains inconclusive. Al-Juwaynī's goal is to establish exactly what is proven or provable and how to prove it.

Yet, despite its lofty purpose, he intended the *Irshād* as an manual for an intermediate level of instruction in theology, or what is known in the western tradition as a "catechism", – that is, a reasoned textbook for religious instruction, often arranged as a series of questions and answers. It is, therefore, not a comprehensive compendium of everything that might be said on its subject or even all that needs to be said, since some areas, as he admits himself, are either too complex or too difficult to be covered at this level. In a few instances he leaves a topic with a comment that it is covered more thoroughly in his own *Shāmil.* Yet in at least one other place he appears to say that the subject of that section ought to be supplemented by oral lectures. In fact, even though al-Juwaynī hopes his *Irshād* might serve as an accessible introduction to theology, he knew that it would work best if it was taught directly to the students by either himself or another scholar who had been properly trained with this work and who had been granted a licence to teach it. This system, which was quite common at the time, ensured authenticity as well as comprehension. But for a modern reader it may seem disconcerting to realize that this book was not written for the casually interested party who happened to want to learn about Islamic theology, especially one who has no teacher at hand to explain all the obscurities in it.

Nevertheless, it is useful to note that its author writes as much about the method of reasoning and what constitutes a proof in matters of belief as about abtruse dogmas and barely intelligible abstractions. His subject is the logic of theology and how the doctrines of Islam can be known definitively and with absolute certainty. That is why he commences the work with sections on the character of reason, on proofs and how they prove what they prove, and on the nature of knowledge itself. Rational proofs are either known to be proven by necessary intuition or by reasoning through a proof that yields the knowledge that the result is as it must be. There are, in addition, proofs given by tradition – that is, by the unimpeachable testimony of a concurring plethora of witnesses who all affirm that what they report is in fact what happened and is thus true. Only after setting out the intellectual premises of what constitutes reason and reasoning does he begin to discuss God and knowledge of God.

At that point al-Juwaynī introduces the first of his three sub-categories of theology: what must be said or stipulated of God – that is, what attributes are His of necessity and belong to Him. These in turn he divides into those that are His in and of Himself and are not due to any cause that arises by virtue of His having that attribute. The latter are God's qualifying attributes, those that entail some aspect of causation, such as God's will, His being purposeful, His speaking, commanding, prohibiting, creating, seeing and hearing. God's attributes of self – that is, those that are true of Him in and of Himself – include His eternity, knowledge, being alive, subsistence and utter difference from all that is temporally produced and is contingent.

In one place, al-Juwaynī indicates that theology includes knowing what must not be said about God or attributed to Him. This area would be his second category. In some works on Islamic theology the subject of what not to say about God could and did lead to a long discourse on the heresies in Islam and the erroneous teachings of various heretics and deviants. Al-Ashʿarī himself had composed one of the most extensive and most interesting of all such works to survive but there exist several others as well.[24] Al-Juwaynī, however, despite suggesting that it should be included, passes over that section quickly and says merely that once what he has said is fully grasped the deviations and aberrations of the heretics should be more or less obvious.

Instead al-Juwaynī proceeds to the third category, namely what is possible in respect to God. Here, then, he discusses a long list of topics and these involve many of the most controversial details of his theology and that of the Ashʿarites in general. He begins with a section on the vision of God and how humans may be rightly said to see Him as promised in the Qurʾān. His principal opponents are the Muʿtazilites who denied that God could be seen in any sense since all objects of sight must necessarily be physical. Next al-Juwaynī takes up the subject of whether or not and in what manner humans have power over their own acts. The Muʿtazilites held that humans alone have the power to do and not to do those actions of theirs that involve moral choices; they may obey God or they may refuse to do so. Al-Juwaynī declares simply that God is the sole creator and He alone has all power. All contingent power is subject to His will and determination. The Muʿtazilites, fearing that such a doctrine would make God unjust if he subsequently were to punish the sinner for sins he did not have the power to commit, insisted that humans have been given the power. Otherwise God would punish the human for something He did. Here al-Juwaynī adds various arguments connected with the theme of justice – whether God is or must be just – and about grace and abandonment, about goodness and badness, about suffering, compensation, and the good and the best.

Still within the third category, al-Juwaynī next discusses the doctrine of miracles, how a miracle proves the prophetic mission of a prophet and that there exists no other proof of the prophet's veracity. Within this topic come abrogation, the inimitability of the Qurʾān, and the other miraculous signs of prophethood. Following these there is an interesting discourse on the evidence given by tradition.

Finally, still apparently within his third category, al-Juwaynī covers a variety of seemingly miscellaneous topics including temporal limits, subsistence, prices, commanding the good and prohibiting the reprehensible, resurrection, the afterlife, reward and punishment, intercession, the meaning of faith, contrition, repentance and, at the very end, the imamate, and the rules for it and for its investiture in various historical individuals. Although many of these last subjects appear less theological than social or political, al-Juwaynī seems to include them here because they properly belong to the broad category of what is possible for God. Thus, God's role in all of these matters is possible – that is, God does whatever He wishes and what happens depends on Him exclusively. The normal and habitual course of events, however likely, is not in itself necessary and, even though it appears to us to be continuous, almost inevitable, He might break or interrupt the natural order at any moment.

---

24 His *Maqālāt al-islāmiyyīn*, ed. H. Ritter, Istanbul, reprint Wiesbaden, 1963.

The Arabic text of the *Irshād* and the present translation

Despite its fame and importance, the Arabic text of al-Juwaynī's *Irshād* remained generally inaccessible to modern scholarship until it was edited and published by a remarkable French North African colonial administrator, J. Dominique Luciani. A Corsican who entered the French civil service in Algeria in the 1870s, Luciani specialized there in what were then called (somewhat quaintly) "Indigenous Affairs" – that is, matters having to do with governing the native Algerians. He was particularly concerned with the administration of Islamic law, and a number of his scholarly activities involved the editing and translating of Arabic works of special importance to North Africa. Perhaps from his interest in Islamic law he developed a second speciality in Islamic theology, an area in which he also edited and published several Arabic works. His appreciation of al-Juwaynī might have grown from either of these topics. In 1919, Luciani retired from government service and devoted himself to scholarly endeavours. One project in this final period of his life was an edition and translation of the *Irshād*. At the time of his death in 1932, Luciani had apparently completed both the edition and his French translation, which were then said to be in press. Unfortunately, he had not finished whatever study he had in mind to serve as an introduction to the work, or a full accounting of how he had put together his edition. Nevertheless, the whole work minus an introduction ultimately appeared, although not until 1938, six years later.

Luciani had used for his edition only three manuscripts – those preserved in Algiers, Tunis and Paris. He also had available to him at least two commentaries by medieval disciples of al-Juwaynī's thought. In part because his edition, published in any case using the slightly awkward and uncommon Maghribi script, was not readily available in the east and in part because he had failed to take into account the evidence of additional manuscripts available in Cairo and Aleppo, two Egyptian scholars, Muḥammad Yūsuf Mūsā and ʿAlī ʿAbd al-Munʿim ʿAbd al-Ḥamīd, undertook to amend the work of Luciani. Their edition of the *Irshād* was published in Cairo in 1950.

This Egyptian edition subsequently became the standard "critical edition" and is frequently cited as such. Two more recent printings of the text in Beirut – one ascribed to the editorship of Asad Tamīm (1985) and the other to Zakariyā ʿUmayrāt (1995) – appear to be no more than copies of the earlier Cairo edition. The 1985 printing even reproduces the footnotes of the 1950 work without, however, fully crediting the real authors of them.

A closer inspection of the original Egyptian text, however, reveals a number of problems. Some of these are due to the poor quality of the print, which has left many words unclear. In addition there are occasional relatively obvious (more or less) typographical errors. More serious are several cases where the Egyptian printers have omitted a line of text which the proofreaders obviously failed to catch. Since the editors note that they began with Luciani's edition as their base, the missing lines, which appear only by collating the newer text with Luciani's, must belong to al-Juwaynī's original. The omission of them in the Cairo edition can only have been inadvertent.

In my effort to translate the *Irshād* into English, I relied primarily on the Cairo edition until I realized that the problem afore-mentioned existed and would affect the reading of text in a number of instances. Thereafter I attempted to refer to both editions, especially when it seemed to be called for by some peculiarity. I have included here a list of a few of the most serious errors in the Cairo edition, particularly for the missing lines of text. It is by no means complete and it is fervently to be hoped that someone will eventually undertake the task of producing a new critical edition of the *Irshād*, this time rechecking the reading of all the known manuscripts as well as the commentaries. Significantly, the two recent Beirut printings appear to preserve the errors of the Cairo edition, including examples of the more obvious typographical mistakes.

In offering an English translation of the *Irshād*, my primary purpose is to present this entire work of al-Juwaynī as one complete example of a theological treatise. The audience for it in this case comprises all those interested parties who do not have access to the Arabic and who are in the first instance not specialists in Islamic theology. This effort was not intended as a means of glossing the Arabic text for the benefit of experts in the subject but rather to render the whole in as readable form as possible. Obviously, that involves a formidable task since the very nature of the work, despite al-Juwaynī's hope to produce an intermediate-level manual that might attract the beginner to this discipline, is highly technical and depends on some prior knowledge of the arguments used in it. Moreover, in aiming to present the whole of it rather than some particular parts or sections, the precise meaning of the Arabic over many pages does not easily convert into an English version that corresponds over the same range. While it is quite possible to translate passages with a desirable degree of technical accuracy, this endeavour tends to break down over the entire volume.

Also, within the tradition of this kind of literature in Islam, a work like this follows certain expected forms that a specialist in theological disputation would understand. Thus, for example, many individual arguments take the form of what are called "questions" and "responses". In Arabic these begin with a standard phrase "*in qīla*" ("if it is said") to which the author answers "*qulnā*" ("we reply"). Where these phrases occur, they might have been rendered simply as "question" and "response" following the well-established tradition of the literature. However, I have preferred to make the English more attuned to the direct give and take in the flow of the discussion as if a dialogue really existed rather than an abstract series of scholastic technicalities.

Additionally, to aid the flow of the work I have adopted here the useful chapter titles added by the Egyptian editors where none (or few) existed in the original. These were inserted by them between square brackets to indicate that they are not a part of al-Juwaynī's text (although most are derived from words or phrases in the same chapter itself). I have translated and included them here also separated where they appear in the translation by brackets. However, for the table of contents I have used these chapter headings without indicating which of them depends directly on al-Juwaynī.

In addition, although the paragraphs in the Egyptian edition were inserted by the editors in a slightly mechanical fashion and are somewhat excessive in number, it seemed preferable to retain them for the most part. The original has almost none as was common in medieval Arabic but a modern reader both in Arabic and in English expects them. And they do help in following the shifts of subject in the text.

Paul E. Walker

A Guide to Conclusive Proofs for the Principles of Belief

Author's Preface

In the name of God, the Merciful, the Compassionate; God bless our lord and master, Muḥammad, and his family.

Praise be to God, who creates life's breath and revives the dead, who measures destinies and disperses nations – some to the guidance of the proper way, some to abandonment in the temptations to commit evil and sin – who reveals the truth by conspicuous proofs and by destroying impiety and falsehood, who, when the people strayed and abandoned the truth, despatched the Prophet – God bless and comfort him – as a herald and warner, as a summoner to God on His behalf, as a beacon radiant.

Convinced that the proofs that confirm God's absolute unity hold the way to salvation and are a connecting link to the infusion of the saving grace, but having noticed that comprehensive works devoted to decisive results and irrefutable demonstration are beyond the comprehension of the people in our time, and seeing coincidentally that the ordinary handbooks of doctrinal beliefs[1] lack conclusive arguments, I resolved to follow a method that allows for definitive proofs and rational argumentation, and is thus a step above the handbook but without being quite as elevated as those prodigious compilations. But it is God who assigns help and success, and it is He who deserves the credit.

1 The Arabic term here is *muʿtaqadāt*, plural of *muʿtaqad* or "what is believed". By extension it means, as in this case, a manual or handbook of beliefs, a catechism.

Section
On the Character of Reason

The first duty of a person of sound intellect, upon attaining the age of puberty or of legal sexual maturity, is to aspire after a correct reasoning that furnishes sure knowledge that the world was temporally produced. Reasoning, in the idiom of the theologians, is the reflection that seeks that which establishes either certain knowledge or the preponderance of conviction. Reasoning is then divided into two: the correct and the false. Correct reasoning is what leads to discovering the method by which a proof is proven and the false is what precludes it. Reasoning, moreover, might be defective by deviating from the rules of proof from the start, or it might become false, even though begun on a proper basis, because of an extraneous factor that intervenes.

Someone might point out here that a group of the ancients denied that reason leads to knowledge and claimed instead that the senses are the faculties that apprehend knowledge. How would one refute them? Our answer is to pose a dichotomy and ask whether these people claim to know for certain that reasoning is defective or do they merely doubt it? If they are certain of the defectiveness of reasoning, they contradict their own doctrine that limits the faculties for knowing to the senses because knowing the defectiveness of reasoning is not within the category of sensible objects.

Furthermore, we would ask whether they came to know the defectiveness of reasoning *a priori* or whether they know it by reasoning? If they insist that they know it *a priori,* that would be truly incredible, since thereafter they will have no way to protect their assertion from its contradiction. And yet if they hold that they perceive the defectiveness of reasoning by reasoning itself, they contravene their own premise in so far as they deny reasoning as a whole and judge that it does not produce knowledge but then adhere to a kind of reasoning and admit to its being a way to attain knowledge.

They may reply: When you affirm reasoning and claim that it leads to knowledge, do you base your claim on an *a priori* necessity or do you establish it on the basis of reasoning itself? If you claim necessity, you are caught in the same bind into which you forced us and the result you aimed for has turned back on you. But if you judge the validity of reasoning by reasoning itself, you affirm a thing by itself which is inadmissible. We answer: Does your arguing in this fashion provide you any benefit or does it yield no benefit at all? If you insist that it does not yield knowledge or furnish a ruling principle, you have confessed to its being nonsense and thus spared us the trouble of a reply.

If they claim that it supplies knowledge of the falseness of our proof, they have employed one kind of reasoning while attempting to deny the whole of it. If they then reply: Our goal is the opposing of a falsehood with a falsehood, we can refute them with the dichotomy in which we point out that the contradiction of a falsehood by a falsehood is itself one means of reasoning. We insist there is no inconsistency in affirming the sum total of reasoning on the ground of one kind only which affirms, in fact, both itself and the rest.

The questioner may then say: I am not sure of the falseness of reasoning and so your dichotomy does not work on me. Rather, I am in doubt and seek guidance. The way to speak to those who want guidance is to say: Your path is to reason through the proofs that are rationally grounded and to pursue a straight and open course. If your reasoning proceeds soundly, and its postulates are ordered appropriately, it will lead you to knowledge. But he who reasons as described and yet persists in denying that correct reasoning leads to knowledge, will have merely made clear his obstinacy and cancelled thereby his wish for guidance.

Chapter: [*On the opposition of reasoning to knowledge, ignorance and doubt*]

Reasoning is in contrast to the knowledge of that thing which is the object of reasoning, and with ignorance of that thing or doubt about it. Reasoning contrasts with knowledge in that it inquires after it and desires to attain it and that is in contrast to the actual realization of knowledge, since, once attained, it is no longer sought after. The way reasoning contrasts with ignorance is that ignorance is belief attached to a doctrine which differs from what really exists but the one described as believing is convinced of it nevertheless, and that is the opposite of inquiry and investigation. Doubting is a fluctuation between two beliefs, whereas reasoning is solely a desire for the truth and thus it is also in contrast with knowledge and with all of its other contraries.

Correct reasoning, pursued appropriately and completely, and in the absence of an intervening impediment that prevents knowledge, brings about the knowledge of the object of that reasoning. For the reasoner, ignorance of what was once proven cannot follow that reasoning as long as he preserves a recollection of it. But reasoning does not "engender" knowledge and it does not "necessitate" it in the manner that a cause necessitates its effect. The Muʿtazilites claim that it does "engender" knowledge, although they agree with us that the recollecting of reasoning, even though it comprises knowledge, does not engender it. This principle of "engendering" will be refuted in its own place, God willing.

They may well say here: Were reason not to engender knowledge nor to necessitate it in the way a cause necessitates its effect, what is the sense in which it "comprises" it? We reply: The objective here is that sound reasoning, when pursued from the beginning and with any later extraneous defect eliminated, provides intellectual surety of the certainty of the knowledge of the object. Their mutual certainty is necessary but without one of them actually "necessitating" the other or "making it exist" or "producing" it. The situation of the two is analogous to the desire for something vis-à-vis knowledge of it, since wanting the thing is inconceivable without knowing about it. Their interconnection, however, does not require that one of them be the cause of the other, or its necessitator, or its generator.

Chapter: [*Sound reasoning and false reasoning*]

Sound reasoning is implicitly connected to knowledge, as previously specified, and false reasoning is not connected to it. Just as it is not connected to knowledge, similarly it is not connected to ignorance or any of the contraries of knowledge other than ignorance. Sound reasoning reveals to the reasoner the manner by which a proof entails knowledge of the thing proven. When reasoning is interrupted by the occurrence of a fallacy,[1] it becomes defective. Fallacy is in no way conducive of conviction in actuality since, were fallacy to be actually conducive to conviction, it would constitute a proof and such conviction would then constitute knowledge. What will clarify this point is that a proof, when it proves on the basis of its essential character [as proof], demonstrates to all who comprehend it the knowledge of what is proven. If there were a role for fallacy in it, the person who understands the real nature of the fallacy [as false reasoning] would be led to ignorance none the less, whereas such is not the case.

Chapter: [*On proofs*]

Proofs are that in which a person, by the correctness of reasoning, reaches what was not known as a necessity of ordinary habit. They are divided into those that are rational and those that are based on tradition.

Rational proofs are what prove solely by means of their own intrinsic and necessary characteristics. For the validity of their existence, they do not stipulate anything other than the indicators of what they prove, as for example, the innovated indicating by the very possibility of its existence the entailing agent that specifies that it has a possible existence. Similarly, mastery and particularization indicate the knowledge of a master or the purpose of the particularizing agent.

Traditional proofs are those that rely on a truthful report or a [divine] command that requires compliance.

Chapter: [*Reasoning is a requirement of the law*[2]]

Reasoning that confers proper understanding [in religion] is obligatory and perceiving its obligatoriness is a part of the law itself and the aggregate of rules

---

1 *Shubha*: fallacious reasoning or paralogism, reasoning that is false in point of form or is contrary to the rules of logic.

2 The law here and later renders the set of terms and concepts surrounding the notion of *sharīʿa*, the sacred or canonical law of Islam.

concerning these legal obligations come either from proofs derived from the tradition or from the premises behind legal cases.

The Muʿtazilites held that it is the intellect that confers the comprehension of obligations and that, among these, one is reasoning itself. So, according to them, its obligatory status is known intellectually. This is a problem that will come up later, God willing. For now, I will mention only that part of it which is specific to the issue of reasoning.

They might say: When you deny that perceiving the obligatory nature of such reasoning is a function of intellect, in taking that approach, you reject the challenge[3] issued by the prophets and shut off thereby the method of validating them. When they summoned the people to reflect on what they had caused to appear and urged them to reason about the miracles they had revealed – these were the miraculous signs which specifically distinguished them – if they were told that reasoning is not required except with regard to the previously established law and its legal impositions which continue thereafter, according to us, no law could have existed to confer those obligations. This doctrine would have thus left them devoid of guidance, persisting instead in unbelief and obstinacy.[4]

We reply: This opinion which you would force on us in the matter of received law turns against you in regard to the issue of intellect. What brings one to know the obligatoriness of reasoning is itself a matter subject to consideration. In your view an intelligent person ought to admit the possibility that a Creator exists who demands that He be acknowledged and expressed gratitude for His blessing and, if that person acknowledges Him, he will be saved and has hope of an ample reward, whereas if he is unfaithful and arrogant, he becomes deserving of a calamitous punishment.

When he compares for himself the two possibilities and notes the contrary outcomes, he will resolve to cleave to the one of them that hints at an enduring happiness and he takes heed of the associating factors in the second that require a painful punishment. The intellect determines by choice the course of salvation and prefers to avoid peril. If the way leading to knowledge of the obligatoriness of reasoning were the inspiration of thoughts in the soul and an intuition of mutually contradictory possibilities, a person who is oblivious to these thoughts and was unheedful of these stirrings of conscience could not know the obligatoriness of reasoning.

In the matter of the comprehension of intellect with respect to neglect and confusion, the opponent here requires what they require of us in the necessity of a law based on tradition. As the presupposition for the discussion concerning the absence of the two thoughts, what we hold them to equals the claim of prophecy

3 *Taḥaddī*: the Prophet's challenge to his opponents to produce a revelation like his if they would deny him and doubt the truth of his claim to prophecy.

4 The Muʿtazilites held that we know the truth and validity of the revelation by virtue of reason and not merely because tradition indicates it.

in the absence of a miracle. The opposite is true for them but what they would assert is not forced on us because a miracle, when it appears and all thinkers have the possibility of grasping it, is virtually the same as the two thoughts in the claim of the opponent. If they happen, the possibility of reasoning in choosing one of the two is like the possibility in the case of a miracle once it occurs.

Here we state: According to us the stipulation of an obligation is the certainty of the tradition that attests to it, in conjunction with the legally capacitated person's possibility of attaining that fact. When miracles occurred and indications proved the truth of the apostles, the law was established and tradition constantly proclaims thereafter legal obligations and forbids what is prohibited. The obligation of something, however, does not depend on the legally capacitated person's knowledge of it, but instead it is stipulated that the person for whom it is intended have the possibility of acquiring knowledge of it.

Someone may ask at this point: From the standpoint of the law, what indicates the obligatoriness of reasoning and inference? We answer: The community has agreed unanimously concerning the obligation to recognize God, the Exalted, and it is evident in the intellect that coming to the acquisition of this cognizance does not occur except through reasoning and that thing in the absence of which one cannot apprehend what is obligatory is itself obligatory.

Section
The True Nature of Knowledge

Knowledge is the recognition of the thing known as it really is. In seeking to define knowledge, this definition is preferable to the various formulas used to define knowledge that have been handed down from some of our colleagues. One of them said that knowledge consists of discerning the known as it really is. Another statement is that of our master[1] – God's mercy be upon him – that knowledge is what causes the one who has it to be knowledgeable. Yet another is the claim of one group that knowledge is what permits the one characterized as having knowledge to do an act masterfully and perfectly.

In regard to the one who says it is the discerning of the known as it really is, in this case, what he intended is that discerning be ascribed to the apprehending of the knowable after having ignored or disregarded it because, at that point, the one who comes to know what he did not says, "I can now discern it." Our aim in defining knowledge, however, is to include in it what comprises both eternal knowledge and temporally produced knowledge.

We also disapprove defining knowledge as that which causes its subject to be knowledgeable. The purpose in a definition is to distinguish precisely the object to be defined, whereas this is a generality since its applications and examples cover every expression that a person might want to define.

It is not correct as well to define knowledge as that through which the person so described achieves mastery because knowing impossibilities and the eternal and enduring existences do not entitle the person described as knowing these things to any sort of mastery. The definition given by this particular person incorporates merely one kind of knowledge which is simply a knowledge that confers expertise and mastery.

In respect to the definition of knowledge, the earlier Muʿtazilites claimed that it is the conviction about something as it is in reality, accompanied by a feeling of certitude. Their definition is shown to be false by the conviction of the person who believes on another's authority that the Creator exists. This is conviction concerning a tenet as it really is, accompanied by the feeling of assurance in respect to that particular doctrine, and yet it is not knowledge. Later Muʿtazilites added to it by stating that it is the conviction about something as it is in reality, accompanied by a feeling of certitude about the particular doctrine when it occurs either from necessity or as a result of reasoning. This again proves false because of the knowledge that God, the Exalted, has no associate and the knowledge of impossibilities such as the union of contraries and the like, for these and others like them, are examples of knowledge and yet are not knowledge

1 The master is Abuʾl-Ḥasan ʿAlī b. Ismāʿīl al-Ashʿarī, the founder of the Ashʿarite school of theology to which al-Juwaynī belonged.

of things. Things, in our view, are what exist, but, in their view, they are both what exist and that which, though non-existent, might exist. Thus, in such a case, there are kinds of knowledge that are excepted from this definition.

Chapter: [*Knowledge is both eternal and temporally produced*]

Knowledge is divided into that which is eternal and that which is temporally produced. Eternal knowledge is an attribute of the Creator, the Exalted, inherent in His essence and connected to the infinitude of things known. This requires that the method whereby God comprehends, may He be sanctified and exalted, is hallowed well beyond being either necessary or acquired.

Contingent knowledge is divided into necessary, self-evident and acquired. Necessary knowledge is contingent knowledge that is associated with either harm or need and over which the servant has no power; self-evident knowledge is like the necessary except that it is not associated with harm or need. Each of these two types is occasionally designated by the name of the other. In the ordinary course of things, necessary knowledge is automatic and there is no escape from it or room to doubt. It is, for instance, like the knowledge gleaned from sense perceptions, or a man's knowledge of himself, or knowledge of the impossibility of uniting contraries or the like. Acquired knowledge is contingent knowledge that is dependent on a contingent power. Moreover, all acquired knowledge is discursive and is what correct reasoning secures in a proof. This is what is customarily given although, in the person so empowered, knowledge comes into being, as does the ability, without previous reasoning. Nevertheless, custom continues to insist that all acquired knowledge is discursive.

Chapter: [*Kinds of knowledge and their contraries*]

The various kinds of knowledge have contraries that are specific to each, that are contrary to their contraries, and that are contrary to the others. With regard to the specific contraries, one of them is ignorance which is to be convinced of an article of belief that differs from its reality. Another is doubt. It is uncertainty concerning two beliefs or more without having a preference for one over another of them. Yet another is supposition which, like doubt, involves hesitation except in that it effects a kind of preference for one of the two beliefs. And also there are general contraries such as death, sleep, carelessness, unconsciousness, which all have meanings that are contrary to the categories of knowing, as well as being contrary to the will and contrary to the contraries of these.

Chapter: [*Intellect is necessary knowledge*]

The intellect is knowledge that is necessary. The proof that it is comprised of necessary knowledge is the impossibility of categorizing it as intellect were it entirely devoid of any and all knowledge.

If someone here says: What prevents the intellect being devoid of knowledge is that its existence is conditional upon the existence of a specimen of knowledge in the same way that the will is conditional upon knowledge of its object, our reply is that our aim is to demonstrate that the intellect carries with it the stipulation of legal obligation. If a person were deprived of it, that person could not know what his obligations are. Since legal capacitation requires that the person so obligated comprehend what the obligations are, that person will not comprehend those obligations except after commencing to know the kinds of knowledge that are the very principles of reasoning, and there is, moreover, no attainment of the knowledge of legal obligation in its absence. Our purpose is to clarify precisely the kind of knowledge we insist must exist prior to the commencement of reasoning and we designate it as intellect. Having explained this intention in regard to the term intellect, the question itself is averted. We do not deny that intellect is an ambiguous term with several different meanings. However, our intended meaning is the one we have just mentioned.

Intellect is not comprised of discursive knowledge because a condition of the commencement of reasoning is the priority of intellect. Nor is intellect the aggregate totality of necessary knowledge since the blind person or someone who does not perceive in that way is described as intelligent despite their lack of various kinds of necessary knowledge. It is clear from this that intellect is a portion of the sum of necessary knowledge but not the whole of it.

The way to make it specific and to determine it precisely is to say the following: All knowledge that is not absent when the intelligent person is aware of it and in which the unintelligent person has no share is intellect. The result of the preceding inquiry requires, therefore, that intellect is the necessary knowledge of the possibility of things that are possible and the impossibility of things impossible – such as the knowledge of the impossibility of uniting contraries, or the knowledge that what is known must be either denied or affirmed, or the knowledge that what exists must either have been temporally produced or is eternal.

Section
The Doctrine of the World's Contingency

Realize, may God guide you in this, that the theologians, hoping to concentrate multiple meanings in a few concise phrases, have agreed on a number of terms that suit their purposes. Among those that they use – one they employ in both lexical and legal usage – is "world", which is all existents save God, the Exalted, and the attributes of His essence. The world consists of atoms[1] and accidents. An atom is what occupies space and possesses a spatially limited volume; an accident is a property adhering to an atom such as colour, taste, odour, life, death, kinds of knowledge, types of will, and powers, that all accompany various atoms.

Another set of terms they utilize concerns "manners of being" [*akwān*]. These include movement and rest, combination and separation. What groups them together is what makes the atom particular to a place or to the determination of place. Body, in the idiom of the theologians, is that which is composite. Whenever two atoms combine, they constitute a body in as much as each one is in combination with the other.

The contingency of atoms is based on several principles. One involves the affirmation of accidents, another asserting their temporal production, another the attestation that it is impossible for an atom to be devoid of accidents, and yet another the assertion that it is impossible for there to be a contingent being that has no beginning. Once these principles are affirmed, it follows from them that atoms cannot precede that which was temporally produced and that which does not come before what is temporally produced is itself temporally produced (and contingent).

In regard to the first of these principles – that is, the affirmation of accidents – a group of heretics tried to deny it. They claimed instead that there exists no other existent than the atoms. The proof that attests to the accidents is our observation of an atom at rest and then subsequently seeing it in a motion which specifies a particular direction towards which it moves and which separates it from its starting point. Since the supposition that the atom could persist in its original state [or direction] is not inconceivable, we know *a priori* that its having this particular direction is something possible and not something inherently necessary. The characteristic that applies can be either in operation or absent. If what has this possibility is to be particularized by the positive instead of the negative, it requires a determining factor that entails its having this affirmative particularity and that is known intuitively as well.

---

1 The Arabic term is *jawhar* which can mean "substance" but in this context refers to the indivisible particle or atom.

Once this fact is confirmed, the determining factor might be thought to be within the atom itself. But, if that were so, the particularity of the direction, in the case we are discussing, would endure as long as the atom itself lasts, without the possibility of its ceasing or of being turned in another direction. This proves that the determining factor is an addition to the atom. It is, however, impossible that the addition be a non-existent since there is no difference between denying the existence of the determining factor and supposing the determining factor to be something without existence. If it is now correct that the determining factor is positively affirmed and is additional to the atom, it must be either its like or something different. But it cannot be its like, since the like of the atom is the atom and, if an atom requires in its particularity another atom for its condition, its particularity in that condition is impossible upon supposing the negation of the atom acting as the determining factor. The matter is not like this. There is no reason why one of two atoms is any more likely to be the determiner than the other.

Thus, if the determining factor is an addition to the atom, and is confirmed now to be something that differs from it, this factor must be either a willful agent or a necessitating property. If, however, it were a necessitating property, its adherence to the atom that is particularized in this condition would be specific to that atom alone because, if the particularity were not specific, the characteristic property would be no more applicable to its case than to any other.

What we have now described fulfils the purpose to which we aspired. If the determiner of the particularizing factor turns out to be an agent and yet the discussion concerns an atom of continuous existence, that would be inconceivable, since the eternally enduring does not act and there is no doubting that an agent acts. The import of all this brings about a proof for the accidents and this is one of the most important objectives in affirming the contingency of the world.

The second principle is the affirmation of the temporal production of the accidents. The goal here follows as a consequence of several principles among which is showing that it is impossible for the eternal to be non-existent, or the impossibility that the accidents subsist in themselves and the impossibility of their being transferred among themselves, and refuting those who profess a doctrine of latency and emergence. It is best to begin by a general proof for the contingency of accidents and for us to bring out these principles in the course of dealing with the associated questions and prove our points by means of our responses.

We maintain that, when it moves, motion intrudes on the atom that was previously at rest, and this intrusion establishes the contingency of this motion, and also the negation of the state of rest by this intrusion entails the contingency of the state of rest, since, were its eternity affirmed, it would be impossible for it to cease to be.

At this point someone might ask: How do you refute those who claim that motion is latent in the atom but then emerges and, because of its emergence, the state of rest becomes latent? We reply: If it were like that, two opposites would merge in the same subject. In the same way as we know the impossibility of something being both in motion and at rest at the same time, we similarly recognize the impossibility of the union of motion and rest.

If movement and rest appear together in one instance and yet movement is concealed in another, this implies the alternation of governing traits which secures here the affirmation of two properties one of which is its being outwardly in motion. The other requires its being quiescent inwardly. In affirming the accidents, the alternation of governing traits and their succession in atoms is the decisive evidence.

If we are to accept emergence and latency as two properties, this requires their emergence upon the emergence of their effect and likewise becoming latent upon the latency of their effect. This sets up a unending chain. Motion by its very definition necessitates that its subject be in motion. If it were possible to affirm motion without this characteristic trait, that possibility must belong to it always but that thereby alters its type and makes it not what it is in reality.

Chapter: [*On the proof that the eternal cannot possibly be non-existent*]

Someone may inquire: What proof is there of the impossibility of the eternal becoming non-existent? We answer: The proof is that its non-existence at a prescribed time makes impossible its being necessary in that the stipulation of the continuance of its previous existence is now precluded and this is known self-evidently to be false. If a possible non-existence were supposed at a prescribed time in conjunction nevertheless with the possibility of the continuance of that existence but without a determining factor, that would also be absurd, since the possible requires a determining factor and non-existence is an absolute negation that cannot be ascribed to any specific agency.

Equally the non-existence cannot be due to the intrusion of a contrary because the intruder is no more likely to be contrary to the eternal than that the eternal precludes the intrusion of what was supposed to be its contrary.

It is not allowed to base the non-existence of the eternal on a requirement that denies any of the conditions of the continuation of the existence of the eternal, since were there to be a condition stipulated for the existence of the eternal, that conditional factor would be an eternal whose non-existence, if likewise supposed, would require itself a determining factor and so on in an unending chain.

At this point someone may say: One of the cornerstones of the proof for the temporal production of accidents rests on the fact that they cannot displace each other. What is the proof that precludes their displacement, if a person could yet claim that the motion that intrudes on an atom is conveyed to it from another atom? The answer is that the very reality of motion is displacement. As long as it exists, it necessarily entails the displacement of the atom. If it were to be conveyed from one atom to another, that requires the intrusion of a condition that was not previously the same as this displacement in it. But this involves a change in its species and changing the species is nonsense. If the displacement is displaced, it also requires displacement, and similarly, that can be said concerning the displacement that is displaced in respect to its being displaced, and this leads on infinitely. Thus, in the sum of what we have just said, it is established that the accidents are contingent and the principles associated with this fact are confirmed.

In regard to the third principle which involves the demonstration of the impossibility of atoms being devoid of accidents, what the orthodox allow in this matter is that the atom cannot be devoid of any and all the varieties of accidents at once, or of any of their contraries, if they possess contraries, and, even if there were but a single contrary, the atom must have one of these two contraries, and moreover were one to suppose the existence of an accident that had no contrary, the atom inevitably sustains an example of that type.

The heretics accept the segregation of atoms from all of the accidents. The atoms, in their terminology, are called "prime matter" [*hayūlā*] and the accidents "form" [*ṣūra*]. Al-Ṣāliḥī[2] allowed this segregation from the total aggregate of accidents at the beginning. The Basran Muʿtazilites would not accept such deprivation in the case of modes of being but did allow for segregation in respect to the rest of the accidents. Al-Kaʿbī,[3] and those who followed him, accepted segregation in the case of modes of being but disapproved with respect to the deprivation of colours. Thus all of our opponents agree with us in rejecting the deprivation of the accidents once the atom has acceded to them. The discussion here is thus required to take note of the heretics only in the matter of modes of being. If the statement in the matter is restricted to only what is necessary, then by the immediate intuition of intellect, we know that the atoms which are susceptible to combination and separation are not intelligible unless they are contiguous or separately distinct.

What makes this clear is that when they are combined in something that will not cease to be, the intellect cannot confirm their union except on the condition of a previous separation in that it supposes this as their existence prior to this union. Similarly, if a separation should intervene between them, we immediately understand that this separation was preceded by union.

Our purpose in seeking to prove the contingency of the world is made clear by the positive affirmation of the modes of being. In our attempt to refute the Muʿtazilites in those areas where they differ from us, we invoke two considerations. One of them involves taking notice of the general agreement that the deprivation of the accidents, once they are attributed, is not admissible. We maintain that

2 Abuʾl-Ḥusayn al-Ṣāliḥī, a prominent Muʿtazilite theologian of the third/ninth century, often reckoned also among the later Murjiʾa.

3 Abuʾl-Qāsim al-Balkhī al-Kaʿbī was famous as the leader of the Baghdādī Muʿtazilites. He died 319/931.

each accident persists and that it is withdrawn from its subject upon the intrusion of its contrary. According to the Muʿtazilites, the contrary only intrudes upon a state in which the withdrawn accident has ceased to exist so that, when white is erased, it is possible that, subsequent to its withdrawal, there is no other colour that comes into existence. This is a result of having approved the supposition of the deprivation of colour at the point of origin. We could pursue this same course of argument for the other types of accidents.

We maintain as well that what establishes the impossibility of the accidents subsisting in the divine essence, may He be praised and exalted, is that, if they did subsist through Him, He would not be devoid of them and this requires that He be contingent. When an opponent approves the segregation of the atom from temporally produced things, although its receiving them is an accepted fact, he cannot thereafter put forth a proof that the exalted Creator cannot possibly be susceptible to the temporally produced.

The fourth principle consists in demonstrating the impossibility of temporally produced things that have no beginning. The significance of this pillar is decisive; affirming its point upsets the heretics' entire set of doctrines. It is a principle for the majority of them that the world will never quit being as it is and that each revolution of the sphere was preceded by another revolution, back endlessly without beginning. In the world of generation and corruption, temporally produced things are continuous and successive and are like this without a beginning; each of them was preceded by its like, each son preceded by a father, every plant preceded by a seed, every egg by a chicken.

Here we say: The necessary import of your principle requires the admission that there are temporally produced things that are without numerical limit, that lack any ultimate term to their respective units, and that succeed one another in existence. The falseness of that is known by the basic axioms of intellect. If we take for discussion the revolution in which we ourselves are at the moment, we would say, on the basis of the heretics' principle, that, prior to the revolution we are in the midst of, an infinite number of previous revolutions have ended. Since what refuses limitation cannot be terminated in a unity that follows on the heels of another unity, if the revolutions that were prior to this one have terminated, their cessation and expiration proves that they were limited. This assessment suffices to prove our point.

Someone may remark here that the duration of the inhabitants in paradise is everlasting and eternal. If asserting that there are temporally produced things that have no future end is not implausible, that the temporally produced have no beginning is also not implausible. We respond: The impossibility is the entry into existence of what is infinite in successive units and there is, in the occurrence of existence in the future, nothing to stipulate the existence of an infinite. It is impossible that, among those things granted power by God, the Exalted, there enter into existence what a number does not encompass and a duration does not count. What verifies this is that the very meaning of temporal production is to have a beginning. Asserting that there are temporally produced things and yet denying origination is a contradiction. Nevertheless, temporal production does not by its very nature mean that there is also an end in the future.

The experts give two examples for these two cases. They say that the example for asserting the existence of temporally produced things without a beginning is as if someone should say to the person to whom he is speaking, "I will not give you a dirham unless before doing so I have given you a dinar and I will not give you a dinar unless before doing so I have given you a dirham." No one would expect, according to the conditions specified, that he would ever be given either dinar or dirham.

The example, however, that is required of us is for the speaker to say, "I will not give you a dinar unless having done so I give you a dirham and I will not give you a dirham unless afterward I give you a dinar." In this second case one might well anticipate the fulfilment of the stipulation.

Having, by previous statements, affirmed the accidents and their temporal production, the impossibility of the atom being deprived of them, and of their foundation in a temporal beginning, the implication of these principles assures that the atoms do not precede them and what does not precede the temporally produced is temporally produced itself of necessity and without the need for reflection or discussion. These thoughts are enough to establish the temporality of the atoms and the accidents. Hereafter we will move on to describe the path that leads to knowledge of the Maker. And in God is the grace.

Section
A Statement Affirming the Knowledge of the Maker

Once having established the temporality of the world and demonstrated the commencement of its existence, it follows that the temporally produced is that whose existence and annihilation are both possible and every moment of time in which its occurrence might happen was but one of the possibilities in other moments that preceded this one. Among the possible eventualities is also the delay of its existence beyond that moment by hours. If the possible existence occurs instead of the continuation of the also possible non-existence, the mind instinctively decides that this requires a particularizing factor that specifies it with this eventuality. That, may God provide you guidance, is clear of necessity and needs neither the investigation of postulates nor a commitment to a programme of reasoning.

Once the temporal's requiring a particularizing agent is clear as a whole, that particularizing agent must be an agent that necessarily makes the temporal happen in the same manner by which the cause necessarily produces its effect, or it must be a natural physical force, as was held by the partisans of naturalistic physics, or it must be a free agent.

It is wrong for it to follow the rule for causes since a cause necessarily causes its effect simultaneously. If the determinant were assumed to be a cause, it must then be either eternal or contingent. If it were eternal, it would necessarily cause the world to exist timelessly as well, and that leads to the doctrine of the eternity of the world, whereas we have already established the proofs of its temporality. If the determinant was temporally produced, that requires yet another determinant and leads to an unending chain of claims about a determining agent for the determining agent.

Those who insist that the determinant is physical nature in and of itself are quite preposterous in making such a claim because nature, for those who affirm it, causes its effect necessarily, if and when any impediments are removed. If nature were eternal, that would entail the eternity of the world; if it were temporally produced, there would have to be a determining agent. This assessment suffices to discredit these people. Perhaps, we will refute the naturalists yet again, God willing.

Thus, if it is false that the determinant of the temporal was a cause that necessitated it, or that a nature involuntarily in and of itself brought it into being, it becomes clear conclusively, as a result, that the determinant of temporal things is an agent that acts to produce them by free choice and specifies their occurrence with certain attributes and at specific times.

Once having grasped the temporality of the world and understood clearly that it has a Maker, the intelligent person must thereafter reflect on the following three principles: one of them is to take cognizance of those attributes that must be applied to God, the Exalted; the second comprises an awareness of those attributes that cannot be applied to Him; and the third includes acknowledging what His governance comprises. In taking proper note of these three principles, the foundational rules of belief will come into play, God willing.

Section
A Statement of What Attributes God Requires

It should be known that among His attributes there are those that pertain to His person in Itself and others that denote His qualities. The essential core is the attributes of self which are all attributes that affirm a self and inhere in it in so far as the self endures apart from any causative factor that might be due to a cause arising out of the subject.

The qualifying attributes are those in the spheres of governance that belong to the subject and are due to causative factors that arise from causes in the subject of the attribution.[1]

An explanation of these two types occurs in the following examples. That the atom exists as a confined entity means that this attribute is affirmed inherently of the atom as long as its essential self persists and is separate from a causative factor that might intrude upon it. Thus, this is one of the attributes of self. In contrast, that a knower is a knower is brought about by the knowledge that resides in the knower. This attribute and those that resemble it are, in our view, examples of qualifying attributes.

Our method in the exposition we follow in this treatise is to establish the knowledge of the essential attributes that are affirmed of God, the Exalted, and we commence it with an investigation of the proof of His existence.

Someone at this point may say: You have verified the knowledge of the Maker in what preceded, but how now do you deny those who consider the Maker to be a non-existent? We reply: Non-existence is, according to us, perfect negation and thus what is denied existence retains none of the attributes of affirmation at all. There is no difference between a maker whose existence is denied and considering the Maker denied in every respect. Rather the denial of the Maker, even though decisively proven to be false, is a doctrine that is in and of itself a contradiction. It leads to the affirmation of a maker who is himself negated by a contradiction. The Muʿtazilites are the only ones who held a doctrine that the Maker is without existence since they would affirm positive attributes for something that is without existence. They decided that a being without existence is one of the properties of the genera.

The method we approve, however, is not to consider existence one of the attributes since existence is the very essence itself. It is not the same as spatial

---

1 The distinction between the two kinds of attributes (*ṣifāt*) the author speaks about in the following section and thereafter is among the most difficult of the concepts in his theology. It is, accordingly, not easy to find an apt English translation for them. The "attributes of self" renders *ṣifāt nafsiyya*, and "qualifying attributes" *ṣifāt maʿnawiyya*.

extension in regard to the atom because spatial extension is an attribute added to the essence of the atom. Existence in regard to the atom, for us, is itself without additional qualification. Leading scholars – may God be pleased with them – expended great effort to include existence among the attributes, but knowledge of existence is simply knowledge of the essence in and of itself.

Chapter: [The proof of the Exalted Creator's eternity]

Here someone may ask: Once having confirmed the knowledge that He exists, what is the proof of the Exalted Creator's eternity and what is the reality of an eternity with respect to the past? We reply: Some leading scholars maintain that the eternal is that whose existence has no beginning.

Our master[2] – may God's mercy be with him – noted that each existent that is continuous in its existence and extends over a prolonged time is called ancient [*qadīm*] in conventional speech. God, the Exalted, has said, ". . . until it returns like an old [*qadīm*] palm-bough" [36:39]. Our purpose, however, is to prove, in the case at hand, that the existence of the eternal has no beginning. The proof is that, if it were temporally produced, it would have had a producer. If so, the same could be said of its producer. The result is the affirmation of a series of temporally produced things which have no beginning term, and the falsehood in that outcome was already made quite clear.

Someone else might remark at this point that affirming an existent that has no beginning is to affirm temporal periods that follow successively without end, since the continuous duration of existence is not intelligible except in terms of temporal units. This leads to the affirmation of a temporal series without a first term. Our answer is that this is an error on the part of those who believe it because temporal units are indicated as such on account of things that exist in conjunction with one another. Each existing thing bears a relationship to the thing which is in conjunction with it and that relationship defines its temporal moment. In ordinary usage this determination shows up in temporal periodization based on the movements of the heavenly spheres and the alternation of night and day.

Thus, although this stipulation applies in respect to the meaning of time, that it be conjoined with another existent is, nevertheless, not a condition for the existence of a thing. Hence the attachment of one of the two to the other is not a requisite intellectual presupposition in this matter. If every existent must have a temporal period and yet the temporal periods are measured by an existent which itself in turn requires temporal periods, this leads to absurdities no reasonable person embraces. Prior to the advent of temporally produced things, the Creator – hallowed is He – was alone in His existence and in His attributes, and nothing temporal was connected to Him in any way.

---

2 As previously, this is a reference to Abuʾl-Ḥasan al-Ashʿarī.

Chapter: [*God, the Exalted, subsists by Himself*]

The Creator – hallowed and exalted is He – subsists by Himself, well beyond the need of a situation in which to locate or a place in which to stand. The various expressions of the leading masters – may God, the Exalted, have mercy on them – differ in regard to the concept of an existent subsisting by itself. Some among them said that it is an existent that has no need of a substrate, but the atom, according to this, would subsist by itself. The leading master and expert, Abū Isḥāq[3] – God be pleased with him – maintained that what subsists on its own is an existent that has no need for either substrate or determining agent. This condition, in his view, is exclusive to the Exalted Creator. Although it has no need of a situation in which to locate, the existence of the atom depends originally on the determination of an empowering agent.

The aim of the explanation in this chapter is to establish a proof that the transcendent holiness of the Lord is hallowed and exalted beyond any need for a substrate. The proof is that, if He were located in a substrate and His existence required that substrate, that substrate would be eternal and He would be an attribute of it, since every substrate is qualified by what resides in it. And yet the attribute cannot be qualified by the characteristic features which of necessity provide it with meaningful properties. We will later clarify the necessity of qualifying the Creator as being Living, Knowing, Powerful.

Chapter: [*One attribute of God is utter difference from the temporally produced*]

Among the attributes of the eternal Self, the Exalted, is His utter difference from the temporally produced. The Exalted Lord does not resemble anything among the things temporally produced nor do any of them resemble Him.

There is no doubt that this section depends from the outset on explaining the facts of mutual similarity and difference. Things that are mutually similar are each of two beings where what is characteristic of one is characteristic of the other. In defining the pair, it is often said that they are two beings that are equal in so far as what is necessary, possible and impossible. However, the first expression is preferable to this. The mutually dissimilar are each of a pair of beings for which the essential attributes affirmed of one cannot be affirmed of the other.

Ibn al-Jubbāʾī[4] and the later Muʿtazilites were of the opinion that the mutually similar are two things that share in the attributes that are most characteristic of them both. They maintained further that sharing what is most characteristic means necessarily the sharing of the other attributes that are uncaused. On this

3 Abū Isḥāq Ibrāhīm al-Isfarāyīnī, an Ashʿarite theologian and Shāfiʿī jurist, who died in 418/1027 in Nayshabur where he taught.

4 Abū Hāshim ʿAbd al-Salām b. al-Jubbāʾī, was a prominent Muʿtazilite theologian and the son of the famous Basran Muʿtazilite teacher of Abuʾl-Ḥasan al-Ashʿarī. Abū Hāshim died in 321/933.

doctrine they built a goodly number of heretical deviations, but it is false regardless. Even though sharing this basic characteristic necessitates sharing the rest of the essential attributes, relying on the most characteristic when they do not share what is most characteristic precludes any association with what differs from it in the attributes that are more general. Thus, when the cause disappears, the effect is automatically nullified. We know, for example, that blackness, which differs from motion in terms of what is most characteristic to each, shares with it in being temporally produced, in existence, in its being an accident and otherwise. Thus, the determination of mutual similarity based on the most characteristic of shared attributes is wrong. What makes it wrong is that a thing, according to them, resembles its like in that in which it differs from its unlike. But knowledge is of necessity dissimilar to power in the very fact of its being knowledge. Denying this is simply to repudiate the facts which, instead, prove the falseness of attempting to base mutual difference and similarity on what is the most characteristic of the two.

The proper method, after having refuted the notion that the most characteristic attribute is the cause of similarity and difference, is to argue that it is necessary to take into account all of the essential attributes in determining mutual similarity. That one item among them should cause it is now clearly false and the only way is to account for all of them as a whole. The Muʿtazilites in fact refuted their own premise when they affirmed of the Creator – hallowed and exalted is He – a temporally produced will, which could not possibly depend on being situated in a substrate, and yet they judged it to be like our will which does depend on a substrate. This is to admit to a sharing in the most characteristic without the requirement of sharing in the rest of the attributes.

Chapter: [*On the mutually similar and dissimilar*]

Someone may ask: Is it possible that one of two mutually similar things have a function that the other does not, or is it also possible that one of two dissimilar things shares a function with the other? We answer: This issue comprises two questions.

The response to the first is that one thing cannot uniquely have an essential attribute that its likeness does not have, but it is possible that it possess alone a qualifying attribute the like of which will only possibly occur in the thing that is similar. An example to explain this is that atoms are alike in that they have the same essential attributes, since one atom does not exclusively possess spatial extension, receptivity to accidents, or any other of the essential attributes. But certain atoms are particularized by the advent of accidents the like of which are, in the rest of the atoms, only possible. As a result the particularity of a thing in having some attributes which are also possible in its likeness does not invalidate the mutuality of their similarity. The thing resembles its likeness because of its essence and therefore, in the application of similarity, one considers solely the attributes of essence. The contingencies that are possible do not modify the attributes of essence.

As for the second matter contained in this issue, the method in its case is to note that nothing prevents a thing sharing with what is dissimilar some attributes that are of a more general nature. Thus blackness, although unlike whiteness, shares with it the attribute of existing, their both being accidents of colour and others.

Our purpose in considering this issue is to refute a faction of the Esotericists[5] who insist that one cannot ascribe to the Creator – may He be exalted above their words – any attribute of affirmation. They claim that, if they were to represent the Eternal as being an existent essence, that would be, on their part, to compare Him with the temporally produced since these later beings are existents and essences. In inquiring about Him, in regard to the attributes of affirmation, they follow a procedure of negation. If someone says to them that the Maker is an existent being, they deny it, and claim instead that He is *not* non-existent.

The idea they put forth here lacks true reality. We can state without exceptions that we know that there is no intermediary stage between denial and affirmation. When and if these people deny the Maker, proofs that affirm knowledge of Him should be established in opposition to them. If they affirm Him, they are caught affirming of Him what they warned against because the temporally produced, once affirmed, comprises His affirmation as well. If they admit that the Maker is affirmed but that we cannot specify of Him an affirmation, that will not help them, since mutual similarity and difference are attached to what is affirmed intellectually, not to what concerns the mere utterances in speaking and naming. The only way left to them is to characterize the Exalted Lord as the only existent and to preclude describing temporally produced things with that term. This way they might achieve the result they hoped for. But what they hold is false in every respect.

Should it be asked whether we hold to the doctrine that, in existing, God, the Exalted, resembles the temporally produced or do we deny it, we answer that it is a matter not susceptible to discussion. For someone to state that the Exalted Lord resembles the temporally produced, and that His essence is thereby qualified by mutual resemblance, involves the Eternal sharing with the temporal in one aspect only. There is in this no scope for general comparison or an analogy to be followed upon by points of more particularity. Rather it should be said that the reality of existence applies in the same way to the visible and to the invisible and that a consideration of those things which they share occurs regardless of the others.

---

5 al-Bāṭiniyya. Most likely the author refers here to the Ismāʿīlīs even though the term "Esotericists" need not apply specifically to them as opposed to some others. However, the theologicial doctrine he cites in this instance is theirs and they were fairly well known for advocating it.

Here it might be asked: Did you not specify that He is unlike His creation while also admitting that He shares with the temporally produced in existence? Our response is that dissimilarity between two unlike things does not follow the rule for the mutually similar, since similarity applies by its very nature to the equivalence of two like things that are so qualified in all attributes of essence, whereas mutual difference does not entail difference in all of the attributes. In that difference cannot be realized other than between two existing things, of necessity the discussion of difference is a consideration of two differing things that share in existing. Since mutual resemblance entails the general sharing of the attributes of essence, we do not apply it here. But dissimilarity is, by contrast, not characterized by difference in all of the attributes.

Chapter: [*Concerning what cannot be attributed to God*]

Someone might remark here: You mentioned that the sharing of the Eternal and the temporally produced in certain affirmative attributes is not precluded. Specify for us now which attributes are particular to the temporally produced that cannot be applied to God. We would respond: We will mention, in the first instance, those that are particular to atoms. Spatial extension is among those that are particular to atoms and the doctrine of the orthodox without exception is that God – hallowed and exalted is He – transcends spatial extension and being particularized by a direction.

The Karrāmiyya[6] and some of the Anthropomorphists[7] hold that the Creator – who is high indeed above their words – is spatially extended and particularized by the direction upward. But the proof of the falsity of what they teach is that what is particularized by direction exists on a par with bodies and everything that is on a par with bodies cannot escape being equivalent in dimensions, or to the dimensions of a part of it, or by which a part of it is measured. Each principle leads either to the measurement of God or to dividing Him into parts, both of which are plainly outright heresies. Beyond that, what measures bodies may be contiguous to them and what allows of bodily contiguity and apposition is itself temporally produced, since the way to prove the temporal production of atoms depends on their susceptibility to contiguousness and apposition, as previously noted. If they generalize the proof of the temporal production of the atom, accepting the temporal production of what they assert is spatially extended must follow. If they reject the proof as a consequence of what they insist upon, the means to establish the temporal production of the atom ceases to be available.

---

6 The Karrāmiyya were a sect founded in the third/ninth century by Muḥammad b. Karrām who was noted for preaching ascetic piety. His sect grew and spread and was still important at the time of al-Juwaynī. Some Islamic heresiographers list the Karrāmiyya among the Anthropomorphists, although al-Ashʿarī himself put them with the Murjiʾites.

7 al-Ḥashwiyya are those who accept literally and uncritically the anthropomorphic descriptions of God as given in the Qurʾān and traditions.

If, moreover, they adduce support from the apparent meaning of God's words: "The Merciful is seated [*istawā*] on the throne" [20:5], our method is to counter with verses that allow us to give this statement an allegorical interpretation. Among these is His statement: "He is with you wherever you are" [57:4], and His saying: "Is then He who stands over every soul knowing what it earns . . . " [13:33]. What is the meaning of these verses? If they construe them as His being with us in terms of encompassing and knowledge, we cannot be prevented from understanding "seated" as meaning supremacy and dominion. This is a meaning widely understood in the language since the Arabs say, "so and so holds [*istawā*] the seat of power" in a case where that person possesses the keys of government and rules over the populace. And mentioning in this instance the throne indicates that it is the most exalted of created things in the minds of men. He mentions it here as a reminder of all that is beneath it in rank.

If one were to claim that "seating", understood as dominion, intends a previous struggle and competition, we reply that this is false because, if "seating" gave that implication, "supremacy" would do likewise [which it does not]. But does seating in the sense of becoming firmly established presuppose disorder and agitation prior to it? That requires, however, admitting to heresy. But, to construe "seating" as the purpose in God's command with respect to the throne is not out of line; this was the interpretation given by Sufyān al-Thawrī[8] – may God have mercy on him. He supported it by God's words: "Then He ascended [*istawā*] to the sky and it was then smoke" [41:11], but here with the sense of "directed Himself to".

Someone might ask why not take the verse in its apparent sense, instead of resorting to allegorical interpretation, by arguing that it is one of the ambiguous verses whose interpretation only God knows. To that we reply: If the purpose of this question is to keep "seating" strictly within the limits of what is meant when using it literally, then it surely means "to become firmly established" and that results necessarily in a doctrine of corporeality. Any doubt in this matter falls under the same judgment and ends up as a belief in corporeality. Deciding that the sense "to become firmly established" is impossible supposes, on the contrary, that the apparent meaning is not applicable in this case. And thus those who demand that the import of the verse remain within its apparent sense have no justification for this position.

Having decisively eliminated any resort to the apparent meaning, there is no longer an excuse not to construe the verse in the sense most appropriate according to reason and yet also in conformity with the requirement of religious doctrine. Avoiding an interpretation as a precaution against the introduction of a suspect belief leads instead to confusion and prejudice, provoking errors among the masses, opening the way for doubts concerning the fundamentals of faith and

8 A widely respected expert in traditions (*ḥadīth*), and a native of Kufa, who died in Basra in 161/778.

exposing portions of God's book to unfounded conjectures. The significance of God's words "and the others are ambiguous" in the verse where it appears [3:7] refers back to those who deny the resurrection which was, for the apostle of God – God bless him and grant him peace – a final hour fast approaching, and the questions being asked about its limits, its location and its conditions. The aim of God's words "and none know its interpretation except God" [3:7] is that none know its final outcome except God. That sense is supported by His words "do they await anything except its interpretation" [7:53] and the verse in which it occurs. "Interpretation" [*taʾwīl*] here is to be understood as the "final hour" in agreement with the view of the orthodox.

Chapter: [*That God is not a body, in contrast to the doctrine of the Karrāmiyya*]

Groups of the Karrāmiyya, according to their own doctrine, professed to speak of the Exalted Lord as a body. The way to begin the argument against them is for us to note that, in its primary linguistic meaning, body denotes a combination and, for this reason, one refers to a person who is fatter and plumper than another as being stouter [*ajsam*] than he or simply bulkier [*jasīm*]. An even greater extent implies the further accumulation of portions. Because, with respect to body, augmentation denotes an increased accumulation, the term "body" itself must at its most basic indicate combination, as in the case of "more knowledgeable", [*aʿlam*] which, since it indicates superiority in knowledge, proves that "knowing" [*ʿālim*] denotes its root meaning.

Here then we say: If you call the Exalted Creator a body and assert that He has bodily characteristics, you expose yourself to two concerns: either you nullify the proof of the temporal production of the atoms, since it was founded upon their susceptibility to combination, contiguity and apposition; or you carry it further and insist that temporal production can be proven to exist within the Maker Himself. Both of these are departures from true religion and a withdrawal from the fold of Islam.

Among these people there are some who claim they do not assert that the Exalted Creator has the characteristic features of bodies but that the sense in which they speak of Him as a body merely establishes His existence. If they say this, answer them as follows: How can you arbitrarily assign your Lord a name that implies some attribute He cannot possibly have in the absence of any intimation of it in law or in established tradition? What difference is there between you and those who say He is a bodily being but then understand bodily being as existence? Here one might claim that, since it is not forbidden to call God a soul, as God's words prove in the following verse "you know what is in my soul and I do not know what is in your soul" [5:116],[9] then it is also not forbidden to speak of Him as a body. We answer: The use of analogy in affirming

9 These are words said by Jesus to God.

the names of the Lord – hallowed and exalted is He – is not tolerated since, if that were allowed, doing likewise would be permitted in respect to bodily being, such as, for example, intending by "soul" merely existence. For that reason it is all right for someone to say *nafs al-ʿaraḍ* and *al-ʿaraḍ nafsuh*, "the accident itself", but it is not correct to say *jism al-ʿaraḍ*, "the body of the accident". Here it is fundamental to follow the letter of the law.

Chapter: [*That God does not accept accidents*]

Among the ways the atom differs from the Divine is its receptivity to accidents and the validity of its being qualified by temporal productions. The Lord – hallowed and exalted is He – transcends susceptibility to temporal contingencies. The Karrāmiyya maintained that temporal contingencies arise in the essence of the Lord – exalted is He above their claims. Then they insist further that He is not qualified by the temporal contingencies that arise in Him. This results in a stupidity not previously attained for they say that a temporally produced statement arises in the essence of the Lord – hallowed and exalted is He – although He is not the one who speaks it but rather only the source of the speaker's capacity to speak.

The basis of their doctrine is that the names of the Lord do not allow repeated applications and, for that reason, they describe Him as being Creator from eternity. Thus, while they refrain from affirming of Him a qualification that is new in either thought or word, they none the less cannot avoid admitting that temporal contingencies arise in Him.

The proof that what they claim is false is that, if He were receptive to temporal contingencies, He would never be free of them, as was determined previously to be the case with the atom, because we have stipulated the impossibility of their not having accidents; and what cannot be free of temporal contingencies, does not precede them. Hence their doctrine veers towards declaring the Maker Himself temporally contingent.

Such a proof, however, is not applicable to the principles set out by the Muʿtazilites in that they hold that atoms devoid of accidents are conceivable within the conditions we specified in their regard earlier, and also they affirm features of the Creator's essence that are renewable, such as newly arising expressions of His will. These are not impossible according to them. They are, however, also blocked from generalizing their argument in this matter because, in that the renewed application of features of God's essence is not disallowed without establishing temporal contingency, likewise the successive application to His essence of the very same accidents is not precluded.

We say to the Karrāmiyya: Your resort to affirming a temporally contingent speech, in spite of your refusing to qualify the Creator with it, is self-contradictory. If a quality is sustained by an invisible substrate without the substrate being affected by its characteristics, it would be possible with regard to the visible as well that words, knowledge, and desires arise in a substrate without affecting the substrate with the characteristics of the adhering properties. That would confuse the reality of things and yield only absurdities. Thereupon ask them: If you admit that specimens of temporal contingencies arise in God's essence, what stops you from agreeing that temporally contingent colours arise in His essence one after another? The same consequences occur in regard to those temporal contingencies which they agree with us cannot arise in God, as, for example, with the temporally contingent power and knowledge which, according to them, arise in God's essence following their principle concerning the words and the will that are temporally contingent. There exists no distinction, therefore, between what they profess and what they reject.

We would inquire further: If you qualify the Exalted Lord as being spatially extended, even though everything spatially extended has volume and bodily mass and bodily things are inconceivable in the absence of colour, is there any reason to deny the possibility of colour arising in the Lord's essence? Such consequences are inescapable; there is no way out.

Chapter: Proving the impossibility that the Exalted Lord is a substance[10] *(some notes for a refutation of the Christians)*

In the idiom of the theologians, substance is what is spatially extended and we have already adduced a proof of the impossibility that the Creator is spatially extended. Substance is also often stipulated as that which receives accidents. We have also already clearly established the impossibility of the Creator – hallowed and exalted is He – being susceptible to temporal contingencies. To whomever qualifies the Exalted Creator as being a substance, the following dichotomy should be posed in rebuttal: If you intend, in speaking of Him as a substance, to characterize Him by the specific properties of substances, the proof of the impossibilities of that was given previously. Alternatively, you might intend the appellation not to carry with it the characterization that fits its property and particularity. However, either kind of appellation derives solely from tradition because reason provides no indication of them and there is no evidence for this sort of naming in traditional sources. It is, moreover, not permitted in any religion to make rules for the naming of the Creator arbitrarily.

The Christians teach that the Creator – hallowed and exalted is He beyond their claims – is a substance and that He is the third of a trinity. In His being a substance, they mean that He is the basis for the hypostases. The hypostases, according to them, are three: existence, life and knowledge. Further they call existence the father; knowledge, the word (also called the son); and life, the holy spirit. The word [*logos*] does not mean speech in this instance because in their doctrine speech is created.

---

10 Although the Arabic term here is *jawhar*, which previously meant the minimum indivisible particle or atom, in reference to God it is preferable to use the word "substance".

Thus these hypostases are, according to them, substance pure and simple without anything added. Substance is one and the hypostases are three. The hypostases, in their view, are not existent beings in and of themselves but rather they are possessions of substance that conform to modal states like the ones affirmed by those in Islam who accept the modes. The modal state is, for example, spatial extension in the case of substance; it is a mode that is additional to the substance's existence. The modal state is characterized thus neither by non-existence nor by existence but is instead an attribute of existence. The hypostases in Christian doctrine are conditions of the substrate to which these modal states apply.

Following this, they claim that the word is one with the Messiah and is clothed in his humanity. Various schools among them have different opinions about this incarnation of the divine in the human. Some insist that it means that the word resides in the physical body of the Messiah in the same way an accident resides in its substrate. The Byzantines hold the doctrine that the word amalgamates with the body of the Messiah and mixes with it as thoroughly as might wine with milk.

These then are the basic principles of their doctrine and, in answer, we say to them: There is no sense in your restricting the hypostases in the manner you mention. What keeps you from claiming that the hypostases are four among which one is power? There is no better reason to exclude power from the list of hypostases than knowledge. Likewise, if it is permitted to argue that existence is a hypostasis, what prevents considering perpetuity a hypostasis? And, in accord with the preceding line of reasoning, such a consequence applies as well to hearing and seeing.

At this point we would say: If you insist that the word becomes incarnate in the Messiah and you explain it as an indwelling, one must respond to you as follows. Is the knowledge which is called the word separable from substance or not? If now they would claim that it is separable, they must necessarily admit that substance cannot have a hypostasis of knowledge, since knowledge is now merged with the Messiah, but this they refuse to accept.

In contrast, if they insist that the hypostasis of knowledge is inseparable from substance, accordingly, it would be impossible for it to dwell in the physical body of Jesus, on whom be peace, due to its particularization in the first substance. It is impossible for an accident to become incarnate in a certain body while that accident adheres to another body. If that is impossible with respect to the accident, even more so is that impossible with respect to the particularity conferred by the situation of the attributes of self. Were it allowed that the word unites with the Messiah, it is also allowed that substance unites with the humanity. The latter is not a different case. None the less, they reject the union of the substance with the humanity.

It might be said to them as well: Since the word unites with the Messiah, why does it not unite with the holy spirit, which is the hypostasis of life? One of the characteristics of knowledge is that it is inseparable from life. All this clearly demonstrates the confusion of the Christians.

The refutation of the Byzantines is essentially the same as the refutation of those who uphold incarnation. They would specify that once amalgamated it bears the attributes solely of animate and inanimate bodies. What possible means is there to argue that the hypostasis is a particular property?

Among some other difficult considerations against them, we ask: How do you deny the claim of someone who maintains that the word was united with Moses – may the blessings of God be with him – and, for that reason, he could change the rod into a veritable serpent, split the seas in two, each side like a towering mountain, and do other miraculous things?

That in which they believe, however, and on account of which their faith is corrupted is what was done by Jesus – God bless him and protect him – such as curing the blind and the leper, and reviving the dead with the consent of God. When they are presented with the miracles of the other prophets – on whom be peace – their doctrine becomes confused and yields no firm result, since their basic principle rests on the notion of union only in the case of the Messiah – peace be upon him.

As for their doctrine that the hypostases are divine, all Christians, regardless of their sectarian differences, agree on the trinity. We say to them: While each hypostasis, in your view, does not have the attribute of existence in and of itself, how can what does not bear the attribute of existence have the attribute of divinity?

We will hereafter prove with ample clarity that God must of necessity be living, knowing and powerful. If the hypostasis of knowledge is divine, it must necessarily be living and powerful. Upon this basis we ask them: Why do you not make the divine four, viz. substance, existence, life and knowledge? That is, assuming you do not rely on a religion that is purely arbitrary.

Nevertheless, the Christians are in agreement that the Messiah is a god and, moreover, they all confess that he is the son and concur that he is of both divine and human nature. This is self-contradictory: to ascribe the name god denotes exclusively a judgment of divinity, whereas the Messiah is not purely divine. Beyond that, they agree that the Messiah was crucified. When confronted, however, they insist that what was crucified was the humanity alone and that the humanity in and of itself was not the Messiah.

We will strengthen the case against them by further asserting the absolute unity of God, although what we have said here should already be completely convincing.

Section
The Knowledge of God's Absolute Oneness

The Creator – hallowed and exalted is He – is one. One, in the idiom of the Metaphysicians, is the thing that is indivisible. If one says that the one is the thing, this should be a sufficient stipulation. The Lord – hallowed and exalted is He – is a unique existent, transcending all possibility of division and difference. Speaking of Him as one means that He has no like or peer. A clear consequence of the reality of the doctrine of absolute oneness is the proof that God is not a composition, because, if that were the case – exalted is He and glorified above that – each separate portion of Him would subsist as knowing, living and powerful in and of itself. And that is an admission of belief in two gods.

The objective behind this doctrine depends on a judgment that knowledge is particularized by what it resides in and likewise on this claim with respect to all of the properties which necessarily lend their characteristic features to that in which they inhere. If it is supposed that there are two components and it is adjudged of one of them that it has knowledge, power and life, that one is God. The other, by this reckoning, is eternal but is not qualified by the attributes of divinity. The falsity of this is something we will clarify at the end of this section. For the moment we will explain in general what one means by the true reality of absolute oneness.

The aim in broaching this subject is to set out clearly the proof that God is one and that a supposition of two gods is impossible. The proof here is that, if we suppose there are two gods and presume that the object under discussion is a body, we may assume the desire of one of the two to move it and the other to keep it still. However, the means leading to this absurd assumption are blocked entirely. Were we to insist on the carrying out of both their desires and both actually occurring simultaneously, that would result in the coexistence of both movement and repose in the same substrate. This proof is based upon the connection of time with place. It is also impossible that the desire of both of them not produce an effect since that would lead to the absence of both motion and repose in the body. This would result in affirming two gods, both impotent and unable to effect their wishes. It is impossible, as well, to insist that the desire of one is carried out but not the other, since that still involves the impotence of the one whose wish was not effective. We will now prove the impossibility of affirming an eternal that is unable to act.

Someone may say here: You have based this proof on the differing of the desires of two eternal beings. How then can you deny those who believe in two eternal beings who each want what the other wants? We respond that this proof applies generally in cases where there is a differing, as we assumed here, but it also covers in general a supposition of agreement as well. If wanting to move the body by one of them coincides with the other wanting it to remain in repose and this is possible, not impossible, everything indicating the resulting impotence and its being characterized by some sort of shortcoming indicates that anything like it is allowable as well. The proof against those who confess to the admissibility of temporal contingencies arising from the eternal which produces the consequence of having to adjudge it temporally contingent comes down to the same stance as those who believe in the actual occurrence of temporal contingencies that arise within it. A means for one of two temporally produced beings to effect its will that is stopped because of being blocked is a sign of a defect, just as much as is its being kept from really doing what it wants. Those who admit the case of its contrariety and those who reject the case of its coincidence are in the same position.

It may now be asked: How do you refute those who claim that the differing of two eternals as to will is neither admissible nor effective? We answer: Were we to suppose the isolation of one of the two, there is nothing in the rules of reason that keeps its will from making the body move at the specified moment; and if we suppose the isolation of the second, nothing prevents its will keeping the same body in repose. The essence, which is not its particularization in respect to the other, does not necessitate changing the basic characteristics of the attributes of either one, and thus what is admissible in regard to each of them when supposed to be together is what one is allowed to assume for each in isolation.

A clever person has pointed out that our purpose with the proof based on mutual hindrance is to establish the impossibility that the two wills can both function. The very affirmation of two eternals, as stipulated in this matter, leads axiomatically to the preclusion of what is admitted for any eternal if we suppose its isolation. This is even more sure a proof of impotence and defect.

This proof does not apply to the principles of the Muʿtazilites, however, since they have adopted the notion that the servant can do what the Lord does not want – may He be exalted above their claims – and yet such a doctrine does not, in their eyes, constitute a recognition of His weaknesses. But if they should say that the Exalted Lord has the ability to compel creatures to do as He wishes, one responds as follows: His intention, according to you, is that servants believe voluntarily in a faith which merits a reward; and He does not wish that they have a faith into which they were forced or of which they are resentful. Thus what He wants He cannot bring about and what He can bring about He does not want.

The masters of the Muʿtazilite school shy away from the proof based on mutual hindrance for the reasons we have just mentioned but it is explicitly cited in the text of God's words: "If there were in them [the heavens and earth] a god other than God, they would crumble in ruin" [21:22].

If someone else says: You ground this proof of absolute oneness in the impossibility of affirming an impotent eternal and for that point you still need a proof, we respond: Were we to suppose the existence of an impotent eternal, it would be impotent on the basis of an impotency that subsists in it eternally. Reason determines, however, that an impotence that is eternal is impossible, since the stipulation of impotency is that, because of it, the occurrence of an act that is possible in itself is inconceivable. Were we to affirm an impotency that is eternal, this would push us into a declaration that the act is forever possible but then rule that impotence makes it impossible. Of necessity thus we realize the impossibility of a perpetual act in the past. This is the equivalent of our firm resolution regarding the impossibility of assuming eternal past movement, since there is no doubt that the movement followed being situtated in a location from which the movement constituted a displacement.

At this point someone might remark: What you mention turns against you in regard to affirming the eternal power because the eternal power entails the possible realization of an act. The consequence of affirming a perpetual power requires admitting to the possibility of a perpetual action. We respond: The stipulation of power does not include its full realization all at once. In the visible world if we suppose a power that persists and if we were to give credence to it, as an example, that it precedes the actual empowering is not precluded. Although continuing to retain its power, the empowering agent may yet be prevented from using its power. This makes it quite clear that we may not set as a condition the conjunction of the possible use of power with the existence of the actual power. But, if it is accompanied by the inability to bring it about, it is impossible, in every respect, for the realization of something to be possible.

Now, if it were to be asked: How then can you reject those who claim that the things the eternal is able to bring about are finite, and yet the argument for affirming the absolute oneness hangs on the denial of a limit to the things that fall within the ability of God? To that we respond: If the questioner intends specifically the issues involved in the assumption of a single eternal, the answer is that those things that can be done, if they were finite in number, despite reason accepting as permissible that the like of what has occurred will occur, cannot actually occur by themselves in the absence of a determining agent. By confining the power within some finite end, additional things like it are excluded from any possibility of realization, since no temporally contingent thing occurs except as the result of a power. The drift of this argument moves in the direction of combining the impossible and the possible in something that is known to be possible.

If, however, the questioner determines that the question concerns the two eternals and thereafter claims that one of them has power over one type of the things that can be accomplished and the second has power over another type, this is a matter of the greatest obscurity. We answer: We picture a body and we undertake to devise a proof of its being subject to motion and to repose. If the inquirer insists they are together excluded from what is possible for either, this would be an absurdity that leads to a body that is neither at rest nor in motion. If repose is within the capacity of one of them and motion is possible for the other, this supposition yields a doctrine of mutual hindrance just as we thought previously.

If someone were to say that motion and rest and some other example of the existences are within the power of one but not of the other, we can decide the proof on the basis of the colours. If there is an objection concerning them, we will pass over them to another type of accident, and continue in the same way until reaching a proof of one of two considerations: either that they participate jointly in having power over a certain type of accident and, as a consequence, there exists a mutual hindrance, since each specimen of the accident is associated with the opposite. If there is an objection, we can restrict the proof to a like pair of each type to settle the matter definitively. If two likenesses are mutually distinct, as we will mention in the course of the discussion, God willing, this is one consequence of the mutual hindrance that we have already noted.

Were the questioner to say: If one of two eternals is alone in having the power to create every kind of accident, it could be asked: Is the second characterized as having the power to create atoms or not? If a questioner says that it is not able to do that, then it is excluded on principle from being powerful. To affirm an eternal that does not have the power to do things, or knowledge of what is known, or is not living, is arbitrarily to demand that of which there is no proof. Our aim, however, in regard to this doctrine here is not to refute this, but rather to establish a refutation of the claim that there can be two eternals that are both assumed to possess the characteristic of a divine being.

In regard to the eternal having necessary existence, if denying it were supposed, nothing would be possible because the possible cannot realize itself. The admissibility that possible things are realized is known self-evidently and that absolutely requires the eternal's existing as a necessity. By determining that it is merely possible, what is necessary becomes only possible. Were we to affirm an eternal that produces no effect, its existence would not be necessary, since its existence holds no possibility of possible actions. If the eternal is possible, its being eternal is precluded since the eternal exists necessarily. But the possible needs for its realization a determining agent and thus the characteristics of possibility and eternity are mutually contradictory.

If the questioner were to object: The creation of atoms is within the power of the one we have not characterized as having power over the accidents, to that we respond: An isolated atom devoid of accidents is impossible, and having power to do something applies solely to what is possible. The real form of having power is the ability to make possible the occurrence of what is within its power. This determination suffices; understand it!

These explanations are enough to establish the knowledge of the attributes which are necessary in and of themselves. We included and described in this what cannot be ascribed to God in so far as we denied of Him the properties of atoms and accidents and we have set out the proofs of His transcendence above the characteristics of bodies. What we have said frees us from having to review many topics treated by the theologians concerning what cannot be ascribed to God, the exalted.

Should an intelligent person be asked about what cannot be applied to his Lord, the simplest expression to offer in response is to state: No indication of His temporal contingency can be ascribed to Him. This formula comprises within it the determination that He is not susceptible to temporal contingencies and is in no need of adhering to a substrate.

All that we have just discussed concerned one of two categories of necessary attributes, which are those of the self. As for the qualifying attributes, we will commence with them beginning now.

Section
Affirming Knowledge of Qualifying Attributes

You should know – and may God the Exalted guide you – that the discussion in this section has various ramifications but the subject itself is of fundamental importance to the defenders of God's absolute oneness. Our aim, in so far as we are capable of realizing that goal, is to state precisely two essential propositions: one attests to the knowledge of the characteristic properties of the attributes; and the other establishes knowledge of the attributes that cause necessarily what is characteristic of them.

In regard to the characteristic properties, we begin this section with the indication that most certainly the Maker of the world is powerful and knowing. But there is no real need, following the premises set out earlier, for us to investigate and elaborate upon the basic assurance that the Maker is knowing and powerful. Since it was determined that the Exalted Creator is the Maker of the world, and the extreme subtlety of the design involved in it is abundantly clear to the thinking person, and fully grasping what attributes the heavens and the earth and all between them possess as to regularity, orderliness, perfection and precision, leads altogether quite forcefully to the knowledge that it was not produced by a being other than one who has knowledge of it and power over it. No intelligent person can doubt that it is an impossibility for this invention to be the product of some being that is ignorant, dead, inert or impotent. Likewise, every thinking person knows *a priori* that a masterful act which is steadfast and well executed cannot have been produced by a being that is or was ignorant of it. Despite having observed the fineness of the line that was written – the letters well apportioned and precise – any person who would think that it was the product of a person ignorant of script has forsaken all reason and wandered into the wasteland of ignorance.

Some theologians have, nevertheless, attempted to test reasoning and the techniques of analysis in pursuit of this problem. Their procedure is the one to which we will refer. They maintain the following: We have found that acts which are impossible for some beings are not impossible for others. When we investigate the types of hindrances blocking these acts, we are drawn by the method of elimination to the fact that the being for which the act is not impossible is the one with power and knowledge. This outcome relies on a claim that is self-evidently necessary, since were someone to insist that the act is not impossible for any being, the way to refute him involves his having repudiated a self-evident necessity. But, if we are forced to this in the end, it would have been preferable to invoke it from the beginning.

If now someone says: The learned are wont to profess that the well-executed thing indicates only the knowledge of the one who executes it and what you are talking about is extraneous to this doctrine of theirs, to this we reply: The correct teaching for this matter, in our view, is that the temporally contingent indicates an autonomous power or that the power holder has autonomous power, and the well-executed thing proves that the being that executes it is knowledgeable. However, the realization that what we have just said constitutes a proof is self-evident without needing an investigation or an inquiry that leads, assuming it is correct, to discovering the way by which it is proven. Therefore understand this point.

Having thus shown clearly that the Creator, hallowed is He, is knowing and powerful, it is axiomatic that you understand Him to be living. Were an intelligent person from the beginning to examine an act believing that it has a maker, he would be compelled to acknowledge that its maker is living – assuming that the false intimations of the naturalists are averted, as alluded to previously. This then is sufficient in regard to this doctrine.

Chapter: [That the Maker of the world is purposeful]

The Maker of the world is truly purposeful.[1] Abu'l-Qāsim al-Kaʿbī[2] taught that the Exalted Creator is not to be described as being purposeful in the true sense, although one attributes this to Him religiously in regard to His acts. What is intended in His being purposeful in regard to His acts is that He is their creator and instigator. Thus characterizing Him as being purposeful with respect to certain acts has the aim of describing Him as the one who commands them. Al-Najjār,[3] however, maintained that the Exalted Creator is purposeful in and of Himself. Then later, after some revision, he stated that what is meant by His being purposeful is that He is subject neither to constraint nor to being overcome.

Some of the Basran Muʿtazilites held that the Exalted Creator is purposeful in respect to temporal contingencies by means of a temporally contingent will that subsists but not in a substrate. They claimed further that for each temporally contingent act of His there is a desire for it by Him based in a temporally contingent will. Every commanded act by the servant is intended by Him. According to them a single will does not pertain to two desired objectives, otherwise volitions will occur that are temporally contingent but are not intentionally so willed.

With respect to the refutation of al-Kaʿbī and his followers, we say: You grant us that the determination of the servant's act takes place at certain moments according to the properties of the attributes in question. This requires that there be a purpose for determining them at that moment and with the special properties

---

1 Or that He has a will, is willing, or intentional in His acts.

2 Leader of the Baghdādī Muʿtazilites.

3 Abū ʿAbdallāh al-Ḥusayn al-Najjār, a famous Murjiʾite theologian of the earlier third/ninth century.

of the attributes they have. In the same way, regularity, orderliness, perfection and precision establish that the expert master is knowledgeable. Likewise the determination in this case proves that His determination is intentional. A rationally valid proof that yields certainty must be true when generalized. Should an intelligent person attempt to conceive assertions in any proof that are not provable, that would exclude it automatically from the conditions for proof at large.

After setting out these points, we reply to al-Kaʿbī: Every means in the visible world that indicates to the intellect that it is an object of will and is intentional applies as well in the case of the act of God because the indications of His act are intrinsically connected to what the act signifies in the visible world. If one could object in order to nullify the proof and void its general applicability, one might admit that mastery in the visible world proves that the expert master is knowledgeable without also proving that the mastery in God's act demonstrates that He is knowledgeable.

Someone may argue: An act in the visible world proves the intention only in so far as the agent of that act cannot apprehend what is invisible to him. Were he not to be characterized as having knowledge of the time in which the act takes place and what is specific to it, there is no doubt about resorting to the determination of intent. However, the Exalted Creator knows the invisible things as actual existents. It is enough, therefore, that He is knowledgeable without having to suppose that He is also purposeful.

This is false in several respects. The most readily grasped of them is that what they have said forces them to conclude that the Exalted Creator, though lacking power, is sufficient in His being knowledgeable. However, there is a distinction in that regard between the visible and the invisible. Here then we might submit to them a visible agent who is cognizant of what act he will do either because a truthful person apprises him of it or because God informs him about it. But, even if this is the case, the act requires none the less the intention to do it. It is therefore wrong to depend on applying this type of indication of the actor's being unaware of what act of his might yet take place.

Moreover, any one who examines the acts that the servants have power over will infer their intention from the acts, and will not conclude that they are unaware of them, or that they are subject to factors that are hidden from them. Hence if, in the visible world, the act reflects the intention in the situation where the actor does not know fully the outcome of these acts, the investigator's inference cannot pass beyond perceiving that ignorance. In fact, a disjunction which is basic to the process of inference precludes ascertaining further knowledge.

Should an obstinate follower of al-Kaʿbī claim that an act in the visible world does not indicate the intent of its agent, and, even should the intent be recognized, it is nevertheless not revealed by the act. To him we reply: This is a repudiation of the obvious; it signifies a devotion to the extremes of stupidity. The easiest way to oppose the person who holds this is to say to him: Mastery does not prove that the master has knowledge, or, if it does establish that the master has knowledge, it does so by a means other than this.

This answer, however, does not cover the basic doctrines of the Muʿtazilites from Basra who are in opposition to al-Kaʿbī. They have rejected proofs in regard to certain principles of beliefs.

Here we will now set out one example that illustrates their position. It is that, according to them, the mastery in an act of the Creator, exalted is He, is a sure indication of His having knowledge. Yet they recognize acts in the visible world that are masterful although, again according to them, are freely determined by the servant. These acts issue from the servant despite his being oblivious to them because of his being unaware of most of the conditions associated with them. If, however, this evaluation of the probative force of masterliness is allowed them, al-Kaʿbī's solution is not available to them, as we clearly demonstrated in delineating the implications that arise in conformity with this proof. This then may suffice as the refutation of al-Kaʿbī.

In regard to the refutation of al-Najjār and his disciples, our approach is to say: Your statement that the Creator, hallowed is He, is purposeful in and of Himself is subject to the following dichotomy: if you mean by it that He is actually purposeful and intentional, as might be inferred from your description of Him as being knowledgeable in and of Himself, the refutation of you and your brethren arises automatically, when we realize our aim in affirming knowledge of the characteristic properties in the attributes and we have just begun to establish the conclusive proofs for knowledge of the existence of the attributes. There is no other way to refute them if they take this approach other than to follow the method that proves the knowledge, power and life.

The Muʿtazilites attempted to pursue other avenues to deny that the Creator, exalted is He, is purposeful in and of Himself, all of which are false. We will point out what they proposed in this regard when we refute the Basrans.[4]

If the adherents of al-Najjār claim that the meaning of His being purposeful in and of Himself is that He is neither overcome nor coerced, one should reply that you have explained an affirmation by a denial. Denying ascendancy and coercion entails affirming the characterizing trait of the attribute itself. Still at this point they are content with denying ascendancy and coercion and, despite our conceding this point, one may nevertheless demand of them a proof that the Divine Being is intentional with regard to His act. If they are precluded from doing that, they are forced word by word to the result to which al-Kaʿbī was forced, according to what we stated earlier, and the only recourse for this school is to revert to the denial of the characteristic function of will.

---

4 The Muʿtazilites in general belonged to one of two schools called the Baghdādīs and the Baṣrīs (Basrans) which, while they may have originally indicated vaguely the city respectively from which some members of each group came, they later designated merely an intellectual affiliation.

The adherents of al-Najjār imposed contradictions upon their own basic premise. Thus we can say to them: If he who is purposeful is the one who is neither overcome nor subject to coercion, the Creator is purposeful in and of Himself in so far as He is neither overcome nor subject to coercion.

As for the Basrans, there are two points that need discussion. One is their depiction of the Creator, exalted is He, as being purposeful, and the other is their determination that His will is temporally contingent.

On the first matter, we inquire what is your indication of the Creator's being purposeful? If they claim that the proof is the particularization of temporal contingencies as to time and characteristics, their indication of acts of will that are temporally contingent, according to their own doctrine, is false. They claim that these acts are not the result of a will. Although they are temporally contingent and particularized by their individual temporal moments, yet they are not the result of a will. They maintain that the will is that by which something is wanted and is not something wanted in itself as will. They often coin examples that misrepresent, as, for example, saying that some sensate beings desire and yet that desire is not desired, or the result sought after is desired and yet the desiring is not desired. Similarly, the willed is not willed nor is it willed by will. These things they mention are assertions devoid of proof. In order to bring accord between something about which there is disagreement and something that is agreed upon, one has to bring forth a decisive proof which requires that the two be in accord with each other. Nor is what they maintain safe from other objections that oppose them.

Should some person say here that knowledge is a tool for acquiring knowledge but is not something known in and of itself, following the course they have already laid out and the analogy of desire and wanting, the argument against him is the same as against them.

We state: Whoever undertakes an act, and was cognizant of his instigation of it at a specific time, without doubt accomplishes its execution at that time, if he had the power to do it and had knowledge of it. The clear certainty of this approaches the perception of self-evident necessity.

Moreover, reason judges that a will which operates at a certain moment and the other events which are temporally contingent are equivalent. Thus it is false for them to base their claim on the will which is not willed. Their irresponsible fumbling on the subject of the will does not exempt them and the result is that it contradicts their own proof. What they relied upon as the indication of the particularization of the will is rendered null against them by the will itself. What they say thereafter creates the conditions for further discrepancy; for them the path by which to prove that the Creator, exalted is He, is purposeful is blocked.

Among other things they should account for is, an answer for the following question: Why do you reject those who insist that the Hallowed and Exalted Creator is purposeful in and of Himself, as, in your view, He is living, powerful and knowing in and of Himself?

They may respond that that is impossible because the field of application affirmed in and of the self, if it entails a conditional relationship, requires that its conditional relationship apply to all related conditions. For this reason He is necessarily the Knower of all things knowable since He knows in and of Himself. Because the self has no particularity for one of the related conditions over another, the outcome here, if He is purposeful in and of Himself, requires that He intend all things that are willed.

This idea, which is one of their quite arbitrary notions, is spurious. Hence it can be said to them: On the basis of what proof do you reject the relationship of the essential field of application to one of the related conditions and not the others? And how do you refute those among the adherents of al-Najjār who maintain that He is in and of Himself purposeful in regard to some of the objects of will? This is tantamount to the specification of contingent knowledge which is conditionally related to its object due to its very being. Here this person cannot say: Knowledge is not specific for blackness, and yet its relationship to blackness is virtually identical to its relationship with the others.

If they should say now: We have adopted this because of God's being the Knower of all things known, we reply: You are quite subjective in making inferences and in introducing examples. For what reason did you claim that it is necessary for the exalted Creator to be the Knower of all things known as a consequence of being the Knower in and of Himself? You knew that the doctrine of your opponents affirms the attributes and as a result admits that the Exalted Creator knows by a knowledge. But then what these people continue with is beset by a contradiction when they state that the Creator is powerful in and of Himself while not describing Him as having power in all possible situations, for the servant's having power is not among God's powers. The Muʿtazilites of later times affirmed certain types of power in the servant which they denied to the Exalted Lord and it did not matter whether having power belonged to the servant or that He simply had not created in that person the power to undertake something as, for example, is the case with ignorance.

They may say: The powers of the servant are not connected to the power of the Eternal Being because it is impossible that having a power depends on separate sources of power. The impossibility here is not to be judged as if it were one kind of having power. We reply: Your evasion here will not save you from the consequences which you have foisted on yourselves. In your view, what the servant will have the power to do is known to God, the Exalted, despite God not having power over it prior to His servant's actually doing it. But none the less the servant does not have power over it. This doctrine yields nothing more than this.

Yet another outcome we must hold them to is to state: Since you concluded that God, the Exalted, renews repeatedly His application of will towards what never ceases to be, what stops you from deciding that these constitute a necessity in Him? If they answer: Were they inherent in Him, He would never not have them or a contrary of them; and the upshot of this leads into proving Him temporally contingent, we respond: If it is permissible that He be characterized by the qualifying applications of temporal contingencies without involving their contraries prior to being actually characterized by them, what precludes temporal contingencies arising in Him in regard to what never ceases despite His having none of the contraries prior to them? Yet it is a fundamental point of yours that life is possible in the absence of will and its contraries. This is also the doctrine of the great mass of them.

Everything we mention at this point relates to the discussion of one of two elements we promised at an earlier stage in regard to the Basrans' refusal to admit that God, the Exalted, is purposeful. As for refuting them in regard to the affirmation of the temporally contingent will, we will take that up when we embark on the proof for the attributes, God willing. Here we are still discussing the proof for the knowledge of the applications that arise from the attributes.

Chapter: [*The Exalted Creator is all-hearing and all-seeing*]

The Creator, exalted is He, is all-hearing and all-seeing according to the people of intelligence, but the people of deviation and innovation follow doctrines that disagree with this.

Al-Kaʿbī and his disciples among the Baghdādī [Muʿtazilites] argued that when the Creator, exalted is He, is characterized as all-hearing and all-seeing, what is meant by these two terms is that He knows the things known as they truly are. Some groups of the adherents of al-Najjār also subscribe to the same doctrine.

The Muʿtazilites of Basra from an earlier time held that the Creator, exalted is He, is all-hearing and all-seeing in actuality, just as He knows in actuality, and they claim that He is all-hearing and all-seeing in and of Himself.

Al-Jubbāʾī and his son are of the opinion that the meaning of His being all-hearing and all-seeing is that He is alive and without impediment. These two uphold the doctrine that the reality of hearing and seeing in the visible is the same as it is in the invisible world.

The sure indication that the Creator, exalted is He, is all-hearing and all-seeing in actuality is that the acts are proof of His being alive, as established previously above, and it is life that permits characterizing Him as all-hearing and all-seeing. Should He depart from being all-hearing and all-seeing, it would be necessary to characterize Him as being subject to an impediment because every thing that is subject to one of two contraries by substitution,[5] without an intermediary between the two, can never be free of one or the other of them. In determining that it is impossible for Him to be subject to an impediment, that He is characterized as being all-hearing and all-seeing is also determined. This

5 If God does not hear and see, He must be deaf and blind, these being the contraries of the former.

is a precise formulation of the proof. Our aim here, however, is to provide an explanation of it by means of questioning and refutation.

Someone may now remark: You founded your discussion of this matter on the Exalted Creator's being subject to being characterized as all-hearing and all-seeing, but how can you refute the person who denies this point and refuses to accept it? Such a person claims that the Creator, exalted is He, cannot possibly be subject to hearing and seeing and their respective contraries, just as it is not possible that He be receptive to colours. We answer: It is clear that the living being in the visible world is subject to being depicted as hearing and seeing. Having determined this we move on following the method of testing and analysis. We note that inert matter is not characterizable by hearing and seeing. Therefore life is the precondition for being receptive to hearing and seeing with the stipulation that there exists no impediment to it. Thereafter, when we examine the attributes of life hoping to locate exactly what confers its receptivity to hearing and seeing, nothing survives the process of testing intact except that it is alive. All other suppositions except this one prove false. Thus, that life is distinct from inert matter is clear from the realization that it is receptive to hearing and seeing in being alive. And from this, the conclusion follows that similarly God, the Exalted, is alive.

Those who deny the soundness of the receptivity to hearing and seeing and the applications consequent to both are not in a happier position than those who would claim that the Creator, exalted is He, is not to be characterized by knowledge and its contraries because of the impossibility of His being characterized by the qualifications that arise from these contraries. This evaluation fulfils our goal.

It might be asked: What proof is there of the prohibition of something being devoid of the qualifications inherent in the opposites, given that being receptive to them individually is possible? We answer: Everything that proves the impossibility of the isolation of atoms from mutual opposites is also a proof of this, as was pointed out previously at the beginning of this section.

It may now be said: One of the principles on which your proof is based is the impossibility of the Exalted Creator's being characterized by the impediments that are contrary to hearing and seeing. What is the indication of that? We respond: This is one of those issues about which the theologians have said a great deal. We are satisfied with none of what they have proposed in the matter and prefer to take refuge in tradition. The leaders, and all who believe in God, the Exalted, have agreed that the Exalted Creator transcends impediments and contradictions.

But it may be said: Unanimous agreement does not prove it rationally. Tradition provides only an indication of its being a proof; even though its pathways are numerous, the root source of tradition is, nevertheless, the word of God, the Exalted, which is itself truth and His utterance is undeniable. Acts do not in themselves offer a proof of the verbal statement itself but rather the method for affirming them is the same as in verifying hearing and seeing, as we will hereafter mention. If the question concerns the statement itself and, by affirming it, we establish the denial of impediments, then, in denying impediments, we depend on the unanimous consensus which is unverified other than on the basis of the statement. But we are attempting to affirm the statement on the basis of what was unverified prior to acquiring knowledge of the statement that supports it. This is an ultimate in futility. We respond: This inquiry is of great import and providing its refutation is clearly required. In our view the approach needed to avert this question is to note that miracles establish the truthfulness of the messengers, on whom be peace, and the messengers, once their truthfulness is proven, convey information about the words validly affirmed of God, the Exalted, in a general manner. They thereafter convey the specific details associated with them. Hence what we want to confirm is known with certainty.

One might object that miracles do not establish the truthfulness of the prophets in and of themselves as in the demonstration for a true rational proof but rather prove it only in so far as it occupies the position of confirming a specific statement, as we will later explain in the chapter on miracles. If a miracle were to constitute a proof in this case because it assumed the role of confirming the declaration, how could a miracle provide proof of the statement itself, given that its means of proving it is to take the place of that statement? Our answer is that this is confused and dubious but the truth becomes clear upon investigation. Say during a great assembly someone were to assert that he is the emissary of a king and declares this publicly, claiming that he is the king's emissary to all those who are present and those who are absent and that he does this with the king's full knowledge.[6] Then he says: The proof of my having been sent is that, if I should request the king to stand and to sit, he will, contrary to his custom, do it. Thereupon, he follows what he has just said by making this request and the king acquiesces. The people of that assembly are thus forced to recognize that he is, in fact, an emissary whose mission has been verified by the person who sent him. But it does not occur to some in the audience that the person who sent him could have spoken. Some others who attended the assembly are those who reject the speech of the soul and believe that there is no speech other than actual verbal expression. Nevertheless, in spite of their differing out of ignorance as to his ability to speak at that moment and in acknowledging it, all those present are equal in apprehending the sure evidence that he is in fact an emissary. Know this and you will be guided rightly.

This chapter does not really suit the magnitude of this doctrine but we can remedy the situation more appropriately through lectures and therefore we really need to discuss this matter again. In God is the grace.

The way to confirm the knowledge that the Exalted Creator speaks is like the method of confirming the knowledge that He is all-hearing and all-seeing.

---

6 More literally "with the king's having fully heard and seen it".

But the goal in this case will not become clear until after we have proven the existence of the speech of the soul and refute those who deny it.

Chapter: [*It cannot be said of the Creator, the Exalted, that He can taste and smell and so forth*]

Someone might say: You have described the Exalted Creator as being all-hearing and all-seeing, and hearing and seeing are two faculties of perception. There exist in the visible world faculties other than these two, such as a perception associated with the reception of tastes, another perception associated with smells, and yet others for perceiving heat, cold, softness and roughness. Would you attribute to the Exalted Lord the applicable characteristics in these faculties of perception? Or do you limit His attributes to His being all-hearing and all-seeing? Our answer is that the exact reality here, in our view, requires attributing to Him the applicability of the characteristics of the perceptive faculties since every perception denied Him is a contrary which constitutes an impediment. Whatever proves the necessity of attributing to Him the applicable characteristics of hearing and seeing is what proves the necessity of attributing to Him the applicable characteristics of the other perceptive faculties.

But the Lord in His hallowed and exalted state transcends being a smeller, a taster or a feeler, since these attributions are founded on a type of contact which the Lord is above altogether. Also they do not impart the actual function of the perceptive faculties. A man might say, I smelled an apple but I did not comprehend its odour. If smelling were an indication of comprehending, that would be tantamount to someone saying, I perceived its odour but I did not perceive it. The same could be said for tasting and feeling.

Chapter: [*The Lord is perpetual and of continuous existence*]

The Lord, hallowed and exalted is He, is perpetual and of continuous existence. The arrangement according to which we have built the discussion of the attributes requires considering this attribute in the sections devoted to remarks about the attributes of the self. What we approve here is that the Eternal is eternal in and of Himself. His being eternal is not because of applicable characteristics which qualifications thereof make necessary. We will explain this later, God willing.

Everything that proves the eternity of God, the Exalted, in the past and the impossibility of His non-existence and the necessity of His being proves as well that He is perpetual.

What we have said serves as a brilliant light that suffices to confirm the knowledge of the applicable characteristics of the necessary attributes. Now, aided by God, the Exalted, we must delve into proving knowledge of those attributes that necessitate the application of specific characteristics to the essence.

Section
A Statement Affirming Knowledge of the Attributes

The position of the orthodox is that the Hallowed and Exalted Creator is living, knowing, powerful, having eternal life, eternal knowledge, eternal power and eternal will.

The Muʿtazilites and those who follow their lead among the adherents of sectarian tendencies agree in denying the attributes. Thereafter, however, they are of various differing opinions regarding in what manner to express God's being qualified by the applicable properties of the attributes. Some hold that He is living, knowing, powerful in and of Himself. Others prefer another formula. They say that these applicable properties are affirmed of the essence because there is to His being a mode which is the most particular of His attributes and that mode requires that He be living, knowing and powerful. Yet others among those who deny the attributes insist that the Creator – who is above what they say – is living, knowing, powerful, but not through some cause or in and of Himself.

Prior to delving into the arguments here, we would offer two chapters, one of which comprises the confirmation of the modes and a refutation of those who deny them, and the other the acceptance of necessary causation in the applicable properties. Once these two points are dealt with, we will follow them with an investigation of these arguments.

Chapter: [*On affirming the modes and refuting those who deny them*]

The mode for the existent being is an attribute that is qualified neither by existence or by non-existence. Further, among the modes, some are fixed in the essences due to a causative factor and others without a cause. In regard to those that result from a cause, each applicable property belonging inherently to that subject of it is the result of a quality that resides in it. Thus the living being is alive; the being possessed of power is powerful. Each qualifying property inheres in a substrate and, in our view, this requires that it have a mode. Moreover, this requirement of modes is not particular to qualifying properties of which life is a condition.

As for the modes that are not due to a cause, they consist of those attributes that are affirmed of their subject but are not due to a cause which adds upon that subject as, for example, the spatial extension of the atom which is an addition solely in its existence. Each attribute possessed by an existent being that does not exist independently and is not caused by an existent being is of this category. Comprised within it are the existent's having accidents, colours, blackness, conditions, knowledge and the like.

Most of the theologians repudiate the modes and insist that the atom's spatial extension is the very basis of its existence. Their doctrine concerning all instances of what we have concluded are modes belonging to the existent but which are additional to its existence are similar to this.

The indication which proves decisively that there are modes is that one has knowledge of the existence of the atom without apprehending knowledge of its being spatially extended. Thereafter, that it is spatially extended becomes clear and, thus, a new fact associated with the object of knowledge comes into play. Determining knowledge of the existence without knowing of the spatial extension is thus quite feasible. Having determined that there exists here knowledge of two different things, the object of this second knowledge must fall under one of two conditions: either it was known by means of the first knowledge or the second is additional to it.

It is absurd that what is known by the second knowledge is what was known by the first knowledge for several reasons. One of them is that the thinker is convinced, upon receiving the second knowledge, that he comprehends something he did not comprehend previously. He perceives something he did not perceive in the first instance. It is also possible, despite having knowledge of the existence of the object, to be oblivious to the spatial extension. If the spatial extension of the atom were its very existence, this would be impossible in the same way that it is impossible for someone who is oblivious to it in any of its various modes to know of the object's existence at all.

Among the other indications of this fact is that, if what is known by two contingent acts of knowing were the same, one could not arrive at a determination of their mutual difference, as would be the case for the two acts of knowing in respect to the existence of the atom and to its having spatial extension. Those who deny the modes often seize on the fact that a thing is known in one aspect and not known in another, but this resort to the aspects is itself an affirmation of the modes. One cannot delve into this area without taking into account the modes, no matter whether one calls them modes, or aspects or attributes of self.

A person with an exacting mind is not likely to be diverted by the chicanery of those who deny the modes and fail to realize that the mode is not attributable to either existence or to non-existence. Most of what they say about it is far-fetched or is an assertion not founded upon a compelling claim and adherence to the evidence. Our understanding is that the things known are classified as existent, non-existent, or an attribute of the existent which is attributable neither to existence or to non-existence.

Having now made our position quite evident, know that confirming knowledge of the eternal attributes requires viewing the invisible world from the perspective of the visible world. Yet be sure to make a judgment in that manner without connecting the two in a way that leads to materialism and heresy and other stupidities the mind rejects. Whoever upholds judging the invisible on the basis of what obtains in the visible but without linking the two worlds together must admit that the Exalted Creator is a limited bodily being since there exists no visible agent that is otherwise. That person, because he sees none that do not follow one after the other, must also assume that temporal contingencies appear one after the other without a beginning. There are other stupidities like these as well.

Thus there is no doubt as to the connection. The link between the visible and the invisible is of four types.

One of them is the cause. Having affirmed that the effect is governed by the cause in the visible world, and provided proof of this, it is necessary to admit that the cause is linked to the effect in the visible as well as the invisible world to the extent that they are mutually inseparable. To deny one of them is to deny the other. This is similar to our asserting that the knower's being knowledgeable in the visible world is an effect caused by knowledge. We will explain this further at the right point in this book when we take up the details of the arguments.

The second avenue for connection is the condition. Having made clear that the applicable characteristic is subject to a condition in the visible world, and affirmed that there is the like of it in the invisible world, it is necessary, by analogy with the situation obtaining in the visible, to conclude that it is likewise subject to that condition. This is similar to our determining that the knower's being knowledgeable is conditional upon his being alive. Admitting this in regard to the visible extends it automatically to the invisible.

The third area is the essence. Whenever an essence is determined for the thing examined in the visible world, this extends to the like of it in the invisible. This is similar to our judging that the essence of the knowledgeable person is his being the one in whom there is knowledge.

The fourth connection is the proof. Because the proof proves the thing proven rationally, there is no proof in both the visible and invisible worlds that does not prove it. An example here is that creation establishes the existence of the Creator.

This was one of the two chapters promised here.

Chapter: [The causation of the necessary and the refutation of those who reject it]

The second chapter concerns the causation of the necessary and the refutation of those who reject it. What led the Muʿtazilites to the vanity of their doctrine which denies the positive attributes of God is their acceptance that the Creator, exalted is He, must of necessity be knowledgeable. Yet the necessary being, in its being necessary, is free of having a determiner determining it. But the knower's having knowledge, because it is both feasible and possible, is not like that in the visible world; rather it requires, accordingly, a specifying agent or a determining factor.

The Muʿtazilites equate the applicable quality in being necessary and being possible with necessary existence and possible existence. The hallowed and exalted Eternal is necessarily existent and therefore His existence is not linked to an enabling agent. But the temporally contingent is of only possible existence and an occurrence of it requires an agent to bring it about.

This claim of theirs is pointless. Say to them: On what basis would you reject those who insist that the applicable necessary quality is connected to a necessary cause and the applicable possible quality is connected to a possible cause?

As for their attestations based on existence, they yield no result. We are not convinced by what they say concerning the necessity of the existence of the Eternal, hallowed and exalted is He, but instead we have determined, in this regard, that there is no origin to the existence of the Creator, hallowed is He. Because for every action there is a commencement, what has no beginning cannot possibly be connected to an agent. Thus, for that reason, it is impossible that He be connected to an agent and it is impossible also for Him to be connected to a cause. Existence in this case is not the result of a cause either in the visible or the invisible world.

At this point we say to them: You have decided that what is caused is what is possible and you determined that the applicable property results solely from its being possible. Then you invert the fact of being possible and insist that the necessary is not the result of a cause, but what you have said becomes null and void afterwards in all ways.

As for the causation of the possible, it is false in regard to existence itself. It is possible, however, in respect to the temporally contingent but without being itself the result of a cause.

They might say: The existence of temporal contingent things, even if not the result of a cause, is nevertheless connected to an agent. One of the applicable features of being possible is that it be affiliated with something that determines it. Thus, as such, the determinant is a cause and, therefore, is it not an agent? We respond: Existence is, according to us, a mode possessed by the atom. The atom was the atom even when it did not exist and only thereafter did the mode of existence come upon it. Why then do you not claim that a knower's being knowledgeable in the visible world is a mode superimposed on the essence that is qualified by the most characteristic of the attributes either in [the mode of] existence or non-existence? This leads to the denial of causes in the visible world; there is no escape from it.

As for their doctrine that the necessary being is free of causes by virtue of His necessity, this is proven false by several factors.

Among them is that the knower's being knowledgeable in the visible world, if accepted, is connected with necessities in that what has transpired cannot be denied in such a way that it is as if it had not happened, and so it is necessary that the mode which now exists was not the result of a cause.

The proof for this depends on two principles of the Muʿtazilite school. One is their maintaining that the temporally contingent thing does not acquire power in the mode it was created with but that the power was connected to it prior to its creation. However, for the temporally contingent, upon coming to exist, to be free of this attachment to the source of power means that likewise the mode upon its occurrence is free of the necessitating of a cause.

The second principle is their affirming attributes which they designate as being consequent to creation and they claim that these do not fall within the power because of being necessary and they reckon among them the spatial extension of the atom and the subsistence of accidents in a substrate.

Another is that the knower's being knowledgeable is because of knowledge. If they would include the mode about which we are in dispute among the necessary attributes that are consequent upon creation, they would exclude it from being subject to power but not exclude it from being caused. The upshot of all this proves that necessity is not incompatible with causation.

Among the things that negate what they have said is that they generalize the condition of the visible and invisible and declare that the knower's being knowledgeable is conditional upon his being alive but then judge that it is, for this reason, that the Exalted Creator is knowing and powerful. Having not made a distinction between necessity and possibility in respect to the applicability of this condition, the distinction is not permitted them in respect to the applicability of the cause. This evaluation will suffice for what we have proposed here.

Now that the content of these two chapters is in place, we can proceed to the details of the arguments. At this point then, based on the assistance of God, we will advance against the opposition three proofs, each of which secures certainty.

The first approach is for us to say: You have conceded to us that the knower's being knowledgeable is an applicable quality affirmed of the subject, just as the willer's being purposeful is an applicable quality affirmed of the subject. But then you object to the Exalted Creator's being purposeful in and of Himself. Yet everything that deters you in this regard concerning His being purposeful must be assumed in His being knowledgeable. The connection is obvious after testing and analysis.

To this we say: The impossibility of the Hallowed and Exalted Creator's being purposeful in and of Himself is not free of the following. Either it is based on the necessity of the causation of the applicable property in the invisible world, just as it is affirmed of its causation in the visible. And, if the matter is like this, its import implies a causation in the Exalted Creator's being knowledgeable as an interpolation based on the cause that is presumed to exist in the visible world. If what we have noted in regard to the applicable feature of will had been based on their follies, it would mean that, if He were purposeful in and of Himself, He would will every object of will. But we have already shown the falsity of this when we discussed the application of will.

Otherwise, having proven false their attempt to reject the Exalted Creator's being purposeful in and of Himself, nothing remains except our position. The purposeful being's being purposeful does not follow the same course as the agent's being an agent. In His being purposeful, the purposeful being has in reality a qualification and a mode, but there is no mode that the agent has in being an agent. This approach is decisive in respect to what we seek to establish.

The second approach is to say: That the knower's being knowledgeable in the visible world is agreed to and it results from a cause which is knowledge. The rational cause is inseparable from its effect; one cannot be supposed without the other. Thus, if it were possible for the knower to be knowledgeable in the absence of knowledge, it would be possible for knowledge to exist without characterizing its substrate as being knowledgeable. Except that they are inseparable, there would be no meaning to knowledge's imparting its applicable qualities. This is not confirmed by the manner in which the powerful confers power on its object. If it were possible to confirm the application because of being necessary but without the cause, the existence of the cause without its application would be possible as well because of its necessity.

In the expressions that have currency among the specialists in religious principles to call a knower knowledgeable entails a necessitating cause which is the locus of agreement and distinction between one essence and another. If this is evident for the visible, it pertains to the invisible as well. And thus if they say: The knower's being knowledgeable in the visible world is only because of its possibility, we have already proven that this is false, both negatively and affirmatively.

Now if they say: The knower's being knowledgeable in the invisible world is different from the knower's being knowledgeable in the visible and, if it is accepted that the application is the result of a cause, causation like it is required for the application in general of any cause, our answer is: The way that knowledge entails its applicable qualities in the visible world also applies in the invisible. If the two examples of knowledge differ, this does not establish that the applicable difference belongs to the two differing applications in the same way by which the cause entails its effect. Knowledge in the visible world, according to us, differs from eternal knowledge in its being temporally contingent, accidental, specific to one object and so forth. Knowledge in such circumstances does not make the knower's being knowledgeable necessary but requires it only in respect to the existence of knowledge. And this is admitted for both the visible and invisible. Thus what they would force upon us in the matter of two differing applications with regard to the application of the cause turns back against them in the matter of this differing with regard to the application of the condition.

The third approach, which was a basic point of our master, may God approve him, is for us to say: The knowledge that is connected to the object of knowing is knowledge itself. If you were to claim that the Exalted Creator knows the object of knowing and that the object of knowing is, in the reality of God, encompassed by Him, then this object of the knowing which He encompasses must be assumed to tie Him to that same connection. What is connected to what is encompassed by it cannot be external to the reception of the object of knowing and there would be no meaning for the connection of knowledge with the object of knowing other than the object of knowing being encompassed by it.

This is quite definitive against the principles of the Muʿtazilites for they say that the connecting of the two examples of knowledge with the single object of knowing requires that they be identical. And, on that, they base the identity of eternal knowledge – once admitted – with contingent knowledge. That is decisive, if one considers it carefully, and in God is the grace.

Those who deny the attributes rely on several methods. One of them, as we have previously explained, is their alleging that the causation of the necessary is untenable. The objections to this earlier ought, however, to have been decisive.

Another method by which they attempt to gain the high ground is to say: If we affirmed eternal attributes, they would participate with the Exalted Creator in this eternity, which is itself the most particular of the attributes of His essence. However, participation in what is most particular necessarily involves participation in all the rest of the attributes and the outcome means necessarily that the attributes are deities.

In mentioning this they propose arguments without proper demonstration. As for their maintaining that participation in the most particular necessarily involves participation in the rest, there exists much dispute among them on this matter. Even if one were to admit it for the sake of argument, we are still separated on whether or not eternity is the most particular characteristic of the Exalted Creator and they have not found a way to prove that.

Here one might say to them: Allowing that both are connected by the same connection and that they participate together in the most particular of the attributes, the will you affirm of the Exalted Creator and which is contingent, although residing in no substrate, resembles your claim in regard to the will affirmed of the servant which does reside in him. You thus affirm of one of them the necessity of residing in a substrate but that this necessity is impossible for the second. This contradicts your pretences about the participation of the two which share in the most particular of the attributes necessarily applying to all of them.

Nevertheless, we would say to them: Your objecting to the causation of the necessary is contradicted by your resort to the commonalty in the most particular of the necessitating commonalties in the rest. If the similarity of two like things is necessary, for you to bring up the causality here is to admit to the causation of the necessary.

Another ground they attempt to occupy is to say: The knowledge of the Exalted Creator, in your view, is connected to an infinity of discrete objects of knowing. Thus, it is subjected to different items of contingent knowledge, since contingent knowledge is not connected at once both to blackness and to whiteness. If the Creator's knowledge is connected to different objects of knowing, it belongs to the domain of contingent knowledge. And, if that is admissible, one has to admit also that the knowledge is subjected to the power, even though power and knowledge are different things in the visible world. The import results in making do with a single attribute for the domains of knowledge, of life and of power.

Seeing that their statement concerning the discreteness of attributes accompanies their attempt to reject the attributes in principle, what they have stated here does not require a rationalized response. But having already made clear our doctrine in this matter, and although it is not incumbent on us to pursue the argument, we say nevertheless: A rational judgment establishes the proof of the attributes as a whole. As for knowledge's being an addition to power, it is something that cannot be attained definitively by rational means. The method in this case involves adhering to the evidence of tradition. Although the theologians have been concerned with both denying and affirming various of the attributes, they agree in rejecting one attribute that has the applications of both knowledge and power. Someone who seeks an affirmation of an attribute that has both applications violates this consensus.

Here it might be objected: If it is not far fetched to admit that a single knowledge has application to many items of knowledge, what prevents our holding that the Exalted Creator knows the objects of knowing in and of Himself and that He has power over them in and of Himself and that He is Himself subject to the applications of both knowledge and power and this implies necessarily an essence that is not in need of the attributes? We respond: This is not a valid inference. You have grounded your contention here in a principle that you yourselves believe is fallacious since the knowledge in which we believe is not admitted by you. How then can you base your doctrine on what you believe to be false?

The point you rely on requires something that you agree with us is false and it is that the essence of the Exalted Creator, if it were subject to the applications of knowledge, would be a single knowledge. This is something no religious person would profess. Abuʾl-Hudhayl[1] has said: The Exalted Creator knows with a knowledge and His knowledge is Himself but His self is not knowledge. This is accounted among his ignominies and his contradictions. Along with other departures from what the rest of the Muʿtazilites reject, he denied that the essence of the Exalted Creator is knowledge and power. The people most deserving of being compelled to this conclusion are the Muʿtazilites for they maintain that, if there is affirmed of the Exalted Creator a knowledge that is connected to what is known by our knowledge, it would be the like of our knowledge. If they adjudge that God's essence as being is subject to varieties of knowledge, they are forced to conclude that His essence is knowledge and this is one of the things they rejected in principle.

If they say: If what you have said is a rebuttal of your opponents, how then would you defend yourself against the same point? You have insisted that reason requires the affirmation of the attributes in general and yet the discussion about discrete particulars falls under the evidence of tradition. We answer: This is one of the issues that extends beyond the limits of this book. What is appropriate

1 Abuʾl-Hudhayl al-ʿAllāf, a well-known Muʿtazilite theologian of the early third/ninth century.

here, however, is to say that reason provides an affirmation of knowledge and then follow by observing that the fact that knowledge is additional to the self is an understanding based on the evidence of tradition. If reason proves the affirmation of knowledge and consensus upholds the doctrine that the being of the Exalted Creator is not knowledge, from the evidence of both tradition and reason, the result is a proof that knowledge is an addition to the existence, and in God is the grace.

Chapter: [The will of God is eternal]

We mentioned the proof that establishes the Exalted Creator's being purposeful when we set out a proof that knowledge is subject to the applicable characteristics in the attributes. The doctrine of the orthodox is that the Exalted Creator is purposeful through an eternal will. The Muʿtazilites of Basra held that He is purposeful through a will that is contingent but yet does not reside in a substrate. This is false for several reasons.

One of them is that His will, if it were contingent, would require that another will be associated with it, since every act is put into action by an agent who knows it and produces it with particular characteristics at a specific moment. There is no doubting that it intends to produce that act. Denying the intention in producing the act, in spite of knowing of it, forces the upholder of this position to deny what is intended in the production of each and every act. If they claim that the will wants what is intended by it but is not wanted in and of itself, their own words have not been heeded and they are forced to accept what we have said as to the impossibility of instigating an act accompanied by knowledge of it without also intending it.

Someone who investigated this deeply has asserted that it is self-evident and he was not off base in asserting this.

If what they say were allowed to the Basrans, Jahm[2] would be allowed to say: The Exalted Creator creates for Himself items of knowledge that are contingent upon temporal contingencies, and by virtue of them He necessarily knows contingent things. It is not necessary, therefore, that he know items of knowledge themselves through other items of knowledge. This is something for which there is no final resolution.

Here we say: You have agreed with us that two mutually similar things require shared participation in necessary and possible characteristics and in what is impossible. But then you make it necessary for our will to reside in a subject, thereby making it also obligatory in regard to the will of the Exalted Creator. Thus, that the will of the Creator – may He be exalted above their claims – resides in an inert thing is forced on them. Although they attempt to repudiate this by saying that the will invokes a specific place, a particularized shape and life, they

2 Jahm b. Ṣafwān, a Murjiʾite theologian, was executed in 128/746.

should be answered: Your affirmation of a will that does not reside in a substrate denies that it has a substrate or a shape or the attribute to which you have pointed. In denying the very principle of the substrate, denying what the substrate provides for is not far off.

Chapter: [The opinion of Jahm that affirms temporally contingent items of knowledge]

Jahm upheld the admissibility of the Lord's having temporally contingent items of knowledge – may He be above the statements of liars. He contended that, if and when the objects of knowing are renewed, the Hallowed and Exalted Creator produces, accordingly, renewed items of knowledge through which He knows these temporally contingent items of knowledge. Thus, in response to successive objects of knowledge that have previously occurred, items of knowledge follow successively.

According to the consensus of Muslims, what he said exceeded the bounds of religion and is incompatible with it. It also forsakes the rules of reason. The method of refuting him from the perspective of reason is close to that for refuting the Basrans in regard to their belief in temporally contingent acts of will, which, in their view, are affirmed of God, the Exalted, but without referring to subjects for them.

We answer Jahm as follows: If items of will need items of knowledge to which they are attached, contingent items of knowledge will require yet other items of knowledge to which they are attached, because they, too, share with the items of knowledge in being temporally contingent acts. And, having admitted this, there is no other outcome but to affirm a flow of items of knowledge that have no limit but are nevertheless temporally successive and contingent and one is trapped into accepting temporal contingencies that have no beginning. But, if not forced to that conclusion, one accepts, on the basis of the independence of items of knowledge from the items of knowledge which are associated with their temporal production, the independence of the totality of temporal contingencies from the items of knowledge that are associated with them.

The items of knowledge that are temporally contingent, according to Jahm, must be affirmed as not in a substrate, nor as residing in bodies, nor as residing in the essence of the Exalted Creator. If he insists that they subsist without a substrate, he is refuted by what refutes those who affirm temporally contingent items of will without a substrate. If he insists that they exist in the Lord's essence, refuting him is like refuting the Karrāmiyya, who declare that temporal contingencies exist in the Hallowed and Exalted Lord's essence. If he insists that they reside in bodies, he must admit that, if knowledge can be sustained by the body and display the applicable characteristic ascribed to another body, extending what he allows here in regard to the residence of knowledge in body means that its application reverts to God, the Exalted. Having proven these three cases false, and there being no other possibility, the invalidity of the doctrine that yields these three possibilities is therefore itself proven false.

It may now be said: The Hallowed Creator knew in His past eternity that the world would come to be and, when it came to be in the everlasting future, that fact is newly known and thus the Exalted Creator is qualified at the moment of the world's coming to be as having knowledge of its occurrence then and there. If the application to Him of an attribute is renewable, and being so qualified entails this, the necessitating of the applicable quality and His being subject to it is also renewed. This requires in Him items of knowledge that are renewed successively.

We answer that God, the Hallowed and Exalted, is not subjected to the renewal of an applicable qualification that has not previously existed. The modes do not appear in Him successively since their succession would mean what the succession of temporal contingencies implies in regard to the atoms. Rather, the Exalted Creator is to be ascribed a unique knowledge that is attached to what has never ceased nor will ever cease. It follows that, even though knowledge that is temporally contingent follows the rule of numbering, He necessarily encompasses the items of knowledge in their details. His knowledge is not enumerated according to the numbering of individual items of knowledge. Thus, as it is not subject to enumeration when the items of knowledge are enumerated, likewise it is not renewed when they are renewed.

What will make clear the truth in this is that the one who believes in the eternal duration of the temporal world but then tries to envision the knowledge associated with the fact that Zayd will come tomorrow, assumes the continuity of the knowledge of the occurrence of his coming until he comes. When Zayd comes, he need not resort to new knowledge of his coming since he previously had the knowledge of his coming at a future specific time. The effect of this is for us to assume a belief in the duration of knowledge, as we envision it here, and not to be under the imposition of another item of knowledge upon Zayd's actual coming, except what was already thought continuous. We maintain that the prior knowledge is not connected to the occurrence. That result implies his being ignorant of its actual occurrence at its specific moment or being oblivious to it, despite the supposition of continuous knowledge of the coming that was anticipated at a time specific, and that is self-evidently false.

It is not part of our doctrine to uphold the permanent duration of temporally contingent items of knowledge, but rational proofs are built on the truths in some instances and on the supposition of beliefs in others. If, in the visible world, for the one who previously had the knowledge of their occurrence in the future, the renewal of knowledge is not required upon the renewal of items of knowledge, *a fortiori* that is not required in regard to the Exalted Creator. Understand that!

Chapter: [*God speaks, commands and prohibits*]

The Hallowed and Exalted Creator speaks, commands, prohibits, informs, promises and threatens. While earlier affirming the applicable properties of the attributes of qualities, we showed, when we based the denial of the imperfections on tradition and directed against us the question of what it is that is proven by tradition, the way to demonstrate knowledge that the Exalted Lord speaks.

That the Exalted Creator speaks is clear and now is the moment to discuss the attribution to Him of speech. Know then, and be protected from heretical innovation, that among the doctrines of the orthodox is that the Hallowed and Exalted Creator speaks with an eternal speech for the existence of which there is no commencement. Those who are affiliated to Islam all agree in affirming speech; no one tries to deny it.

In the matter of God's speaking, no one subscribes to a creed which denies the attributes in the matter of His being knowledgeable, powerful and alive. Nevertheless, the Muʿtazilites, the Khārijites, the Zaydīs, the Imāmīs, and others among the adherents of heterodox opinion, maintain that the speech of the Creator – may He be exalted above the words of the deviators – is temporally contingent and exists only after commencing to exist.

Some of this persuasion, despite being definite as to its temporal production, abstain from labelling it "created" because of what in the term "created" misleadingly suggests fabrication, since fabricated speech is what, in the absence of any foundation for it, the speaker says in a fabrication.

The majority of the Muʿtazilites, however, generally apply the term "created" to the speech of the Exalted Creator and the Karrāmiyya uphold the concept that the speech of God is eternal but that the utterance is temporally contingent although without being produced. The Qurʾān is the utterance of God but is not the speech of God. The speech of God, in their view, is the power to speak. His utterance is temporally contingent and subsists in His essence – may He be exalted above the statements of these falsifiers. He does not utter words that subsist in Him but rather utters by means of an uttering facility. Everything whose existence commences subsists in the essence and it is temporally contingent upon a power without being produced. Everything that commences which is distinct from the essence was produced by His uttering "Be" and not by means of the power. But this handbook of doctrine is not the place to go into these two matters sufficiently.

Our aim in clarifying the truth and refuting those who would deviate from it will not be fully intelligible until after bringing together chapters on the actual nature of speech and its true reality in the visible world. Once having fulfilled our aims in that regard, we will turn towards our main purpose. In this handbook of doctrine, we felt compelled to keep to evidence that is unequivocal because of its small size. We have therefore traced a course which differs from that found in the doctrinal books of the leading masters. Still this condition forces us, none the less, to expand more broadly on the question of speech and into that we must now delve.

Chapter: On the real nature of speech and its definition and meaning

Know, may the Exalted God guide you, that the Muʿtazilites and those who oppose the orthodox ruminate at length on the exact nature of speech.[3] Here we will indicate the gist of their words. Whereupon we will follow with a refutation.

The older group of them said, among other things, that speech consists of letters in combination and discrete sounds that signify real intentions. This is false because each and all objects defined should be subsumed within any definition, whereas here a single letter is capable of conveying a self-contained meaning. Were you to make an imperative from the verb *waqā* or *washā*, you would say "*qi*" or "*shi*",[4] which are both examples of speaking but neither involves several letters or sounds [in combination].

One might object that a single letter cannot be pronounced in isolation and, when you produce the imperative from these particles, you add the pausal *hāʾ* and thus say "*qih*" and "*shih*". Therefore, the single consonant is never isolated and by itself. However, this will not rescue them from the intended objection since the word "*qi*" ["take care"] has a function in speaking and it manifests speech despite being a single letter. Our only purpose was to make that point clear.

Also there is no point in limiting it to the conveyance of meaning since sometimes the uttering of words conveys nothing. One might say, for example, "He speaks but makes no sense", and thus there is no point in the restriction that it has to convey meaning.

We maintain, moreover, that letters are themselves the sounds and there is no point in the repetition. In definitions one should guard against a duplication that produces no benefit. When they say that speech consists of letters in combination and discrete sounds, it is like determining speech to be sounds and sounds. If they were to omit the letters, one says to them: Discrete sounds convey no meanings in and of themselves that are not assigned to them by virtue of previous conventions. If you were to admit this and to accept such an idea, you must accordingly call the conventional chords played on a stringed instrument speech. This evaluation suffices in respect to their definition.

If now someone were to inquire: What is the definition of speech according to you? We reply: There were those among our leaders who refused to define speech. We will explain this in detail as we set the matter out clearly in the course

3 It is worth observing here that what the various definitions of speech imply theologically is not immediately obvious in al-Juwaynī's exposition at this juncture. His aim, however, seeks to keep God from the actual utterance of discrete sounds or the composition of letters which by their very nature are sequentially ordered and are thus temporally contingent. Following the definition of speech given by the Muʿtazilites, in speaking God engages in a temporal act and He thereby becomes Himself involved directly in time and ceases, accordingly, to be eternal.

4 In Arabic script these two imperative verbs appear as single letters r and j; the vowels – here both a *kasra* – are normally not written.

of explicating the true reality of speech itself. All of the intelligibles are not susceptible to definition; some of them can be defined and some cannot, just as some of them are caused and others uncaused. Our Master [al-Ashʿarī], may God have mercy on him, said speech is what renders its subject a speaker. In our view, this merits special attention.

It is preferable, however, for us to say that speech is a discourse that arises in the soul. If we are more specific, it is a discourse that arises in the soul which is manifested in terms of expressions and conventional signs.

Chapter: [*The Muʿtazilites deny interior speech*]

The Muʿtazilites denied that speech arises in the soul and claimed instead that speech consists of discrete sounds and letters in combination. They allow a speech that arises in the soul only in so far as it forms expressions that rely on letters and sounds. At times Ibn al-Jubbāʾī admitted [the existence of] interior speech and he called it "thoughts" [*khawāṭir*]. He insisted that these "thoughts" could be heard and perceived by the sense of hearing. Al-Jubbāʾī also maintained that sounds that are intermittently phonetic do not constitute speech but rather that speech consists of the letters in combination with the sounds. It is not the sounds themselves, but speech is what is heard when the sounds are heard.

The orthodox affirm that speech arises in the soul. It is a reflection that circulates in the mind which is manifest sometimes as expressions and sometimes in conventional signs or other terms similar in nature. The proof that speech arises in the soul is that, when an intelligent person gives his servant a command, mentally that person clearly expects complete compliance on the part of the servant. Accordingly, he indicates his inner concerns by means of some words, or certain kinds of gestures, or even graphic marks which are called writing.

If they should object that what we pointed to as a command is only the desire on the part of the person giving the command that the servant so commanded should obey the order, this is false in that the person giving the command might order the recipient of the order to do something he does not expect him to do and, despite the existence of this reservation in the soul, the command none the less entails the result indicated by the [external] expression. We will explain later that those who issue a command and impose an obligation do not necessarily want the act that is commanded to be performed.

If here they say: What he senses in himself is a will to make the phrases that issue from him a command, as either a recommendation or an obligation, this is false in several ways. One of them is that the utterance itself lapses even while the feeling of what is entailed persists in the soul. The past is no longer wanted, but instead regretted, and thus necessarily we realize that what we sense after the words are finished is not regret for the thing done. A fact that will clarify this is that the utterance is a rendering of what is in the conscience. This is something the mind verifies. The utterance is not a rendering of the will to make it be such and such, but rather it is a rendering of the entailment or of the obligation. Those who consider this carefully will not deny it.

Should it be asserted that the entailment is a form of belief, this is impossible. A belief is an opinion, or knowledge or ignorance of something, or yet another of the various forms beliefs take. What one finds in oneself that imposes an obligation is definitely not an item of knowledge, nor an opinion, nor ignorance of something, nor an intuition, nor a conjecture. What verifies this is that what they insist forces us to make of the obligation a will and a belief forces them to admit the same in respect to reasoning. If someone says here that reasoning is the wish to know that about which one reasons or is one type of belief, they cannot escape from the fact that it makes clear that reason is something other than desires and beliefs, without, by taking this route, supporting us in establishing our own claim.

Another proof for the existence of interior speech is that, in someone saying "do it!" this might express a preference or it might demand an obligatory act or might mean an authorization or even might impose an interdiction. If it establishes an obligation, it is impossible that the word is the obligation in and of itself because the form of the word that intends an obligation is the same as the form of the word that intends a preference. The word is formed merely of distinct sounds and the sounds differ in their phonetic composition only within a narrow range of allowable variations. Therefore, it is necessary to recognize that the obligation is itself a trait in the soul. Thereafter, various types of signifiers mould that trait into expressions and other forms of outward signification.

Someone may now retort: What you impose on us in accord with your view of the matter turns against you in arguing that the word indicates what is in the soul, since the indication of an obligation requires that it be distinguishable from the indication of a preference; we respond: The distinction between the two does not revert to the sounds themselves but rather to the observable conditions and associating factors that accompany the utterances which compel the person addressed to perceive the intention of the speaker. However, what we have mentioned here as the associating factors is not speech, according to our opponents. Our examination at this point is more than enough for rational evaluation.

If here we rely on the testimony of the lexicographers, we realize without doubt that the Arabs speak of the "speech of the soul" and of "statements that circulate in the mind". They say, for example, "There were words in my soul" and "I found an expression in my soul". This is so well known it needs no citation of examples either from prose or from verse. Al-Akhṭal[5] has said:

> The words are in my heart; it is they that cause the tongue to signify the heart.

An opponent might now claim that the utterances that produce a self-contained meaning are called by the intelligent, in general, speech and they admit that

5 Ghiyāth b. Ghawth b. al-Ṣalt, known as the "loquacious" [*al-akhṭal*], who died before 92/710.

saying "we have heard a speech" indicates the expressions they comprehend. To this we reply that the acceptable rule, in our view, is that the expressions in reality are called speech and that, as a discourse, speech arises in the soul. The combination of these two statements precludes the assertion of discord by opponents.

There are among our associates those who maintain that real speech is what arises in the soul and that the expressions denote speech metaphorically, just as they denote knowledge metaphorically, by implying the apprehension of an expression that is itself only an indicator of something known, though often the figurative sense is so commonly used that it passes for the real meaning.

Chapter: [*That the speaker is the one in whom speech occurs*]

The speaker, according to the orthodox, is the one in whom the speech occurs. And speech, in the view of those among them who affirm the modes, requires a mode in its subject which is its having speech. Speech occupies thus the same position as knowledge and power and other like attributes that of necessity require their subjects to possess these characteristics.

The Muʿtazilites, and all others who say that the speech of the Exalted God is temporally contingent, hold that the fact of a speaker's being a speaker is one of the attributes of action. A speaker, in their opinion, is the one who performs the act of speaking. Thus, in performing his act, the speaker exhibits no characteristic that is grounded in his essence, since, in their view, the implication of the agent's acting is merely the occurrence of an act of his. As a direct consequence of this, they do not stipulate that speech arises in the speaker in the same way as it is not necessary for the act to belong to the agent. This is one of the most important of the points we have to examine in this chapter.

We maintain the following: If a speaker were the one who does the act of speaking, one would not know that the speaker is speaking without knowing that he speaks the words, but the matter is not like that. A person who hears speech that issues from a speaker is certain that he is speaking, although the fact of his being the agent for his speech or being forced to speak never enters his mind. If then one believes that he is speaking, despite having to avoid these follies, it establishes, accordingly, that the fact of a speaker's speaking is not equivalent to his being the producer of speech. What makes this perfectly clear is, whereas we believe that there is in reality no agent save the Exalted God, despite being resolved on this article of faith, we still have certain knowledge of the speaker's being the one who speaks.

One way to reinforce this is for us to observe: Speech, according to you, consists of discrete sounds and letters in some sort of ordered combination, but, if one of us were then to say, "I am going today to Zayd", this would issue from him as speech and he would be the speaker of it. If the Exalted God by necessity created in the servant these sounds in that very arrangement, an adversary cannot escape, seeing as we have already determined that there is speech here, either of two consequences: either that the substrate of speech must be the speaker; or that it must not be so. Should he insist that the substrate is the speaker, he cannot have recourse to the idea that the speaker is the one who produces speech, since, in the way it is determined here, speaking is an act of God. Should he claim that the substrate of speech or the whole of which the substrate of speech is a part does not speak, he opposes and denies what is nearly completely self-evident. We hear the one in whom speech resides saying: "I am going today to Zayd", as if we have heard him saying that freely on his own.

If our objective in this chapter were based on the principle of ours to separate radically the Sanctified Lord from creation and on the impossibility of any other thing being a creator, that principle would make clear the falsity of trying to insist that the Exalted Creator is a speaker solely on account of being the agent for speech. But instead He is the agent of the speech of temporally contingent beings but He is not the speaker of that speech.

Here then the consequences imposed on the Najjāriyya[6] become obvious. They agree with the orthodox in holding that the Exalted Lord is the creator of the servants' deeds. However, it is no longer allowed them, although it is their doctrine, to claim that the speaker is the one who produces speech. Speech, according to the opinion of our opponents, consists of sounds. Were the speaker the one who produces speech, the one who makes the sound would be the one who causes the sound to be produced. The upshot, according to the declaration of the deviants, makes the Exalted Creator be, in so far as He is the agent who produces the sound, the maker of the sound.

Having proven wrong by decisive arguments those who hold that the speaker is the one who produces speech, there is nevertheless no doubt about speech being a particular property of the speaker in some manner. Since it cannot be by action, there remains, by the method of survey and elimination, and following upon the nullification of what we have been discussing, nothing other than what we approve, which is to insist that the speaker is the one in whom speech arises. Affirming this principle entails that speech is necessarily a feature possessed by its substrate, namely its being a speaker, since any attribute that resides in the substrate necessarily confers on it that characteristic.

These preliminaries serve well enough for our purpose in refuting opponents but we will also direct against them a few inquiries prior to delving specifically into the main objective of this particular question. We note that speaking about the particulars of speech depends on affirming that the Exalted Creator speaks. How then would you repudiate those who claim that He does not speak at all?

They insist that a speaker is the one who produces speech and that the Sanctified and Exalted Creator has the power to create speech and bring it into

---

6 These are the followers of al-Ḥusayn al-Najjār. They were a Ḥanafī sect principally of the early third/ninth century. On them see "al-Nadjdjār" and "al-Nadjdjāriyya" in the *EI2*.

existence. To that we respond: We have proven, in earlier argumentation, and contrary to your opinion, the falseness of your maintaining that the speaker is the one who produces speech. What you have mentioned allows you to accept that speaking is within the power of God. Why then do you insist that His having the power is an event, even though not everything that intelligence ascertains to be within the power of the Exalted Creator must necessarily have come to pass? That would require, in so far as the things within that power are without limit, the actual occurrence of an infinity of temporally contingent events.

They may say: We only realize that speech has come into being and that the Exalted God is to be characterized as speaking because of miracles and unnatural signs which testify to the truth of those who claim to be prophets. The prophets offer information about the speech of the Exalted God and of its occurrence, and they are those whose truthfulness and inspiration is confirmed by authentic signs and trustworthy proofs. Yet, in holding fast to their argument, they now say: You ground the knowledge that rejects imperfections upon tradition and yet you base the affirmation of the Exalted God's speech on miracles. How then do you reject those who follow your own method in this regard? We answer: Our opponents among the Muʿtazilites and those who take the same tack are, in the first place, prevented from affirming the miracles and pursuing the means to understand the aspect of them that indicates the truth of those who are embraced by the miracles. We will explain this, God the Exalted willing, under the subject of miracles.

At this point we add: What makes our doctrine hold good will not support your contention. In attempting to establish our claim we cited the example of the king and, in accord with his rank, his presiding over an assembly at an appointed time and known place, surrounded there by those of his retainers especially dedicated to his service. At that point, one person asserts before all those present that he is the king's emissary to all the seen and unseen, and this is with the king's full knowledge. Under these conditions as testimony to prove his apostleship he offers an order issuing from the king that violates the habitual arrangement the king normally follows. But thereupon the king responds positively to his wish and confirms his claim. This is a situation that indicates that the king provides validation for the claim by means of a statement that is inside his soul and by an external act which interprets it and which occupies the role of a convention in prompting the comprehension of meaning.

So this is our method but it will not work for the Muʿtazilites because, according to them, the meaning of the Exalted Creator's being a speaker is that He produces speech. There is nothing in the appearance of signs to indicate that the Exalted Creator creates discrete sounds in some particular body which thereby constitute speech. Rather miracles are linked to the verification of those who manifest them. Such a form of verification is characteristic of them. Those who are so authenticated actually receive their validation in that manner. The veritable characteristic in question does not depend on an action that reverts to an agent. Therefore miracles do not provide evidence for the existence of speech.

Something to make our aim here quite clear is that we have explained by sure proofs that the one, in this case, who verifies a thing does not verify it by producing a verbal statement in the verification, although verification is a form of speaking. We have already stated the falsity in general of the doctrine of those who hold that the speaker is the one who produces speech. This includes verification since it is a form of speech.

Therefore, that the Exalted Creator verifies the apostles by a verbal statement, as is the doctrine of the Muʿtazilites, is false, as it is also false that miracles prove the truth of the prophets by putting the miracle in the position of verification on the basis of a verbal statement. Accordingly, their appeal to a proof based on miracles is clearly nullified by the corruption in their beliefs and the contradictory nature of their principles. By invalidating the evidence of miracles, no other course remains that will lead to an affirmation of a verbal statement. And thus does God deal with all unbelievers. These are the questions directed against them prior to delving more deeply into the matter at hand.

In regard to another demand of theirs, we ask: How do you deny those who claim that God, the Exalted, is a speaker in and of Himself, just as, according to you, He is alive, knowledgeable, and powerful in and of Himself? They see this as a consequence of His being purposeful in and of Himself. Should they maintain that it is impossible that He be purposeful and a speaker in and of Himself because, since the application applies to all other objects within the field of its application, an attribute that is affirmed of the self requires of necessity that its application be universal; therefore, since He knows in and of Himself, His knowing applies to all objects of knowledge. The point they are trying to make is futile. In respect to this issue, one might say that the Exalted Lord is purposeful in and of Himself in regard to some purposes and not others. This is the same as the particularization inherent in a will that is contingent upon the object to which it applies.

If now someone asks: Why would the will be particularized by the object to which it applies and why does its application not extend to every other situation? Among the answers of those who know the truth is that applying what is specifically its own proper application does not cause the thing itself to become particularized. Rather it is particular in and of itself, just as it applies in and of itself. And we do not agree with them that God's being knowledgeable in and of Himself indicates that He knows all objects of knowledge. But there is another proof for this.

There is no way out of this objection in that they contradict their own premise when they admit that the Exalted Creator is powerful in and of Himself but then insist that His being powerful does not apply to all objects of that power because, in their view, the things a human has the power to do are not subject to the power of the Creator. But God is exalted above their words. This is an attribute of the self which, in accord with their own claim, they would make particular.

If they maintain that speech consists of combined letters and discrete sounds, there is no way to affirm speaking that originates in the soul. To hold this on their part is to rely on what was determined previously to be false, since we have confirmed that there is a speech that arises in the soul which does not involve letters or sounds or melodies or tones. Our purpose in bringing up this topic is to be assured of exactly this.

Know now, as a result, that the debate with the Muʿtazilites and other opponents on this issue is a matter involving both denial and affirmation. What they affirm and determine to be speech is actually affirmed of His self. Their statement that it is the speech of God, the Exalted, if reduced to its particulars, brings speech back to a function of languages and nomenclature. The meaning of their declaration "These expressions are the speech of God" is that they are His creation. For our part, we do not deny that they are a creation of God but we do refuse to designate the Creator of the speech as the one who speaks it. We are thus of one mind as to the meaning but in disagreement, despite this accord, over how to designate it.

That form of speech which the orthodox judge to be eternal is the speech that arises in the soul. Our adversaries deny it altogether and refuse to affirm it. Following upon its being affirmed, they debate whether it is temporally contingent or eternal. If we move on to these arguments, it involves affirming the existence of something of which they deny the very principle. We say: That the Exalted Creator speaks by means of speech is proven and the intelligent adjudge that His speaking is peculiar to Him in some way. There is no need to impose the burden of offering a proof of this.

The particularity in this instance, which is agreed to by all the schools of doctrine and is required by reason, must either exist as an aspect of the Creator's action, or exist as an aspect of a particularity given by another of His attributes, either one that is essential or one that is qualifying. But it is wrong to argue that the particularity occurs in the speech as if it were an act of the Exalted Creator. In presenting earlier the way to refute those who maintain that the speaker is the one who produces speech, we have already made that clear. It is equally false to assert that the particularity in the existence of the speech lies in the knowledge of God, or His will, or hearing, or sight. These are modalities proper to the speech of humans who are appropriately characterized by the resulting and corresponding particularities.

It is not right to say that speech is in any way made particular by the Exalted Creator's essential attributes, since that condition applies to all generally and is not a claim of particularity, and we are in the process of dealing with the specific case. For someone to say that speech is a particularity of His, or of some attribute of His essence generally, without moving on to explicate the exact manner of that particularity, establishes nothing at all.

Since it is false to ascribe the particularity to the aspects mentioned above, there is nothing left except to conclude definitely that the speech of the Exalted and Sanctified Creator is peculiar to Him because of being particular in its mode of subsistence. Having determined this and because of having recognized the proof of the impossibility of His being susceptible to temporal contingencies, there follows the impossibility of His being temporally contingent. The falseness of these claims leaves nothing else but the doctrine of the orthodox who characterize the Exalted Creator as being a speaker who speaks an eternal speech that had no beginning. The techniques available for rational proofs are abundant but there is already enough here for conviction.

Chapter: [*Some doubts of the adversaries*]

One of the arguments they rely on is to say: If you affirm an eternal speech, one of two options follows: either you admit that the eternal speech consists of a commandment, a prohibition, or an announcement; or you do not judge it to be so.

If you claim that there was from all eternity a commandment, a prohibition or an announcement, you are faced with an inconsistency. An essential feature of commandments and prohibitions is that they coincide with the existence of the subject to whom the command or prohibition is directed and there cannot have existed from all eternity someone to whom it is addressed or who stands in need of being impelled to do something or restrained from doing something else. One cannot comprehend a command that has no recipient; one cannot command an impossibility.

If, on the contrary, you insist that speech in eternity does not have the characteristic features that delimit natural speech, you maintain something incomprehensible and the discussion of such a doctrine, whether for refutation or acceptance, suggests none the less that it is comprehensible. One of our partisans, ʿAbdallāh b. Saʿīd b. Kullāb,[7] may God have mercy on him, held that the eternal speech cannot be characterized as a command, a prohibition or an annunciation, except where the respondents exist and in combination with the conditions that subject them to commands and prohibitions. Once God brought humans into existence and made them understand His speech as being a matter of command or requiring restraint or entailing some information, that speech must accordingly be characterized by these properties which, in his view, are attributes of actions equivalent to the Exalted Creator's bearing the characteristic accorded by His being unceasingly a creator, a bestower, the source of good and of abundance.

---

7 An important pre-Ashʿarī theologian who died about 241/855. The later Ashʿarites, like al-Juwaynī, regarded him favourably and considered him to have been quite orthodox in his teachings.

This approach, although it averts controversy, is not acceptable. The correct way is that approved by our master, may God be pleased with him, which is to say that eternal speech never ceases being characterized as a command, prohibition or announcement. The non-existent being is, in principle, subject to the eternal command only upon the eventuality of its coming into existence, even though the eternal command in and of itself is characterized, when it should actually exist, as entailing what will come to be. Their attempt to deny this on the basis of the impossibility of the non-existent thing being subject to a command yields them nothing.

Firstly, the way to counter them is by one of their own principles that blocks this course of argument. It is their doctrine that, when the command was issued for the human to act, the subject of the command did not exist but that the action, prior to his existence, was nevertheless demanded of him. When he does come to exist, however, it ceases to be demanded of him in the state he comes into, just as, according to their principle, he ceases at that moment to be subject to God's power. There is no intermediate position between the denial and the affirmation. If an established positive act is not demanded of him, the import of the command still subjects him to the negation of that act. If they do not consider improbable the thing demanded's not having existence, one cannot allow them to consider improbable that the person commanded may not have existence.

What they say that is even more improbable concerns our admitting that the not-yet-existent is subject to the command upon the determination of its existence and thus, when it comes to exist, its being subject to the command is a reality, although we do not admit such a determination of being subject to command in its being not-yet-existent. If the Exalted Creator knows that it will not come into existence, its eventual existence as being subject to command is thus impossible and, under those conditions, there attaches to it no imposition based on the command. The Muʿtazilites have decided that the not-yet-existent is subject to command but that, upon coming into existence, its being subject to command ceases. This is their way of resolving the problem of the application of the command[8] to the non-existent.

Here we observe that all Muslims are in accord with us that, in our own time, we are subject to the command of God. The majority of the Muʿtazilites, in contrast, hold the doctrine that the Lord God does not speak in our present time and that the speech of His that once existed exists no longer. Since they do not view our being subject to command as improbable and yet there is no longer a command, they are left with nothing in their version but a muddle.

Another point: The Sanctified Lord was in His eternity powerful and among the properties inherent in the powerful having power is that there exists something over which He has power [or, something He has the power to effect]

---

8 Reading *al-amr* with some of the manuscripts in place of *al-ʿilm* in the edition.

and, although the coming into being of actions in eternity is impossible and self-contradictory, this latter thing is both conceivable and possible. Since His having power from eternity is not unthinkable, despite the particularity that occurs with the advent of an effected thing within the eternal, it is not unthinkable to so characterize speech that entails something to be in the future.

Another of the points they invoke is for them to say: Prior to the appearance of this dissension, the Muslims were in unanimous agreement that the Qurʾān is the speech of the Sanctified God. They all recognized that it consists of *sura*s and of verses, of letters in combination and of words. It is heard in actuality and it has a beginning and an ending. It is the miracle of the apostle of God, God bless him and keep him, and is a sign confirming his authenticity. A miracle cannot take place except by an action that interrupts the normal course of nature, occurring in support of the challenge issued on behalf of the prophet, God bless him and keep him. In that no particularity belongs to an eternal attribute in respect to one advocate of monotheism over another, it is impossible for the eternal to come to be a miracle. Were it feasible for eternal speech that exists in the soul eternally to constitute a miracle, one would need to admit that eternal knowledge, for those who affirm its existence, might constitute a miracle.

These doctrines of theirs are mere fantasies devoid of significance. As for their attempt to provoke discord by arguing that the Qurʾān, according to the consensus of Muslims, consists of *sura*s and verses and that it has a beginning, internal divisions, a starting point and a conclusion, to that we respond as follows: In the first place, the majority of you hold the doctrine that it is the speech of the Exalted God which, from the moment of its creation, consisted of sounds and which thereafter functioned independently and expired. Therefore the recited version that is memorized and written down is not the speech of God. This is the doctrine of all those later Muʿtazilites who pretend to be especially clever, but it leads to the denial of the Exalted God's speech and is more repugnant and disgusting than the arguments about the attribute of speech.

When al-Jubbāʾī became fully aware of this and was therefore certain that, if one held to this doctrine, it would result in a rupture of the consensus of the community, he devised a doctrine with which he tore off the cover of respectability by denying what had to be. He said that the speech of the Exalted God co-exists with the recitation of every reciter. Moreover, this speech, according to him, consists of letters joined to discrete sounds that issue from various points of articulation but they are not the sounds themselves. He claimed further that they exist also in the writing. Because there is a harmony to the well-ordered letters and the impressed patterns, the letters found in the scripture are not simply the shapes that are apparent nor the lines that are plainly evident. Next he insisted that the letters that are heard during recitation, although they are not the sounds, are not those seen while in the process of writing the lines.

He taught also that one who recites the words of the Exalted God is confirming with his uvula the letters which form his recitation but they are distinct from the sounds. The letters are the speech of God and yet they are distinct from the recitation and the sounds. When the reciter leaves off reciting, the words of the Exalted God cease to be in him, although in reality they continue to exist and inhere in something else.

Another reprehensible doctrine was his saying that, if a group of reciters assembles to chant a verse, the speech of God exists in every one of them and thus what exists in the whole of them is one and the same speech. Merely to state this doctrine is enough; the wise will have no need of being supplied a rebuttal as well.

As for their arbitrarily insisting on affirming that the letters are distinct from the sounds, it goes against the judgment of reason and invents a doctrine for which there is no evidence. The letters, according to the understanding of the intelligent, are themselves the discrete individual sounds. Thus, if, upon hearing the sound, it is permitted to assume the perception of something that is not a sound, what prevents assuming seeing the letters when arrayed in an orderly fashion and neatly imprinted in methodical lines?

As for holding that one and the same speech may reside in several locations, that denies evident necessity. No person of learning harbours any doubt about this point. This handbook of ours will not trouble with examining how to refute it.

Another of his abominable doctrines is holding that the human expects God, through forming and selecting the sounds and intonations, to create the words used during adoration of Himself. This is a self-evident abomination that no intelligent person would tolerate.

Here now after dealing with their objections, we say: You have claimed that the Qurʾān is the speech of God and yet, when asked for the justification of attributing speech to the Exalted Creator, you provide no means for making such a specification other than its being an action of His. Concerning what you claim is His act you receive support for it from our own doctrine. It represents the ultimate purpose in your attribution of speech to the Exalted God. Therefore, we both agree in attributing speech to the Exalted God, although a disagreement remains about the denotations and the connotations of it. It is not, in our view, unthinkable to attribute an act of the Exalted God to God if the law clearly permits it. This protects us from all the mischief they try to stir up.

At times the term "al-Qurʾān" implies the idea of reciting. It is the verbal noun derived from the verb "to recite". There is an example of this in the poet Ḥasan b. Thābit, who said in praise of ʿUthmān, may God be pleased with him:

> They sacrificed an old man with marks of prostration on him; he passed the night glorifying [God] and reciting [the *Qurʾān*]

The meaning here is that he passed the night glorifying and reciting. The Exalted Lord Himself called prayer "Qurʾān" because it is comprised of recitations [of the Qurʾān]. Thus He says, great is His name: "Indeed the recitation of the morning prayer is well observed" [17:78], which means that the morning prayer is observed by the angels of the night and of the day, the ones rising and the others descending. According to traditions, the apostle of God, God bless him and keep him, said: "God listens to nothing like He listens to the prophet who excels in the chanting of the Qurʾān." It means to excel as a chanter in the process of recitation.

As for what they cite as the consensus of the Muslims in regard to the Qurʾān being the miracle of the apostle, along with the certainty that miracles must be confined to acts that break the normal rule of nature, we respond to them: One of your principles is that the prophet's, on whom be peace, challenge to the Arabs – they who were most eloquent and pure of language and most devoted to discussion – was not the speech of the Exalted God and what the Exalted Lord had created Himself had then expired. However, the challenge of the apostle, on whom be peace, was merely to produce something similar. For this reason, it is you who deserve more to be known as the violators of the consensus than your opponents. It is your declaration that every reciter brings forth a likeness of the speech of the Exalted God. But the Lord, great is His name, has said: "Say, if humans and jinn were to join forces to produce the like of this Qurʾān, they could not produce its like" [17:88].

Moreover, for what they have proposed, they receive co-operative support and general collaboration, since they claim that the words of God are the miracle of the apostle, on whom be peace, and they mean by the speech of God a speaking which is His act. We maintain as well that the speech which He produced is a miracle of the apostle, on whom be peace. There thus is nothing exclusive to their position with respect to this meaning and all of their misrepresentations ultimately fade away.

Another of their attempts to stir up trouble and achieve control over the masses is for them to say that God's words: "Take off your shoes!" [said to Moses; 20:12] is the speech of the Exalted God; and to suppose that this was, prior to the creation of Moses, on whom be peace, attributed to God in eternity is both an obscenity and is unintelligible.

The way to deal with it, if they cling to it, is to respond: "Take your shoes off", according to the agreement of the Muslims, remains a statement of the Exalted God still in our own era and Moses is not the one addressed now. If this is not unacceptable at such a later moment, it was not allowable in times past.

The reality of all this is that the opponents consider speech to be letters and sounds and, based on what they believe, they think it impossible to speak to a non-existent being by means of letters that follow one after the other. The matter is, however, not as they imagine it to be. Speech, in the opinion of the orthodox, is a trait that arises in the soul which consists of neither letter nor sound. Eternal speech pertains to all the things appertaining to speech in its totality. It is a command in relation to the subjects of command, a prohibition against the prohibited, and an announcement of information. Moreover, it applies variously to things that are temporally renewable without being temporally renewed in itself.

Our approach in determining this matches that for eternal knowledge. It existed eternally and pertained previously to that eternity and its characteristics – for example, the non-existence of the world and the fact that it will come to be in the everlasting future. Upon the temporal production of the world, the eternal knowledge applies to the event of its coming into being but without any alteration in itself. Similarly, eternal speech existed in anticipation of the moment for the communication to Moses and, when he came into existence, it was a communication to him in actuality. The newly existing thing was, however, Moses, not the speech.

They might, however, say here: Discussing rejection or acceptance only applies to a doctrine that is well understood. What you affirm as arising in the soul is unintelligible and you thus cannot have a discussion about it. If they take this approach, the way to proceed is for us to say: Someone who gives a command to his servant finds himself imposing obedience on the servant and he calls upon the servant to comply. A person who denies this rejects the obvious. What the mind decided upon is, according to us, the speech that arises in the soul and it is something understood and known. If they would change this imposition into something else that is other than what we allude to, that represents, on their part, an unreasonable resort to argument for argument's sake. In proofs of ours advanced previous to this, we have clearly shown that the imposition is exactly as we claim it is and what we are about to demonstrate now blocks their attempt to cause controversy by claims of ignorance.

Chapter: [*That the speech of God is eternal according to the literalists*]

The Ḥashwiyya, who take their evidence only from the literal wording, hold that the speech of the Exalted God is eternal and everlasting. Moreover, they insist that it consists of letters and sounds, and they are certain that what is heard as the sounds of the reciter and their intonation is the very speech of the Exalted God itself. The lowly riff-raff among them even declare that what is heard is the voice of the Exalted God Himself. This is ample confirmation of their unbridled foolishness. Furthermore, they maintain that, when the words of the Exalted God are written down and physically inscribed, wherein these bodily forms become graphic signs and imprinted letters – that is, lines and words on a page – they are still in their essences the eternal words of the Exalted God, even though, at that moment, they have become contingent bodies, which only thereafter revert to an eternal state. They deem what is seen as a line to be the eternal speech, even though it consists of letters and sounds.

It is a principle of theirs that, although discontinuous and consecutive, the sounds were nevertheless established in eternity as subsisting in the essence of the Creator – may God be exalted far above their notions. The concepts behind their doctrines are built on a denial of the plainly self-evident; they affirm that there is for the eternal speech, which they recognize, a beginning and an end.

Thus, they make out of it something that precedes and something that is preceded. The second letter of every word is preceded by what comes before it and thus every preceded letter has a beginning to its existence. We know by necessity that the existence of that for which there is a commencement is itself temporally contingent. There is no hiding their violation of otherwise quite obvious reason when they declare the temporally contingent to be eternal.

What further confirms their ignominious disregard for the truth is that the letters, even if depicted as composed of certain substances, are nevertheless, according to them, the very words of the Exalted God. The iron from which the letters are moulded ceases to be iron. But we actually perceive the pieces of iron formed into a body. How can there be any need for these people to go to such extremes?

In their ignorance, they are convinced that, when written, the name of God, in the inscription that one sees, is God Himself in actuality. He is the object of worship and the one to be invoked.

Moreover, their principle that eternal speech becomes incarnate in bodies although it does not separate from its essence makes idle sport out of religion, loosening the tenets of the Muslims, and imitating the doctrine expressed by the Christian in their holding that the word inheres in the Messiah, who is equipped with human form. If it were not that many people are deceived into embracing these notions, the situation would not warrant paying attention to these obvious disgraces and outrageous abominations.

Chapter: [*Our creed concerning recitation*]

The recitation, according to the orthodox, consists of the sounds of the readers and their intonation, which are acquisitions of theirs, commanded of them in the state required by certain acts of ritual obeisance or recommended at many other times. For these, they are censured if they refuse, rewarded if performed and punished for omission. On this, all Muslims are in agreement. It is certified by traditions and abundantly communicated in reports. Reward and punishment appertain to no other thing than to what humans accomplish. It is impossible that an eternal attribute, which exists outside the realm of possible and realizable things, be connected with the imposition of an obligation, a desire or a rebuke.

Recitation is something that is agreeable on the part of one reader and disagreeable when done by another. It can be defective or regular and exact. The eternal attribute, however, transcends all of the things to which we allude here. No person of true discrimination would ever think that the sounds that make hoarse his throat or engorge abnormally his jugular veins, and which, in accord with proclivity or desires, may be pronounced incorrectly or correctly, loudly or furtively, are the actual words of the Exalted God. This is our creed with regard to the recitation.

Chapter: [*Our creed concerning what is recited*]

In regard to what is recited in the process of recitation, a part of the recitation is grasped and understood and it is the eternal speech which the expressions signify but which are not it. Moreover, what is recited is not incarnate in the reciter nor does it subsist in him. The situation of the recitation and what is recited is like an invocation and what is invoked. The invocation belongs to the statements of those who invoke, and the Lord who is invoked, hallowed and glorified is not the invocation, nor the hallowing nor the glorifying.

The Arabs coined different terms for what is variously signified by different expressions: the imparting of poetry is called "reciting" [*inshād*]; a communication about things absent which are not susceptible to speech is called "commemoration" [*dhikr*]; and the signs that signify the speech of the Exalted God by means of sounds are called "recitation" [*qirāʾa*].

Chapter: [*The Exalted God's word does not inhere in copies of the Qurʾān*]

The words of the Exalted God are written in copies of the Qurʾān, preserved in the breast, but they do not inhere in the copy nor subsist in the heart. The writing, by which it is expressed, either through the movement of the person who writes or through inscribed letters and imprinted lines, is altogether temporally contingent. What the lines signify and what is understood from the writing is the eternal speech. This is tantamount to declaring that the speech of the Exalted God is written in the copies of the Qurʾān, except that what is meant is not His becoming attached to bodies or His subsisting in physical forms.

No one who subscribes to the truth would hold that the speech resides in the line of writing – except al-Jubbāʾī in various follies of his that we have reported. It is related of al-Najjār that he held that the impressions themselves are the physical forms of the Exalted God's speech and the speech is the sounds made during the recitation, as well as the physical forms made during the writing. All this muddles and confuses the quest for what is correct, while forsaking altogether the search for truth.

Chapter: [*The speech of God is heard*]

According to the common usage of Muslims, the speech of the Exalted God is heard. There is testimony to this in the book of the Exalted God when He says: "If any of the idolaters ask you for protection, grant it to him until he hears the words of God" [9:6]. Furthermore, hearing is an equivocal term; its meanings are not all the same; nor does it have only one connotation. What might be intended by it is a sense perception; or it might imply comprehension and understanding; or it might lead to obeying and submission; or yet further to acquiescing.

As for hearing with the meaning of sense perception, it is completely obvious. "Hearing" with the meaning of comprehending and knowing is widely used and is not in doubt. The Exalted God characterizes those who are obstinate in unbelief as being deaf, intending not that there is a defect in their sense perception, but rather that they refuse to grasp the meanings or comprehend what they are warned about and to heed the signs of the Exalted God.

If someone should relate in his own manner the words of another, the one listening to the sounds transmitted might say: I have heard the words of so and so, and he would mean the absent person, the sense of whose words were those communicated to him.

What one must conclude with certainty is that what is heard and comprehended in our own time are the sounds. But, if the speech of the Exalted God is heard, it means that it is grasped and understood through the sounds that are actually perceived by the senses and heard physically. In the precepts of the law and as agreed to by the community, there exists evidence that the Exalted Lord selected Moses, and others of the chosen among humans and the angels, and He caused them to hear His mighty speech without an intermediary. If a listener to the recitation by a reader were to perceive the very speech of the Exalted God by the senses, Moses, may the blessings of God be upon him, would not have been singled out as being addressed directly and as having perceived the words of God without the aid of a intermediate transmitter or of a messenger to convey them.

Chapter: [*The meaning of the revealing of the Exalted God's speech*]

The speech of the Exalted God was revealed to the prophets and many verses in the book of God indicate that. However, the meaning of revelation [*inzāl*: "making descend"] is not to move something downward from above. "Descending" [*inzāl*] with the meaning of "transposition" is particular to bodies and physical things. Those who believe in the eternity of the speech of the Exalted God and its subsistence in the essence of the Creator, may He be sanctified and exalted, and the impossibility of its separating from that to which it is attributed, will have no doubt at all about the impossibility of its being transposed. And those who believe in the temporal contingency of the speech and hold that it is an accident among accidents are likewise not allowed a doctrine that admits the transposition because an accident does not separate and does not move [from its atom].

What is meant by revelation [*inzāl*] is that Gabriel, may the blessings of God be upon him, perceived the words of the Exalted God while he was yet in his station above the seven heavens. He then descended to the earth and caused the apostle, may God bless him and grant him peace, to comprehend what he himself had understood when he was before the Lotus of Paradise.[9] This takes place without any transposition in the words themselves. If someone remarks that the message of the king descends to the palace, he does not intend the conveyance

9 The lotus tree at the highest limit of paradise, from the Qurʾān 53:14 and 16.

of the actual sounds the king has made or the relocation of the actual speech of his that subsists in his soul.

Chapter: [*The speech of the Exalted God is one*]

The speech of the Exalted God is one, although it pertains to many in its applications. His other attributes are the same. He knows all objects of knowledge by a single knowledge; He has power over all subjects of power through a single power. A similar statement applies to life, hearing, seeing and willing.

The conclusion that there is unity in the attributes is not a determination of the intellect but rather depends on a decree of the law and is required by tradition. In regard to establishing that knowledge is unitary, there are differences of opinion; and there is no way to affirm it against those who deny it except by resort to rational proofs. But this applies in the case of a single knowledge. As for the supposition of a second knowledge, no theologian adhering to Islam would accept it; if it is to be characterized as being eternal, all agree in rejecting it.

Here someone might say: If we concede to you what you have stated concerning knowledge and power, what approach does one apply in respect to will and speech? We respond: The purpose here is to make clear the concluding of a consensus that by necessity must be observed, and it denies the existence of a second eternal speech. On the basis of what we have said previously, this has been established firmly and without any ambiguity

Someone may now ask: What causes you not to rely on the determinations of intellect in this section? We reply: We found that eternal knowledge pertains to the objects of knowledge that give rise to differing sorts of knowledge in the visible world. Nothing in the intellect rules definitively in favour of the impossibility of eternal knowledge occupying the place of power, nor is there in it something that leads to requiring that the single knowledge pertains to all objects of knowledge. Every attempt to prove this by rational determination fails. This belief is simply not susceptible to thorough examination, of what is said either for, or in refutation of, it.

Chapter: [*The attributes are not distinct from the essence*]

Those who affirm the attributes cannot speak about them as being distinct from the essence. Our purpose in this chapter, however, is to bring to the fore the investigation of the real implication in recognizing two distinctly separated entities.

What the later authorities among our masters approve concerning the implication of two distinct entities is that they are two existents that might be separated one from the other by time or place or existence or non-existence. This is preferable to the statement of those who say: Two distinct entities consist of every pair of things one of which can exist without the other. The person who accepts the eternity of atoms and the impossibility of their non-existence is certain, nevertheless, of the distinction between two bodies, despite his failure to allow one of them not to exist. One cannot realize the knowledge of what is truly certain except by first recognizing what is really real.

A statement that would clearly fix the meaning of distinct entities cannot be definitive, in our view, because rational arguments cannot be used to establish it, nor are there convincing proofs for it in tradition. We are not able to prove with certainty the falsity of the statement of those among the Muʿtazilites who say: Two things are always distinct. The issue here reverts to the application of preference and metonymy in dealing with terms that are equivocal in meaning.

Should it be said: Since you are not sure about what your master mentioned in regard to the true nature of distinct entities, are you certain of the prohibition against the application of distinctiveness to the attributes of the Exalted Creator and His essence? We respond: We are certain that this is prohibited because an agreement of the community prohibited such an application of it. None the less, just as the attributes are not to be described as being other than the essence, one should not say that they are the essence. We avoid any statement implying that the attributes are existing entities and that knowledge and the essence together are two existing things, or any other statement like this about any of the attributes.

Our masters in general refrain from stating that the attributes differ one from another, even though the imam and *qāḍī* Abū Bakr [al-Bāqillānī],[10] may God approve him, maintained that they do differ.

Chapter: [*What we say about the attribute of perpetuity*]

The scholars among our masters held the doctrine that perpetuity is an attribute of the Perpetual Being which is additional to His existence, as knowledge is in the reality of the knower. For us, however, it is preferable to admit that perpetuity is nothing other than the continuation of existence, rather than something added to it. Were we not to follow this approach, we might be forced to characterize the eternal attributes as being perpetual and thus to affirm that they have perpetuity. Going down that route leads to basing the characteristic [of one attribute] on the characteristic of another. Were we to admit that the perpetual is eternal, we must qualify the latter with perpetuity and this yields us an endless regression.

Someone may say: The proof that establishes the existence of the attributive characteristics is the advent upon their subject of their particular properties. For example, when we witness a substance that does not move, which thereafter comes to possess the attribute of motion, it establishes that this characteristic is newly imposed. This is exactly the situation with respect to perpetuity, since the atom at the moment of its temporal production can no longer be characterized as being perpetual. Only if its existence as it was were to be prolonged could it be

---

10 A major Ashʿarite theologian and Malikī jurist, who died 403/1013.

characterized as being perpetual. We respond to that: Being characterized by perpetuity depends on the continuity of existence and this is the same as eternity. What exists but came into existence recently cannot be called eternal. If it ages and becomes old, one might well say that it is "ancient" [*qadīm*] but that does not prove that antiquity is an attributive characteristic.

Someone may say: If you relate perpetuity to the perpetual being itself, what causes you to deny the statement of those who maintain the perpetuity of the accidents? To that we reply: The accidents cannot possibly be perpetual because, if they were to endure, it would be impossible for them not to exist. Thus, if we were to suppose the perpetual duration of white, for example, and that its existence is permanent, we could not imagine its cessation and the subsequent replacement of it by black. Were black not the negation of white and its opposite, white would prefer to repulse black and keep it from occurring.

Moreover, there is no sense in envisioning, as some people do, that what is perpetual will cease to be when God makes it cease to be. Annihilation is non-existence and non-existence is pure negation. There is no sense in applying power to pure negation. The effect of saying that the Creator has the power to make the existent non-existent can be reduced to the claim that He has the power to not have exist what exists.

Someone might ask: What is the meaning of the annihilation of the atoms? We respond: The accidents are not perpetual and thus, should God desire the annihilation of an atom, He deprives it of accidents by not creating them and the atom thereupon ceases to exist accordingly, because it is impossible for an atom to exist without accidents.

The Muʿtazilites denied perpetuity but nevertheless claimed that the majority of accidents are perpetual and that what ceases to exist of the perpetual things does so only by the superimposition on it of its contrary. They agree with us in regard to the impossibility of the perpetual duration of sounds and volitions – this in a protracted and confused encounter. They insist that atoms cease to exist when the Exalted God creates an annihilation in something that is not a contrary of the atom and which is itself an accident subsisting on its own. Furthermore, according to them, the annihilation of some of the atoms while others persist is impossible.

Section

A Statement of the Meaning in the Names of God, the Exalted

Chapter: [*What should be said about the designation and the name*]

For the orthodox, a designation refers to the term used by those who name something, but the name in itself does not signify this term but rather that to which the designation refers. Were someone to say "Zayd", his statement is a designation and yet also what is understood by it is a name. In this situation, the name is the thing named, and the attribution and the attribute are virtually the same as the designation and the thing named. The attribution is the statement of the one who attributes; and the attribute is what the attribution signifies. However, the name is often given where the intention is a designation and the attribute is employed when what is intended is an attribution. Statements made in this matter thus never attain the level of certainty.

The Muʿtazilites maintained that there is equality between the name and the designation and between the attribution and the attribute. For that reason they were forced into a reprehensible deviation for they also said: The Creator had in eternity neither attribute nor name because the name and the attribute are the terms of those who name and those who describe. In eternity there was no statement by them. But someone who claims that his Exalted Lord did not have in His eternity the attribute of divinity has left religion aside and departed from the consensus of Muslims.

Furthermore, the proof that the name is distinct from the designation and from what the name-giver intends by it lies in various verses of the Exalted God's book, among them His saying: "Sanctify the name of your Lord Most High" [87:1]. What is to be sanctified is the being of the Exalted Creator, not the terms that are mentioned by the worshippers. He of Great Power and Glory also said: "Blessed be the name of your Lord" [55:78], as well as: "What you worship other than God is nothing but the names you and your fathers named" [12:40]. It is well known that the worshippers of idols worshipped not the term and the words but the things named and not the designations for them.

If someone says here: The Muslims attest that the Exalted God has ninety-nine names and, if the name were the thing named, that would be a declaration that there are a multiplicity of gods.

There are two ways for us to answer that.

One is for us to say: Often the intention in the name is the designation and this is something that we do not deny. The intended sense in the uttering of the name is to indicate the thing named.

The second is that each name that indicates an action is a name and thus the names are actions and they are multiple. What pertains to the eternal attributes does not preclude multiplicity; and what pertains to essential attributes are modes which also do not preclude their multiplicity.

Chapter: [*The law and the names of God*]

Whatever names and attributes the law uses to refer to the Exalted God, we also use; and whatever the law forbids as a reference for God, we likewise forbid. In regard to those for which there is neither explicit authorization nor prohibition, we offer no judgment, neither endorsing nor forbidding them. The ruling of the law derives from the sources of tradition and, if we were to determine an endorsement or a prohibition without legal precedent, we would be affirming the application of a judgment that is outside of tradition.

Still, in regard to allowing the application of a term, we make no stipulation that there be a definitive ruling on it in the law. Rather, it will suffice for the conduct required in practice, even though not necessitated by explicit evidence. Nevertheless, despite the use of legal analogies in determining the requirements of practice, adherence to them is not permitted in regard to the designation of the Lord and His attributes. Understand well!

Chapter: [*The meanings of the names of God*]

Our chief, may God be pleased with him, divided the names of the Lord, may He be sanctified and exalted, into three categories. He stated that among His names are those by which we say that He is He. These are all those in which the designation for Him indicates His very existence. Others of His names are those by which we mean what is other than He. These are all those in which the designation for Him indicates an action, such as Creator and Sustainer. Yet other names for Him are those by which one does not mean that it is He or that it is other than He. These are all those in which the designation indicates an eternal attribute, such as Knower and Powerful.

One of our leading masters remarked that each name is the thing named in itself and this led to saying that the Lord, may He be sanctified and exalted, when He is called Creator, Creator is the name and it is the Lord God. Creator, however, is not the name for creating, nor is creating the name for the Creator. He further generalized this for all the other categories.

The better approach, in our view, is that of our master, may God be pleased with him. Here the names occupy the position of the attributes. When employing a name without entailing a negation, they refer to a positive certainty. Thus, when we say: God, the Creator, we are obliged to comprehend in that term a positive fact which is the fact of creation. The meaning of Creator is the one because of whom there is creation. But there is no attribute from creation that actually applies to the essence. The term Creator indicates nothing but the affirmation of creation. For that reason our master stated: The Exalted Creator cannot be characterized in His eternity as being a creator, since there existed no creation in eternity. Were He to be described in this way so as to imply thereby that He is all powerful, it would be metaphor only. He adduced from this also that knowledge and power, just as they are two attributes, are also two names. The discussion concerning this matter goes back to the dispute about whether to employ a term or whether its use is forbidden.

All of the names of the Sanctified Lord are divided according to whether they signify the essence or the eternal attributes and what signifies actions or the negation of anything the Sanctified Creator is hallowed above. At this point we will provide a brief explanation of the names that are sanctioned by tradition.

"Allāh" most exactly is the equivalent of the proper name of God, may He be sanctified. There is no etymology for it. Nevertheless, some say that its root is *ilāh* to which is added the *lām* of exaltation. Others say *alilah* from which they subtract the intermediate *hamza* and assimilate the *lām* for exaltation with what follows it. Yet others say that its root is *lāh* to which is added the *lām* of exaltation. Some lexicographers maintain that it derives from *al-taʾalluh* which is worshipping. Thus the meaning of *allāh* is the one who is the object of worship.

"Al-Raḥmān al-Raḥīm" [the Merciful, the Compassionate] are two names taken from the word *al-raḥma* [mercy]. Their meaning is the same according to the most competent authorities, much like *al-nadmān* [repentant] and *al-nadīm* [regretful]. Nevertheless, al-Raḥman designates specifically the Exalted God and cannot be applied to any other. Furthermore, *al-raḥma* denotes, in the view of the best authorities, the desire of the Exalted God to confer favour on His servant. The two names are among the attributes of the essence, although some scholars see in the word *al-raḥma* this very idea of conferring favour and would therefore have "al-Raḥmān al-Raḥīm" belong to the attributes of action.

"Al-Malik" [Sovereign] means the One who possesses sovereignty. But thereafter they disagree as to the meaning of sovereignty. Some explain it as meaning creation so that the sovereign is the Creator and this then is the name of an act. Others say that sovereignty is the power to originate [*ikhtirāʿ*] since one says "so-and-so possesses the advantage of his fortune", meaning thereby he achieves power by means of it. In that way this name is the name of an attribute. The Exalted Lord is always and will always be sovereign.

"Al-Quddūs" [Most Holy] on the model of *faʿʿūl* from *al-quds* is purity [*al-ṭahāra*] and righteousness [*al-nazāha*]. It means to be exempt from the effects of defects and of the indications of contingency. It is one of the names that exclude and deny. The Holy Land is called "holy" [*muqaddasa*] because it is free of the pollution of tyrants. Similarly, paradise is called the "precinct of holiness".

"Al-Salām" [the Sound]: It is said that it means the One who is secure from every defect and imperfection and thus it is one of the names for exemption. It is also said that it means the One who keeps humans away from peril and ruin and thus depends on having power. It is said further in this vein: It is the One who saves [holds safe] the believers in paradise and thus goes back to the eternal speech and words. The Exalted God has said: "Peace [*salām*], a word of salutation from the Most Merciful Lord" [36:58].

"Al-Muʾmin": It is said that its meaning is the One who attests [*al-muṣaddiq*] since faith is assent [*al-taṣdīq*] and the Exalted Lord attests to Himself and His apostles by means of a statement of truth. Thus the name reverts to speech. Others have said about al-Muʾmin that it means that the Exalted God preserves the pious from the supreme terror. On that basis the term allows taking it in the sense of discourse because the Exalted Lord will keep safe His servants on the day of the last judgment and will cause them to hear His words: "Fear you not, nor grieve" [41:30]. It is also possible to take this name in the sense of the power to create safety and tranquillity and in this case it would be one of the names of actions.

"Al-Muhaymin" [the Supervisor]: Some say it means the witness [*al-shāhid*]. The term "witness", however, may be broken down into several senses. Thus, it might be taken as the Omniscient from whose attention not the slightest atom escapes. Possibly, it could be construed as discourse signifying that the Exalted Lord makes each soul bear witness to the acts it has performed. Al-Khalīl [b. Aḥmad][1] said in his explanation of "al-Muhaymin" that it is the overseer [*al-raqīb*]. We will provide further explanation of this meaning later. Some others held that the sense of "al-Muhaymin" was originally *al-muʾaymin* and later the *hamza* was changed into the *hāʾ* by analogy to their saying *haraqtu* and *araqtu* both having the same sense, or *harajtu* for *araqtu* and *arajtu*. The word *al-muʾaymin* means faithful, which is to say, someone who keeps his promise.

"Al-ʿAzīz" [the Mighty]: It means the One who dominates. Domination reverts back to a question of power. Among the sayings of the Arabs is "Whoever is mighty triumphs" [*man ʿazza bazza*], meaning whoever dominates becomes hardened. Hard earth we call hard [*ʿizāz*] because of its rigidity. Yet others say that the name "al-ʿAzīz" has the sense of "without likeness" and, for that reason, this name belongs with those of exemption.

"Al-Jabbār" [the Omnipotent]: It means the One who brings about the best. The Arabs say: "I have restored the broken bone", and it was brought back to proper repair. It is thus accordingly one of the names of actions. It is also said that "al-Jabbār" means the One who prompts the servant towards what He wants for him. As such the name goes back either to an action or to the power for doing it. Others say that "al-Jabbār" means someone who is not affected by the intentions of those who try to get something or of those who try to obtain control over him by trickery. If the palm tree grows lofty and towering and passes out of hand's reach, one says that the palm tree is "mighty" [*al-jabbār*]. The sense of "al-Jabbār" then approaches that of "most high" [*al-mutaʿāli*] as will be explained later.

---

1 Khalīl b. Aḥmad al-Farāhidī (d. 170/786 or 175/791) was an important early Arabic philologist and lexicographer. On him see "al-Khalīl b. Aḥmad" in the *EI2*.

"Al-Mutakabbir" [the Overwhelmer]: Its meaning and that of the High [*al-ʿAliy*], the Most High [*al-Mutaʿāli*], the Magnificent [*al-ʿAẓim*] are all the same. Among the scholars there are those who take these names in the sense of transcendence and hallowedness above the signs of contingency and the marks of imperfection. There are among the masters some who take these names as having the character of all those attributes of the divine by which the Lord differs utterly from His creation. This approach has embedded in it accepting the concept of transcendence and it is therefore preferable. There is nothing wrong with a single term that presupposes separate connotations divided by being negative and positive.

"Al-Khāliq, al-Bāriʾ, al-Muṣawwir" [the Creator]: The sense of "al-Khāliq" [the Creator] is clear enough. One intends by "creation" the "making of something new" [*al-ikhtirāʿ*], and that meaning is the most obvious. One might intend by it "determining it to be" [*al-taqdīr*]. For that reason the shoemaker is called *khāliq* ["maker"] because he patterns various pieces of the shoe one upon the other. The Commentators take God's saying "So blessed be God, the best of creators" [23:14] as meaning "Determiner" [*al-taqdīr*]. "Al-Bāriʾ" has the same sense as the Creator [*al-Khāliq*]; and "al-Muṣawwir" means the originator of forms [*mubdiʿ al-ṣuwar*].

"Al-Ghaffār" [the Much-Forgiving]: It means the One who shields [*al-sattār*]. *Al-ghafr* in lexicography means cover [*al-satr*] and hence a helmet is called *mighfar* [head covering]. Moreover, it is possible to take *al-satr* [cover] as not applying the punishment, or in the sense of a benefaction which deflects from him doom in this life and the next.

"Al-Qahhār" [the Subduer] has an obvious meaning. One may also understand it as power and it is not far fetched to see in it the actions which make tyrants despised, such as causing ruin or something similar.

"Al-Wahhāb" [the Giver] is the One who confers blessings.

"Al-Razzāq" [the Provider]: It signifies the One who creates sustenance and brings the condition of being gratified by it into existence. We will later return to the meaning of *rizq*.

"Al-Fattāḥ" [the Revealer]: Some say it means the One who renders judgment among the creatures and that *al-fatḥ* [opening] in lexicography means *al-ḥukm* [the deciding factor]. The Arabs refer to the judge as the "One who decides" [*fattāḥ*]. It has this sense in God's statement: "Our Lord, decide [*iftaḥ*] rightly between us and our people" [7:89]. It means make a judgment between us. When it is taken in the sense of judge, it is possible to consider it as an eternal statement, or one may also consider it an act by which justice is granted to the oppressed against the oppressors. Yet again it is said that *al-fattāḥ* is the creator of success [*al-fatḥ*] and victory [*al-naṣr*].

"Al-ʿAlīm" [the Omniscient] signifies a knower at the most distinguished level. It is formed on the model of *faʿīl*, which is a form indicating the greatest intensity.

"Al-Qābid and al-Bāsiṭ" [the Gatherer and the Spreader] are examples of attributes of action. Al-Qābid [the One who holds in] means to be confined in regard to things desired and al-Bāsiṭ [to be expansive] is to expend one's wealth however one likes.

"Al-Khāfiḍ and al-Rāfiʿ" [the One who diminishes and the One who raises] are also attributes of actions and their meaning is obvious.

Similarly, "al-Muʿizz" [the One who gives power], "al-Mudhill" [the One who humbles], "al-Samīʿ" [the All-hearing], and "al-Baṣīr" [the All-seeing] are all quite obvious in their meanings.

"Al-Ḥakam" [the Judge] has the meaning of al-Ḥākim. It is possible to consider it a statement of God which assigns to each soul recompense for its deeds. It is also possible to consider it the actions that requite by way both of reward and of punishment.

Some say that *al-Ḥakam* and *al-Ḥākim* go back to the meaning of preventing. For that reason one calls the bit [*ḥakama*] of the bridle *ḥakama* since it prevents the riding mount from bolting. Also the sciences are called wisdom because they keep those characterized by wisdom from the dispositions of ignorant people.

"Al-ʿAdl" [the Just] which means the One who is just. He is the One who does what he ought to do.

"Al-Laṭīf" [the Kind]: Said by some to be the One who treats kindly [*al-mulaṭṭif*] like the courteous [*al-jamīl*] which has the sense of the One who is gracious [*al-mujammil*]. It would thus be an attribute of action. Others say *al-laṭīf* signifies the One who knows the hidden meanings of things.

"Al-Khabīr" [the Knowing] which means omniscient [*al-ʿalīm*].

"Al-Ḥalīm" [the Magnanimous] which means the One who is not provoked by the lapses of those who disobey and does not hasten to their punishment before the proper moment for it. Thus this name goes back to the idea of transcendence and being beyond being characterized by haste. Some others say that *al-ḥalīm* is the forgiver [*al-ʿafūw*] which meaning may be divided either into bestowing blessings or into not seeking retribution. The two are quite close.

"Al-Shakūr" [the Grateful]: It has the meaning of recompensing His servants for their gratitude towards Him. This name thus carries the sense of reciprocity. Another meaning for *al-shakūr* is the One who gives a great deal for a deed of minor importance. Others say that *al-shakūr* is the One who praises highly the chosen among humans and in this sense it reverts thus to a question of speech.

"Al-Ḥafīẓ" [the Guardian]: some say its meaning is Omniscient [*al-ʿalīm*] and that "retention" [*al-ḥafẓ*] is to know [*al-ʿilm*]. Accordingly, one can say: so-and-so "retains" [by heart, *yaḥfaẓu*] the Qurʾān, which means that he knows [*yaʿlamu*] it. Others say that the guardian [*al-ḥafīẓ*] is the custodian [*al-ḥāfiẓ*]. He is the overseer of creatures and the One entrusted with keeping them from harm.

"Al-Muqīt" [the Provisioner] is said to mean the creator of nourishment. Others say it means the allotter [*al-muqaddir*] and the innovator of every thing in its right measure. Yet others say it means the one who holds the power [*al-qādir*]. The poet declaims: "The possession of malice satisfies my soul since I have the power [*muqīt*] to harm him." It means being the one powerful enough even to harm him.

"Al-Ḥasīb" [the Reckoner]: Some say it means the self-sufficient [*al-kāfī*]. The Arabs say: I gave him what satisfied him, which means, I gave him enough for him to say *ḥasbī*, that is, I am satisfied. Others say that *al-ḥasīb* has the meaning of the reckoner of accounts for people [at judgment]. It would thus be a name for speech.

"Al-Jalīl" [the Great] means the august [*al-ʿaẓīm*], which we commented on earlier.

"Al-Karīm" [the Generous] is said to mean the giver of bounty. Others say it has the same sense as "forgiving" [*al-ghafūr*]; others say "highest" [*al-ʿaliy*]. Treasuries of money are called *karāʾim*; and every precious thing [*nafīs*] is valuable [*karīm*].

"Al-Raqīb" [the Overseer] means the All-knowing from whose knowledge nothing escapes.

"Al-Mujīb" [the Answerer] goes back to the concept of answering the prayers of those who pray and would thus revert to an aspect of eternal speech. It is possible to construe it as an action which entails providing relief for those in need. One says: I responded [*ajabtu*] positively to so-and-so's request and gave him what he needed.

"Al-Wāsiʿ" [the All-comprising]: It is said to mean the knowledgeable [*al-ʿālim*]; others say the "munificent" [*al-jawād*], since one describes the munificent person as having an expansive breast and not being tight-fisted. Yet others say that this term has the sense of the self-sufficient [*al-ghaniy*], but we will explain self-sufficiency further in the section on justice.

"Al-Ḥakīm" [the Sage] is said to be equivalent to Omniscient [*al-ʿalīm*], although others mention the "judge" [*al-Ḥākim*], as we explained earlier. Yet others say it means perfect mastery [*al-muḥkim al-mutqan*].

"Al-Wadūd" [the Very Loving] is said to mean the One who bestows love [*al-wādd*], which is explained as the One who gives love to his friends. Later there will be an explanation for love on the part of God, God willing. Another meaning is that the loving [*al-wadūd*] is the beloved [*al-mawdūd*].

"Al-Majīd" [The Glorious]: Al-Zajjāj[2] held that it means "benefactor" and he based this on the Arab saying: The livestock were well nourished [*majudat*] once they encountered abundant fresh pasturage. And also: the herdsman found them good pasture [*amjadahā*]. From this comes the saying of the Arabs: In every tree there is fire but the *markh* and the *ʿafār* have the most. The *markh* and the *ʿafār* are two kinds of trees from which the Arabs kindle fire. *Istamjada*

---

2 Evidently Abū Isḥāq al-Zajjāj, the grammarian and lexicographer, who died either in 310/922 or 316/928.

means to contain a large portion of something. In this way *al-majīd* approaches in meaning the idea of "beneficent" [*al-jawād*]. The term *al-jawād* might be construed as provider of blessings [*al-munʿim*] or as having the capacity for giving existence and grace. *Al-Majīd* might also be taken as the generous [*al-karīm*] since *al-majd* generally has the sense of generosity.

"Al-Bāʿith" [the Resurrector] is the One who resurrects the dead on the day of Congregation [*al-ḥashr*]. Another meaning for *al-bāʿith*, according to some, is the One who sends apostles to the nations.

"Al-Wārith" [the Survivor] is He who remains after the annihilation of His creation. "Al-Shahīd" [the Witness] is said to mean the Omniscient as previously stated. "Al-Ḥaqq" [the Real] means the One whose existence is necessary. It is also said to mean the One who always does right [*al-muḥiqq*] and, in this sense, it is almost an attribute of action.

"Al-Wakīl" [the Trustee] means the guardian who sees that His creatures have what is best for them. Another meaning is the one entrusted with the supervision of creation. "Al-Qawī" [the Strong] has the sense of the one having power [*al-qādir*] but some say it means unshakable [*al-matīn*].

"Al-Walī" [the Protector] means the One who provides help [*al-nāṣir*]. It is also said that it means the One in charge of the affairs of creatures.

"Al-Ḥamīd" [the Highly Praised] means the One praised. The word *al-ḥamd* actually means praise [*al-thanāʾ*].

"Al-Muḥṣī" [the Numberer]: It is said that it means the Knower who comprehends all the intelligibles. Others say it means the Powerful but both senses are quite obvious in linguistic usage.

"Al-Mubdiʾ" [the Initiator], "al-Muʿīd" [the Returner], "al-Muḥyī" [the Revivifier], "al-Mumīt" [the Bringer of death], and "al-Ḥayy" [the Living] have obvious meanings.

"Al-Qayyūm" [the Self-subsisting] has the meaning of the Director of Creatures both in the present and in the future. It is an attribute of action.

"Al-Wājid" [the Opulent] is said to mean the One who has no need to seek anything. The Exalted God has said: "Lodge them in your own homes according to your wealth" [65:6].

"Al-Mājid" [the Noble] has the same sense as the "glorious" [*al-majīd*]. "Al-Wāḥid" [the Unique] means to be one, that is, to be above any division into parts. Others say it means the One that there is none like, not in His essence, His attributes, His actions, or in His names. "Do you know any other of the same name?" [19:65].

"Al-Ṣamad" [the Impenetrable] is said to have the meaning of the lord [*al-sayyid*] but it is also said about the term *al-sayyid* that it is the king [*al-mālik*]. Another meaning is the "magnanimous" [*al-ḥalīm*]. Ibn ʿAbbās[3] commented on

---

3 ʿAbdallāh b. al-ʿAbbās (Ibn al-ʿAbbās), a cousin of the prophet, who died about 68/688. He is usually regarded as the father of the science of Qurʾānic exegesis.

the statement by God in reference to the attribute of Yaḥyā, peace be upon him, as being "princely [*sayyid*] and chaste" [3:39] that it means "magnanimous" [*ḥalīm*]. According to another view, *al-ṣamad* is the person one turns to in matters of need. Yet one more is that the *ṣamad* [impenetrable] is the One that is not hollow inside.

"Al-Qādir" [the Powerful], "al-Muqtadir" [the All-powerful], "al-Muqaddir" [the Regulator], "al-Muqaddim" [the One who advances], "al-Muʾakhkhir" [the One who retards], "al-Awwal" [the First], "al-Ākhir" [the Last] are all well understood.

"Al-Ẓāhir" [the Patent], "al-Bāṭin" [the Latent]: About *al-ẓāhir* it is said that it means the victor [*al-qāhir*] as in someone saying: so-and-so vanquished [*ẓahara*] so-and-so. Others say that it has the sense of being known by indisputable proof.

"Al-Bāṭin" signifies that He is concealed from His creation by obstacles He creates in their vision. It is also said to mean the Knower of hidden things.

"Al-Barr" is the Creator of creation. "Al-Tawwāb" [the Merciful] goes back to His bestowing blessings on those who free themselves from the binds of persisting sins and return to the obligation of obedience. Repentance [*al-tawba*] means "return" [*al-rujūʿ*].

"Al-Muqsiṭ" [the Equitable] means the just [*al-ʿādil*] and thus one says *aqsaṭa* [He acted justly] when He is just and *qasaṭa* when He is unjust.

"Al-Nūr" [the Light] has the meaning of the Guide [*al-hādī*]. "Al-Badīʿ" [the Originator] is said to be al-Mubdiʿ [originator]. Others say that it is the One without peer.

"Al-Rashīd" [the Leader] is said to mean the One who guides on the right path. Others say it is the knower; yet others that He is the One who transcends things of the world and all marks of imperfection.

"Al-Ṣabūr" [the Very Patient] has the same meaning as *al-ḥalīm* [the magnanimous] which we commented on earlier.

Chapter: [The two hands, the two eyes, and the face]

Certain of our masters maintained that the two hands, the two eyes and the face are proper attributes of the Lord God and that this is proven by tradition rather than rational proof. But what is correct, in our view, is that the hands should be construed as power, the eyes as vision and the face as existence.

Those who affirm that these are attributes as determined by tradition hold also that they are additional to the ones indicated by reason, adduced, for example, from the statement of God in reprimanding Iblīs for refusing to prostrate himself [before Adam]: "What prevents you prostrating yourself before what I created with my own hands" [38:75]. According to them, there is no way to take the hands as meaning power because all originated things are inventions that the Exalted God created by means of His power. In construing it like this, it loses its specific implication in the case here. This is simply not right. Reason attests that creation cannot occur except by means of the power or by the All-powerful having power. Thus there is no reason to think that the creation of Adam, peace be upon him, took place other than by means of the power.

What will make our point quite clear is that Adam, may the blessing of God be upon him, would not deserve being prostrated to if he were not singled out from creation by the hands [of God] and this is in agreement with what is required by the rules of reason. But the prostration becomes incumbent only as a consequence of the command of God and the obvious sense of the verse entails the execution of the prostration specifically to Adam because the context of this verse applies uniquely to Adam. Thus, as a consequence, the literal sense must be abandoned and yet reason may still determine that that by which creation comes about is power.

Furthermore, it is not unreasonable for certain humans to be honoured by particular mention. There are many examples of this in the Book of God. He, powerful is His name, ascribes to Himself the Kaʿba, but it has no special distinction merely for that reason. He further ascribes to Himself the believer's attribute of worshipfulness. Likewise, He ascribes to Himself the spirit of Jesus, on whom be peace. Ascription is divided into the ascription of attributes, ascriptions of possessions and ascriptions of nobility.

As for the verses which contain a mention of the eyes, that the literal meaning is to be abandoned is generally agreed to. Thus, for example, God's statement in regard to the arc of Noah, upon whom be peace: "She sails under Our eyes" [54:14]. No one who has a proper regard for the truth would affirm that the Exalted God has eyes. The meaning of the phrase in this verse to the effect that "she sails under Our eyes" is that the arc is in a position wherein We have surrounded it with angels, protectors and caretakers. In a situation where he is under the king's care, shelter and protection, one says that so-and-so is under the eyes and ears of the king. It is said that what is meant by *aʿyun* [eyes] in this verse are the springs [*aʿyun*] that erupt from the earth and which are ascribed to the Exalted God as His possessions. This is not unreasonable.

As for His statement: "Forever abides the face of your Lord, majestic, splendid" [55:27], there is no way to construe "face" as an attribute, since no such attribute of the Exalted God is specified as remaining after the annihilation of creation. Rather it is God who remains alone with His necessary attributes. Thus the most obvious way to construe "face" is existence. Some others say that the intention with "face" is direction [*al-jiha*] by which one really means the right way to approach the Exalted God. One says: "I did that for the face of God", meaning thereby, "in accord with obedience to the command of God". The meaning of the verse then is that all that is not in accord with the face of God is useless.

Those of our colleagues who prefer to affirm these attributes on the basis of the literal meanings of these verses are forced, as a consequence of their argument, to make attributes, in their adherence to the literal sense, out of sitting on the throne, coming, descending and having a side. But, if allegorical interpretation is permitted for the items where it is generally agreed upon, it is not an unreasonable method to apply for those we have just mentioned. We were trying not to speak of the literal sense but, since the subject has come up, we should pay some attention to its general situation in the Qurʾān and the Sunna. These are the items upon which the riff-raff among anthropomorphic literalists rest their case.

Another question that is often raised in this regard concerns the statement of God: "God is the light of the heavens and the earth" [24:35]. This is said by some to mean that God is the One who guides the inhabitants of the heavens and the earth. Those who are properly devoted to Islam would never say that the "light" of the heavens and the earth is God Himself. The intention of this verse is to furnish allegorical expressions and the verse itself is a metaphor as a whole. The thrust of the verse confirms what we have just stated. Thus God says: "God coins allegories for the people" [24:35].

Another point of contention is God's statement: "Alas for me in my neglect of the side [*janb*] of God" [39:56]. The meaning of this verse cannot be in doubt to anyone except a gullible numbskull. Given the tenor of the whole passage, one simply cannot take the word *janb* [side] to indicate a part of the body, especially in speaking of "neglect" in this context. There is no way other than to construe *janb* as an aspect of the Exalted God's command and the operation thereof. The word *janb* might also mean high dignity [*al-janāb*] or protection [*al-dharā*]. One says, for example, that so-and-so is safeguarded by the protection of so-and-so. The one who seeks shelter at his side [*janb*], finds protection in his majesty [*janāb*]. Moreover, what we state here is not some form of interpretation. We know definitively that to take the word *janb*, which is associated in this case with neglect, as a body part is wrong.

Yet another potential problem is God's statement: "The day wherein the shin [*sāq*] will be exposed" [68:42]. The sense of this verse informs about the terrors of the day of resurrection, the terrible conditions attendant upon it, and the tortures that will be inflicted on the evil doers. When the command to fight appears, breasts fill with rage, eyes stare with hatred, noses flare, the combatants grapple in close combat, then it is said that "the war is now in full swing [at shins, *sāq*]". No person with any learning at all could conceive taking the word shin [*sāq*] as a body part.

One more item of concern is God's statement: "And your Lord came, and the angels rank upon rank" [89:22]. Similar to this is His statement: "What do they look for except that God come to them in the shadow of the clouds, and with the angels" [2:210]. The meaning here of "coming" is neither to change from one place to another nor to alter position. God is above that. Rather the meaning in His saying "And your Lord came" is that the command of your Lord – His decisive ruling and His just verdict – went into effect [that is, came, *jāʾ*].

It is quite a common way of speaking to signal an order by one of the qualities of the person giving the order if the intent is to extol that person. Thus one says: When the commander arrives the others withdraw. The intention in saying this is not to indicate the commander's physical movement but the commencement of the effective execution of his commandments and restrictions. If there exists wide latitude for interpretation and the various possibilities offer ample room for discussion, there is no sense in construing the verse in such a way as to require acknowledging traits that are marks of contingency.

One of the areas where caution is necessary is in opposing the literalists on the basis of verses where they accept the allegorical interpretation of them so that when they pursue the method of interpretation in one case they open themselves to the use of that same method in areas of controversy. Among other points of contention, for example, is God's statement: "And He is with you wherever you may be" [57:4]. If they would take that literally, it must dissolve the knot keeping them attached to the idea that sitting on the throne actually means that He is sitting there. They are thus forced into admitting shameful things that no person of intelligence would accept. If, on the contrary, they take His statement "He is with you wherever you may be", and His saying "There is no private conversation among three people but that He is the fourth of them, nor five but He is the sixth" [58:7], as meaning that God comprehends all secrets, they will have given an authorization for interpretation. This evaluation of the literal meanings of the Qurʾān should be enough.

As to the *ḥadīths* on which they base their arguments, they are isolated examples which cannot determine doctrinal certainty. If we were to ignore them all entirely, that would be quite permissible. However, it behoves us to mention the interpretation of at least those that appear in the collections of authentic *ḥadīths*. One of them is the "*ḥadīth* of descending", in which it is related of the prophet, God bless him and keep him, that he said: "The Exalted God descends each Friday night to the earth's heaven and proclaims: 'Is there anyone who repents, so that I may forgive him? Is there someone who seeks mercy that I might grant it to him? Is there someone who calls out that I may answer him?'", and so to the end of the *ḥadīth*. There is no way to take the word "descending" [*nuzūl*] as implying a change of place or vacating one place and occupying another because that is a characteristic of bodies and a sign of physical matter. To allow this would lead to a double-sided contradiction, one side of which is the determination that God is contingent and the second a violation of the evidence for the contingency of bodies.

The better way to construe the word "descending", even though it is used in relation to the Exalted God, is as the descending of His cherubic angels. This is quite allowable and is not unreasonable. Similar to this is God's statement: "This is the requital of those who make war against God and His apostle" [5:33], which means, this is the requital of those who make war on the friends of God. It is not unreasonable to omit the antecedent [*al-muḍāf*] and put in its place the noun in apposition to it [*al-muḍāf ilayhi*] by appropriation.

One way to follow in interpreting the *ḥadīth* is to construe the word "descending" as God's showering His blessing upon His servants despite their continuing to show animosity, persisting in disobedience, being distracted at night from contemplating the signs of the Exalted God and, in regard to the life to come, being mindful of only present concerns. The term *nuzūl* [descending] is employed with respect to the case of someone like us who wishes to display humility. Thus one says: The king descends [*nazala*] from his august eminence to a worldly rank when he feels indulgent towards his subjects and he lessens the presumption of his vast authority, even though it is still none the less possible for him to increase his oppression towards them.

One sure indication that "descending" [*nuzūl*] does not stipulate a displacement is its employment in relation to the Qurʾān itself, knowing, as previously noted, that it is impossible for the words themselves to move about.

Another question that comes up concerns something related from the prophet, God bless him and keep him, that he said: "On the day of resurrection, the people of paradise will come to abide in felicity and the people of hellfire in the inferno; the fire will say, 'Are there any more?' Thereupon, the tyrant will put his foot in the fire and the fire will say, 'Enough, enough!'"

This *ḥadīth* is among those related by Muḥammad b. Ismāʿīl [al-Bukhārī][4] in his *Book of Commentary on the Qurʾān* within his collection of authentic *ḥadīths* [*al-Ṣaḥīḥ*]. There is ample scope for interpretation in this *ḥadīth*. For example, it is possible to take "tyrant" as a bully among men who is, in the knowledge of God, one of the most arrogant. The fire is inspired just anticipating him. It continues to demand more until the foot of that tyrant finally settles into it. At that point the fire will say: "At last, at last!"

In the evidence of the *ḥadīth*, moreover, it is reported that the footsteps of the pious, as well as the impious, pause at the side of the inferno which appears as if it were so much congealed fat. When these feet touch it, the fire swallows those that belong to it, for it knows them better than a mother knows her own child. The confirmation for taking "tyrant" in the sense we mention is what is related from the prophet, God bless him and keep him, that he said: "The inhabitants of the fire are the haughty and tyrannical, the insolent, gross and arrogant."

Possibly, the word *al-qadam* points to a nation of people that deserve hellfire according to the knowledge of the Exalted God, and that its apposition to the word *qadam* indicates the king of that group.

Another passage that the literalists cling to are the following words of the prophet, God bless him and keep him: "Verily, God created Adam in his image." This *ḥadīth* is not recorded in the collections that are most authentic. But even

4 This person is the famous traditionist who died in 256/870.

if it were authentic, there is an explanation for it that the literalists pay no attention to. It is related that a man struck a slave he owned who happened to have a beautiful face. Thereupon, the prophet, God bless him and keep him, told him not to do it, explaining: "God created Adam in his image." The pronoun *hāʾ* refers back to the slave whose beating he forbade. It is also possible that the *hāʾ* refers to Adam himself and the meaning of this *ḥadīth* would, in that case, be that God, the Exalted, created Adam as a human being but without having either father or mother. The purpose of the *ḥadīth* then is that Adam, on whom be blessings and peace, appeared not as an ordinary part of creation but rather that God invented him with his own form.

For those who have properly comprehended what we have said here, finding answers to explain other questions that might be asked will not be difficult. After careful investigation and avoiding haste, one will find an interpretation for the contested *ḥadīth*.

At this point we have said enough, may God's mercy be with you. It is conclusive in affirming knowledge of the necessary attributes which we have divided into those that are essential and those that are qualifications. In the course of the exposition in this section what cannot be said about the Exalted God was laid out clearly as well. Having then treated these two fundamental areas, there remains nothing but to enter into a discussion of what is possible for God and, once that is accomplished, this handbook of doctrine will be complete and able to stand on its own. But in God is the grace.

Section
A Statement of What is Possible for God

This section contains two parts covering many individual themes which comprise within them principles of the greatest importance. We choose to begin the whole with an affirmation of the possibility of the vision of God, the Exalted.

Section

Proof that the Vision of God is Possible

Chapter: [*Affirming perception*]

It is best for us to bring forward here the various points that apply particularly to the arguments of the orthodox which separate them from the specious doctrines of those who oppose us. One of the most important is the affirmation of perception in the visible world.

What the orthodox and the majority of the Muʿtazilites uphold is that those who perceive in the visible world are perceptive by means of a perception, as, for example, the person who is knowledgeable in the visible world knows by means of knowledge. Ibn al-Jubbāʾī and his followers, however, maintained a denial of perception, either in the visible or invisible worlds. They held that the one who perceives is a living being without impediment.

Everything that serves to prove the existence of the accidents also proves the existence of the perceptions. Thus, if we adduce the existence of knowledge from the renewal of its characteristic qualities – that is, of the knower's having knowledge – then by the process of examination and elimination, in accord with the method used previously to attain a proof of the qualifying attributes, we are drawn to an indication affirming knowledge of those who perceive in fact. Much as the renewal of the knower's having knowledge in the visible world does not make the same necessarily valid in the invisible world, a similar condition applies to those who perceive being perceptive.

The person who construes the idea that the one who perceives has perception as implying simply that he is alive and absent of any impediment has no way to make a distinction between this and those who adhere to this very course of argument in regard to knowledge, power and will. If one takes perception as the reception of a particular form, it is not unreasonable also to take knowledge as a particularized form. Without pursuing the details, the sum of the matter is that denying the perceptions is to follow the method that rejects, as objectionable, the affirmation of accidents.

Having established the existence of perception in what we have just alluded to, you should know that perception does not depend on particularized form and that such a point is false from several perspectives. The most accessible of them is that a single perception subsists only in one atom alone. Moreover, the atoms that surround the locus of that perception have no effect on it, because every atom is particularized by the space that is proper to it and which is qualified by its own accidents. There is no effect of one atom on another. The characteristic qualities of an atom exist because of the accidents that arise uniquely in it and thus likewise no accident that arises in one atom has any effect on any other atom.

In accord with what we have just mentioned, it is now established that the atoms that one determines to be associated with the locus of perception, but without having an effect on it, have an existence that is the same with respect to the feature they impart as they would if non-existent. Altogether then this entails definitively denying the stipulation of special form and of a composition with a particular qualification. That, for our purposes, is decisive.

Also what strengthens the case for denying the stipulation of special form is that the stipulation applies equally both in the visible and the invisible worlds. For this reason the Muʿtazilites say that, since the alive having life is a condition for its having knowledge in the visible world, a similar determination must apply in the invisible. As a result of what this stipulation forces upon them, we can ask them the following: If the perceptive being having perception in the visible world were conditional to its being structured, it would follow necessarily from the attribution to the Creator of His being perceptive that one should describe Him as being structured. May God be exalted beyond the statements of those who preach false doctrines.

Now, having affirmed perception and verified that it does not require a special form and that its subsistence is possible on the basis of a single unique atom, we can build on that principle an argument that makes clear the falseness of Muʿtazilite pretensions. These are their claim that the one who perceives by the perception of eyesight does not perceive except after a ray is emitted from the eye of the seer and reaches the object of sight. When the ray is rightly directed and its emission from the sense organ really goes to the object of sight and makes contact with it, the other side encounters the object of sight and, if it does not miss it, it sees accordingly.

If there should exist between the object and the seer a thick curtain that prevents the ray from passing through, it will not see the object. If it is a far distance away, because of the rays going astray and perishing, a distant object will not be seen. Because also of excessive closeness to the observer, the excessive closeness prevents the emission of the ray and it is not seen. It is for the same reason, according to them, that one cannot see behind the eyelids.

They understand the vision the observer has of himself when looking at a polished object in a similar way. Thus they maintain that the rays are emitted and, if they fall upon a polished surface, they will not adhere to it since the polished surface has no roughness. Instead it reflects the ray back to the observer and it returns there. If and when that happens, he perceives himself. When the rays become split because of squinting or something else, the one who has the perception does not perceive the object as it really is due to an irregularity in the course of the ray. In regard to this matter, their ravings are too extensive for an explanation of them to be contained in this handbook of doctrine.

All of their senseless talk is based on the emission of rays, which are themselves subtle and radiant bodies, from the organ of sight and the impermissibility of supposing their emission without a special form of the eye.

Since we have proven the falsity, in what preceded, of requiring perception and the one who perceives having perception to depend on the special form, this ensures the absolute untenability of what they would make consequent upon the existence of the special form.

Furthermore, the rays consist of bodies, in their view, inside the eye which are emitted from it when the eyelids open. It might thus be asked of them: What is it that provokes their emission? Why do they not remain fixed in place? What makes them hold back or alternately spread out? If they should claim that there are, in the organ itself, tendencies that provoke the defusing of the rays, this answer depends on the false principle of theirs concerning production, but they do not support each other in this. Moreover, it is their view that the tendencies are inherently descending, like the tendencies of a heavy weight, or ascending, like flames of fire when stirred up. As for the rest of the directions, the tendencies towards them are either induced or acquired artificially. The observer does not procure a tendency towards a direction as he would bring it about in trying to push a heavy object either to the left or to the right.

If they say that the ray is sent out by the movement of the pupil and the eyelids, that is impossible because someone who has had his eyelids removed can see even when his pupil is still. Thus, accordingly, it is proven that there is nothing inducing the emission of the rays. If considered as a creation of God, one must allow the possibility of the absence of the creation, even admitting the possibility that the living being who has perception and is without impediment, might open his eyes, all obstacles having been removed, but God, the Exalted, does not want the emission of the ray and, for that reason, he will see nothing. This is, for these people, something that is completely impossible.

One objection that is quite difficult for them to deal with is our saying: If an atom were seen because of the ray reaching it, what happens in the case of seeing its colour which is an accident. One sees it but it is not possible for the ray to touch the accidents. Here should they maintain that he sees only what the ray touches or that upon which subsists what the ray touches, we will answer that the import of this forces you to admit the possibility of seeing tastes and odours, since they also subsist upon what the ray touches.

We say to them as well: It is your view that a single atom, if it were to appear in the path of the ray, would not be seen, even though the ray following a straight line touched it. Should we then suppose the annexation of other atoms to that one, the first will not receive a particular ray but only what touched it when it was alone. All of this proves the falsity of the emission of rays from the observer and their making contact with objects of sight.

If opponents hope to find proof of their belief about the emission of rays from the observer and their making contact with the objects of sight in what we explained at the beginning of this chapter, and to derive support for it from the mention of nearness and distance, the deviation of rays and their reflection from polished surfaces, for what they are trying to claim there is nothing here to give them comfort.

A concise answer to all that they may have imagined is for us to say: Why have you not based the existence of the vision in the one case or its negation in another upon your supposition about the emission of the rays and their reaching the object? On what basis would you refute the statement of those who say: Everything that you deny and affirm depends ultimately on the continuation of habits determined in the matter as God wished them to be. They follow the same course as in the succession to food and drink being satiety and quenching, although they are not the necessitating factor for them. If the normal course of habit is broken, seeing a distant object from far away or one that is excessively close is possible. As well it is possible then to see what is behind a screen. If one puts to them these facts, they have no recourse except something plainly unreasonable which proves nothing. The way to oppose them rests on all the things they agree with us to be the necessary consequence of established habits.

Chapter: [*The perceptions are five*]

The perceptions are five: one of which is sight which pertains to the category of visible things; the second is hearing which pertains to sounds; the third, the perception associated with odours; the fourth, the perception connected to tastes; and the fifth, the perception that applies to heat, cold, soft and rough. The organs of sense, in the idiom of the scholars, are bodily members only some of which have the functions of perception. The perceptions are designated metaphorically by smell, feeling and taste.

These expressions, according to informed persons, make known the contact between the senses and the bodies that are perceived and whose accidents are perceived. The contacts are not perceptions themselves nor are they conditional upon them, although they habitually accompany them. The proof of this is that you say: I smelled something but I did not perceive its odour, and I tasted it but I did not discern its flavour; I felt it but I did not perceive its heat. This confirms that one does not intend by uttering these expressions to specify the perceptions in themselves.

Our masters, may God be pleased with them, consider a part of the perceptions the sensation of being alive in itself, with pains, pleasures, and the rest of the characteristics that are a condition of life. There is no way to maintain that the sensation of these characteristics is knowledge of them. A person is often forced to recognize the pain caused to others and he finds in his own self an appropriate pain corresponding to it. He thereupon distinguishes intuitively between his own sensation of that in himself and his knowledge of the pain in another.

Chapter: [*Every existent may be seen*]

The orthodox agree that all that exists can be seen. The greater authorities among them hold that each perception may be associated in the normal course of habit with a category of existing objects, and thus the possibility of this association within its own category extends to all of the existents. What makes it possible for a thing to be perceived is existence and that may be generalized for all the perceptions, as we shall explain by means of proofs, God willing.

The parameters of this discussion touch on matters that those who seek guidance ought to comprehend. For example, should someone ask: Is it possible that the one who perceives perceives his own perceiving? The approved answer, in our view, is that it is possible for the perceiver to perceive his own perceiving. If he does not perceive it, it is solely because of an obstacle that prevents the perception. Thus there would be an obstacle to the perception and an obstacle to determining that he perceives it himself. Is it possible that the perception of another be attached to the other's perception and the obstacles to it? This question is much too subtle for us to explore here.

Chapter: [The obstacles to perception]

All of what it is possible to perceive is perceived. When the perceiver does not perceive it, he fails to perceive it only because of an obstacle that intervenes to block the perception of what it is otherwise possible to perceive. An enumeration of the obstacles conforms to an enumeration of possible perceptions. They are finite in number since one must admit that there is a limit to the number of objects of perception.

The Muʿtazilites denied the obstacles that we affirm to be contrary to perceptions. They insist that the obstacles to them are excessive closeness and distance and the failure of the emitted ray to maintain a straight line and make contact with the object of sight. Following their principles, a curtain that is dense and opaque would be one of the obstacles. They consider blindness to be a defect in the organ of sight. Everything that establishes the existence of the accidents proves that blindness, as with all obstacles to perception, is a property. If it were possible to consider blindness to be a defect in the structure, one could as well imply the same for omissions, negligence, suffering and other things like these.

Anyone who understands the way proofs apply will quickly see how to generalize the proof we are aiming at. If, however, one wants to renew familiarity with the method of proving the existence of the accidents, let him go back over word by word what we have written concerning the existence of the accidents. These are fundamental premises that must inevitably come before any others.

Chapter: [The vision of God, the Exalted]

We have said that, in the doctrine of the orthodox, God, may He be sanctified, can be seen. We have also reported the contrary view of our opponents. Moreover, the majority of the Múʿtazilites are in unanimous agreement that the Exalted

God will not be seen Himself. According to the belief of these people, it is impossible to see Him by the senses; and He cannot possibly be seen by other means than an organ of sense. A small group of the Muʿtazilites held that the Creator will show Himself but that temporally created beings are precluded from seeing Him because they cannot see except by means of an organ of sensation and by the contact of the rays. Al-Kaʿbī and his associates held, however, that God the Exalted will not be seen, nor will He show Himself, or another being – this was the doctrine of al-Najjār.

By the dictates of reason, that upon which one establishes the proof of the possibility of the vision is to say: In the visible world, we have a perception of diverse things that consist of atoms and colours. The actuality of existing is common to this diversity of things; their differing is due only to their modes and their own attributes. Vision does not pertain to the modes. Everything that is seen and distinguished from another by the judgment of perception is the actual essence and the modes are not essences. If then it is determined by the necessity of reason that perception pertains solely to existence and the reality of existence does not vary, therefore, if an existent being can be seen, necessarily the vision of all existent beings is possible, just as it is true that seeing one atom means necessarily that seeing all atoms is possible. This is quite conclusive in proving what we wanted to prove.

If it is said: If the vision cannot pertain to anything other than an existent being, those who perceive would not perceive the diversity of the objects of perception. This is a question raised by the followers of Abū Hāshim [b. al-Jubbāʾī].[1] It was one of their principles that perception does not deal with existence but only with the distinctive characteristics of the thing perceived.

What they have said, however, represents the most extreme kind of self-contradiction. Ibn al-Jubbāʾī precluded describing the mode as knowable separately, cautioning against imagining that the mode is an essence. Thus he insisted that it is this which is perceived, not the essence or its existence. But how could an intelligent person accept finding that he perceives what he does not know, despite the certainty that the operation of knowledge is more comprehensive than that of perception. Knowledge pertains to both existence and non-existence and perception pertains solely to the essence that is qualified by existence.

If now they ask: What is the mode that is known when perceiving existence? We respond: Our doctrine concerning knowledge of the modes upon perception of existence is like your doctrine concerning knowledge of existence when perceiving the modes. Thus, it is not unreasonable in the rules of thought that the two aspects are interconnected which is tantamount to the connection of pain to the knowledge of it, or the substrate and the accident and other similar cases.

As for those who deny the possibility of the vision, some of them base this on the fact that, if the Exalted Creator were to be visible, we would see Him at

1 Literally the "Bahshamiyya", a standard name for the followers of Abū Hāshim b. al-Jubbāʾī.

the present moment, since the obstacles that would preclude a vision of Him do not exist. They are excessive closeness and distance, an opaque barrier, or the like. Thus, since we do not see Him, it is an indication that we do not see Him because the vision itself is impossible.

So here we say to them: Why have you limited the obstacles to those you mention? Why deny factors that are additional to them? In investigating the matter at issue, they base themselves on their own claim as follows: We have looked carefully into the obstacles and eliminated all those except the ones we have specified. To them we respond: In your detection of exactly what obstacles there are, you did not achieve comprehensive certainty. You were definitely open to errors since you were not necessarily infallible nor capable of comprehending the totality of things and their full realities. Therefore, you have based yourselves accordingly on nothing but vacillations and dissipated efforts.

Furthermore, we would ask them: How can you deny those who claim that we do not see Him only because of an obstacle that affects the organ of sense which prevents perceiving Him? They say that this doctrine leads to accepting the belief that it is possible for there to be, in His presence, tall hills, lofty figures, phantoms of towering heights and mountainous solidity. Yet one does not see them because the perception one might have of them has not been created yet. The upshot of this is ignorance and a violation of the laws of reason.

Here we say: What you have mentioned relies on an exaggeration that comes to nothing and which promptly turns against you in the example of those who close their eyes and believe in God's having the power to create what He creates, in the briefest of moments and with the greatest rapidity anticipatable, what you would impose against us. But how can one believe, when blinded or head bowed, that there has come to be in front of him, by the invention of God, towering mountains and hills? A person who accepts that will accept anything.

Similarly, those who adhere properly to Islam agree that God has the power to create man fully and perfectly formed, without having to go back and forth through various degrees of creation consisting of drops of liquid and mixing. Anyone who sees a complete human and has doubts about his having been given birth in direct conformity to what is made possible by the power of the Exalted God plunges into the thrall of ignorance. It is not impossible that rivers will flow with the blood of fresh slaughter and mountains will change into pure gold. But, if a sane person considers this possible in his own time and supposes that it might happen in his own era, he is crazy and possessed by demons. On the same basis, it is definite that there is nothing in front of us that we do not see.

This takes us back, may you be preserved from heretical innovations, to the permanence of habits and their persistence, despite there being no rational requirement for it to be this way. How is it otherwise, when the prophets are singled out by the ability to see the angels which their companions cannot see. That age was a time when the habitual order was broken and when miracles occurred that set aside the normal course of things.

One of their sophisms is an argument which, if you examine it carefully, goes back to no more than a mere assertion. An example is their statement: The seer must necessarily be standing opposite the object of sight or virtually opposite. Here it may be asked of them in reference to this example: Do you know what you claim self-evidently? Or do you know it by reasoning? If they claim self-evident knowledge and yet they accuse their opponents of denying it, arguing with them ceases to have meaning and their lies become obvious. Then one may direct toward them a charge of anthropomorphism which is, in fact, represented in their own claims.

One among them might say: Of necessity we know the impossibility of the existence of a being that is neither associated with the world nor disassociated from it. This assertion cannot be refuted other than by a reason similar to that we used to reject the sophism of those who deny the vision of God. The Exalted Creator sees His creation from all directions and thus it is possible that He will be seen in a situation that lacks a specific direction.

It is essential for the beginner in this field not to be reticent in refuting them by knowledge – that is, God's being an object of knowledge – in everything they latch on to in their attempt to deny the possibility of the vision.

Chapter: [*The vision of the Exalted God will take place in paradise*]

It is proven by the dictates of reason that the vision of the Exalted God is possible and this chapter is dedicated to showing that the vision will take place in paradise in accord with God's promise, given sincerely and by true statement. The proof of it is in the text of the Scripture. It is God's statement: "Faces that day will be radiant, looking towards their Lord" [75:22–23].

The word "look" [*naẓar*] comprises several meanings linguistically and different connecting prepositions stand after it according to its various connotations. If one wants to indicate by it intimacy and attentiveness, one uses it without a preposition. God says, in regard to the situation of the hypocrites and their way of speaking to the believers after a separation has come between the two: "Wait for us [*unẓurūnā*] that we may borrow your light" [57:13], which means, "have regard for us". If one intends by the word *al-naẓar* ["reflecting"], it has affixed to it the preposition *fī* ["on" or "about"] and you say, "I reflected on the matter" [*naẓartu fiʾl-amr*], having meant thereby, "I considered it carefully". If one indicates by it an expression of mercy, it is followed by a *lām* and you say: "I looked after so and so" [*naẓartu liʾl-fulān*]. If one means by it catching sight of something, which is to say, the vision, it is followed by the preposition *ilā* ["at" or "towards"].

The use of *naẓar* in the verse that is the subject of our controversy is followed by the preposition *ilā* ["towards"] and is predicated of the "faces" [*wujūh*] that are looking expectantly in anticipation of the joyful event. The word *naẓar* here constitutes proof of the vision. If someone were to oppose us with

God's statement: "No eyesight will perceive Him, though He perceives the eyes" [6:103], we reply: Several ways are used to explain this verse. One of them is to say that the Exalted Lord will not be perceived but that one will see Him. This way implies accepting the verse literally. One is precluded from taking this approach, however, because it specifically cites perception as having the purpose of "taking in" [*iḥāṭa*] and its implying the attaining of some object. Since God transcends, in His exaltedness, being confined within limits, it can only mean "attain an object" with limits. Still these people are not prevented from understanding "taking in" in the sense of "knowing" [*ʿilm*] and thus they may say: "The Exalted Lord is known in reality though no one encompasses Him." Therefore one sees Him but does not perceive Him. Furthermore, nothing in this verse denies the possibility of perception and that is the matter in dispute, which thus depends still on the discernment of reason.

Moreover, this verse has a unrestricted sense and is not specific to any set time but rather to all generally. In contrast, the verse we drew upon as providing proof of the vision relates to a defined moment in time. Accordingly, one may, in following the path of interpretation, construe the general sense in the particular and thus take the denial of perception here as applying to the time of earthly life.

They may raise an objection against us on the basis of God's statement in answer to the request of Moses, on whom be peace: "You shall not see me" [7:143]. But this verse is, in fact, one of the truest indications proving the possibility of the vision. Surely, the one God has chosen to be His apostle – the very person selected and distinguished for prophethood, singled out by God's favouring him and honoured by God's speaking to him – cannot have been ignorant of the true nature of God which the scum of the Muʿtazilites cannot comprehend.

Those who deny the vision accuse those who accept its possibility either of the equivalent of outright heresy or of holding a position that contributes to misguided delusion. The prophets, on whom be peace, are certainly exempt from this error. How is it possible then that our opponents defend their impeccability from all forms of error? If one of them were to say: Moses, on whom be peace, merely asked for indisputable knowledge and he expressed it as a request for a vision, he should be answered: Vision that is connected to the word *naẓar* to which is added the preposition *ilā* designates formally "seeing". Furthermore, this answer needs to be construed as corresponding to the message as a whole. Why then do the Muʿtazilites take the phrase "you shall not see Me" as denying the vision but consider the question at the beginning of the verse as not indicating a vision? If one of them were then to claim that he only requested the vision so that his people would cease definitely to make their excuses, since they used to ask him to show them God openly, answer him as follows: This is contrary to the text itself. He, may there be on him peace, related the vision he asked for to himself only when he said "show me" [*arinī*].

Moreover, how does one suppose that, for the sake of his people, Moses, the one whom God addressed, could ask his Lord for something he knows that God does not have the ability to do. When they asked him, after having crossed the sea, that he make them a god, he declared in reply: "Truly, you are an ignorant people!" [7:138].

A small faction of the Muʿtazilites maintains that Moses, peace be upon him, used to believe mistakenly in the possibility of the vision. Then God, the Exalted, informed him that it is not possible. This horrendous error is greater than any of the words that issue from their mouths. It shows extreme contempt for the prophets. If that were permissible, it would be possible for the prophet to have believed that his Lord is a gross body, and that only subsequently did God inform him and reveal the truth to him.

If then it is confirmed that the request by Moses, on whom be peace, establishes the possibility of what he asked for and, furthermore, that his request for a vision of God occurred at that moment, for a prophet to be baffled about knowledge of invisible matters does not detract from prophecy itself. He, God bless him and keep him, thought that what he believed was actually possible and attainable. Thereupon, the Exalted Lord informed him that it is concealed by His invisibility. Since his request was for a vision at that moment, it is obvious that the denial is to be taken as applying solely to the situation in which the request occurred.

Chapter: [*The difference between the vision and smell, feeling, and taste*]

Should someone say: You stipulated previously that it is possible for all the perceptions to be applied to every existing thing. The upshot of that, however, forces you to admit the possibility of the application of the five means of perception to the essence of the Creator and His attributes and, as a consequence of this, to arrive ultimately at the determination that the Exalted Lord can be smelled, touched and tasted. To this we respond: We have mentioned that feeling, taste and smell are expressions for the avenues of transmission rather than the perceptions themselves. As for the perceptions themselves, it is certain that they are not the transmissions and so it is possible that they are applicable to every existent thing. All of this proves the possibility of seeing every existent thing and that may be applied generally to each of the perceptions.

If someone says: On the subject of the necessary attributes, you earlier declared that the Exalted Lord is All-hearing and All-seeing, and you affirmed certain knowledge of hearing and seeing. Are the rest of the perceptions also affirmed as belonging to the Creator? We answer: It is correct, according to us, that they exist. Affirming knowledge of hearing and seeing establishes also that the rest of the perceptions exist.

The preceding chapter covered what is possible in the applicable qualities of God. What applications there may be of His powers in regard to His creating and instituting things is connected to the creation of acts and to matters that require an understanding of the applicable properties that are within the power of humans.

Section

A Statement about the Creation of Acts

Before the appearance of heretical innovations and partisan tendencies and prior to the agitation caused by subjective opinions, the forefathers of the community agreed together that the Creator and Innovator is the Lord of the Worlds and that there is no other Creator nor any other Maker except Him. This is the doctrine of the orthodox. Moreover, all temporally contingent things were brought into being by the power of God the Exalted, without a distinction between those that result from the power of humans and those that fall exclusively within the power of the Lord. This principle carries with it the implication that all empowerment belongs to the one who has power and that God, the Exalted, is the One who holds the power; He is the One who brings it into being and the One who gives it existence.

The Muʿtazilites, and those who follow them among the people of deviant tendencies, agree that humans are the authors of their own acts which they bring into being by means of their own powers. They agree also that the Lord, may He be high above their claims, is not to be described as having power over the empowerment of humans just as humans should not be characterized as having power over the empowerment in the Lord God.

Moreover, the earlier Muʿtazilites used to refuse to apply to humans the designation "creator" in accord with the closeness of their period to the consensus held among the forefathers that there is no creator except God, the Exalted. But the later Muʿtazilites had the audacity to call the human being a creator in the true sense. A few of the later figures even invented notions that broke away from the fold of religion. They maintained that the human is the creator and that the Lord – may He be immune above the preaching of falsifiers – is not to be called creator in the true sense. May God protect you from these heresies and such persistently mistaken impieties.

At this point we will lay out against the opposition three methods of dealing with this issue. The first involves adhering to rational certainties that preclude humans from being the ones who originate. In regard to the second, we will mention the implications imposed on the Muʿtazilites by the rules of reason, the goal being to make clear the contradictions in their doctrines. Finally, under the third, we will specify the proofs in received tradition that establish the soundness of the doctrine adopted by the orthodox.

Chapter: [*That the human is not a creator*]

The first issue in this discussion has as its purpose what can be kept to two arguments. One of them is for us to ask our adversaries: You claimed that what a human has power over is not what the Exalted God has power over, since you hold to the impossibility of affirming the same empowerment on the part of two holders of power. Therefore, we ask you: Prior to God's empowering His servant and before actually bringing him into being, was He then to be characterized as having the power to do what He knew that He would eventually empower the one He would bring into being to do or not? If they insist that He is not to be characterized as having the power to do what He would eventually empower the human to do, that is plainly false, since what He would eventually empower the human to do is itself due to the power of God, because it is one of the possible things that may come to pass by the application of human power in accord with the way we have formulated the question at hand.

If the application of God's having power to the empowering of the servant was precluded by the impossibility, as held by our adversaries, of an empowerment by two distinct holders of power, it is not necessary to preclude what He has power over but will eventually empower the servant to do being with Him before He empowers the servant to do it, since the contingent aspect of the power has not yet come into effect. Because it is necessary that what God empowers the servant to do be within the power of God, prior to His empowering the servant to do it, when He empowers the human it is impossible that what was previously within the power of God ceases to be within His power.

If, in the belief of our opponents, it appears contradictory for it to remain within the power of God even while human power intermittently applies to it as well, it would make more sense for it to persist as being within the power of God and deny that it is within human power than in terminating the application of God's power to it because of its falling intermittently within human power. If the necessity of what the human has the power to do being within the power of God is proven, everything that he has the power to do, God is its Producer and Creator, since it is impossible that the human alone bring into being what God has power over.

One point that our masters held firmly was the doctrine that actions that are done perfectly betoken the knowledge of those who bring them into being. Yet there are acts that have issued from humans in a state of carelessness and confusion that are well ordered and arranged, displaying the qualities of competency and proficiency, even though the human was himself unaware of what he had done. Still, it follows that the authoring of the act must betoken the knowledge of the one who brought it into being. The only conclusion from that, in the view of the orthodox, is to declare that the one who brought the act into being was God, the Exalted, and that it is He who knows them in reality.

Those who hold that the human brings into being his own acts and yet that he is ignorant of them, as in the case we are using to adduce this proof, have ceased to accept that competency and proficiency indicate that the author of them is competent and proficient. But that is in contradiction to rational proofs.

Furthermore, if one were to accept that a masterful act occurs which its author is ignorant of, one would hold false also that an action proves the existence of someone who has the power to do it. This leads on to saying that it is false for an action to prove the existence of an agent.

If now they were to turn against us what we referred to on the subject of "performance" [*kasb*] and to say here: Being the one who performs necessarily means having knowledge of what one performs, but it is possible that there issue from him a few actions while he is confused and negligent, we reply: According to us, the dictates of reason do not require the performer of an act to be knowledgeable about what he does and thus it is possible for him to accomplish a small number absentmindedly, since, if that were necessary in regard to a large number of acts, it would be equally necessary also for a small number. If they say: In accord with the principles you have laid down, it is possible for a large number of acts to issue from a human being without his knowing about them, we answer: This is allowable according to the rules of reason but it is precluded from actually happening by the prevailing habitual order of things. If that were to be broken, what you want us to admit would be then quite possible according to reason.

At this point they may say: In the course of your discussion about proving God's having knowledge, you specified that this is only known self-evidently rather than being obtained by reflection and reasoning. This is what you have declared acceptable. But it is contradictory to the premise you now rely on with respect to your doctrine that the masterful act signifies that the one who brought it into being knows about it. We answer: This is a deception on your part. There is no contradiction between what we said earlier and what we now adduce in this regard. In effect we have said that we know of necessity that a masterful action does not issue except from someone who has knowledge. Thus the real truth in this statement centres on the masterful action proving that its agent has knowledge of it, without any need to reflect about its being a proof. Just as proofs are of various kinds: one of them is, for example, not known as being a proof except by reasoning; another is a proof known self-evidently. What we are discussing now is of the second type. There is no meaning in something being a proof for what it proves except in that knowledge of it necessarily yields knowledge of what it proves. This is the effect of the mastery that proves the knowledge of the one who perfects it. This then is the argument concerning the first topic.

As for the second issue, it consists of objections into which they are forced which are decisive and from which there is no escape. One of the strongest is that, by their own principles, the contingent power applies exclusively to existence, not to any other of the attributes. But the reality of the existence that belongs to the contingent being does not vary. The variation in different things depends on the modes it has that are additional to its existence and they are an effect that is due to the power. One of the principles of this group is that a power that applies to something applies to its likenesses and to its opposites. Existent beings participate in the reality of what the power applies to and thus necessarily the application of a contingent power pertains to all contingent things, such as tastes, colours, and atoms. In the same way, in their view, it is necessary for the power that moves to apply as well to all things in a similar situation. There is, for them, no escape from that conclusion.

They may now say: What you forced upon us in the matter of creation turns against you in regard to the application of the power to perform. If power applies to any of the accidents, you must admit yourself what you tried to force us to concede which is the possibility of its application to all of the contingent things. And, if you do not admit what turns against you, the objection you raised no longer stands. To this we respond: According to us, the contingent power does not apply to existence pure and simple but to the essence and its modes. The essences vary with their modes. Thus we need not admit, on the basis of our determination of the power's application to one thing, a determination also of the possibility of its application to something that differs from it. This argument has great effect against the Muʿtazilites in that they maintain that the power applies solely to existence, even though in its reality existence does not vary at all.

Another point that has great effect against them is that they maintain that the contingent power cannot bring back what was brought into being in the first instance. Yet it is known that the resurrection is all but the same as the first creation. For this reason the adherents of Islam infer the Lord's having the power to resurrect based on His having the power to undertake creation in the first place. The scripture speaks to this very point and the Lord advances the first creation as an argument against those who deny the resurrection.

If the Muʿtazilites avow that, concerning that of which reason admits in general its possibility, the contingent power will not serve for its resurrection, on this basis it must be admitted that it is not of service for the commencement of creation. If, however, they force on us the applicability of the contingent power to the future life, we accept it and consider it not unreasonable. If God restores human empowerment, it is also possible that He restores His power over it.

Another objection against them consists in saying: You accept with us that, with the exception of existence, none of the attributes of action develop from a power that is contingent, although they themselves come and go, just as existence comes and goes. What then is the difference between existence and the attribute that is added to it?

If you say: When the existence of motion is established, proving its existence affirms necessarily that the characteristic properties that belong to it also exist; power only has its effect in what is possible not in what is necessary; but the attributes that accompany existence are necessary; how then could the power effect them? To this we reply: It makes no sense for them to be necessary, since it is possible to suppose their non-existence when the existence does not exist.

They may now say: The meaning of their being necessary is only that they are necessary when the existence is affirmed. We respond: Likewise the existence is necessary when they are affirmed, since, just as it is impossible that the contingent is affirmed without the attributes which accompany it, similarly it is impossible for the attributes that accompany it to be affirmed without the contingent thing. There is no escape from this conclusion and there is no trick our adversaries can use to refute this outcome.

As for the third issue in this discussion, our purpose here is to apply the proofs from tradition. They fall into two types: those taken from circumstances in which the consensus of the community was present, and those adduced from the text of the Holy Book.

Those taken as an expression of the community have various aspects. One of them is that the community is in accord on supplication to God, the Exalted, and to voice to him the desire that He bestow on them faith and certitude and that He shield them from unbelief, impiety and disobedience. But, if recognition were not within the power of God, this widely used prayer and its universal desire is connected to a request for something that the Creator has no power to do.

Should they now say: This desire may be construed as a request for the power to acquire faith and for assistance to that end by the creation of power, we reply: This is not correct, according to your own principles, because, if every person that has the capacity, had power over faith and the Lord did not deprive him of having the power for it, there is no way to construe the prayer as a desire for what already exists. But the person offering the prayer seeks something not yet attained and previously lacking.

Furthermore, just as the righteous ancestors asked the Exalted God for faith, similarly they requested Him to shield them from unbelief. The power for faith is a power for unbelief, according to the principles of the Muʿtazilites. Thus, if the Lord were to help with the acquisition of faith by creating the power for it, it is also necessary that He assist in the acquisition of unbelief by creating the power for it. This case becomes even stronger against our adversary when we suppose that the argument concerns someone about whom God knows that, if He grants him the power, he will become an unbeliever. Should, therefore, He give him the power under these circumstances, He will be aiding unbelief more surely than faith.

Among the prayers of the prophets to this effect is the statement of Abraham and his son Ismail, may God's blessings be upon them both: "Our Lord, make us submissive to You" (and the rest of the verse) [2:128]. Another of them is the statement of Abraham, on whom be peace: "And preserve me and my sons from worshipping idols" [14:35].

Also among the points we adhere to, based on the received expression of the community and the consensus of its leaders, is that Muslims, prior to the appearance of the Qadariyya,[1] were in unanimous accord that the Exalted Lord

1 The term Qadariyya applies, as is the case here, generally to those who believe in human free will and hold that humans have power over their own acts independently of God's power over

is the sovereign over all created things and Lord of all that was temporally produced. It is an impossibility that the Exalted Creator be sovereign over what He has no power over and a god of something not considered among those things within His power. There is no doubt that all created beings have a lord and sovereign. If the servant was to be the creator of his own actions, necessarily he would be their lord and god in so far as he holds the power over them by and of himself. This is a great effrontery to religion that would be accepted by no successful person. The sense of the revelation indicates as much. God said: "For then, each god would govern what he created, some of them holding themselves above others" [23:91].

Yet another received item from this source is for us to maintain that the creation of understanding, submissiveness, and good works is more admirable than the creation of bodies and their accidents, which are not in the same category as submissiveness. If one were to attribute to the servant the creation of understanding, that would be a more admirable creation than that of the Lord. It would be more appropriate for him to serve himself and to provide guidance and save himself from sin and perdition than his Lord. A person who insists that the servant serves himself better than his Lord has broken from the consensus of Muslims and separated himself from religion altogether.

They might say: If it were not for power over faith, there would be no possibility of the servant acquiring faith, and thus having such power is more useful and better. To that we reply: As a result of this idea, the upholders of this dogma are forced to make the power for unbelief more evil than unbelief itself in so far as unbelief is impossible except as a consequence of that power. The power is effective equally for two opposites and one of them is not then preferable to the other. If thus God, the Exalted, were to ameliorate his situation by giving him the power to find faith, He would also hinder him by giving him the capacity for unbelief. This evaluation fulfils our intention in respect to sources based on the expression of the community.

As for the text of the Holy Book, one of them is God's statement: "That is God, your Lord; there is no god besides He, the Creator of all things" (the verse) [6:103]. This verse requires that the Exalted Creator stands alone in creating all created things. The inference in it is reconfirmed by our knowing that the import of it comprises the glorification in His being the Originator and Innovator and in being alone in creating all things. If there were another creator and innovator other than He, the glorification due for creation could no longer be taken in its particular meaning. The servant would then be allowed to glorify himself for being the creator of all things, even though what is meant is merely that he is the creator of some things.

---

them. It can, however, mean the opposite, namely that God has absolute power over all acts and He in fact determines them all Himself. See "Ḳadariyya" in the *EI2*.

Here they say: What you have latched on to is a generality. Scholars have two doctrines concerning formulae that are general: one denies that the words entail a generality and the second upholds the generality, provided that it is subjected to interpretation. But all literal forms are subject to various ways of being construed. Thus one cannot rely on them to reach a definitive result. To this we respond: We do not adhere to a simple formula except after having made clear its connection to the desire for glorification. We demonstrated conclusively that this glorification is what is understood, as required by the verse itself. Construing the verse in the particular is no longer tenable seeing as we have obtained certainty in respect to glorification. What is understood, although not adduced from the formula in isolation, is nevertheless derivable from associated factors.

In this same way, one infers from God's statement: "Or have they ascribed to God associates who created as He created, so that creation is all alike to them, say God is the Creator of all things" (the verse) [13:16]. This verse is prime evidence in regard to the topic under dispute. If they claim: The apparent meaning does not apply as, similarly, it did not in the subject of your previous inference, since the literal implication in both verses requires that the Lord be Creator of all things and the specification here of things covers both the eternal and the contingent, we reply: The one who communicates and who speaks in these situations does not fall within the class of those spoken to. The like of this is someone saying: "I have not found an eloquent adversary, nor an accomplished debater, but that I silenced him." No person of intelligence would imagine this declaration to include that he himself fall within the judgment imposed by his statement – that is, to suppose his having silenced even himself. The decisive meaning of the text will not be found by evasions and trickery.

We can adduce in every verse in the Book of God an indication to glorify the Exalted Creator as having power over all things. The Muʿtazilites do not have this sense available to them, since, for them, the meaning in God's statement: "God has power over all things" [2:284] is that He has power over His own actions but He does not hold power over the actions of others. The matter being like this the servant also has power over all things, according to this interpretation. As a result the glorification of the Exalted Creator ceases to mean anything.

Another passage that can be invoked is God's statement: "And God created you and what you make" [37:96]. We will dedicate a special chapter to the meaning of guidance and going astray, the sealing [*khatm*] and the occlusion [*ṭabʿ*] and the gladdening of hearts [*sharḥ al-ṣudūr*] and in it we will keep strictly to the text and spirit of the Holy Book. For the moment, it is time to mention the doctrines defended by the Muʿtazilites and their sophisms which are divided, according to their own teaching, into the discernment of reason and the dictates of tradition.

One of those they adhere to from the discernment of reason is to say: The intelligent person judges between what is within his power and what is not within his power. He, for example, perceives a difference between his voluntary motions and the colours around him over which he has no control. The way to distinguish between the two categories is that he finds that what is within his power occurs as a direct consequence of his intentions and requirements, and what of it that does not happen does not occur due to his refraining and turning his attention away from it. If something comes up that occurs on account of his intention and requirement, he doubts not that he was the reason for its happening. Moreover, it would not have happened were it not contingent. Thus the human being must be the producer of his own actions. If his actions did not occur because he made them occur, they would be in the same category as his colour and the rest of his attributes over which he has no power.

We say: What you rely on here is a claim that is not connected to the evidence. As for your statement that what is within the power occurs as a consequence of the requirement and intention, it is false for several reasons. One of them is that this cannot be generalized for all states nor does it include all actions. Instead the matter needs a distinction: sometimes an act occurs as a consequence of the intention and sometimes it does not occur because of it. Thus, for example, the acts of an intelligent person who is careless might not occur in accord with his intention and requirements. They are similar to any act a sleeping or an unconscious person might do.

Thus, since what they say cannot be generalized to encompass all acts, the occurrence of only some of them in response to the requirement does not prove that they are acts produced by the human being. It happens that a person is sated upon eating, his thirst is quenched after drinking, that cloth acquires desired colours by dyeing, that the person addressed understands when given information, that he has shame and has fear upon being shamed or frightened. But these acts, although they take place in accord with what is intended, are not the acts of the person who has the motive or the intention.

In addition we maintain that the one who believes that there is no Creator except God will not be incited to create by any requirement at all. With this belief it would not be correct for him to intend to produce. The actions of the majority of creatures do not occur as a consequence of an intention. What happens by intention and occurs because of the human being is, according to our adversaries, contingently produced. Since it is now clear that, in the cases of those we mentioned above, the act is not consequent to the intention, their hoping to take refuge in the idea of motivation is vain and that on which they rely for their argument is corrupt.

Furthermore, we say: It is not unreasonable, in your view, that the Exalted Creator creates in the human involuntary modes of being, and that He creates in him motivations towards them that are generally involuntary. If the situation is like this, the modes of being occur in response to the motivations. But we cannot decide, in that case, that the involuntary modes of being which occur in response to motivations are the acts of the person who has the motivation. Therefore what they rely on is false in every respect.

What they mentioned in regard to the perceiving of the difference between what is within and not within the power is correct, but the distinction is a tool for perceiving the application of the power in one case and not in the other. It is like the difference between what is known and what is supposed as probable, even while knowing that knowledge and supposition have no effect on that to which they apply.

Chapter: [The distinction between the claim upon the servant with respect to his colours and his body versus the claim upon him with respect to his acts]

Among the points they insist upon – one which is a major contrivance of theirs – is for them to say: God, the Exalted, demands obedience from the servant. But it is absurd and lacking in reason for the servant to be asked for something he cannot do. They continue: Being empowered, in your view, is tantamount to the power itself in that both occur by the power of God, the Exalted, and the servant has no role at all in causing to occur the things with that power. What then is demanded? What is the sense of demanding? What is the distinction between the claim upon the servant with respect to his colours and his body versus the claim upon him with respect to his acts?

Perhaps they will attempt to resolve this quandary by saying: We will not hold you, in this instance, to the concept of a command that applies to the reprehensibleness or worthiness of the action. Nevertheless, all upholders of religion agree that what led to the imputation of a contradiction in the speech of God, the Exalted, and which deviates from good sense, is false. It is nothing but foolish talk for someone to say to the person from whom he demands something: Do what I am myself doing and create what I am already creating.

Our method of opposing this quandary of the Muʿtazilites commences from a number of different points. Among them is for us to note that one of their principles is that the non-existent is a thing and an essence with properties that qualify it. That being so what is the sense of demanding a positive affirmation of what is already affirmed? There is no sense in an object of knowledge having existence unless it is affirmed as an essence possessing qualifying properties. Our objection to their doctrine here, in fact, removes any meaning that creating might have in their view from the scope of God's activity, may He be sanctified and exalted.

As for those of the Muʿtazilites who deny the modes, they have no expectation of finding a way to disassociate themselves from the consequence we have just mentioned. Those among the partisans of this school who uphold the modes might perhaps claim that the thing demanded is existence and that it is a renewable mode of the essence. But that is absurd because, if the mode were to be particular to the affirmation of existence over non-existence, it would be an essence. Anything imagined to be non-existent which is then believed renewable in essence occurs subject to the separate and unique power that transforms it.

Therefore, it is itself an essence. If one were to allow the transfer of the effect of a power to the mode, it would be possible to claim that an atom became still after being in motion, and its being in repose is a mode determined by a power without any need to stipulate a repose that is an accident additional to the essence. But that entails the denial of accidents. There is no way for them to avoid this consequence.

Among other points that refute their specious argument is for us to ask: According to you, the servant from the beginning is asked to reason and yet when afterwards he believes in the demand imposed, how can he arrive at knowledge of the demand prior to ascertaining firmly that there is a being who ordains the commandment?

What they rely on to force us to admit that the spoken demand is itself a contradiction refutes instead their own claims in a way from which there is no escape. This is for us to note: It is among your principles that the Exalted Lord, in imposing upon them the obligation to obey Himself, acts in the best interest of His servants. We postulate a doctrine against you in which the person about whom God, the Exalted, knows that, if he dies not having reached the age of reason, he will be saved from eternal punishment, or, alternatively, if He leaves him to reach intellectual maturity and grants him full facilities, he will become ungrateful and rebel. That being his situation, it would most assuredly be in his best interest for him to die. If anyone were to question this, further discussion with such a person is pointless; his argument is simply untenable. All discussions about requiring an imposed obligation are bound up with an intention for the best result.

Here there is no greater example of contradiction than for someone to say: I am giving you an order and my purpose in giving you an order is your best interest, despite my knowing that you will not be best served, since, if I do not give you the order, you would be saved from the grievous sins of eternal damnation and the ruination of everlasting perdition. This – may you be safeguarded from such innovations – is the ultimate in contradiction and grasping this fact is easy for any intelligent person.

Also what opposes them is that the prescriptions and restraints of the law are connected to the conditions determined to be in accord with the causes proper to them. An example is the supposition in the law with regard to a command that the person obligated by it be upstanding and knowing. There is no way to deny it, based either on the sources of the law or the requirements of tradition. Thus the knower's being knowledgeable, although a useful presupposition in terms of the demand made of him, is not due, according to the principles of our opponents, to a being that demands it of him. Nothing occurs as a result of the power except the coming into existence of an essence. The modes are necessitated by the causes and necessarily come to be as a consequence of this contingent relationship. If then supposing demanding what will not occur by the agency of the demand's subject is not improbable, the consequence, on the basis of which they would oppose us, is thus actually valid.

At this point we say: What you founded your contrived ideas on is a pure fantasy. We continue: You were already aware that your opponents do not believe in the servant who is subject to command and prohibition being the one who makes his act occur, and you knew of the consensus of the religious community that the commands are directed to the person under obligation. Yet you would insist, despite these two principles, on the impossibility of demanding of someone what he cannot make happen by and of himself.

To summarize the discussion, we now state: What you claim as being impossible must fall under one of two conditions. Either you base your claim on self-evident necessity, or on a proof that backs up your argument. If you claim necessary knowledge, in making such a claim, you run into the opposition of the majority of the community and you must certainly be considered unconscionable. Nor can you save yourselves from the objections to your claims by one similar to it. If you try to base the soundness of your claim upon reason, reveal it so that we can speak against it. Do not be content with an empty claim.

In the matter of appropriation, one of our leading masters pursued a method that refutes this sophism of theirs, as we will later explain in a chapter devoted to the true reality of appropriation. What he said was that the contingent power comprises within it the existence of a mode belonging to the thing empowered by it, and it is to this mode that the demand applies. Creating, according to the principles of the Muʿtazilites, does not include the coming into existence of the essence, since, in their view, essences exist both as non-being and as being, in either case having their own qualifying attributes. Coming into being involves the existence of the essence and that is a mode, according to the most competent of the Muʿtazilites.

Another sophism of theirs consists in their saying: Should you judge that the contingent power does not produce an effect on that to which it applies and so its function is the same as knowledge in respect to its influence on the thing known, from what this entails comes the application of the contingent power to colours, bodies, the eternal and all contingent things, in so far as they are analogous to things known. In this they misconstrue their own claim, while yet searching for a way thereby to prove it. Anyone who wants to establish a comparison between one thing and another should seek evidence proving the likeness between them in the way desired by the person making the comparison.

Thus, if they maintain that the link between powers and knowledge is their both equally not producing an effect in that to which they apply, we reply: Why have you not said that the application of knowledge is general, since it leaves no trace of itself? They cannot free themselves from this objection, nor can they bring forth a proof and they are not about to be shown a way to find it. Moreover, vision produces no effect in the visible object nor, according to the doctrine of the adversary here, does it apply in the case of any other of the beings. Knowledge about a specific determined object does not apply to any other than it, even though there is no effect of the knowledge in the thing known by such knowledge. Thus the contention they relied on proves false.

In addition what they have argued turns against them in a way that leaves them no means of escape. This is that the true nature of contingency does not vary. For our opponents, it is an effect of the power. The attributes by which contingent things vary are not effects of the power. How then do you not uphold the application of the contingent power to all contingent beings, seeing as there is no variation in the application of the contingent power and its effect on them all?

Yet another sophism of theirs is for them to say: The servant is rewarded on the basis of his action, or punished, reproached, or praised. All this proves that his act was brought about by him, since it cannot be considered good to reproach him or bestow praise for what he did not bring about himself, as in the manner of his coloration or corporeal functions. This argument of theirs yields nothing because reward and punishment and what attends them in the way of blame and honour do not, in our view, result from the acts of the obligated person by necessity. If God, the Exalted, were to enter His servant into either abiding happiness or painful punishment, both of those are perfectly possible and not unthinkable. The acts of the servants are, according to the rules of the law, merely signs and tokens of the regulations of God, the Exalted. It is not inconceivable to set up such a sign which does not actually pertain to the one who has been marked by it. We will confirm this in the chapter on reward and punishment, God, the Mighty and Glorious, willing.

Chapter: [*On the application of the contingent power to what it empowers*]

Someone might say: One argues a particular doctrine, either in refutation or in acceptance, in the situation where it is intelligible, but what you believe in regard to the servant's appropriation of an act is nonsense, since, if the power has no effect on what is empowered by it, the empowerment cannot have occurred because of it. There is no meaning for the application of the power in this case. Our answer is that our masters expressed differing opinions as to how the contingent power applies to what it empowers.

Some among them argued that the contingent power produces an effect in so far as it brings about a mode which the empowered thing has and on the basis of which the act of appropriation is distinguishable from necessity. If we were to stipulate a necessary motion in a certain direction, and we suppose also another in the same direction that is moving appropriatively, the appropriating movement belongs to an additional mode that comprises an effect associated with the application of a contingent power to it. By it the act of appropriating can be distinguished from the necessary. As for contingency and the production of essences, only God, the Exalted, causes them to exist.

But this procedure is not acceptable and does not follow the rules laid down by the orthodox. In adopting it, one opens the door to many errors that must be avoided. Among them is that, in having power, the servant cannot possibly be isolated from the Exalted Lord. If we stipulate that the contingent power has an effect and we affirm that it belongs to the servant, we violate the belief which requires that the Lord has power over all things that are subject to power. It is impossible to hold that the stipulated condition occurs both as a result of an eternal power and a contingent power and, if this is impossible, allowing its stipulation here is to allow the supposition of a creation stemming from two creators.

Nevertheless, the partisan of this procedure passes on in his doctrine to a claim of an unknown mode which he cannot explain clearly, despite our having proved definitively that the appropriating movement corresponds to the necessary. To suppose the existence of unknown modes is a departure from propriety and opens an access for corrupt notions to enter into the principles of religion.

The sound procedure is to understand conclusively that the contingent power does not produce its own effect in what is subject to the power, and it is not a condition of the application of an attribute that it produce an effect in that to which it applies, since knowing is intelligible in its application to the thing known, despite not producing an effect in it. In a similar way, a will that is associated with the act of the servant does not produce an effect in its object. Should now our opponents find this still inadmissible and revert to the concept of the servant being the one accountable, we have provided here sufficient justification for a convincing refutation.

Chapter: [*On being guided, in error, under seal and stamp*[2]]

Understand, may God, the Exalted, help you to reach His gracious approval, that the Book of God, the All-mighty, contains verses indicating the unique role of God, the Exalted, in providing guidance for people and in leading them astray, or in placing a seal on the hearts of the unbelievers among them. These are texts that prove the falseness of the doctrines of the opponents of orthodoxy. Here we will first review our point in regard to the verses concerning "being guided" and "in error". After, we will follow with the verses that contain a reference to "sealing" and "stamping".

Among those that carry the most weight against them are the following statements of God, the Exalted: "And God summons to the Abode of Peace and guides whomever He will to the straight path" [10:25], His saying: "You do not guide those that you like but rather God guides whoever He wishes," [28:56], His saying: "Whoever God wants to guide, He expands his breast for Islam, and whoever He wants to lead astray, He makes his breast narrow and tight" [6:125], and the statement of God, the Mighty and Glorious: "Whoever God guides he is rightly guided; whoever He leads astray, they are the losers" [7:178].

2 *al-hudā*, *al-ḍalāl*, *al-khatm*, *al-ṭabʿ*.

Understand that "being guided" in these verses cannot be construed otherwise than to indicate the creation of faith. Likewise one cannot construe "being led astray" in any other way than as the creation of error. We do not reject adducing from "guidance" in the book of God, the Mighty and Glorious, a meaning other than the one we have indicated here. It is used in the sense of the "summons", as in God, the Exalted, saying: "Surely you will guide to the straight path" [42:52], where its meaning is that you will surely summon.

The connotation of guidance and what is intended by it is conducting the believers onto the paths to paradise and the roads by which they may reach it on the Day of Resurrection. God, the Exalted, said: "He will not let their deeds go astray; He will guide them and set their minds aright" [47:4–5]. God, the Exalted, mentions those who are warriors in His cause, specifically meaning the Emigrants [*al-Muhājirūn*] and the Helpers [*al-Anṣār*].[3] Next, He declares that He will guide them. Hence it is necessary to understand this verse to mean what we indicated previously. Further God, the Exalted, said, in reference to the unbelievers: "Guide them to the path of hell" [37:23]. It means to show them to the path to hell. The implication in His saying: "As for Thamūd, We guided them" [41:17], is to "summon" and the sense of the verse is that We summoned them but they preferred to remain blind to the guidance to which We summoned them.

We indicate here the various significations of the terms "being guided" and "being led astray" simply so that you will perceive that we do not deny that either "being guided" or "being led astray" are used with a meaning other than "creating". However, we are specifying that this particular inference for them is in accord with the verses we cited at the beginning of this chapter. For them there is no way to construe either as meaning "summons". Indeed God, the Exalted, distinguishes between "summon" and "guidance" in saying: "God summons to the Abode of Peace and He guides whoever He wishes." Thus guidance is particular and the summons is general, and this entails the understanding we adduce from these verses. There is no way to construe them as providing guidance towards the road to paradise because God, the Exalted, makes guidance conditional on His will, and His wish and His choice. Anyone deserving of paradise imposes on God, in the view of the Muʿtazilites, the obligation to admit him to paradise. God, the Exalted, saying "Whoever God wants to guide He exposes his breast for Islam", speaks explicitly about the situation in this world. To open the breast or to close it up and the mention of Islam are the best confirmation of what we have been saying.

If, in wanting to construe guidance as meaning summons or something else commensurate with their beliefs, the Muʿtazilites attempt to draw their evidence from the verses we cited, we have only to answer that it is not inconceivable to

3 The *Muhājirūn* are those who emigranted from Mecca to Madina and joined Muḥammad there. The *Anṣār* are the local inhabitants of Madina who entered his cause after his arrival.

understand what you take as evidence implying what you have mentioned. It is only that we infer in the verses a distinction specifying that guidance is for a certain group and being led astray for another, especially in conjunction with a mention of Islam and the opening and closing up of the breasts. There is simply no scope in the texts from which we have adduced our proof for their fancifully embellished interpretations.

As for the verses mentioning "stamping" and "sealing", they include God, the Exalted, saying: "God placed a seal on their hearts" [2:7], His saying, "Rather it is God who put the stamp of their unbelief on their hearts" [4:155], and His saying, "We have thrown veils over their hearts that they may not understand it and in their ears a deafness" [6:25], and His saying, "And We made their hearts harden" [5:13].

The Muʿtazilites have argued about these verses and the opinions they hold are in turmoil. A group of the Basrans believe in construing them as God, the Exalted, denoting unbelievers by the repudiation inherent in unbelief and error. This then is the meaning of "putting a stamp".

Obviously, this way of speaking is pointless. The Exalted Lord is praised in these verses and declares through them His having dominion and power over the conscience and secrets of the servant. It shows that the hearts are under His authority and that He alters them as He wishes. He makes this explicit in His statement: "We shall turn their hearts and their eyes even though they did not believe in it the first time around" [6:110]. How could one accept to understand these verses as mere denotation or naming? Now could a person of intelligence allow that? None of us is incapable of giving names and denotations. With all of His awesome authority why try to discern the effect of the Lord in this?

Al-Jubbāʾī and his son construe these verses in a disgusting manner that advertises their inattention to matters of religion. Thus they say: Whoever disbelieves, God marks his heart with a sign that the angels will recognize. Having had a seal placed on the hearts, for the angels the hearts of the unbeliever will be distinguishable from the hearts of the pious. Therefore this is the meaning of the seal, according to them. But what they cite is contrary to the text of the Book and the sense of the revelation. The verses are textual evidence that, by means of the stamping and sealing, God, the Exalted, turns away from the practices of proper guidance whoever among the servants He wants to turn away. God, the Exalted, has said: "We put over their hearts a veil that they not understand it and in their ears a deafness." The verse entails the veil being an impediment to the comprehension of faith. But the mark they contrive to declare doctrine would not preclude such comprehension.

Having exceeded our aim to deal with matters succinctly, the truth is nevertheless now clear and fully manifest. The obstinacy of the opposition in their interpretation is thus quite evident. But it is God who makes one successful in reasoning correctly.

Section

The Doctrine of Capacity and its Characteristic Property

The servant has the power to appropriate it and his power over it is confirmed. The Determinists maintain a denial of the power and they insist that what is termed the servant's "appropriation" of an act of his can be said to be so only by extension or metaphor. Voluntary and wilful motions have thus the same function as trembling and shivering.

The proof affirming the power is that, when his hand trembles and then he moves it with intention, the human finds a difference between its state while subject to the motion of necessity and the state he chooses and appropriates; and the distinction between the state of being subject to necessity and the one freely chosen is known by self-evident necessity. Moreover, it is impossible to attribute it to the difference of the two motions because the necessary one is definitely equivalent to the voluntary one; each of the two motions proceeds in the same direction and is conveyed towards it. There is no room to claim a distinction between them due to the influence of an unknown attribute. That would pre-empt the very means of knowing that two equivalent things are in fact equivalent. Therefore, if the distinction cannot be ascribed to the two motions themselves, it must have its origin in an attribute of the person who moves.

Thereafter, as previously in the verification undertaken in our attempt to provide a proof attesting to the accidents, we apply the method of survey and elimination to confirm the power. Here we say that ascribing this difference solely to the agent in and of itself is inconceivable without an additional factor, for, if that were the case, the function attributable to the agent in and of itself would persist as long as it did itself.

If the distinction is ascribable to a factor added to it, this addition must be either a mode or an accident. It cannot be a mode because an immaterial mode does not supervene upon the atoms. Rather it arises as a consequence of a previously existing thing, as we stipulated earlier. If, on the other hand, this added factor is an accident, it must be a power, because there is no other attribute of the one doing the appropriating than the power. Otherwise, its existence would be conceivable, even if having power were denied, but the majority of the attributes other than power would be denied if the power existed.

In the preceding discussion here, we have not tried to cover all the points thoroughly but were content instead with an outline of it. It may now be asked: For what reason do you reject those who ascribe the distinction to the existence of will and loathing? We respond: The intelligent person perceives a difference between his moving his hand and his trembling, even though, in situations of carelessness and inadvertence, he has no purpose in doing the former.

Then they may say: How do you refute those who ascribe the distinction to the health of the limbs or a special physical condition or to the absence of that? We answer: This is false for several reasons. The nearest to our goal in this instance is that a person who is vigorous and of healthy physical constitution distinguishes between moving his hand by himself intentionally and having something else move his hand, even though the condition of his hand is the same in both situations. These postulates having proven false, the conclusion here validates precisely the power. And this is our method of validating all points under contention.

Chapter: [*The contingent power does not persist*]

The contingent power is one of the accidents, according to us, and it does not persist. This is a characteristic property of all the accidents, in our view. The Muʿtazilites are in agreement among themselves that the power persists. The proof, however, of the impossibility of any of the accidents persisting is that, if they were to persist, they would never be non-existent.

We stipulate this proof in the case of the power and then we demonstrate its generalization to all the others. Hence we say: If the power were to persist and then its non-existence were supposed, the doctrine here must follow one of two results. Either its cessation is ascribed to the intervention of a contrary, which is the doctrine of our opponents, or to suppose that its cessation is due to the cessation of a condition it has. It is false to ascribe its non-existence to the intervention of a contrary, since the intervening of a contrary to nullify the power has no precedence over the power repulsing the contrary and preventing it from intervening. Moreover, if the contraries occur subsequent to each other, the second will exist when the first ceases. If its non-existence is realized, what went before it has then ceased to exist and there is no need for the contrary.

It is also false to hold that the power ceases upon the cessation of a specific condition it has since its condition must be either an accident or an atom. If it were an accident, the procedure in regard to its persistence and cessation is like the procedure in regard to the power. If it were an atom, one could not conceive, once holding that the accidents persist, the cessation of atoms, because the process in its ceasing to exist must nullify also the accidents attached to it. Yet, if one judges that the accidents persist, one cannot conceive their non-existence; and, if supposing that their non-existence is precluded, the non-existence of atoms is also precluded. We dealt with some aspects of this notion under the subject of the attributes.

It is wrong, moreover, to hold that the power ceases to exist because God abolishes it, since abolishing existence is non-existence and it is an absolute negation. It is impossible that the subject of power is annulled because there is no difference between saying there is nothing subject to the power and saying that what is subject to the power is non-existent.

Chapter: [*Once more on the contingent power*]

Having now established the impossibility of the contingent power persisting, it is inseparable from the coming into being of the thing it empowers and it does not precede it. Were we to admit to the notion of the contingent power's persisting, that it precedes the occurrence of the thing it empowers would not be considered impossible. For this reason, it is an absolute necessity that the eternal power precedes the occurrence of those things subject to it. Hence, having established that the contingent power does not persist, there follows from this the impossibility of its preceding what it empowers, since, if it were to precede it, what it empowers would occur despite the cessation of the power. That is impossible, as we will explain, God, the mighty and glorious, so willing.

Chapter: [*The contingent being in the state of coming to be is subject to the power of God, the Exalted*]

The contingent being, in the state of coming to be, is empowered by the eternal power. If it has an association with a contingent power, it is also subject to that power. If an empowerment in those subjects of the Creator's power should persist and, even if it is the atom, nevertheless none other of the contingent beings persists. As long as it persists and continues to exist, by general agreement, it cannot be characterized as being subject to power.

The Muʿtazilites maintain that the contingent being, in the state of its coming into being, cannot be subject to the power of either the eternal or a contingent being. This is tantamount to a being enduring everlastingly. The power applies only to what it has power over in the state of its non-existence. They say in generalizing this: The capacity must necessarily precede the empowered subject. The conjunction of the power's essence with the advent of the thing empowered by it is possible without also continuing to apply to it once it has come to be.

The proof that the contingent being is subject to a power and that the capacity is concomitant with the act consists in saying: The power is an attribute of application and it cannot be considered in isolation from the thing to which it applies. If then we were to postulate a power that precedes and a thing subject to power coming after it in two successive states, the power, according to the principles of the Muʿtazilites, cannot be determined to apply to the subject of power. If we consider carefully the first state, one cannot conceive in it the occurrence of an empowered subject. If we then consider the second state, the power has no application in it. Hence, in the first state, there is no realization of what is possible and, in the second, the empowerment cannot be determined to exist. Thus the application of the power does not have a meaning that persists [from one to the other].

Following upon this, we strengthen our argument on the basis of two points: One of them is that the subject of power must be either non-existent or existent.

It is impossible that it be non-existent because that is a pure negation. But the existent being, according to our opponents, is not subject to the power. The second point is that they insist that the contingent being is tantamount to the everlasting in the impossibility of its being subject to a power. Thus the possibility in the first state depends on the existence of the power and the state that comes to exist subsequently is a state in which there is no application of the power. If one allows this, an enduring thing in the first state is empowered by the power, just as the contingent being was empowered by the power prior to its occurrence in the first state. For them there is no escape from this conclusion.

If they say: The contingent thing occurs and exists and it requires the power to make it occur but, when the occurrence of the contingent thing is realized by it, the need for the power ceases and the contingent thing acquires the status of something that persists continuously we respond: What you mention proves false on the basis of the characteristic that is caused in a thing by a necessary cause. The characteristic in the condition of its coming to be links it to the cause. No one can say that, when the characteristic has come to exist, there is no need to presume, given its having come to exist, that there is a cause linked with it. Likewise, the productive cause accompanies the occurrence of the caused thing and makes that necessary in it, as we will mention afterward on the subject of capacity, God, the mighty and glorious, so willing.

In conceiving it, a truly intelligent person will discern three states: the state of being non-existent, the state of coming into existence subsequently, and the state of persistence after having come into existence. As for the state of being non-existent, it is merely the continuation of nothingness. In the case of the second state, if there were to be no application of power in it, the non-existence would continue. When the power applies, the existent replaces a non-existent that might have continued. In the third state, the existent endures and thus there is no need to presume the intervention of the power.

Here the Muʿtazilites are forced into a conclusion that is quite obviously erroneous. They maintain that, if the power precedes the subject of power in one state, it is possible that there occurs in the second state an incapacity that is the contrary of the power. Subsequently, the incapacity will manifest its effect in the third state following the existence of the power and that will constitute a second state for the existence of the incapacity itself. Thus, according to them, it is possible in the second state for the subject of the power to occur in tandem with the incapacity. In that way, were the agent of power to die in the second state, one could nevertheless still envision the occurrence of the subject of the power alongside the dead, since the act of empowerment is not here made conditional upon being alive. But no person of reason would entertain such an idiotic notion.

Should someone say: Every pair of applicable contrary attributes is attested on the basis of a single premise, despite being contradictory in their application, and when you judge that the contingent power accompanies the subject of the power, you are forced to judge also that the incapacity accompanies the subject of the incapacity and that is impossible. Man has no present capacity to effect what will take place only in the future. One of our associates declared in a cowardly fashion that the incapacity precedes what is the subject of the incapacity, in opposition to the case of the power. That is false. The incapacity must have an application commensurate with that of the power, despite the admitted contradiction between the two contraries. For that reason the incapacity cannot be conceived in what cannot be conceived to have the power to do it.

Understand this and be quite certain that those who say that the human is incapable of effecting bodies and colours is speaking metaphorically. What he means by incapacity is figuratively the cessation of the power. This is as if ignorance were a form of belief or to consider the person heedless of a thing to be ignorant of it, even though he believes in nothing. The result of this requires the one who trembles involuntarily also to be at the same time capable of not trembling, in the same manner that the one who moves by free choice has the power to move at the moment he moves.

Chapter: [*What is subject to the contingent power is a single thing*]

The contingent power applies only to a single subject. The Muʿtazilites maintained that the power applies to contraries and the majority of them held that it applies to different things that are not mutually contrary. Thus it is a principle of theirs that, among the various subjects of the power, the contingent power applies to things that follow each other in an endless temporal succession. They are in agreement that a single power does not bring about the occurrence of two similar things together in the same subject at the same time. Two like this would occur only as a result of two powers. If the number of like things increases despite the coincidence of place and time, the powers increase in conformity with their number.

However, it is preferable to settle this question on the basis of what preceded it. Thus, in rejecting the application of the contingent power to two contraries, we say: If it applies to them, they will be joined because of their mutual connection and they will be mutually connected as a necessary requirement, and this is self-evidently false. The impossibility of combining two contraries is understood *a priori*. Were we to postulate now the hypothesis concerning different things that are not mutually contrary, we would say: If the same power applies to all that is correctly within the power of the human, it is necessary that the power that gives power to the crawling thing be the power to acquire all knowledge and desires and other possible kinds of power analogous to these. The falsity of this is known without requiring extensive reasoning or meticulous investigation. Moreover, the basics underlying the previous question extend to this particular point.

Hence we say to those who oppose us: If you judge that the same power applies to two contraries, how can one of them be singled out as having come to be as a result of the power rather than the other? If they say: Of the two contraries, only the one occurs that is the focus of the intention and therefore it is singled out by coming to be, this is false in two ways. One is that the heedless and the sleeping person produces one of two contraries without wishing it. The benefit of the power for what occurs is the same as its benefit for what does not occur. The second calls for us to ask: If desire occurs as something subject to the power, and loathing, which is its contrary, is likewise subject to power as well, how is it that desire alone occurs, seeing that, according to you, the desire is not intentional? For the Muʿtazilites, there is no way out of this dilemma. For us what transpires is the subject of power and for that reason occurs as the creation of the power for it, and certainly it confers no benefit to anything other than that on which it falls.

The Muʿtazilites are forced into another consequence in this argument. Say to them: Heedlessness is contrary to having knowledge and for that reason knowledge becomes non-existent, in your view, upon the supervention of heedlessness, in the same way blackness ceases to exist when whiteness supervenes. It follows necessarily that the agent of the power to know something has the power to be heedless of it, but it is known definitely that heedlessness is not the result of having a power. On that issue the Muʿtazilites wander about in such a confusion that this handbook will not permit a thorough review of it.

Now if they were to say: The course open to the agent of the power allows it to choose between undertaking something and refraining from it. That, however, is realizable only on condition of having the ability to accomplish either of two contrary things. Should the power apply solely to a single subject of empowerment, the human would be committed to it without finding any means to desist from it. But for them to cite this is merely gratuitous and a résumé of their own doctrine. The power to accomplish something is not conditional on having the power to abstain from doing it. The course of the application of the contingent power to what is empowered by it is like the application of knowledge to the known thing. It is not a condition for the application of knowledge to the object of knowing that it also applies to its contrary.

Furthermore, another point of theirs that will not hold up is for them to maintain that the person prevented from doing something has the power to do what he was prevented doing. It is a principle of theirs that the person being held in restraints and tied up has the power to walk about or rise up in the air. If they are allowed to declare in favour of the power coming to exist, even while precluding the occurrence of being the subject of the power, it is not far fetched for us to affirm the existence of the power to do something without having the power to do its contrary.

Chapter: [*On obligating what cannot be done*]

Someone may say: It is public knowledge that the doctrine of your leader allows the obligation of what one does not have the ability to do; explain what you accept of this doctrine and, after presenting the question at issue, support it with a proof. We respond: The obligation to do what one does not have the ability to do takes many forms. Among its forms, one is to make obligatory the union of two contraries and the production of something that exceeds the limit of the powers available. The correct doctrine, in our view, is that this is feasible, within reason, and not impossible. The answers of our leader, may God approve him, varied in respect to the permissibility of imposing an obligation on the person who does not know, as in a person who has fainted or the dead.

The proof for the possibility of obligating the impossible is the unanimous agreement on the possibility of obligating the human to stand up when the order is given to him even though he is seated. We have already established a definitive proof that the person seated does not have the power to stand up by himself. If he is ordered to stand up prior to having the power to do so, although that is impossible, the imposition obligating the impossible is no longer impossible.

Should it be said: Standing up is within the general realm of the possible in contrast to the union of two contraries, reply: Standing up occurs as the result of having power and, without the power, it is impossible, as is the union of two contraries. The one commanded to stand up can do so only when also empowered to do so.

It might be said: The person ordered to stand up is forbidden not to do it. If he was seated and while seated did not have the power to stand up as commanded, he nevertheless had the power to be seated as he was forbidden to do. This is an application of the obligation. This is, in fact, the most easily understood way of putting the case but, upon close examination, it proves false in two respects. One is that the command to rise up in the sky consists of an obligation to do the impossible, according to those who deny it, whereas remaining on the earth can be done and is quite possible. It is, however, the opposite of rising up and flying about the skies. The other is that, even though being seated is forbidden, being seated is not the objective but rather the objective sought is something the person does not have the power to do, namely fly about in the skies.

They might however say: The commandment to do two contraries implies doing both of them together. Seeking both together requires wanting them done simultaneously, but wanting the union of two contraries is impossible. We respond: This assumes that what is commanded to be done must be what the person giving the command wanted done but the situation is not like that, in our view. The Exalted Lord commands the unbeliever to have faith, even when the unbeliever is, in His judgment, damned and He does not intend him to find faith.

Someone might here ask: Is what you recognize as happening, on the basis of reason, in agreement with religious dogma? To that we reply: Our leader maintained that it is within religious dogma for God, the Exalted, to command

Abū Lahab[1] to confess to the truth of the Prophet and believe in him and all that he gave account of. But, according to what is reported about him, he did not believe in the Prophet. Thus he was commanded to confess the Prophet's truth by commanding him not to confess to it and that is an example of the union of two opposing contradictions. Moreover, verses of the Book of God, the Exalted, speak of asking for exemption from being obligated to do what one does not have the capacity to do. Thus God, the exalted, says: "Our Lord, do not impose on us a burden beyond our capacity to carry" [2:286]. If that were truly impossible, seeking exemption from it would not be tolerated.

Chapter: [*The power over colours, tastes and the like*]

Someone may say: How do you know that colours, tastes and the like are outside of the power of humans? We respond: If those things were within their power in general, when they are unable to do them, they would be qualified by the incapacity to do them, because the substrate in question has to be qualified either by the thing or by its contrary. It may be said: What causes you not to believe that they do not have the capacity to do those things? We reply: If they did not have the capacity to do them, they would sense their own incapacity, since incapacity is a thing one senses like knowledge, desire and the like. The proof is that the incapacity to do what is possibly within one's power to do must, should any impediment blocking that knowledge be removed, be perceived necessarily. Moreover, perceiving it does not follow necessarily because of its being an accident, nor because of any other attribute other than its being an incapacity to act. Thus, for that reason, it follows that all incapacity is perceptible. Since the incapacity for colours is not perceived, nor is having the power to effect them, we know with certainty that they are outside the scope of the things humans have the power to do. But God alone provides the grace to reach the truth successfully.

Chapter: [*The power of God, the Exalted, to do what will not come to pass*]

The contingent things that the Creator, may He be sanctified, knows will not come to exist or happen are nevertheless within His power. This can be made clear by the following example. The advent of the Final Hour is within God's power at this very moment, although it is known that it will not occur imminently. The theologians have gone back and forth on this matter without result, in my opinion, due to a serious disagreement about it.

The meaning in something being known not to be about to happen even though it is within the power of God, the Exalted, is that it is in and of itself possible. The power to do such a thing is in and of itself quite appropriately His and there

1 Abū Lahab was the Prophet's uncle, a half brother of his father, whose opposition to Muḥammad's mission earned him and his wife the special condemnation of a Qurʾānic *sura* (no. 111).

is no restriction on Him as to its application, as there are restrictions on the application of the contingent power to colours. This is the meaning of His having the power. Otherwise, what God knows will not happen, will certainly not happen.

Chapter: [*Those things that comprise the refutation of the upholders of the doctrine of production*]

A contingent power applies exclusively to what exists in its subject. What occurs apposite to the subject of the power does not fall under that power but rather occurs as an act of God, the Exalted, without the human having any power over it. If a stone rolls away when a human being leans on it, the stone's propulsion is not a result of the human's having that power, according to the orthodox.

The Muʿtazilites maintain that what occurs apposite the power's subject, or to the whole context in which it exists, might happen as a product of an empowering cause that is attendant to having the power. When the stone is propelled after being leaned on, its propulsion is a product engendered by the leaning that arises within the subject of the power. Furthermore, the production, according to them, is an action belonging to the agent for the cause and he has the power to do it through the intermediacy of that cause. Among the things so produced, there are those previously in the power's subject, such as discursive knowledge generated from reflection which arises in the subject of the power in response to confusion, protracted investigation and controversy concerning what is and is not produced by such generation. But it is not our objective here to survey fully the details of their doctrine.

The proof of the validity of the doctrine of the orthodox is that what they characterize as the product must be either subject or not subject to power. If it were to be subject to power, this would be false in two respects. One is that the cause, according to their own principles, produces the effect necessarily, assuming the absence of any impediments. Since, when the cause begins to exist and thereafter, the effect follows necessarily, it must be independent by virtue of its necessity, and thus is in no need of the power's causing an effect in it. If we were to imagine believing in the doctrine of production and we accepted the existence of the cause and the removal of impediments, and yet we believed none the less in denying the power all together, the effect would still come to exist upon the existence of the cause, in line with what we specified previously in regard to these beliefs. The second aspect is that, if it were subject to power, one could conceive the effect's occurrence without the mediation of the cause. The proof is that, when an empowerment that is subject to God occurs, since the human is not instrumental to it, it occurs as an empowerment subject directly to God, the Exalted, without requiring the intermediacy of another cause.

If they now say that the Creator, may He be sanctified and exalted, is powerful in and of Himself but the human being has power only through this power, what is powerful in and of Itself differs from what has power by virtue of this power. For that reason it is described as having power over various classes of things that humans with power do not have the power to do. We reply: This is inconsequential because the power, according to you, has no effect in bringing about the having of power in the visible world but what brings about the act is only the powerful having power. Moreover, this characteristic in the visible world is caused by the power and it is invisible and is not the cause because of its being necessary since the necessary cannot be caused in your view. For this reason you claim that the effect of the powerful having power, both in the visible and invisible worlds, is creation and you declare that the human is accorded an empowerment over an unlimited number of things. But after that nothing saves you from your having contradicted your own principle in ruling that certain types are outside of the powers accorded humans. You are thus, in this issue, to be held accountable for what you have already rejected. Reliance on corrupt rules will provide you no benefit. The issue against you here concerns the reconciliation between the visible and invisible worlds with respect to the characteristics of the things subjected to power.

Having then by what we have said proved false that intermediate production is within the power of humans – that being the part we were most concerned to prove false – this also proves the falsity of the doctrine of the whole of the Muʿtazilites. Nothing remains but to judge that the production is not empowered. To admit this is to declare by clear pronouncement that it is not an action stemming from the agency of the cause, since a condition of the action is its being subject to the agent's power. If it were possible to affirm an action that has no agent, it would be possible also to hold that what we know of the atoms of the world and their accidents are not God's act, but rather they result from a cause empowered necessarily to produce everything else. But that departs from religion and forsakes the doctrine of Muslims.

Furthermore, to uphold the doctrine of production brings those who believe in it to reprehensible positions which are utterly unreasonable and whose untenability ought to be grasped *a priori*. Such is the case wherein a person shoots an arrow but then death overtakes him before the arrow reaches its mark. Subsequently, it arrives at its mark and strikes a living being. The wound continues to bleed for some years until finally causing that person to die. All this occurs after the death of the shooter. This bleeding and the pain are the work of the shooter even though it all happens after he has died and his bones are perhaps already scattered about. But yet there would be no greater error than to ascribe the killing to a person long dead.

All the aspects we cite as proof that the Creator, may He be sanctified, is uniquely responsible for creating each contingent thing functions in this chapter as a refutation of those who insist that intermediate products are brought into being by the agency of associated causes.

They might say: We have found that the effects occur in response to intentions, exigencies and the range of the associated causes, as similarly the things being empowered that are associated with the power, which arise in its subject occur in response to exigencies and intentions. But this point they invoke here is among those items we have already discredited in regard to the creation of acts. We have shown clearly that it is futile to rely on it.

Moreover, items which they admit are not intermediately produced in fact prove this falseness in a way that supports our contention. Some examples are satiation, quenching, sickness, health and death, according to the majority of the Muʿtazilites, and the heating from the friction of rubbing one body forcefully against another, the sparks flying from a flint when struck, the comprehension of those spoken to, their shyness and fear when made to understand and caused to be shy or to have fear. All of this and what runs along the same vein are not, according to our opponents, an intermediate product, even though the general rule they cite in regard to the occurrences conforming to the intentions should cover these cases as well.

If, however, they now say: Those items you bring up as evidence each represent, in fact, different cases that cannot be covered by the same generalization, to this we reply: But it is the same in the case of the shooting, the wound, the lifting of a weight and transporting it, and everything else under contention here.

Chapter: [*Concerning forces and intellects*]

The philosophers assert that the processes of generation and corruption, by which they signify the compounding of the four elements and their subsequent decomposition, are the effects of natures and physical forces. The involuntary transmutations that take place in the world below the moon and its orbit are all natural effects, while what transpires in the world above, which is itself devoid of fire, air, water and earth, are effects of the souls of the spheres and their intellects. Moreover, these effects, in their view, depend on the first spiritual being who, in turn, depends on the first existent being who is the Creator, according to their claim, and He is the cause of causes and their necessitator.

Their principle entails, not that the first existent freely created a thing by bringing it into existence, but rather that He necessarily gives rise to the first spiritual being and then the first spiritual being necessarily produces the sphere and its soul and intellect. What they say about the highest sphere is the same for those that follow it, down to the sphere of the moon. The celestial effects mutually correspond; there is no variation in them; nor are they susceptible to the alternation of forms. The sun cannot be envisioned having a disposition other than the one it has. It is only the prime matter of the world of generation and corruption that is susceptible to the diversification of forms. In this matter, they speak of prime matter in place of atoms and form in place of accidents.

However, the truth of their doctrine is that the higher world and the world of generation and corruption do not have a beginning. They exist simultaneously with the first existent, like the effect with the cause. Thus it is best for us to establish at the outset a decisive proof for the temporal contingency of the world and all the existences in it of things subject to successive alterations. And by affirming this we refute their basic principle.

What they have said is purely arbitrary and without merit. On these issues, which they refer to as metaphysics [*ilāhiyyāt*], they never cease to persevere in considering the views of speculative thinkers and testing them by means of rational arguments. They admit this themselves and insist that the science of metaphysics can only be attained by the training of the natural disposition and the study of mathematics which deals with the special properties of numbers, and by geometry, physics and the science of music. Those who train in these subjects receive knowledge of metaphysics without preliminary argumentation.

One of their strange declarations is for them to reject the convincing proofs given by the theologians by insisting that they are sophisms, that the best of them are merely dialectical, and that none of them consists of demonstrative syllogisms. Yet, in regard to what they research, they accept, without argument, what conforms to nature, despite admitting that it is a matter as obscure as it can be. It might be asked of them: Why do you not consider the first existent to be the necessary cause of every other thing? What is it that proves to you the necessity of the first spiritual being and then the necessary causing of what is lower by that spiritual being? Is this not a purely arbitrary judgment lacking merit? This belief yields no more than that.

As for what they term the natures in the sublunary sphere, there is no merit in it. What they allude to is the combining of elements in certain proportions. However, if they mean by their being combined that they intermingle internally, that is impossible because an extended body cannot occupy a space where another extended body already exists. If an extended body could occupy the space of another extended body, the whole world could revert to the space of a single mustard seed without assuming the non-existence of any part of it. That this is false is known axiomatically. If the elements were to intermingle with one another, the same space might combine in itself heat which is the form of fire, humidity which is the form of air, cold which is the form of water, and dryness which is the form of earth, and that is also known to be false as an axiom of reason. If they claim that the elements adjoin one another and that each element is particular in its own space and is discrete by virtue of its form, it must follow that they remain simple bodies, having the same forms and the same centres. The elements, however, are extensions, since they take up portions of extended space and possess shapes. They are portions of primary matter having forms. That ought to be sufficient for you in this handbook of doctrine.

Chapter: [*On willing things that come to exist*]

Seeing that this chapter concerns the functional characteristics of will, the creation of acts, and the applications of powers, we find it helpful to commence with matters of principle. We thus begin by citing the doctrine of the orthodox concerning the willing of things that come to exist and refuting the dogmas of those who oppose them. Our doctrine is that God, the Exalted, wills the coming into existence of every contingent thing. But the Creator's will does not have particular application to any one type of contingent thing over another. Rather, He willfully determines the occurrence of all contingent things, the good and the bad, the beneficial and the harmful.

There are among our masters those who uphold this in general but not in specific detail. Thus, if they were asked whether God, the Exalted, wills that unbelief exists, in answering, they would not specifically admit the application of will in respect to it, even if they believe it to be the case. Instead they would refrain from admitting it to avoid any chance of being accused of serious error on that basis, since many people imagine that whatever God, the Exalted, wants, He commands and makes happen. However, often a term is employed to signify a general rather than particular sense. Thus, if you were to say: The world and all it contains is God's, but then, if the question led on to the matter of a son and a wife, you would not say that God, the Exalted, has a wife and a son. Those of our masters who were most correct ascribed the application of the will to all contingent things, in both the general and the particular sense, and both at large and in specific detail.

Among the items about which the orthodox differ as to whether to acknowledge or not are matters involving God's liking and approval. If someone, for example, asks: Does God, the Exalted, like the unbeliever to disbelieve, and does He approve of it? Among our masters, there are some who do not admit this and they disapprove of it. Thereafter, they are divided into two parties. One of them maintains that liking and approval express God's beneficence and favour. These are among the attributes of His action. When one says: "God, the Exalted, loves a human", that does not suggest an affection or sympathy for him but rather indicates God's beneficence toward His servant. The love of the human for his Exalted Lord indicates his submission and obedient compliance towards Him. God, the Exalted, however, transcends in His sanctity either favouring or being favoured. Another construes liking and approving as meaning willing. Thus instead he says: When will applies to the beneficence accorded the human, it denotes liking and approving. When it applies to the chastisement inflicted on the human, it indicates displeasure. The person who regards liking as an attribute of action would construe being displeased as such as well.

The most correct of our masters forcefully resisted the bugaboo of the Muʿtazilites and maintained that liking means willing, as also does approving. The Exalted Lord likes the unbelief and approves of it as an unbelief meriting punishment. Once it is affirmed that liking is willing, there follows from this a consequence that runs throughout this chapter without having been intended here. This is that you understand that liking is not really applicable to the Exalted Lord, since willing applies only to something yet to come and the Exalted Lord is eternal and without beginning. It, in contrast, implies the future existing of what does not exist but whose existence is possible and the non-existence of what has the possibility of being non-existent. But the being whose eternality is proven and who cannot be non-existent, cannot be the subject of will. What confirms the truth here is that, having admitted that the uniting of two contraries is impossible and that this impossibility is necessary, this will preclude a person's wanting the impossibility of uniting two contraries. Similarly, a person who believes that black is necessarily black cannot possibly want black to be black if he is already convinced of its necessity and considers that it continues to exist as such. Here we will redirect our discussion back to the real purpose of this chapter.

The Muʿtazilites maintain that, except for those involving wishing and loathing, the Exalted Lord wills His actions. He wants those acts done by the human that consist of obedience and good works; He loathes those that are forbidden. With respect to those that are simply permissible or those within the power of animals and children and which also do not fall under an imposed obligation, the Lord, in their view, neither wishes nor loathes them.

We have two rational methods available to examine this. One is based on the creation of acts in that we have explained that God, the Mighty and Glorious, is the Creator of every creation. Accordingly, His willing every contingent thing, purposely bringing it into existence, and creating it, is necessary. The second is for us to restrict the intellect to methods not dependent on the previous premise by introducing tradition and the requirement of sacred law.

Of the points we can prove this way, one is for us to say: Those who affirm the existence of the Exalted Maker agree together that He is beyond and transcends all marks of imperfection and the stain of impotence. Persons of intelligence agree also that the most valid sign of authority and the most authentic indicator of perfection is to be able to accomplish what one wants and the contrary indicates its opposite. If the Muʿtazilites claim that the Lord, may He be sanctified and exalted, has a loathing for most of what the human being does and yet it takes place despite His loathing, they have judged Him impotent. They are saying: The Lord wants what will not be and there is something in existence He did not want. Thus His will has no effect on His creation; His wishes carry no weight in His kingdom and many contingent things occur there, however and whenever the devil and his legions want them to.

To defend against this, the Muʿtazilites attempt various ruses that are readily grasped by nearly anyone and thus easily avoided. We will review here what they believe works to this end since they think little of the common person and the masses. What they cite is to say that the Exalted Lord is able to compel the people and force them to have faith by causing the appearance of a sign towards which the necks of tyrants would bow in submission. He must necessarily be thought impotent if He were not able through compulsion and subjugation to manipulate the people as He wishes. But what they say presents a worthless hoax, since they are of one mind that the Lord does not create the faith of the believers or the obedience of the obedient. According to them, the meaning of compelling is only the causing of a sign to appear that is so terrifying the unbelievers will believe when they witness it. But, even saying this is worthless, since it is quite conceivable that, no matter how awesome the miracles, a group of the unbelievers will, even so, persist in their lack of faith and never concede the truth. This is not unlikely nor impossible rationally. What is asserted here is that the Muʿtazilites maintain that perhaps there exists a human about whom God, the Exalted, knows it is not within possibility that God has a grace He could bestow on him such as to cause him to believe. If this is not inconceivable in regard to grace, it is not unreasonable in respect to terrifying miracles.

What closes off this contention is for us to say: If they were compelled, their faith would not merit reward, in your view, and, if that were admitted, it would be repugnant. The Lord, may He be sanctified, wills nothing repugnant, according to your own claim, but rather He only wants the faith that can be rewarded. It is a requirement of free choice that it be devoid of compulsion and coercion. What they want in this case cannot be realized; and what is realized is impossible to want. But God is high indeed above the doctrine of the falsifiers.

If they say now: If it were possible for there to be what God forbids but not what He commands, this does not preclude also that there occurs what He loathes and not occurs what He wants. This, however, evades the question, since what he commands but does not occur does not occur only because He does not wish it to occur. The non-existence of the occurrence is not due to other than He in such a way as to implicate God with an incapacity. If what He wants does not occur, the ineffectiveness of the will is [not] brought about by something other than He. Thus there is a great separation between what they held against us and what they now are compelled to accept.

Among the things that strongly support our doctrine is that, prior to the appearance of deviation and the agitation of diverse opinions, there was general agreement among the earlier generations of the righteous upon a formula that was accepted without any number of the elaborations susceptible to invented interpretations. This was to say: What God wants happens and what God does not want will not happen.

Of those things that sow confusion in their minds one is the fact that the scholars, without exception, agree that the debtor is acquitted of his liability when he says: "By God the amount due my creditor will be satisfied tomorrow, if God, the mighty and glorious, so wills." If the term fixed and the period of waiting lapses, and he does not satisfy it, he has not broken the oath he swore because of his exception based on God's being willing. It is as if one were to say that he will satisfy his debt tomorrow, if Zayd so wills. But Zayd's willing is doubtful and uncertain. If the Exalted Lord wanted the debt satisfied inevitably this would be the same as if he had said: I will satisfy the debt due my creditor tomorrow, if Zayd wills. Then subsequently Zayd so wills and he does not satisfy it. In that case the debtor would have indisputably broken his word.

Another point in support of our position is for us to say: The Exalted Lord, according to you, wants the faith of the unbelievers and that is obligatory upon His having made a determination of it. Explain then, you Muʿtazilites, what we raise as an issue here. Specify for us the moment at which His will is determined, since it is your doctrine that the will is contingent. They will certainly be incapable of indicating here a specific moment in time and they will thus find no corroboration for their opinion.

Another specious argument of the Muʿtazilites – one of those they are devoted to and to the discussion and refutation involved in it – introduces a principle about which there is contention. This is for them to say: The commanding of something implies that the commander is purposeful and it is impossible, according to the dictates of reason, that the person commands something he loathes or rejects. Similarly, the prohibition of something implies its being loathsome to the prohibiter. It is impossible, by the very nature of interdiction, for the person making the prohibition to have wished for what he prohibited. They insist on this point and maintain that coupling a preemptory command to the display of loathing for what is commanded by it involves a mutual contradiction which is tantamount to combining together the command for something and the prohibition of the same thing. Thus there would be no distinction between a person saying, "I command you to do such-and-such and I forbid you from doing it", and that person saying, "I command you to do such-and-such and I disapprove of your doing it". It now being clear that all things commanded are willed by the commander of them, it follows from this that the Exalted Creator wants the faith of the person whom He knows will not believe because He commands that person to believe.

This can be answered in several ways. One of them is to explain that, in the commander's loathing of what He had ordered done, what they consider inconceivable is not implausible in the visible world. The compilers of collections have given examples that fulfil our purpose but we will do with but one of them. This is of a man who applies correction to slaves of his but is excessive in curbing and subduing them and continues to beat them. News of this spreads and reaches the sultan at the time who sets about to reprimand the man who is excessive in his correction. When the man is brought before him and his case is unfolded in front of him, the man responds with the excuse: I did only what I did because of the insubordination of my slaves and their recalcitrance and their open display of opposition to me. But the sultan doubts the matter and does not trust what he has said and his irritation against him persists. The master of the slaves, wishing to verify his statement and remove the suspicions in the matter, says to the sultan: "As the sign of my veracity, I will summon my slaves and give them, in your presence and hearing, a decisive order that has no room in it for ambiguous interpretations. If they refuse me and disobey my order, my veracity will be perfectly clear to the king. If they obey me, I will then be subject to his anger." But, when thereafter he summons them, commands them to do something, proscribes them from it, or reprimands them, there would still be no doubt but that he really wants them to act against him in order to confirm the excuse he has just given.

If they should now say: What was issued in this supposed case was not a command in reality and its purpose was not actually to require obedience, to that we reply: This is to deny the evidence since the command issues from the master in association with adjoining conditions that decisively entail obedience and is of such a nature that the slaves can have no doubt in the matter but rather must certainly comprehend its entailing obedience from them as necessarily being what is sought and desired. How would it be possible to construe the command, which is connected to the associated circumstances, differently from what it is plainly and self-evidently known to entail? How could the command be like this and yet the excuse of the master would only be valid on condition that his order was peremptory and its significance unambiguous? If the command could be like that, his excuses would be unacceptable and his explanation out of order.

Among the things to prove that what is commanded does not require that it be desired by the person commanding it is the principle of abrogation which is the revocation of a ruling subsequent to its first being issued. It is impossible to assume that what is abrogated was actually intended. If the obligatory becomes interdicted and forbidden, it requires, according to the principle of the Muʿtazilites, that what was once wanted becomes reprehensible. But that is inadmissible in the decisions of God, the Exalted, according to unanimous agreement. If upheld, this would indicate something new in Him, but God, the Exalted, transcends all that. Having established that abrogation falls unexpectedly upon what is commanded by it, and determined that approbation does not change into disapproval, it follows, as a result, that what was first commanded did not occur in accord with the wishes of the commander.

They may say here: Abrogation does not comprise the annulment of the original rule but indicates nothing more than the time period during which the act of worship applied in line with a special application of the rule; for them to hold this, is to make abrogation altogether invalid and imposes instead the doctrine of its rejecters, such as the Jews and others. We will discuss abrogation and its true reality and refute those who reject it in the section on prophecy, God, the Mighty and Glorious, so willing.

In the matter of what is commanded, perhaps, not being desired by the person issuing the command, the leading masters found support in the story of Abraham and his son, the sacrificial victim, on both be peace. He, may God bless him and grant him peace, was commanded to sacrifice his son but that was not actually what was wanted of him.

To avoid God's own argument, the Muʿtazilites recklessly proceed in ways that saved them not at all from the issue posed here. Among these is to say: Abraham, on whom be peace, was not ordered to sacrifice his son in actuality. He only envisioned the command in his dream and then took it as a command. This is a horrendous slight and belittling of their stature. How is it possible for a religious person to ascribe to Abraham, the friend of the Most Merciful, a resolve to sacrifice his son without being decisively commanded to do so? How could it be believed that the prophet did not know with certainty whether he had been commanded to do it or not? To admit this is to reject all credence in the commandments of God, the Exalted, which these prophets have conveyed.

Another way of theirs is to say: He was only ordered to seize and tie him, turn him prostrate on his face, sharpen the knife, and prepare the steps leading up to the sacrifice but not the sacrifice itself. But this is of the same sort as the first. We know with certainty upon believing in the story that Abraham, on whom be peace, was deeply upset at having to sacrifice his son and it caused him enormous suffering, as God, the Exalted, said: "Truly that was a manifest trial" [37:106]. His being ransomed with the great sacrifice is the best sign of this. It is not permissible to believe that the prophet saw in the commandment of God, the Exalted, something other than what it entailed.

It may be said: The proof that he was not ordered to make the sacrifice is that, when he tied his hands and feet solidly and laid him prostrate on his face, it was said to him then, "You have already confirmed the vision" [37:105]. This indicates his having complied with the requirements of the command and fulfilled it completely. But this is careless of them and overlooks the truth in the matter. It was not said, "You have realized the vision", but instead, "You have verified the truth of the vision", which is to say, you now believe it to be true and you hasten to do what you were ordered to do. Desist now from executing the order. You are relieved of it; your son is ransomed from the sacrifice you were commanded to perform because of the great sacrifice.

They may say: Abraham had cut the throat of his son and severed his jugular vein but, as he cut another part, what was cut previously mended and rejoined, and this continued like that until the blade exited from the other side, thus he had been commanded to perform the sacrifice and God wanted that of him; what they say here is a great calumny and an affront to the sense of the Holy Book. God said, in speaking of Abraham and his son: "So when they both submitted and laid him on his face, We called out to him, O Abraham" (to the end of the verse) [37:103–104]. The obvious meaning requires that, when he had laid him down, God called for him to let up. His having been ransomed is the most definite proof that he had not fully complied with what he was commanded to do. Furthermore, what they bring up here is not called a sacrifice. Sacrifice must consist of cutting through the throat and esophagus and severing the jugular veins in connection with this action, continuing to separate them, until the sacrifice is completed. Thus their tricks prove vain and the argument in God's own statements turns against them.

What they cite as the contradiction inherent in combining a command to do something and manifesting disapproval of it is simply a point for contention. In our view, no such contradiction occurs in combining the two. How could one allow the claim of the contradiction in it, when commandments of God, the Exalted, apply universally to all those subject to this obligation, and in addition there are passages in the Book of God, the Exalted, that are not amenable to divergent interpretation to indicate that God does not desire the unbelievers to have faith and the sinners to obey. If the commandment applies universally and if the verses that we draw upon indicate that He, may He be sanctified, intends the erring of the one who goes astray and the guiding of the one who is guided, that proves the falseness of their misrepresented claims.

A proof of this is that if one of us should say to his servant, I have taken away your illness, I have restored your strength and I have brought your preparedness to completion to such a point that, you may make an effort to acquire blessings, hasten to good works, protect the frontiers, even though I know for certain that you will sin, commit highway robbery, spread corruption in the land and employ the means I have provided you to a bad end, that would be considered contradictory either in customary usage or in the absolute sense. God, the Exalted, according to the principles of the Muʿtazilites, intends the best for the person He grants the respite of time, even though He knows that, in the time allowed him, he will pursue evil and follow passions, whereas, if he were to have died prior to maturity, he would have been saved and successful. If this is not contradictory, in their view, when assumed in the commandment of God, there is no contradiction in the situation where they claim that it exists.

A point they often invoke is to say: Will acquires the characteristic of the thing willed by it. If what was willed was stupid, the willing of it was stupid. This fantasy of theirs is, however, worthless. One ought to seek of them a proof for it and not let them resort simply to such ungrounded allegations. Moreover, if willing stupidity were stupid, the willing of obedience would be obedience. The upshot of this would be that God, the Exalted, would be obedient because of His having willed obedience. This, however, violates the unanimous agreement of Muslims and runs away from correct religion. Furthermore, the will according to us, is eternal. Only if it were contingent and had a beginning could it be characterized as stupid or its opposite. What verifies this is that whoever seeks to acquire knowledge of abominations and the impieties of the impious, without being pressed to do it, that constitutes a stupidity on his part. The Exalted Lord knows all things known, both the good and the bad, but the fact of His having knowledge does not characterize Him by the traits that are attributed to any of us who acquires knowledge of something.

These are the fundamental arguments behind their sophisms. In warning against them and outlining various ways to avoid them, we have shown how to pass beyond them to others.

Chapter: [*Various arguments of the Muʿtazilites*]

The Muʿtazilites draw inferences from the exterior wording of the Book of God, the Exalted, and do not delve into its essence and grasp its true significance. Here an example would be God's statement: "And He does not approve ingratitude in His servants" [39:7]. There are two ways of responding to this verse. One is to deduce from it the necessity of adhering to the doctrine of those who distinguish between approval and will. The other way is to construe the word "servants" as those granted the grace of faith and the inspiration of certitude. They are the ones honoured by being mentioned here in direct connection with God, may He be sanctified. This verse has the same sense as God's saying: "A fountain from which the servants of God drink" [76:6]. What is intended here is not all the servants of God but rather the chosen who are destined for eternal bliss.

Another verse they rely on is God's statement: "The polytheists will say, 'If God had so wished, we would not have been polytheists'" (to the end of the verse) [6:148]. They maintain that the indicator of a proof in this verse is that the Lord, may He be sanctified, Himself reports it. He explains clearly that they said: "If God had so wished, we would not have been polytheists." Then He rebuked them and repudiated their contention. If they had been speaking correctly and openly declaring what was true, they would not have been reprimanded.

We say: They deserved the rebuke because they had ridiculed religion and sought to oppose the prophets' entreaties. They had already heard that the laws of the apostles consign all matters to God, the Exalted. Thus, when they were requested to embrace Islam and submit to its regulations, they sought to apply the arguments they had used against the prophets. They said: "If God had so wished, we would not have been polytheists (to the end of the verse)." It was not their intention to mention the content of their own beliefs. The proof of this is the continuation of God's statement: "Say, is there any knowledge among you; if so, produce it for us. But instead you follow only conjectures." [6:148]. How could the matter not be like this, seeing that faith in the attributes of God, the Exalted, derives from faith in God Himself; and not to believe in these verses is not to believe in God Himself.

One way they have of abusing the common people is to make inferences from God's statement: "I have not created the jinn and humans except to worship Me" [51:56]. This verse is general in its formulation, though susceptible to particularization for those who uphold its generality. It is ambiguous for those who deny its generality. Furthermore, it is not allowed to draw inferences pertaining to matters of certitude from items susceptible to interpretation or of an ambiguous character. It is a doctrine of the Muʿtazilites that generalities, if they are taken in the particular sense, become ambiguous with respect to the rest of the things designated. Thus there is no disagreement that children and the insane are specifically exempted from the obligation contained in the verse in question.

Furthermore, one could say that the object of the verse was to make clear that God, the Exalted, is not in need of His creatures, while they are reliant on Him. This is its purpose. A sign of this is God's stating next: "No sustenance do

I require of them, nor do I want them to feed me" [51:57]. It is as if the meaning of the verse in question is: I have not created the jinn and humans for them to benefit me. I created them solely in order to command them to worship Me.

Moreover, the root meaning of "worship" is self-abasement. A passable road is one reduced by being subjected to trampling, shoes, hoofs and the feet of travellers. Thus the intended meaning in this verse is: I have not created them except for them to humble themselves before Me. Those who submit humbly reveal their self-abasement. In regard to those who rebel and abjure, plain and obvious evidence indicates their self-abasement, despite their false accusation and calumny. Interpreting the verse in this way is preferable to finding in it a contradiction. Since the Exalted Lord knew that the majority of people would not believe, one might assume the following meaning: And I have not created those I knew would not believe except to receive My grace. But that cannot be.

They also invoke God's statement: "Whatever good happens to you is from God, whatever evil happens to you is of your own doing" [4:79]. To that we respond: The verse preceding this verse contains definite proof of the falseness of your doctrine. There it says: "If some good happens to them, they say this comes from God; if some evil befalls them, they say this comes from you [the Prophet]. Say: all is from God. What is it with these people, they hardly understand anything that happens" [4:78]. The word "happen to" is evidence denying freedom of choice because it is not used except in regard to something humans receive without seeking. One does not say that walking or an occupation happened to so-and-so, but one does say that a sickness, happiness or madness happened to him.

The meaning of the verse is that the unbelievers among the Quraysh would say, when faced with drought or earthquakes: These are evil omens concerning Muḥammad and his mission. But, if conditions were good for them, they said: This is due to us and our gods. So God, the Exalted, disapproved of them and spoke to His Prophet, on whom be peace, about them; they are the ones meant when He said: "Whatever good happens to you" – meaning here in the way of benefits – "is from God; and whatever evil happens to you" – that is to say, hardships – "it is recompense for your actions." Accordingly, the Muʿtazilites do not uphold the obvious and literal sense of the verse since, in their view, good and evil emanate from the acts of humans. They occur by the power of the human, outside of the power of God, the Exalted. Thus, according to them, the human produces both [good and evil].

Occasionally, they adduce, in regard to the creation of acts, God's statement, may He be hallowed and exalted: "So blessed be God, the best of creators" [23:14]. They claim that this indicates that humans are qualified by being able to create and invent. But this is mere fancy on their part and is erroneous. The word "create" [*khalq*] signifies, in this instance, "to measure". An example of this is to call the shoemaker *khāliq* because he measures the size of one shoe by another. Another is the saying:

And you indeed have cut what you measured [*mā khalaqta*]
But some people measure [*yakhluqu*] and then do not cut.[2]

God, the Exalted, having mentioned the effusion of sperm at the various stages of creating, at determined moments and times fixed and specified by Him, He then states: "So blessed be God, the best of the *khāliqīn*." It means the best of those who measure. But, for the Muʿtazilites, the human would be a better creator than God Himself, may He be exalted above their words, since the best of the creators is the one whose creation is best and, among the creations of the human, is faith in God and that is a better creation than the creation of bodies and their accidents.

Following this, in regard to the issue of produced things coming to occur by the will of God, the Exalted, we here derive support from texts of the Holy Book. God, the Mighty and Glorious, has said, "Even if We were to send angels to them", continuing to His saying, "They would not be believers unless God so wills" [6:111]. And God's statement: "If God had so willed, He would have gathered them together unto guidance" [6:35]. Also His words: "Those whom God wishes to guide, He opens their breast for Islam and those whom He wishes to lead astray He makes their breasts closed up and constricted as if they were climbing up to the sky" [6:125]. The texts we have invoked when speaking about guidance, being led astray, the stamp and the seal all prove exactly that to which we subscribe.

Chapter: [*On grace and abandonment*]

The bestowing of assistance is the creation of the power to obey and the abandonment is the creation of the power to disobey. It follows that the recipient of assistance will not disobey, since he does not have the power to disobey. The inverse of this statement is the same. The Muʿtazilites turn the bestowing of assistance into the creation of a state of grace in which the Exalted Lord knows that the human will have faith. Abandonment is construed as the preclusion of this grace. However, the things known to God, the Exalted, do not include the right to this grace for every one but rather some of them – those God knows will have faith if He grants them grace. And in regard to some of them, He knows that what gives others faith will, in them, only increase the tenacity of their tyranny and the persistence of their hostility.

The sum of these principles forces them to maintain that the Exalted Lord cannot be said to have the power to bestow the state of grace on all creatures but this is contrary to religion and the clear texts of the Holy Book. God, the Exalted, has said: "Had We so wished, We would have brought each soul its own guidance" (to the end of the verse) [32:13]. And He also said, "If your Lord had

2 The poet is Zuhayr b. Abī Sulmā; see his *Dīwān*.

so wished, He could have made of the people one nation but they continued with their differences" [11:118], and other verses like these.

Impeccability is this assistance in its very essence. When it is general, it is the bestowing of general assistance; when it is particular, it is the bestowing of particular assistance.

Chapter: [*On censuring the Proponents of Qadar*[3]]

People of religions are in agreement about censuring the Proponents of *Qadar* and they curse them. The apostle of God, God bless him and keep him, said: "The Proponents of *Qadar* have been cursed by the tongues of seventy prophets." No one refuses to curse them. But some people attempt to avert from themselves these discarded notions by using arguments that do not serve that end. They say, for example: You Proponents of *Qadar*, if you believe in attributing the power to God, the Exalted, this is both astonishing and impudent. The apostle of God, God bless him and keep him, has said: "The Proponents of *Qadar* are the Magians [Majūs] of this community." He compared these people to them because of their making a distinction between the good and the bad in the application of will and volition in the same manner as the Magians in ascribing the good to Yazdān and the bad to Ahriman. The apostle of God, God bless him and grant him peace, said: "When the Day of Resurrection dawns, a crier will cry out among the people of conformity, 'Where are the opponents of God, the Exalted?' And the Proponents of *Qadar* will stand up."

That being peculiar to them is obvious because the orthodox consign all of their affairs to God, the Exalted, and do not protest against anything He does. Those who ascribe the power to themselves and believe it to be one of their own attributes, are more aptly qualified by the term *Qadarī* than those who ascribe it to their Lord.

These explanations are conclusive in the matter of the creation of the acts, the capacity and whatever pertains to them. We precede now to delve into the various aspects of justice and injustice, and imploring God, the Exalted, to assist us, we consign all our affairs to Him.

3 As mentioned previously the word *qadar* can mean both radical predestinarianism in which God has predetermined the fate of all humans and its opposite wherein that power belongs to the human being. Al-Juwaynī is not quite clear about what he refers to but it may be, in the first instance, simply the attribution of evil to God.

Section
The Doctrine of Justice and Injustice

Chapter: [*Preliminary points and the issues*]

Know, may God guide you in the best way, that this important principle and momentous matter contains within it two preliminary points and three issues. One of the preliminary points involves rejecting those who hold that the intellect ascertains what is good and bad. The other is that God, the Exalted, is not obligated by the dictates of intellect. As for the three issues: the first concerns the explanation by the various adherents of religions of God's inflicting pain on those servants and creatures of His whom He causes to suffer pain. This question includes, as subdivisions, the discussions of reincarnation and compensations. The second issue concerns what is suitable and what is most suitable; and the third is about grace and its significance.

Once we have finished examining these fundamental principles, we then will broach the question of miracles and we will delineate the proofs of the prophets, as recorded in the traditions that are the foundation of belief. But it is God alone who leads us to what is correct.

All matters that we will explain up to the end of this creed are comprised in the third of the parts that we have planned. That one is an analysis of what one can say about the characteristics of God.

Chapter: [*The good and the bad*]

The intellect does not ascertain the goodness of a thing or its badness in matters pertaining to the governance of religious obligation. Something's being good or bad falls solely within the disposition of the law and the requirements imposed by tradition. The principle behind this doctrine is that nothing is good in and of itself, nor by virtue of the class of things to which it belongs, nor because of a quality inherent in it. The doctrine concerning what is bad is the same. According to the law, a thing may be good of which the like and equal of it in the sum of its characteristic essential attributes would be bad.

Having established that, for the orthodox, goodness and badness do not derive from a genus or an essential attribute, the meaning of goodness is that for the doing of which the law confers praise, and what is meant by the bad is that for the doing of which the law confers censure. The Muʿtazilites hold that goodness and badness are perceived by the intellect in a general manner, that the perception of them is not subordinate to the tradition, and that the good is good because it has the attribute of goodness. They make a similar declaration in regard to the bad. This then is the basis of their doctrine. At times, however, they become confused about it and, in expounding the doctrine, are unable to convert the good and the bad into two attributes of goodness and badness.

One point that must be grasped, prior to plunging further into the matter in question, is that our leaders were quite tolerant in articulating their doctrine. They said: Goodness and badness are perceptible only in the law. But this attitude could allow misconstruing goodness and badness as being factors ancillary to the law in that the very perceiving of them is subordinate to the law. The matter, however, is not like this. Goodness is not an attribute whose perception is ancillary to the law but is merely an expression applied to the person on whose action the law confers praise. It is the same for badness. When we describe an act as being either obligatory or prohibited, we do not mean to imply that, by specifying this, we are distinguishing the quality in an act that is obligatory from another in the one that is not obligatory. What is meant by "obligatory" refers merely to the act which, because the law commands it, is obligatory. What is meant by "prohibited" is the act which, because the law forbids it, is prohibited and proscribed.

The Muʿtazilites next make subdivisions for the good and the bad and claim that, in certain instances, the perception of the goodness or badness of an act occurs by necessity and intuition without the need for reflection. In other instances, the goodness or badness of it is perceived as a result of rational reflection. For the latter, the method by which they reason is to appraise the rational in comparison to the intuitively self-evident instances of things that are good or bad, and, in assessing the entailment of the badness and goodness in the intuitively self-evident, it can be related to the other. Thereafter, one correlates the entailments that are shared by them. Thus the badness of unbelief, according to them, is known intuitively. It is the same for unmitigated harmfulness in which there is no real purpose, and other like examples of their fantasies.

Our course is to direct against them the following statement: About what you insist is self-evidently good or bad, it is under contention and your assertions are rejected. If it is false to claim intuitive self-evidence in the sources, it is false also to correlate speculative things with them. This procedure, in brief, demolishes the principles of the Muʿtazilites regarding badness and goodness. If these principles are self-contradictory and their doctrines about what is suitable, about grace, the subjects of reward and punishment, and the rest are based on them, then all the openings for the discussion in the chapters devoted to justice and injustice have been close to them.

Here we ask them: Why did you claim an intuitive knowledge of the good and the bad, when you knew that those in opposition to you in this matter cover the face of the earth? The smallest group of them exceeds the minimum number of witnesses required for certitude. It is not acceptable to distinguish one group of scholars as those who, despite all being equally able to perceive it, have a special kind of intuitive knowledge?

They may now say: You had agreed with us in regard to the good and bad in situations of self-evidence. You oppose us only in the means that lead to this knowledge. You insist that what indicates the good and the bad is tradition and not reason. Difference among scholars about necessary knowledge is not inconceivable in regard to this point, since reports attested by multiple concordant witnesses comprise themselves self-evident knowledge. Al-Kaʿbī and his followers held that the path to knowledge is what is reported by multiple and concordant witnesses from which a proof is adduced, and that is not infringed by the occurrence of self-evident knowledge in regard to what is reported in this manner.

But what they have said here comes to nothing. Our detailed analysis of their doctrines, given previously, showed how it falls apart. We repeat now only that the good and the bad are not attributes of what is good and what is bad, nor are they aspects arising from them. There is no meaning for the good or the bad other than the advent in and of itself of the command or the prohibition. What the Muʿtazilites affirm about the good and the bad being attributes and characteristics we have denied on the basis both of reason and tradition. All of this shows that, over and above the differing methods we use leading to it, we are clearly not in agreement about this matter. This should be quite obvious to anyone who considers it carefully.

Among other things that will make the truth clear in regard to our rejection of the claims for self-evidence is that what they claim is known intuitively to be bad, their opponents agree in considering it to take place as an act of God, the Exalted, even in regard to being certain that it is good. They maintain, for example, that the Exalted Lord can inflict pain on one of His servants spontaneously without his having come to deserve it, without compensation for the pain caused, and without incurring a benefit or averting an injury equivalent to the pain.

Moreover, just as they hold definitively that this is to be considered possible in God's determining judgments, for that reason also, they know with certainty that, if it happens, it is good. There is no way to deny this. In this instance, reason declares a thing good, although it has a form which the Muʿtazilites determine is bad on the basis of self-evident knowledge. But, however they would arbitrarily determine something on the basis of self-evidence, it is now clear that they are not safe in their claim from being contradicted by its opposite. Self-evident knowledge adjudges good what they declare bad and bad what they find good.

They may say here: The proof that bad and good are perceived by reason is that those who deny the revealed laws and reject the prophetic missions know nevertheless that injustice and infidelity are bad and gratitude is good. If the situation in regard to these matters depended solely on tradition, those who deny it would not comprehend the good and the bad. It yields them, however, no benefit to say this. In the first place, it is to argue over a situation involving self-evidence, according to their own claim, and reasoning does not apply in a situation which is self-evident.

Now we say: There might be a way to continue with what you are saying, if one conceded that the Barāhima,[1] who deny the revealed law, know the good and bad. But that is a contested point. It is not inconceivable for sects to persist in their beliefs under the impression that they are true when they are not true. This is the situation of those who accept belief in religious principles blindly.

What confirms our point here is that the Barāhima, who, like the Muʿtazilites, hold, according to their own claim, that determination of the good and the bad is a rational matter, would therefore believe that the slaughtering of animals, subjecting them to pain, and exposing them to hardship and overwork is bad. Their believing this, however, does not represent true knowledge, but rather ignorance. As it is not inconceivable that they should persist in such ignorance, likewise it is not unthinkable that they will persevere in a belief that is not true.

Another point the Muʿtazilites rely on for their claim of self-evidence is to observe: If a need offered itself to an intelligent person, and his purpose could be served by reaching either the truth or the false and there was no advantage in one over the other in making it possible for him to either acquire a benefit or avert an injury – if they were truly equal for him and the same in every respect – the intelligent person would inevitably go after the true and spurn the false. That person would choose the false only if he envisioned in it an interest which would add to what he would realize with the truth. But, if the objects were equal, reason would shun the false and go for the true. That cannot be the case unless the true is good according to reason.

What they say here is false in several respects. One is that it tries to draw the argument from a situation which they all agree is one of self-evidence. And the second is that what they say and conceive is contradictory. If the false is bad in and of itself, the person who did it previously deserves blame, censure and punishment in a general way; and it is to be characterized as vile and disgraceful. This is the necessary result of the doctrine of the Muʿtazilites. But then how can they picture the equality of the true and the false and presuppose the sameness of the interest in both, as in the doctrine of theirs we have just cited?

What verifies exactly our aim in this matter is their having said that the intelligent person inevitably goes after the true when his interests are equal. Thus it is necessary for them to exclude here the true from the rule of legal obligation, and the deserving of rewards for doing it and punishment for not doing it. There is no reward due the person compelled to do something imposed on him because he, in fact, did what he was forced to do. It is necessary that what is true follows the analogy of what they maintain is the rule for what intelligence forces on the intelligent person. What they hoped to sustain depended, however, on

1 The term Barāhima refers to the Indian Brahmans but it was used in the Islamic context to indicate those who do not believe in prophetic or revealed religion of any kind. For more detail see the study by Sarah Stroumsa, "The Barāhima in Early Kalam," *Jerusalem Studies in Arabic and Islam* 6 (1985): 229–41.

generalizing their argument from situations where the revealed laws, in fact, already determined that falsehood is bad and truthfulness is good.

If they were to reply: We limited our discussion to those who deny the revealed laws or those whom the laws have never reached, and the intelligent person, under these conditions, will prefer the truth, we answer: That can only be valid if the person you imagine that the discussion is about believes that falsehood deserves censure on the basis of reason. But this is not allowed and must be avoided. If we picture this in someone who does not hold that reason determines the bad and the good and whom the revealed law has not reached and for whom the good and the bad are equivalent in every respect, we do not concede that, under these circumstances, he will prefer the truth inevitably. Instead he would be prevented from having a preference either for the truth or the false. Your misrepresentations thus surely prove false.

Yet another point they invoke is to say: If the good were not known by reason prior to the coming of the revealed law, one would also not understand it when it did arrive. This is the weakest sort of argument. If, in regard to the rule of the legal obligation, we ascribed the goodness and the badness to the advent of the command and prohibition, that does not preclude presupposing its advent prior to its actual arrival and understanding the same situation. This is tantamount to the very knowledge of prophecy itself. We know, prior to the appearance of the miracles, that what establishes the truthfulness of the one that may be sent is an unprecedented disruption of ordinary events. We believe this even prior to the actual coincidence of the miraculous events with a claim of a prophetic mission.

Often they provoke discord by basing matters strictly on ordinary habit. They say: Persons of intelligence regard doing good as good, as for example, the rescuing of the drowning man and the saving of a dying man, and they consider injustice and enmity bad, even if they have no tradition that says so. But this is deceitful and fraudulent. We have not denied the natural tendency for pleasure or aversion to pain and other examples of this sort which they invoke, but our argument refers only to what is good according to the dictates of God, the Exalted, and what in it is bad.

The proof of what we hold is that, for instinctual habits to function, as in their claim, as the basis of the intelligent person's considering something bad or good, it would likewise mean that men of intellect persistently and continually declare reprehensible leaving male and female slaves alone to engage in debauchery with each other within the sight and hearing of their masters who have themselves the capability of keeping them away from each other. If they were to leave them alone and the conditions were these, according to the method they laid out, this would be considered reprehensible, even if it is certain that it is not bad according to the dictates of God.

Someone might say: These arguments of yours simply follow closely upon those of the opponents but what is your proof for what you would consider correct? Why have you changed the proper order and commenced the examination of the question by citing their dubious theories? To that we reply: We only undertook this because of our opponents claiming self-evidence in regard to the principles of badness and goodness. If we had begun with our own course of argumentation, they would have rejected it as running counter to what they believe on the basis of a claim of self-evidence in regard to the principles of badness and goodness.

And as for those who persevere in claiming this – and it is the doctrine of most of them – the best way of arguing with them is that just used. For those who desist from claims of self-evidence, we would argue against them in the regular manner. Thus we say here: When you characterize a thing as being bad, one of two conditions must apply. Either your saying that it is bad is based on the thing in and of itself or on an attribute of that thing, or it is not based on the thing in and of itself nor an attribute of that thing.

If one says that it is based on the thing in and of itself or an attribute of that thing, this is false for several reasons. The most readily accessible of them is that the killing that is unjust is the equivalent of the killing that is a punishment or revenge. Those who deny the equivalence of the two acts and the similarity of the two killings, deny what cannot be denied, and must repudiate all trust in the similarity of two like things. The falseness of this result is clear on the basis that what an intelligent person might do would not be qualified as being bad, despite actually having been done, if it was done by a youth prior to the age of legal capacity. Some of them dissent about this and they insist that what is done by a youth not yet of age is nevertheless bad. If they were to hold this, we would confront them in the first way.

Having proved false the bad thing being bad in and of itself, the only procedure after this is to hold either that the meaning of its being bad is due to the intervention of the revealed law that prohibits it, as we maintain and which is the plain truth of the matter; or that it is bad because of a factor other than the revealed law and is other than the bad thing in and of itself. If they should now hold this latter point, it should be said to them: If the thing is not bad because of itself and its being bad does not derive from the application of a prohibition, it is impossible that an attribute be bad because of another attribute. That attribute would not be either essentially or substantially an attribute for the bad thing. The sum of all this established the falseness of declaring an act either bad or good in regard to the rule of legal obligation.

In this chapter we exceeded the limits of conciseness a little but it set the stage in principle for everything that is to follow afterwards in regard to the characteristics of justice and injustice. You will find that the issues to follow are based on that foundation and, in grasping them, the falseness of everything else will be proven. This is one of the two preliminary points promised earlier.

Chapter: [*That neither humans nor God are subject to the obligations of reason*]

The second preliminary discussion consists of the refutation of those who maintain that the intellect indicates a necessary obligation. This point has two parts. The argument in one of them applies to the supposition of an obligation covering the human and the second is devoted to the refutation of those who believe that something is necessary for God, may He be exalted above the words of those who make false claims about Him.

The first part resembles the preceding question concerning badness and goodness. All of their specious arguments and claims of self-evidence that we cited and which we rejected as objectable and against which we set out arguments, return again in the present question.

To prove that the obligation of gratitude towards the benefactor is known rationally, they have recourse to another formula. This is to say: The intelligent person, having recognized that he has a Lord, even at the beginning of his reflection, considers it likely that the Lord, who is his benefactor, expects from him an expression of gratitude. If he thanks the Lord, the Lord will reward him and confer on him an abiding place of rest. If he is ungrateful, the Lord will punish him and bring about his destruction. When he contemplates the two possibilities, the intellect instructs him to prefer what leads him to security against the chastisement and to an anticipation of rewards. They coined the following example for this: A traveller encounters two paths on his journey. Each of them leads to his goal but one is free of dangers and devoid of harmful things while the second may involve hazardous accidents, brigandage and the attacks of savage beasts. He has no interest in pursuing the course of danger, and thus reason determines that he follow the course of safety.

In citing this situation, they have limited the conditions of the reasoning process so that, if pursued to its end, it will cause them to reach the truth. But should the same person reflect about what they said, he may come across another thought that runs contrary to the first. This is for him to realize that he is a possessed slave, submissive and subservient, and that the slave can do nothing but what his owner permits him to do. Although he may exhaust himself and expend great effort, without his lord's permission, he will be simply overworked and troubled. This thought will be even stronger when he realizes that the Lord who is his benefactor has no need of the gratitude of the grateful since He is above needing anything. He, who is the Mighty and Glorious, having begun beneficence before it could have been deserved, He requires nothing in exchange for it. If this thought were raised against what they have mentioned, the intellect would order the person confronted with the original two options to abstain from deciding altogether.

What confirms our point is that, should a great king give one of his slaves a piece of bread and afterwards that same slave wants to proceed systematically through the orient and the occident, praising the king for his beneficence and his generosity, and proclaiming his munificence, no one would consider that a good thing since, in relation to his power, what the king did was an insignificant trifle, a paltry commonplace. And, in relation to the power of God, the Exalted, all beneficence, added together, would be of less value and greater insignificance than the piece of bread among the king's possessions.

Should we want to refute what they had said in another manner, we might direct the discussion to someone who did not initially recognize his benefactor. Having then generalized their condition of confronting two options, we now say to them: This doctrine of yours concerns someone to whom thoughts occur and who reflects on them. What do you hold about the heedless and distracted person to whose mind nothing occurs. Such a person has lost the means to know about the obligation or that gratitude is required of him. This is a potent objection against the opponents.

It might be said: There is no doubt that God, the Exalted, put into the mind of the intelligent person at the beginning of the perfection of his mind the thoughts we mentioned. But to say this is to play games with religion. How many persons of intelligence procrastinate in the midst of their errors and continue their heedlessness without what they mention ever entering their minds! Furthermore, such thoughts at the commencement of reasoning constitute doubts, and doubt about God, the Exalted, is unbelief. The Creator, however, according to the principles of these people, does not create unbelief.

Were it to be said: God, the Exalted, will send to every intelligent person an angel to put a stamp on his heart and to utter in his soul a message he will hear, we say this is truly outrageous and is, moreover, an affirmation of speech without letters which is contrary to their own principle that speech is inconceivable without letters and sounds.

Should we want to settle this question definitively, we say here: The Exalted Lord is the Creator of all creations and there is no other Creator besides Him, as we have clearly specified. What the human appropriates is a creation of God's. There is no sense, therefore, in the intellect's indicating the necessity of anything to the human, given the impossibility of his making it occur. In fact, if the Exalted Lord requests something of His servant, the request is established according to the description we outlined in speaking about the specious arguments of our opponents concerning the creation of human acts. However, since we believe that the human does not make his act happen and that no request was previously directed at him, there is no sense in determining whether it is necessary, just as there is no meaning to determining the necessity in the actions of the atoms. Understand that well and be guided by it. This is one of the two parts to this chapter.

The second part comprises the denial of an obligation on God, the Exalted. Nothing is obligatory for Him. This question is a corollary of determining the good and the bad. The way to set out a proof in this matter precisely is for us to ask the person who believes that God, the Exalted, is subject to some obligation:

What do you mean by His being obligated? If he answers: I intend by this the directing of a command to Him, that is absurd by universal agreement, because God is the Commander and the command of no other being applies to Him.

If he says: The meaning of His being obligated is that, if He does not do what He must do, He will anticipate some loss, this is also absurd. Surely the Exalted Lord transcends acquiring benefits or suffering loss; and, seeing as God is exalted high indeed above these, there is simply no meaning for benefit and suffering loss or pains and pleasures. Then he says: The meaning in His being obligated is His doing good and being bad if He does not do it. He thus insists that His being good is an attribute He has in and of Himself but we proved that is false in a manner quite convincing.

Moreover, another thing they would require of God, the Exalted, is the recompense of deeds. We will dedicate a special section to this issue, if God so wills. Here we will observe in this regard a detail that accords with their doctrine. Thus we say: The deeds of humans are an acknowledgment by them of the blessing of God, the Exalted. In your view this is enjoined upon them, but reason does not dictate the requirement of compensation for discharging an obligation. If the human had a right to compensation for fulfilling the acknowledgment imposed on him, it would be necessary that the human has the obligation of a new acknowledgment of God, the Exalted, whenever He grants him a reward, if, in fact, the reward itself is obligatory. They have no way out of this and never will. As far as requiring of Him the best and grace, we will introduce that subject later.

This evaluation accomplishes our purpose in regard to the two preliminary points. Now we will take up the issue of God's causing pain to humans and beasts in the present world.

Chapter: [*On suffering and its characteristics*]

Pains and pleasures do not fall within the power of any being other than God, the Exalted. Since they happen as an act of God, the Exalted, they are good in respect to Him, whether they occur instantaneously or come from Him in time, as what is called reward. In presupposing them to be good, the orthodox have no need to assume the prior meriting of them, or to expect them to fulfil a commitment for compensation, or to begin to procure a benefit or repulse some harm that is concomitant to them. Instead whatever of them should occur is good on the part of God, the Exalted, and cannot be held against Him in judging Him. Those who do not accept the assignment of all matters to God, the Exalted, have become disordered in their opinions.

We will relate here a summary of the tenets of the unorthodox sects. Thereafter, we will delineate briefly a statement refuting each group decisively, God willing. The subject of this discussion is the causing of suffering to children who have never been guilty of unbelief and have not committed a sin, and also a statement about inflicting suffering on beasts.

The Dualists,[2] who affirm two governors of the world, have said that suffering is unjust and bad in and of itself, no matter how it is taken. Suffering, in its totality, issues, according to them, from Ahriman and not from Yazdān. The Bakriyya,[3] which is a small group related to Bakr b. Ukht ʿAbd al-Wāḥid, maintained that beasts do not suffer at all and it is the same with children who have not reached the age of reason and submitted, by virtue of the ability to reason, to the commandments.

Groups of the Ghulāt[4] among the Shīʿa and others believe in reincarnation. They say that animals suffer only because their souls were previously in bodies and shapes that were better than those of animals but they yielded to grave sins and committed grievous crimes. For these they were transferred into other bodies in which to be punished. Once they complete their penalty and receive the punishments they have earned, they will be restored to a better form. The premise of their doctrine is that the Exalted Lord does not inflict suffering unprecedentedly but only after having been previously merited. Nor, according to them, is suffering good in anticipation of recompense or to acquire some benefit by means of it. Forms and individuals are classed by rank and degrees of lowliness and vileness. They are exposed to various kinds of suffering and their souls are transmuted in rank and degree in accordance with the sins they commit.

Another principle of this group is that all animals are under legal obligation and are cognizant of what suffering might happen to them as a penalty and punishment. If they were not cognizant of this, the suffering would not act as a restraint, keeping them from repeating sins like those they committed previously. One of them even held that every species of animal has a prophet sent specially to that particular species. Another maintained that none of the things in existence are inanimate. Everything that people imagine to be inanimate is actually alive and possesses a soul susceptible to punishment.

Their doctrines with regard to the commencement of legal obligation differed. One of them insisted that the Exalted Lord placed the souls under obligation from the beginning even though a necessary result of that was hardship and suffering. The rest of them, however, held that He did not impose obligations from the beginning but rather that He gave the souls the power to choose and they imposed on themselves the obligation. Some of them fulfilled the obligation and carried it out; others ignored it. According to the doctrine of yet others, the Lord imposed obligations on the souls from the beginning of their creation but not what involves hardship. Thereafter those who disobeyed disobey; those who complied comply.

2 By Dualists he obviously means here the Zoroastrians.

3 This group is all but unknown in Islamic heresiography.

4 The Ghulāt are the extremists who, generally speaking, believe in the superiority of ʿAlī b. Abī Ṭālib to Muḥammad. They are thus a part of the Shīʿa, although considered on the heretical fringe, even by the mainstream Shīʿa. Although some factions of these Ghulāt did believe in reincarnation it is unclear which ones the author refers to in this case.

The Ghulāt among the Proponents of Reincarnation denied the resurrection and eternal life. They claimed that there is nothing more than the transmigration of souls into various bodies and being subjected in them accordingly either to punishment or to reward.

As for the Muʿtazilites, they hold, when asked about the suffering endured by children and beasts, that suffering is good for several reasons. One is that it is merited by previous acts. Another is that it procures a compensatory benefit that is clearly superior. Yet another is that it facilitates the prevention of an injury more harmful than it. In regard to the suffering of beasts, they hold that it is good because the Lord will compensate them in the Abode of Reward with something that more than makes up for the suffering they were exposed to. Finally, the majority of them hold that the compensation consequent upon suffering is a degree less than the recompense consequent to legal obligation. They differ, however, as to whether this compensation endures as long as the rewards or not.

Their answers are mixed also as to whether to conceive the bestowal of favours as equivalent to the compensations from the beginning or not. Some of them held that this is impossible, just as it is impossible that the bestowing of favours is on a par with the rewards for the obligatory acts, the impossibility of that being generally agreed upon. Those among them who rely on the most detailed analysis maintain that the bestowal of favours proportional to the compensations is possible and is not inconceivable. Those who hold to the impossibility of the bestowal of favours being equivalent to the compensations allow that the occurrence of suffering is for the sake of a pure compensation. Those who admit that the bestowal of favour is equivalent to the compensations do not, in their view, regard suffering as good because of compensation. Rather they maintain that it is good only in two conditions which must be found together: one is that compensation is necessary and the other is that the suffering be an example for those who have not suffered and be thus a grace holding back those in error from their errors.

ʿAbbād al-Ṣaymarī[5] held that suffering is good purely in setting an example, without the presumption of a compensation for it.

These are the principles of the Muʿtazilites in regard to the infliction of suffering on beasts and children. Moreover, a complement to their principle is that the thing for the sake of which pain is considered good, when it is known, is also looked upon as good when one believes or presumes the thing for the sake of which suffering is regarded as good, according to the common habits of ordinary people. They say: It is similarly looked upon as good in the habits of learned people who impose hardships on themselves in hopes of obtaining benefits greater than these, even though the actual result of it is hidden from humans. The knowledge of hidden things belongs to God alone.

---

5 ʿAbbād b. Sulaymān al-Ṣaymarī (d. ca. 850/864) was an earlier Muʿtazilite. There is a short notice on him "ʿAbbād b. Sulaymān" by W. Montgomery Watt in the *EI2*.

Chapter: [*On compensations*]

What the Dualists hold in claiming that suffering is unjust and bad in its essence is quite obviously false. We know that for a sick person to drink a distasteful and repugnant medicine hoping by so doing to keep himself from being ill would not be considered, in the custom of intelligent people, a bad thing. It is not the same as a healthy person deliberately wounding himself without seriously intending to obtain some benefit or avoid some harm. Those who deny this are in league with those who reject the self-evident.

It might be asked of them: Is the good and the inclination to it recommended or not? If they deny that it is recommended, they have forsaken their own doctrine, in so far as the intellect advocates good deeds and warns against the bad. If, on the contrary, they say that the good is recommended, ask them: For the person who deviates from it, is there blame and suffering as punishment or not? If they respond: Evil does not necessarily enjoin punishment, they thus keep the company of evil and avoid the good; it is necessary for them not to cast blame on the person who does evil or to single out the person who does good with admiring praise. All of this proves the falseness of their doctrine about the intellect's determining what is good and what is bad. If now they say that the blame and suffering inflicted on the evil-doer, as well as his being subjected to anguish and distress, is good, they again contradict their own doctrine that suffering is bad in itself.

Chapter: [*Again on compensation*]

The Bakriyya deny self-evidence and reject intuition. We know self-evidently that beasts and children suffer pains, that they are tormented when they suffer pains, and that they have a strong aversion against what they know will cause them pain. If it were allowed to deny this fact, one could deny also that they are alive and proceed to claim that they are inanimate objects, unable to feel, or to suffer, or to perceive. But this ought to be enough to refute them.

As for the Proponents of Reincarnation, what induced them to make innovations and break with the community involves a point that can also be held against the Muʿtazilites and everyone else who maintains that the intellect determines what is bad and what is good. They hold that inflicting suffering from the beginning without compensation is bad and that, given the power to bestow favours equal to or many times more than the compensation, it is also not good simply to compensate for it. Nor is it good because of the intention to make an example for those who have not suffered, since it would be looked on as bad to inflict pain on Zayd to teach a lesson to ʿAmr. The only avenue remaining is to consider good the inflicting of pain by assuming that it constitutes a punishment for a previous case. That necessarily involves the prior imposition of obligation and the proscribing of opposition to it; and that the advent of later suffering is a punishment for what preceded.

We will explain later that the arguments of the Proponents of Reincarnation are directed against the Muʿtazilites but here we ask them what their doctrine is in regard to the commencement of the imposed obligation. If they should answer that the Exalted Lord made obligatory things the obeying of which is troublesome from the beginning, they envision being made to suffer and suffering without having committed a crime. In so answering, they contradict their own principles in every respect. If in hoping to escape from this, they now say: The good in imposing suffering from the beginning depends on a commensurate reward of great consequence, at this point we ask them: Why do you not regard as good the infliction of suffering on beasts and children in view of compensations to come? Should they answer: Bestowal of favours equal to compensation is possible but the bestowal of favours equal to the rewards is impossible, their statement here is merely arbitrary. There is no ultimate sum to the blessings that the Lord, may He be sanctified, has the power give, whether in bestowing favours, rewards or compensations. We will allude to that further when discussing the arguments of the Muʿtazilites.

If they now reply: God has not imposed hardships on humans, what they have said is false because, if He had not imposed hardships on humans, there would be no imposition at all and the matter would be disregarded as futile. How would one understand the commission of a crime? And in what way would the suffering be deserved? How could that be supported by those who ground the foundation of their doctrine on the determining of what is good and what is bad? If they reply: The Exalted Lord imposed on humans pleasures in which there is no hardship, respond: That is absurd. It is a self-evident corollary to the imposing of a religious obligation that the person under obligation believe in the necessity of what is imposed upon him. In requiring belief on his part and in punishment being the result if he does not believe in the necessity of what is imposed on him, he is exposed to quite obvious distress.

Moreover, the aim of imposing the obligation is to turn one's mind towards the rewards. It is only considered good in the intellect, according to the principle of determining good, if it provides a reward for those acts that were troublesome. If then it is allowed to limit the application of reason to the grant of reward only for those pleasures that are free of hardships, it is also permitted to repudiate the foundation on which they base the intellect's determining the badness of inflicting suffering.

If they say: The Exalted Lord delegates the imposition of obligation to the discretion of the souls, reply: If suffering is bad without being deserved, being exposed to it is also bad or being allowed to choose it or not. There is no escape for them from what they have forced upon themselves.

For us, however, there are two ways to proceed. One of them means ascribing to them the denial of the self-evident in their saying that beasts reason and that their own prophet summons them and that they apprehend the transmission of the message. But this is a rejection of the obvious evidence. To allow it is to allow that flies and worms ponder the most subtle of the sciences and that some of them come to understand from others after being exposed to argumentation, inferences, questioning and parrying the objections. But this is a ridiculous inanity no person of sense need accept. The second way is to prove to them the religious laws if they have not received them. Once these laws are established, the law will show them the falseness of their doctrines which circumvented the sources of the law. In attempting to refute them, this evaluation should do.

As for the Muʿtazilites, we mentioned that they hold that inflicting suffering is to be considered good for several reasons, and defaulting in which or in some particular of which is a bad thing. We will now examine successively each of these reasons and refute and dismiss them one by one.

As for their doctrine that suffering is to be considered good by virtue of being a punishment for a prior act, it is a matter of contention and calls for them to offer a proof. Ask them therefore: Why do you hold that suffering is considered a good thing if it constitutes a punishment? If they respond: We hold this because the intellect dictates that for the person who is treated unjustly or is oppressed and caused to suffer pain, whether without precedent or out of animosity, it is considered good that he demand justice from the one who mistreated or wronged him. If a slave misbehaves, no person of intelligence would consider rebuking him a bad thing. We then ask: On what basis do you reject those who claim that this would not be considered bad merely because the person seeking justice receives a benefit in his obtaining justice which is the appeasement of his rancour and the abatement of his anger and fury? Does the matter not thus turn out to consist of averting suffering by suffering? But our discussion is about the Exalted Lord inflicting suffering on whomever He wishes, even though He may dispense with doing it and is high indeed above anger and fury, and has no need to appease rancour. Did you not say yourself that the suffering He inflicts is not a good thing should He be able to dispense with it and has no need to do it? But what governs God in this does not follow the rule for humans! There is no way for them to escape from this.

If now they say: If the Exalted Lord could dispense with punishing criminals and, if He actually refrained from punishing them, that would constitute an encouragement of immoral acts and the commission of crimes and mortal sins, their notion here, however, is proven false by their own acceptance of repentance, since it, according to them, imposes an obligation on the part of God and, in that, there is the encouragement of sin by tempting the person to risk it because of believing that, when he repents and expresses contrition, his repentance for the wrongdoing will be accepted. We will return to this again in the section on rewards and punishment. In regard to the aspect of the issue under discussion here, however, this analysis is sufficient for our present purpose.

As for their doctrine that suffering is to be considered good by virtue of a compensation that provides a greater benefit, this is false in two respects.

One of the two is that the Exalted Lord has the power to bestow favours that are equivalent to what would constitute the compensation. But there is no point to the prior occurrence of suffering and then the compensation for it, when the power to grant such a favour was there from the beginning. That is like a person inflicting suffering on some poor fellow in order later to give him a piece of bread, when the same person already had the power to grant him the equivalent of it in the first place. This is even more certain for the dominion of God, the Exalted, whose power is so absolute that with Him no gift is grandiose or generosity extravagant. Humans, by contrast, are exposed to hardship and tightened straits and are in need of whatever they are given, even if it is little.

If now one of them should say: It is not possible to bestow favours equivalent to compensation, that is ridiculous. The compensations are either benefits temporary in nature or permanent and eternal. Whichever is the case, it is within the power of God, the Exalted, without presuming the infliction of previous suffering. Thus, if they maintain that, if the bestowing of favour were possibly equivalent to the compensation, the bestowing could be equivalent to the rewards, we answer: This is our doctrine exactly and we are refuting those who deviate from it.

In this matter, they have other confusions that I will come to explain in the section on rewards and punishment, God, the Mighty and Glorious, so willing.

The second method for discrediting the idea of suffering being good by virtue of compensation is for us to observe that, if a human commits a crime against another person and hurts him by cutting or wounding him or some other way, he is required to provide suitable compensation for the suffering, even without consulting the injured person or obtaining his permission. It is necessary for us to consider that good because it is good on the part of God, the Exalted. But the Muʿtazilites judge the functioning of God's activities according to the actions of human beings.

They may say: The suffering that comes from God is to be considered good only because He knows that there will be a compensation for it. Humans, however, have no means of knowing the outcome of their own activities. They do not have the right to cause suffering because of something the occurrence of which they cannot know for certain. This is false. The human can inflict suffering upon himself in the expectation of some benefit commensurate to the pain and fatigue he has undergone, even though that benefit is merely presumptive and not known with certainty. If that is good in regard to his own self, despite the outcome being hidden from him, it is good on the part of others.

Thus that on account of which they attempt to establish a distinction between the operations of God, the Exalted, and those of humans proves false. Whoever truly grasps what we have just said above will find it easy to deflect quickly all questions they might pose about issues we have not mentioned here.

The third method in the subject of declaring that suffering is good concerns saying this is so because it averts a harm greater than it. This is false and has no application in the domain of God, the Exalted. There is nothing harmful that one might hope to avert by some suffering except what God, the Exalted, already has the power to avert without that suffering. Thus there is no valid purpose for inflicting the suffering. The situation here is like that of a person who makes it possible for a child to avoid the attack of a ferocious beast by obliging him to proceed along a leisure path on which there are no dangers. But the condition in such a case, where the alternate course involved proceeding along a rough and uneven path full of thorns, would not be considered good for that reason.

Those among them who hold that the suffering is not considered good simply by virtue of the compensation unless it comprises also the intention of providing an example to another, uphold the absurd. If the intellect does not consider good the inflicting of suffering on some person for an objective, it would not consider it so because it provides a lesson for someone else. It does not regard decreeing the molestation of one individual in order to provide a lesson for another as being within the realm of justice. They might object and now claim that it was applicable only if we understand the inflicting of suffering as an example pure and simple. To that we reply: This will not save you from what you intended by it, since, if the simple fact of compensation does not keep the suffering from being unjust, that it exists is the same as its not existing and its providing an example remains merely abstract. What will make this clear is the following: someone who is informed by a prophet that, in his being inflicted with suffering, there is a lesson for someone else, he still has no right to inflict pain on him even if compensation would be required and is the result of being an example, a fact known to him because of having been informed of it by a truthful person of absolute unquestionable integrity.

Such are the methods by which to refute the Muʿtazilites consistent with our aim in this handbook of theology. All that we have said against these groups was based on close examination of the errors in their beliefs but, if we had confined ourselves solely to our own doctrine that repudiates the concept of the intellect determining the bad and the good, in so doing this would alone belie all of their principles.

This subject which concerns the doctrine of suffering and its function in relation to the good and the bad has now been covered. It is God from whom we seek assistance. From here we will next proceed to investigate the area of the good and the best and we will mix in with it the subject of grace, even though we kept the two separate when setting out the order for the introduction of principles in this book.

Section
[The Doctrine of the Good and the Best]

The Baghdādī and the Baṣran Muʿtazilites hold different ideas about this subject and their opinions vary widely. The doctrines of the leaders of the Baghdādīs support the notion that it is obligatory on God, the Exalted – may He be high indeed above what they say – to do what is best for His servants, both in their religion and in this terrestrial world. It is not possible for Him, given His wisdom, to omit anything that can be done towards the betterment of the present and future life. Rather, it is incumbent on Him to do the utmost that is in His power in order to provide the best for His servants.

They say also, in conformity with their doctrine, that the commencement of creation obliges God, the Mighty and Glorious, and is necessary as required by wisdom. When He creates those on whom He knows He will impose legal capacity, He must perfect their intellects and abilities and remove their defects. Everything that humans secure in the present and the future, according to these people, is what is best for them. They even go so far in generalizing this principle that they repudiate the obvious evidence. They would say that holding those people damned to the fires of hell in shackles and chains is better for them than being released. Similarly, in the present world, it is best for the impious to be cursed by God, that He make their deeds come to nothing, and that He withdraw the reward for their good works, if they should die before repenting.

The Baṣrans have denied most of this, although they agree with their brethren in the error of affirming obligations on God, may He be exalted and sanctified above their claims.

One area of agreement between the two groups is the necessity of rewards for the hardships of legal imposition and of compensations for undeserved suffering. They are in accord that, when the Exalted Lord creates a servant and perfects his intellect, He should not abandon him. Instead it is incumbent on Him to cause him to think and make it possible for him to locate the right way to salvation; if He imposes an obligation on the servant, He must, given His wisdom, bestow on him grace and do the utmost that is possible within His knowledge to bring the subject of the imposition to believe and obey, as we will mention in a special section devoted to the subject of grace, should God, the Mighty and Glorious, so will.

The authors of works on sectarian tendencies report that these people hold, in general, that it is necessary for God to do the best in religion and they differ only about doing what is best in the present world. This report is a bit exaggerated. Outwardly, it appears to condone errors. One might imagine that, according to the Basrans, it is obligatory that God begin by perfecting the intellect in order to make the imposition. But that is not the doctrine of any of the Muʿtazilites.

What the Basrans maintain is that God, the Exalted, confers out of generosity the perfection of the intellect at the beginning but bringing the impetus for the imposition into existence is not obligatory for Him. Should He impose the obligation on His servant, however, then following upon the imposition, He must make it possible and within his capacity and accord him also the grace of the maximum good. This is the sense of the statements by the leading masters who report their doctrine.

Among the points upon which they all agree is that it is obligatory on God for impious acts to spoil the effect of those of obedience, and that He accept repentance, and others that we have enumerated in the *Shāmil.*[1]

Our purpose now is to set out clearly the proof that counters the aberrations of the Baghdādīs. Then, having explained that refutation clearly, we will turn to the Basrans. We will array one faction against the other as a technique of identification so that, if they become mixed up, the guided person will perceive the real truth in among their confusions. And God is our supporter.

One argument we would invoke against the Baghdādīs, once having conceded to them, for the sake of debate, that intellect determines the bad and the good, is the following. Your principle entails that, in all cases susceptible of improvement, it is necessary for God, the Exalted, to do the very best possible. But, when you are pressed about what you hold, you adduce examples from the visible world in which you imagine the bad and the good being perceived by reason. Having come to believe that, you then attempt to trace the invisible back to the visible. If this is truly your doctrine, it is proper that each one of us must necessarily do the very best possible in service to others in accord with the obligation of doing the best in both the visible and invisible worlds. However, if you do not make doing the best obligatory in the visible world, and yet that is the principle on which the discussion is based with regard to the invisible world, you have contradicted your own premise and blocked off that avenue of argumentation.

We presume that what we have said applies to the human's own improvement of himself. They agree with us that it is not obligatory for the human to try to achieve the very best on his own behalf in the present life, seeing that he has the possibility of acquiring only such benefits and pleasures as those already furnished him.

They may say: It is unnecessary for the human to do the very best on his own behalf and that of others only because to be under such an imposition would exhaust and trouble him, then it is permitted not to impose the maximum or utmost extent. But the situation is not like this in regard to God's operations, since He has the power to benefit another and to do what is best for him while yet being high above suffering any pain in doing what He does. But this argument of theirs goes nowhere. If being exposed to trials and tribulations were different

1 The *Shāmil* was al-Juwaynī's major compendium of theological doctrine; only part of it survives.

in the visible world from the invisible, as in the objection we raised against them, the same difference is necessary in what, by agreement of all, is obligatory on humans. Thus one would hold that it is not obligatory for the human to do anything that causes him to suffer hardship.

If they say: The rewards obtained for acts of obedience exceed those for bearing hardships, reply to them: In regard to procuring the best, pursue the same path as in the topic of compulsion; you are not relieved, by the assertion of exposure to adversities, of not having to respond to it. But this will not provide a way out.

We add here: The human is more appropriately under obligation to do the best, according to your erroneous principles, and what you cite in looking for a distinction establishes the contrary of what you have said. Bearing up to hardships procures the one who endures them a bounteous reward and thus for the hardships endured he receives the best in this world and a reward in the next. One cannot say of God, the Exalted, that He exerts Himself. The imposition of things that comprise hardships is not good, according to them, except in the way we have mentioned. They are then necessarily forced to make a connection between the visible and invisible worlds from which there is no escape.

One point we adhere to and which is close to what we have already said is that supererogatory prayers, and pious acts freely accompanying them, are good for the humans who perform them. What verifies this is that the Exalted Lord calls for and incites them. But, according to these people, the Exalted Lord recommends only what is best. If then it is clear that performing them is beneficial, what is beneficial to them must therefore be considered obligatory for humans. If, however, the matter is not like this and the acts of humans are divided into what is obligatory and what is recommended as being desired by God but without obligation, then the acts of God are divisible into those required of Him and those considered generous. If they seek a distinction, as we mentioned, between the visible and invisible worlds, we would respond with what we said earlier.

They may say: The Exalted Lord divides the operations into obligatory and meritorious only because He knows that it is best this way. He understands that, were He to declare the pious deeds obligatory in their entirety, humans would disobey and disregard the burden of the imposed obligation and turn towards the easier and less burdensome way of life. Thus God, the Exalted, determined what is best. We reply: This is ridiculous and refutable with minimum consideration. The performance of supererogatory prayers is a good that one is called upon to do and there is no way for them to deny it.

Having conceded this, however, the consideration of its occurring in God's knowledge, which they hope saves them, provides them, in fact, no help, since, in formulating their doctrine concerning the obligation to do what is best, they do not make the involvement of knowledge a consideration. For that reason, they say: If God, the Exalted, knows anyone who, if obligated by an imposition, will be cruel, oppressive, rebellious, vicious and arrogant and, if his life terminates before his intellect reaches maturity, will be successful and saved, it is obligatory on God, the Exalted, to offer him an elevated rank, despite knowing that he will perish before attaining it. Why could they not have said: Since performance of the supererogatory act is good, it is necessarily rendered obligatory without taking into account the fact that it is known to God? There is no way out of this. They have tricks along all the avenues they follow whose baselessness should be obvious to anyone who understands the contents of this handbook. Here we point out for each avenue only the most obtuse of their deceits.

A point of the greatest importance in opposing them is for us to say: Your determining that God is obliged to do the best puts you in the situation of denying self-evident things. When the Holy Book reaches its term and every person carries their acts suspended from the neck and the unbelievers are sent to an eternal life in hellfire, it will be incumbent on the Lord to do the best for His servants. The best for the inhabitant of the fire is to remain there eternally, having their skins stripped off bit by bit, partaking the fruits of the *Zaqqūm*, instead of drinking water from *Salsabīl* and the pure sealed wine.[2]

If they should say: This is better for them than to be in paradise, it is useless to discuss the matter with these people and their obstinacy becomes quite obvious. They may say: God subjects them eternally to painful punishment only because He knows that, if He absolves them of it, they would return to doing what He forbad. They would then require even more severe punishment than the one afflicting them presently. For this reason, keeping them where they are is better than exposing them to a punishment far greater. But this in fact leads nowhere.

There is a good deal more to their response. We, however, are content to relate, from among the points made by the leading masters, the following question: Why did God not cause them to die? Or why did He not terminate their punishment or retard their intellects enough so that they would not disobey Him? That realm is not a realm of imposed legal obligations in which the exposure to such obligation is required. Moreover, if it is not unreasonable to hold that the best consists in imposing an obligation on someone God knows will become an unbeliever, why does one not say: The best is to absolve the person the Lord knows will revert. This is more likely. Deliverance from punishment is a clemency implemented, whereas imposing an obligation in the case of the one who will disobey induces a hardship without the expectation of reward. We will have occasion to return to press the Muʿtazilites about the moment assigned for reward and punishment, should God, the Mighty and Glorious, so will.

A point in support of our position is for us to say: If you judge that everything the Lord does for His servant is an obligation on Him, it is proper for

2 *Al-Zaqqūm* is the horribly bitter tree of hell mentioned in the Qurʾān (37:62, 44:43, and 56:52); *Salsabīl* is a fountain in paradise from the Qurʾān (76:18); and the "sealed wine" comes from Qur'an 83:25: "Their thirst will be slaked with pure wine that is sealed."

you to judge that He does not require thanks and praise for any of His actions, in the same way that the delivery of reward to those who deserve it does not merit praise in the next life. According to their logic, reason rules that those who fulfil an obligatory act do not deserve thanks for having done it, no more than the person who returns a deposit or repays a legitimate debt.

If they say: The reward is a compensation and the compensation is not due a compensation; it is no more than an initial benefit, we reply: If the two [reward and compensation] are equally obligatory and imposed, distinguishing between them has no effect on your argument. Moreover, the acknowledgment of the human is compensation for the benefits received and it is comparable to the reward. Hence relying on the argument they try to make proves vain in every way.

A matter which the Baghdādī Muʿtazilites thrash out at length is for someone to say to them: You have imposed on God, the Exalted, the obligation to do the best in this world but the things within the power of the Exalted Creator relating to the pleasures are infinite. By what measure then do you determine exactly what is the best, since there is no restraint on the pleasures nor limit to what is possible? Every level of goodness has the possibility of being added to.

If they say: The Lord measures the best in accord with the situation of the human by the amount beyond which He knows an increase will cause him to become insolent, to that we respond: The pleasures constitute immediate benefits and are independent of the knowledge that the human will subsequently become insolent. The person about whom the Lord knows that, if He gives him the power and allows him free choice, he will prefer impiety and disobedience, ought, according to your doctrines, to be subject to the imposed obligation in order to offer him its benefits, despite knowing that he is about to perish and is on the point of destruction. Why not generalize this to the pleasures, without insisting on knowing what will be the future outcome? And there is no answer to any of this.

The opinion of these people violates the consensus of the community and stands in opposition to the leading masters. Having declared doing the best an obligation on God, there remains no room for an act of generosity and it can no longer be said of the Lord that He is generous. But God is far above the words of the liars. We know with self-evident certainty, based on the information provided in the religious law, that the Lord bestows His generosity on whomever He wishes and withholds His beneficence from whomever He wants. However, according to the Muʿtazilites, God is not free in His actions nor in bestowing His generosity. For them to say this is to malign the divinity. It displays an aversion for the Sacred Book. God Himself said, in regard to His own preferences and choices about His dominion over His servants and His having power: "Your Lord creates whatsoever He will and chooses freely; they do not have the choice" [28:68]. But a small part of what we mention here demolishes the basic premises of the Muʿtazilites and punctures the balloon of their pretensions.

With regard to the Basrans, we will contend with them over the first principle. We barred them from holding that the intellect determines the good and the bad and we specified clearly that there is no obligation on God, the Exalted. In so doing they were prevented from attaining the end they desired. If, however, we forsake all that and, for the purpose of argument, concede it, we now pose to them the following: You declare that, after imposing the obligation, it is incumbent on God to do the best in matters of religion. Why did you not declare it incumbent on Him to do the best in matters of the present world? What is the difference between them after the creation of the world and after the creation of pleasures and appetites?

Here we will apply the specious arguments of the Baghdādīs against them, and it is a matter of serious difficulty for them. We say: Your sources are reason and what transpires in the visible world. It is known that whoever possesses inexhaustible rivers and streams that flow abundantly without interruption and has no need for them, if before his eyes there stands a human gasping with a thirst quenchable by a simple gulp, to interpose an obstacle that prevents the person from obtaining the means to live would not be considered good and to drive him away from the approach to the water would be considered bad. If that were not considered bad, there is nothing bad according to reason.

The goal, in this course of argumentation, is to show that in relation to what is within the power of God, the Exalted, the best in the present world is less than a handful of water in relation to those rivers. They are finite in extent while the things within the power of God, the Exalted, are infinite. One of us is damaged by making a sacrifice, even if it is a small matter and we are only dimly aware of the harm it involves. In contrast the Exalted Lord transcends susceptibility to harm.

This puts the Muʿtazilites in a corner, if they determine the good and the bad by means of reason. But, if we were to accept what they say, we refute it immediately by the punishment of the people of hellfire. We say: If the human commits a bad act in the visible world, to forgive him is good according to the rules of morality, even though it exposes the master to the harm caused by fury when he forsakes revenge and retaliation But what about the disobedient condemned eternally to be chained and shackled, having repented of their past deeds, and the Exalted Lord is the most merciful of the merciful?

There is a point peculiar to the Basrans which brings up a topic that can be dealt with separately. On that issue we say: You declare that, once the imposition exists, doing the best is obligatory in religion and you consider the imposition good because it directs the subject of the imposition towards eternal reward. If, however, the Lord knows that, should He cause his death prior to attaining puberty, he will be saved; but, if He allows him to live, grants him free rein, empowers him, facilitates in him the ability to reason and makes it easy for him, he will resist obstinately and renounce his belief, how could one support saying that the Lord wants the best for the person He knows this about? Or how could an intelligent man tolerate saying that doing what is best is the imposition of obligations on him, given that if he were to die, he would be saved? Herein the truth comes out and its strictures bear down heavily against them.

On this issue we will now bring out the truth by offering the following example. We say: An affectionate father knows that his son, should he be furnished with ample funds, will become insolent, engage in corrupt activities, and scorn correct conduct. But if, in contrast, he is tight-fisted towards him, he will do well. In this situation, he wants what is best for his son, but he provides him with ample funds, despite knowing that he is causing the son to become a rebel and is bringing about his destruction, even though we know self-evidently that being tightfisted is better for the son than liberality. Were the father to say, after providing for his son, supplying him with provisions, and making him well connected, I intended only to furnish him the means to live well, despite my knowing it will be the opposite of that, it is quite obvious that the man is not following the dictates of reason.

They may say: It is only that the father is not paying attention to him, since he does not grasp thoroughly the amount required to assure that he will have the good things in the future if and when he follows proper conduct. The Exalted Lord knows the exact amount of reward that the subject of the imposition requires if he is to remain faithful. But this is playing a game with religion. Knowing the amount of reward has no bearing when it is also known that it will not be obtained. What good is it to the servant that God knows the amount of a reward he will never have. What reveals clearly the truth in this matter is that one considers good of the Prophet, on whom be blessing and peace, that he persists in appealing to those about whom the Lord informs him that they will not believe, even though the Prophet, God bless him and keep him, is completely unaware of the amount of reward that those subject to the imposition will obtain.

What supports our assertion is that if the imposition in the case of those the Lord knows will be unbelievers were good, it would be good also for those who have not reached the age of legal capacity, given the knowledge that, if they reach it, they will not become unbelievers, to ask God, the Exalted, to let them live until they become unbelievers, since it is a right of the servant to ask God to do what is best for him. At that point the merit in Muʿtazilite principles ceases altogether to have any prospect of validity.

Among issues we address to the Basrans, we maintain that the Lord has the power to bestow favours equal to the rewards. What purpose is there in exposing the servants to misfortune, hardship and calamity? They may answer: One does not attribute to the Lord the power to do this. Were we to assume this, God would be thereby the granter of favours but receiving a merited remuneration is preferable to the acceptance of a favour. We reply: These are words of someone who does not accord God His due worth. What you mention only leads to rejecting the acceptance of divine favours and that might apply only among equals. But what bound slave is too proud to accept the favour of God?

The proof of it is that, along with commencing the imposition of obligation, the Lord is the bestower of favours, according to you Basrans. Thus the reward results from something God instituted by bestowing favours. Moreover, we say: You have forgotten your own principles which refer to what transpires in the visible world. It is known that, if a king in our own era were to bestow favours on someone, honour him in his own abode, grant him a generous stipend, raise him to a high rank and, if he should also hire a domestic servant and pay him his wage after he had expended the sweat of his brow and worn himself out in manual labour, the one of them who received the favours of the king is more rightly judged fortunate, respected and well regarded. We will return to this matter later, God willing.

We add here: It is exceedingly strange of them to hold that to expose a person who disbelieves to doom is better for him than to bestow a favour on him. There can be no greater blindness than this. May God protect us from heresies.

Chapter: [*The doctrine of grace*]

Grace, according to the Muʿtazilites, is an act by which the Lord knows that the servant who is its subject will obey Him. It is designated by no genus of its own. Some thing might be a grace leading to the faith of Zayd but not a grace for that of ʿAmr.

The term grace [*luṭf*] is sometimes employed as a complement to the term unbelief [*kufr*] and one calls what occurs as unbelief in the unbeliever a grace. Moreover, it is a principle of the Muʿtazilites that it is incumbent on God, the Exalted, to extend the utmost grace to those under imposition and they say, following up on this course, that God, the Exalted, does not have within His power a grace such that, were He to use it on the unbelievers, they would all believe. But God is high indeed above their statements.

As for the orthodox, grace, according to them, is the creation of the power to be obedient and that is always within God's power. We ask the Muʿtazilites: Why do you consider grace to be obligatory in matters of religion? Why not say that God withholds the grace in order to intensify the trial and expose the subject of imposition to greater hardships, or that withholding acts of grace leads to a more substantial reward in the next life? If they answer: The goal is to have them believe, we respond: What purpose is there in imposing an obligation on someone who will never believe? If we were to judge solely by the rules of reason, ending the life of the person who follows this course is a grace for him without exposing him to the impositions, given the knowledge that there is no grace known to Him that will make the subject of the imposition come to believe. This then achieves all our aims in regard to the subject of the good, the best and grace.

Section
A Statement in Proof of the Prophetic Missions

The proof for the prophetic missions is one of the most fundamental principles in religion. Our purpose, in that regard here in this handbook of theology, will be limited to five topics. First, proving the possibility of the prophets having been sent, thereby refuting the Barāhima; second, miracles and their conditions, and in what way they are to be distinguished from marvels and sorcery, and how they set apart those who claim prophecy; third, explaining clearly the manner by which miracles prove the truth of the prophets; fourth, the specific indications of the prophecy of our Prophet, Muḥammad, God bless him and keep him, and the refutation of those in the other religious communities who deny it; and fifth, a statement of the regulations concerning the prophets and what is obligatory on them and what is permissible for them.

Chapter: [*On proving the possibility of prophetic missions*]

The Barāhima deny prophetic missions and reject them as not being rational. They consider it impossible that a human being was sent as an apostle. We will mention here the specious arguments they accept as beliefs and rid ourselves of them at the outset. One of their allegations is to say: Were we to assume the arrival of a prophet, what he proclaims must be either perceivable by the operation of reason or not. If what he proclaims is something the intellect could discern on its own, there is no benefit in his having been sent. And something that lacks a genuine purpose is frivolous and silly. On the other hand, if what he proclaims is not part of that to which reason attests, it is unacceptable, since the only things that are acceptable are those attested by reason.

These specious arguments of the Barāhima are based on the intellect's determining the good and the bad. Were we to gainsay them on that subject, none of their deceits would endure but, for the sake of argument, we will concede to them that intellect determines it. It, however, will not set right this principle and we will demonstrate the falseness of their contentions, despite having conceded this. Thus we say: Nothing precludes the proofs attested by reason from confirming what the prophet proclaims. This is analogous to using several rational proofs to support a single objective. Even if it is sufficiently proven by only one proof, the others do not become frivolous accordingly. Moreover, if God dispatches an apostle, nothing that is known of Him precludes his having been sent as a grace in regard to the judgments of reason and that, when sending the apostle, it is the people of intellectual ability who are entrusted with these matters. Thus, if what we have said is not impossible, their insistence that the sending of the prophet lacks purpose is wrong.

Furthermore, we would ask here: Why did you not claim that, if what the Prophet, God bless him and keep him, proclaims is not attested by reason, it is false? And how would you refute those who insist that it is the same situation as a sick person who goes to a doctor seeking from him something to make him better? The sick person knows in general that he wants something that will cure him but he does not know specifically what it is that will provide the cure. It is the doctor who indicates to him what will cure him. It is the same way with the one sent by God to the people. They do not know, prior to the prophet's mission, specifically what there might be in the things the prophet will be sent to convey that would benefit them. But then, subsequently, when he is sent, he indicates what is good conduct and shows clearly the proper course to follow.

They may also be asked: Why do you not claim that reason can do without the dispatching of the Prophet, God bless him and keep him? Do you not admit that it is possible the prophets were sent to indicate foods and medicines and to distinguish them from deadly poisons and noxious plants? None of these things are perceived by reason. If they respond: Long experience of trial and error leads to this sort of information, we then reply: Until they are established, not having the experiences leads to injuries and the incursion of loss. If proper guidance existed from the beginning, one would not need to practise with poisons and to try to distinguish them from the other substances.

Another argument they invoke consists in saying: You will find that the law of yours includes matters that reason regards as bad, even though we know that the sage did not command abominations and did not recommend reprehensible acts. They add: The laws embrace, for example, the slaughtering of animals and subjugating them, but reason judges these things to be bad. We respond: What you mention turns against you by the fact that God, the Exalted, inflicts suffering on animals and children who have not previously committed a sin and bear no responsibility. If they say: This is a wisdom on the part of God, we answer: If doing something is an act of wisdom, then it is not inconceivable that ordering it done is also wise. This will suffice to achieve our present purpose.

Occasionally they allude also to other delusions that no person of intelligence would take seriously. They say for example: There are things in the laws that reason would not allow, such as bowing in the act of prayer, falling prostrate on the face, displaying grief, disrobing, the hastening, running back and forth between the two mountains, throwing the stones without aiming at something, and other things like these that these people would make a mockery of.

The method that opposes them best and from which they will find no escape is for us to state: The Exalted Lord often harms his servant, impoverishes him, strips him naked and abandons him like a piece of meat on the butcher's block, his genitals in full view. However, if one of us were to strip bare his servant, despite being able to provide him a covering and conceal his genitalia, that would certainly incur blame. But the Exalted Lord does whatever of this He pleases. He is never asked to account for that, whereas they are held to account. It is He who withholds reason and forces the insane to consume the thing that perpetuates their torment, despite His having the power to restore their minds. If this example we offer as the work of God, the Exalted, is not inconceivable, one must also admit that it takes place by order of God.

If they say: If what you mention takes place as acts of God, the Exalted, there are in it hidden benefits the knowledge of which is reserved to Him alone, yet we respond: You must also then admit the same conditions for matters you judge to be inconceivable.

These people have specious arguments that assail prophetic miracles and we will cite the major ones in the course of our discussions, God willing.

The proof of the possibility of God sending prophets and instituting laws for their communities is that it is not one of the impossibilities that are precluded from happening by their very natures, such as the occurrence of two contraries in the same instance, the transformation of genera and the like. In respect to God's ordering a human being to commence observing the regulations of the law, there is nothing to preclude it from the point of view of the determination of the good and the bad.

That having been clarified, we say: Next there are two ways to go. One of them is for us to deny the principle that reason determines the good and the bad, after which there remains only the certainty of the possibility. The second is for us to concede for the sake of argument its determination of the bad. We would say here: The dispatching of the prophet is not in itself bad, as would be injustice, evil for evil's sake and the like. Nor is its badness derived from a matter associated with another thing. Thus nothing prevents understanding the sending of the prophet as a grace which, when present, causes the intelligentsia to believe and they are thereafter bound to the dictates of reason. Were it not so, they would reject faith and remain obstinate. This conclusively proves the possibility of prophetic missions.

Another of the decisive proofs of this is the affirmation of prophetic miracles, as we will describe them. They are proof of the truthfulness of those who invoke them as signs of their missions. Having demonstrated clearly that they are proofs of the truthfulness of those who claim prophecy, we will have located the most unambiguous refutation of those who would deny prophecy.

Chapter: [*On prophetic miracles and their conditions*]

You should understand first of all that the term "miracle" [*muʿjiza*] is taken from the word "impotence" (or "incapacity") [*ʿajz*] and that it is an expression used currently in an extended, figurative and metaphorical sense. The one who renders something incapable is, in reality, the creator of the incapacity; and those to whom the challenge of the Prophet is addressed were not incapable of opposing him, God bless him and keep him. If the miracle is something beyond the capabilities of the human, one could not conceive that the human is incapable of doing it. One is incapable of doing only what one can otherwise do. If, on the contrary, the miracle is something within the power of the human being, one could not conceive the incapacity of those who invoke the miracles as proof of their mission, since the incapacity accompanies the thing of which one is incapable. If they were incapable of contesting, the contestation would have existed necessarily and the incapacity would have accompanied it, as we have investigated thoroughly in the book on the power. Thus the meaning of "rendering incapable" [*iʿjāz*] is to proclaim the impossibility of the contestation, without involving the existence of the incapacity, which is the opposite of power.

One often employs the term "incapacity" metaphorically as the absence of power, as one says metaphorically about ignorance that it is the absence of knowledge. Moreover, in calling a prophetic sign [*āya*] a miracle [*muʿjiza*], there is another metaphorical usage and that is to ascribe the rendering of something incapable to the miracle in and of itself, whereas the Lord God is the one who renders creatures incapable of producing the signs. Nevertheless, they are called miracles because they cause the impossibility of the people's contesting them.

Know also that miracles have a number of specific characteristics that should be grasped thoroughly. One is that it is an act of God, the Exalted. A miracle cannot, however, be an eternal attribute, since an eternal attribute cannot be particular to one claimant to prophecy rather than another and also, if the eternal attribute were a miracle, the very existence of God would be a miracle. The miracle is one of the acts of God, the Exalted, only in performing the function of God's announcing, in regard to those who claim prophecy, "you are truthful", as we will explain later in discussing the way in which the miracle proves the truth of the apostle. What we are speaking about applies to something that does not fall within the power of humans.

If someone should ask: Is it possible that someone walking on water or rising up in the air and circulating about the heavens is a miracle? To that we respond: Assuming that to be a miracle is not inconceivable, if all the characteristics are fulfilled. Movement in the various directions is within the capacity of humans but it is more proper for us to say that the power to execute these movements is a miracle and is an act of God, the Exalted. It is not within the powers of the human being. As for the movement itself, those who believe that it is an act of God do not regard it inconceivable that it is a miracle in so far as it is God's act but not in so far as it is an acquisition of humans. In this sense both the power and the movements are miracles.

If someone asks: Should a person who claims prophecy say, "My miracle is that it will be impossible for the people of this region to stand up during a time period I shall set; this would be an obvious miracle and yet it is not an act but rather the absence of an act." Our master, God have mercy on him, has said: The miracle is an act of God, the Exalted, intended to confirm a declaration, or to take the place of the act indicating the intention of the confirmation. He thus indicates what we have mentioned. My own position, however, is that the miracle consists in continuing to remain seated, despite attempting to stand up, and therefore the miracle is, in fact, based on an act. If someone were to point out that sitting is an ordinary activity and miracles are extraordinary things, we reply: Being continuously seated, despite attempting to stand up, is extraordinary, if it occurs among a group consisting of innumerable persons. And this is one condition of a miracle.

Another of its conditions is that it be extraordinary, since, if it were commonplace and ordinary and happened equally for the pious and profligate, the virtuous and the vicious, those who rightfully claim prophecy and those who fake their claims to it, the presumed miracle would serve neither to distinguish nor to designate the truthful person. That is so obvious we must insist on it.

The Barāhima have several questions that must be dealt with at this point. One is for them to note that something extraordinary cannot be precisely defined. Something found as rarely as only once or twice and which belongs thus to the class of extraordinary things, if repeated and it multiplies, it becomes an ordinary thing. But one cannot, at that point, precisely specify how it became an ordinary thing and thus distinguish it now from the extraordinary things. And thus what one claims about it is based on ignorance.

This line goes nowhere, however. It revolves around denying rational evidence for worthless fantasies. We know necessarily that reviving the dead, parting the seas, and the like are not ordinary acts. Not knowing the number of times required to make them become ordinary does not invalidate this evidence. Often something cannot be specifically defined either in number or in quality although it is known by necessary evidence. This is the same situation as in the multiple transmission of reports that lead to necessary knowledge of the thing reported by them. We have no way, even if we want, to specify precisely the minimum number of transmissions required to yield certainty. One number in that regard is not more likely than another.

The most that we can say is that the number which the law indicates for witnesses is not the number required for historical transmissions and we have no other number that conveys decisive certainty. Someone who addresses another with words that humiliate that other person and the other person becomes angry, realizes with the certainty of necessary knowledge that he is angry. It is not possible to tie knowledge of his being angry with factors such as a reddening of the face and other indications of it, since each of the factors indicated may be found in states other than anger.

The Barāhima may say here: According to your principles, the rupture of ordinary events and their inversion is within the power of God, the Exalted. It is thus not impossible that the thing becomes ordinary and its likeness familiar. If it becomes generalized, it ceases to constitute a miracle. When a prophet makes a claim to his mission and invokes as proof of it a rupture of the ordinary, should we not believe that it is the beginning of an ordinary thing which will become common? If it becomes generalized, it is not a miracle.

A statement that responds to this completely would be lengthy. But the simplest way to rebut them is for us to say the following: If a prophet were to say, "my miracle is that God will change an established habit and institute another contrary to it", that would be the truest of the miracles that prove the prophetic missions. If one rare event proves it, when the habitual resumes being commonplace, how much more appropriately does the advent of a new habit that is contrary to what preceded prove it. If, however, they persist in their distortions in respect to the rare event that a prophet invokes as his challenge, what would they say about him, should that rare event occur to him, and the days and eras follow without that rare event ever happening again? It thus cannot be the commencement of a continuing habit.

One of the most outrageously false arguments they use in that regard is for them to ask: How can the intelligent person be sure that what the prophet produces is truly extraordinary, given that he himself is acquainted with the discoveries of the scholars concerning the special properties of bodies and the marvels of celestial influences, up to and including the changing of copper into pure gold, the moving of heavy bodies with light instruments, and other marvels of science and the products of penetrating investigation? In addition to these examples, everyone knows about the stone that has the special property of being able to attract iron. Should we not believe that the person who claims prophecy simply came across one of these secrets and publicly feigned his claim based on it?

We answer: That leads to the denial of intuitive knowledge and the casting of doubt about matters of self-evidence. Everything that led to rejecting necessary knowledge is false and not self-evident. What demonstrates this is that we know self-evidently that human powers and scholastic investigations together cannot restore life to scattered bones, cure the blind and the leprous, change a staff into a snake that swallows up the lying inventions of the sorcerers. A person who admits attaining things like these by the sciences and the comprehension of special properties has left the fold of rational men.

One should recognize that it is not inconceivable in some remote corner of the earth there is a region in which animals sprout and grow like plants, so that when the plant reaches fruition the animals acquire intelligence and produce examples of wisdom and marvels, and other inanities.

Moreover, should a prophet issue a challenge on the basis of something we consider extraordinary and, if it were not really extraordinary, people would eagerly seek to contest it, to subject these claims to exposure and to denigrate his assertions. If, on the contrary, the assertions are broadcast, their signs, the challenge they convey and the people's incapacity to produce anything like them spreads, this demonstrates that it was an extraordinary event. This is, in fact, what we aimed at in that regard.

The third condition of a miracle is that it applies to proving the truthfulness of the claim of the person for whose sake it appears. This condition divides into three aspects that must be understood.

One is that the prophet issues a challenge in virtue of the prophetic miracle and that it appears in conformity with his claim. If a sign should be manifested by a person who is silent and makes no declaration, that sign would not be a miracle. We state that a prophetic miracle only establishes a proof in that it assumes the place of verification by means of a verbal statement, as we will mention shortly, and that cannot occur without the issuing of a challenge. If the person who claims to be the representative of the king were to state in his presence and hearing: If I am your representative, stand up and sit down. Thereupon, if the king did that, it would be tantamount to his saying, You are truthful. If the representative were not to make this claim but rather to declare himself an envoy in a general sense and still the king stood up and sat down, actions of the king would not prove the man's veracity. Therefore there is no doubt about the necessity of the challenge.

Moreover, it suffices in issuing the challenge that he say: The sign of my veracity is that God will restore life to this dead person. It is not a condition of issuing the challenge that he say: This is my miracle and no one can produce another like it. The aim in issuing the challenge is to tie the claim of prophecy to the miracle and that is achieved without saying: No one can produce its like. This is one way in which the prophetic miracle applies to the claim of prophecy.

Another aspect of it is that the miracle does not precede the claim. If the sign appeared first and had passed, someone might say: I am a prophet, and that which has passed is my miracle. No one would pay attention to this since what has passed does not apply to his specific claim. Someone may say: If we were to examine a box and find it empty, then we locked it and left it where we could see it. And at that point a claimant to the prophecy said: The sign of my prophecy is that you will discover in this box clothes. If we open the box and find in it the clothing as he had described, that would be a confirming sign. We reply: Even though we recognize the possibility that the fabrication of those clothes preceded his claims, his statement about something invisible is a miraculous sign and is in conformity with his claim. Understand that well.

If it is asked: Is it possible for the miracle to come after the claim of prophecy? we respond: If it follows later and conforms to the claim, it is a sign. That would be like the prophet saying: "The sign of my veracity will be the extraordinary occurrence of such and such tomorrow morning." If that actually happened as he promised and was truly extraordinary, it would be a sign.

Someone may say: If the claimant to prophecy were to say, "My sign will appear after my death", at a moment specified by him, and if what he said were to occur after his death in conformity with his claim, that would constitute an extraordinary event. Our way of dealing with this is to say: If he imposes on the people the obligation of following the religious law immediately and yet the miraculous sign were being held in abeyance, his imposition on them would exceed proper bounds. If, on the other hand, he were to designate the regulations and their being compelled to follow them at the moment in which his sign appears, that would be proper. The Qāḍī Abū Bakr [al-Bāqillānī], may God be pleased with him, rejected what I consider proper. But there was no reason for him to deny it. The truth is more deserving of being followed.

Another aspect of the miracle's application to the confirmation of truthfulness is that they do not manifest the pretension of the false prophet, as for example, were a claimant to prophecy to assert his case saying: The sign of my veracity is that God will cause my hand to speak. If God were to make his hand speak, it would reveal his lies. It would say: "Know that this man is an impostor, so beware of him." But that is certainly not a confirmatory sign. Or he could say: "My sign is that God will restore life to this dead person", and then, when God revives him, he rises and speaks sharply saying: "This person you associate with is a slanderous liar and God, the Exalted, has sent me to disgrace him", and he falls on his face dumbfounded. The Qāḍī Abū Bakr, may God be pleased with him, said that this is indeed a sign in regard to the false pretender but does not prove prophecy.

My view with respect to this is that, if declaring it false is an extraordinary event, it is that which denigrates the miracle, as in the situation of the hand that speaks to say it is false. In the case of the dead who was restored to life and who declared it a lie, his declaration of the falsehood is not extraordinary. The prophet may perhaps say: The sign consists solely in his being restored to life and his declaration of my falseness is of no greater value since it is similar to the declarations by the rest of the unbelievers.

Chapter: On the affirmation of saintly marvels and on distinguishing them from prophetic miracles[1]

The orthodox accept the possibility of the natural order being broken in the case of the saints. The Muʿtazilites agree among themselves in precluding this and the scholar Abū Isḥāq [al-Isfarāyīnī],[2] may God be pleased with him, inclined to a view close to their doctrine. Furthermore, those who accept saintly marvels divide into several factions.

Some hold that the condition of a marvel that breaks the habitual order is for it not to be produced or chosen by the saint. This group thus maintains that a marvel is distinguishable from a prophetic miracle for this reason. But this is not correct for reasons we will indicate later. Those who uphold the possibility of the

1 The two Arabic terms used here are *karāmāt* (saintly marvels) and *muʿjizāt* (prophetic miracles). Both words mean "miracles" but the former is normally reserved for the miraculous acts done by a saint and the latter for prophets. As will become clear al-Juwaynī certainly admits that prophets perform "marvels" or acts like those attributed to saints and these acts might be called miracles (as they might for the saints), but the saints do not share with the prophets in the *muʿjizāt*, which must accompany the issuing of a challenge.

2 Leading Ashʿarite theologian and Shāfiʿī legal scholar in Nīshāpūr where he died in 418/1027. On him see the article "al-Isfarāyīnī" by W. Madelung in the *EI2*.

marvel occurring as a result of choice but who also preclude its happening in a matter involving a claim, say: If a saint makes a claim to sainthood and attempts to assert the preference of his claim by something that breaks the habitual order, that is not acceptable. This group presumes that this creates a distinction between the marvel and a prophetic miracle. This approach is also unsuitable. It is not impossible, as far as we are concerned, for the rupturing of the natural order to appear in connection with a claim proffered by a saint.

Certain of our associates maintain that what has occurred as a miracle belonging to a prophet cannot occur also as a marvel of a saint. According to this group, it is impossible as a marvel of a saint for the sea to part or for a staff to turn into a serpent or the dead be restored to life. The same applies to the other signs of the prophets. But this approach is likewise incorrect. The approved way, in our view, is to acknowledge that all examples of the rupturing of the natural order may occur in connection with the appearance of saintly marvels.

Our aim in declaring these approaches spurious and in affirming the correct way in our view and in distinguishing between the marvel and the miracle will be made clear by our explaining the principles on which those who deny the marvels base themselves, by our repudiation of them, and by our reliance on a decisive proof in defence of the reality of the marvels.

One argument alleged by those who deny the marvels is to say: If it were possible for the habitual order to be broken in any manner at all, that would be possible in all ways. It follows from this that what was a miracle of a prophet may appear at the hands of a saint. This leads the prophet to being declared false by the one challenged by his miracle in saying to the person whom he challenged: No one can produce the like of what I produced. But, if producing its like is possible for the saint, this fact makes the prophet liable to being accused of lying.

This is specious reasoning that goes nowhere, since there is no disagreement that the same example of a break in the habitual order might constitute a miracle for one prophet after another. Furthermore, its appearance in the second instance does not make false the prophet who first issued his challenge by means of it. They may say: The prophet made his claim specific in addressing those whom he challenged. He should have said: No one can produce its like except those claiming prophecy who are truthful in making this claim. We reply: If qualifying the claim were allowed in the way you mention, nothing precludes the prophet also saying: No pretender to prophecy can produce the like of it, nor a cheating impostor, nor someone seeking to declare me false. The marvels of saints, however, are not included among these cases and no restriction seems more appropriate than any other.

Another argument of theirs is to say: If we accept the rupturing of the habitual order on behalf of saints, we have no assurance that it will not happen in our own time. This leads to sensible people having misgivings about whether the Tigris will not flow with fresh blood, the mountains will not change into pure gold and a human will not come into existence without having been in the womb or undergone parturition. Accepting the possibility of this is sophistry and the doubting of self-evident facts.

We say here: What you mention turns against you for the time of the prophets. Those who lived in the period of the interval between two prophets – that is, between the ascension of Jesus, on whom be peace, and the mission of Muḥammad, God bless him and keep him – were not permitted, in attempting to deny the marvels, to accept what you preclude accepting. Once the prophet had been sent, his signs had appeared, and the habitual order of things had been broken, the minds of the intelligent were assured that breaks in the habitual order would not continue to occur.

This is our method in dealing with the objection made against us. We are now sure that what they presumed might happen will not happen. If God determines that it should occur, He will invert the habitual order and put an end to the self-evident knowledge that what they presumed might occur will not happen. Thus what they say proves false and, by repudiating it, we affirm the principle of the saint's marvel.

Someone asks: What is your proof of its being possible? We respond: It is axiomatic that there is no case of breaking the habitual order that is not within God's power. The occurrence of a thing is not precluded by reason judging it bad, as we have already determined in previous discussions. There is nothing in the occurrence of a marvel to demean the prophetic miracle. The miracle does not constitute a proof in and of itself but rather constitutes proof by its connection with the claim of the prophet to his apostolic mission. It takes the place of a verbal confirmation. The king who confirms the claim of the person who asserts that he is his envoy by an act that confirms and corroborates the claim he has announced could also promulgate something similar to it as a way of bestowing honour on one of his saints. Aiming to bestow honour as a means of providing confirmation cannot be considered unworthy. This is only too obvious to those who think about it.

If someone asks: What is the difference between the marvel and a prophetic miracle? We answer: There is no difference from the point of view of reason except that the miracle occurs in relation to the claim of prophecy and the marvel occurs without any claim of prophecy.

Those who affirm the marvels prove it by a method that is irrefutable from the point of view of tradition. The inhabitants of the cave and what happened to them in the way of miraculous signs cannot be denied and they were not prophets, as all agree.[3] Similarly, Mary, on whom be peace, was singled out by several signs. Zakariyyāʾ, may the blessing of God be on him, found her with winter fruits during the summer and summer fruits during the winter and he said in astonishment: "From where did you get this?" [3:37] Fresh ripe dates fell at her feet, and there are other examples of her miraculous signs. Similarly,

---

3 The story of the inhabitants or companions of the cave is from Qurʾān (18:9–25).

the mother of Moses, on whom be peace, was quite obviously divinely inspired about matters concerning him. The birth of the Prophet, peace be upon him, was attended by signs that no true Muslim would deny. And that was prior to his becoming a prophet and being chosen for his mission because the miracle does not precede the claim of prophecy, as we specified earlier.

If one of them were to stray and insist that the signs we adduced as proof were the miracles of the prophets of every period, that would be a headlong leap into ignorance. If we investigate the periods that were devoid of prophets, we do not find that the signs we acknowledge are connected with claims of prophecy. On the contrary, they occurred in the absence of any challenge by a claimant. If they say: They occur to the prophets without their making a claim, the condition of a miracle, however, is the claim. If it is lacking, the ruptures of the habitual order are simply marvels belonging to the prophets. With this we achieve our purpose of affirming the marvels. There was, moreover, no prophet at the time of the Prophet's birth to whom his signs could be ascribed. Thus the possibility and actuality of the marvels is clear both in reason and in tradition.

Chapter: [*Sorcery and what is connected with it*]

[This chapter] concerns the proof of sorcery and how it is to be distinguished from the prophetic miracle. In it we will affirm the jinn and the satans[4] and refute those who deny them.

Sorcery really exists. We will first describe it and then prove the possibility of it rationally. Next we adduce from the context of tradition its having actually occurred. Finally, in the course of our exposition, we will mention what distinguishes it from miracles. It is not impossible that the sorcerer might rise up in the air, that he circulate through the atmosphere of the heavens, that he become thin and enter through tiny slits and windows, and that he do examples of other things not within the power of humans. Movement in the several directions is the kind of thing human beings have the power to do. It is not impossible rationally that God, the Exalted, makes happen, upon the request of the sorcerer, what he wants to do by providing him the power to do it. Everything that is within the power of humans occurs, according to us, by the power of God.

The proof of the possibility of this is like the proof of the possibility of the marvels. The way of distinguishing sorcery from the miracle is like the way of distinguishing the latter from the marvels. There is thus no need to go over it again. Several bits of evidence in tradition testify to the actuality of sorcery. Among them is the story of Hārūt and Mārūt.[5] Another is the Sūra of the Dawn

---

4 The Arabic here is *shayāṭīn*, the plural of *shayṭān* (Satan) and thus, although the English rendering "satans" instead of something like "devils" is slightly odd, it is literally what the Arabic says.

5 On Hārūt and Mārūt, see Qurʾān 2:102 and the standard commentaries on this verse.

[al-Falaq][6] about which the commentators agree that the cause of its being revealed was the sorcery of Labīd b. Aʿṣam, the Jew, over the Prophet of God, God bless him and keep him. He cast a spell over him by means of a comb and a tuft of hair placed under the bottom stone of the well of Dharwān. Ibn ʿUmar was also under a spell and his hand became unusable. A servant belonging to ʿĀʾisha, may God be pleased with her, was also under a spell.

The legal scholars agree on the existence of sorcery and differ only about its effects. These are the ones who have the power to decide and through them a consensus is constituted. Given their agreement, there is no point in taking into account the opinions of the Muʿtazilites. Thus it is established that sorcery is both possible and a reality.

Moreover, understand that sorcery is a manifestation only of the impious; the marvels are not manifested by them. This is not a requirement of reason but is accepted by unanimous agreement of the community. Even though a marvel is not under the control of those who announce their impiety, it does not testify definitively to sainthood either, since, if it were to so testify, the author of the marvel would have assurance of what would result, but it is agreed that this does not happen to a saint in regard to the marvel.

If they now request: Explain precisely your doctrine in regard to the jinn and the satans, we answer: We uphold their reality. The majority of the Muʿtazilites deny them, but their denying them proves how unmindful they are and how weak is their faith. There is no rational impossibility against affirming their existence. Proof texts in the Holy Book and in the Sunna proclaim their existence. And those intelligent people who are attached to the bonds of religion admit what reason affirms possible and the law declares a reality. For those who deny Iblis and his legions and the satans who were overcome in the time of Sulayman, as reported in innumerable verses of God's Book, there remains no attachment to religion and no interest in it to hold on to. God alone guides to the truth. This was our purpose in this subject.

---

6 The 113th *sūra* of the Qurʾān.

Section

A Statement of the Way in Which a Miracle Proves the Veracity of the Prophet, God Bless Him and Keep Him

Know, may God, the Exalted, guide you, that a miracle does not prove the veracity of the Prophet in the same manner as rational proofs prove what they prove. A rational proof applies to what it proves in its very essence and it cannot be conceived in the mind as not proving it. The force of a miracle is not like this.

One can explain this by examples in two cases. Because the existence of a contingent thing proves that there exists something that causes it to come into being, one cannot conceive its having come to be without its being proof of that other thing. But the transforming of a staff into a snake, if it happened spontaneously as an act of God, the Mighty and Glorious, in the absence of a prophet's claim, would not prove the veracity of the claimant. Miracles thus bear no resemblance to the proofs of reason.

If someone asks: Then in what way do they prove it? We answer: This causes considerable embarrassment to those who do not know this subject well. The approved doctrine, in our view, is that a miracle proves the veracity in that it occupies the place of verification by verbal affirmation. Our point will be made clear on the basis of the following two examples.

We state: Suppose a king were presiding over a gathering of the people, allowing his subjects to come inconveniently close to him, the people gathering and thronging together, and [at a time when] preoccupations have troubled the populace. Once everyone has taken their seat and all the people are arranged by position and rank, one of the inner circle of the king stands and says: "O assembled people, a grave matter has befallen you and a momentous danger threatens you. I am delegated by the king to you, and am the one entrusted with the responsibility for you, as his guardian over you. I make this claim in front of the king and within his hearing. If, O king, what I have said is true, then contravene your ordinary habits, set aside your natural dispositions, and stand up in your splendour and majesty and then sit down." Whereupon the king in conformity to the request just made does exactly that. Those present then certainly know of necessity that the king was confirming the man's veracity. The act that he performed occupied the place of a verbal statement proclaiming his veracity.

This was precisely the point of this example. Now we will go on from there to several questions that we would put aside except that those we would dismiss comprise within them matters of the greatest importance.

One of the most important of these questions is one posed by the Muʿtazilites when they ask the following: If you accept that the Lord leads his servants astray, misguides them and brings them to perdition, why not believe then that miracles are produced by impostors in order to lead the people astray? Our doctrine, they add, which regards God, the Exalted, as transcending acts of injustice and the leading of humans astray shelters us from the objections forced on you. The miracle proves veracity because we know that the Lord reserves it for those who are truthful and will not permit it to the impostor in order to lead the people astray.

The answer to this is for us to say: Those who witnessed the assembly of the king, in the example just given, knew necessarily that the king confirmed the declaration of the person claiming to be his delegate, even though it did not occur to most of those present to contemplate, ponder or even speculate whether or not the king might misguide his subjects and oppress his followers. If the miracle's proving the veracity was subordinate to knowing that the one who produces the miracle will not terrorize or lead astray, those recognizing the delegation by the king would be limited to the ones who realized this fact and had taken notice of it. But the matter is quite obviously not like this. What reveals the truth is that, if the king were unjust and tyrannical, no one would trust his impulses. But the act stipulated here concerns a person of such a character as to provide confirmation of the claimant's having been delegated. To reject that is to deny the obvious.

With that we ask the Muʿtazilites: How would you prove the miracles? If they answer: It follows from our knowing that God, the Exalted, will not lead His servants astray, we reply: The knowledge that you claim to have is tied to commonplace acts in the same manner as it is to extraordinary acts. Thus you consider it possible that an ordinary act might occur which, in your belief, could be the distinguishing mark of a prophet. If they answer: There is no doubt about a miracle having a character that is particular to the way it proves what it proves, we respond: Show it to us and we will discuss it. They will either persist in their vague wanderings and confusion or return towards the truth. If they explain any other reasoning, except the corrupt beliefs they seem to hold, we would say: A miracle does not appear at the hand of the impostor because, if it did appear, it would prove his veracity; and proving the veracity of a liar is impossible, according to the rules of reason.

Someone may ask: Do you admit that a miracle could possibly take place in conformity with the claim of an impostor? Or do you maintain that it cannot happen? We reply: What we accept, in that regard, is that a miracle cannot possibly take place in conformity with the claim of an impostor, since it comprises a declaration of truthfulness and what is impossible is not something that can be done. A miracle is necessarily particular to the claim of a truthful person, just as a connection is necessary between suffering and being aware of it under certain situations. The category of miracles covers someone lacking a preexisting claim but it precludes any occurrence in conformity with the claim of an impostor. Understand this well!

Someone may ask: If what you affirm, in the example you gave, is established, on what basis would you relate the invisible world to the visible world, given your knowing that there is necessarily a link between them? Wanting to join them together without such a connecting link verges in the direction of materialism and heresy.

Often they support this query with another. They say: We only know of the prophetic mission of the one who claims it because of associated circumstances and what experience we have of these. But such things are lacking and non-existent in the domain of God.

This is the final difficulty in the matter of prophecy. Once resolved, after it, there remain no ways for the detractors to sow disorder. Taking recourse in God, the Exalted, we say: What we cited of the visible world served to make us comprehend better and to provide examples for clarification. We did not invoke them in order to prove them. The thrust of the matters we mentioned is self-evident and need not be proven. But illustrative examples could be given.

We will now explain the like of what we mentioned both for the visible and the invisible worlds together. We say: A miracle is probative only in the case of someone who believes that the Lord has the power to do whatever He wishes. In speaking to those who previously believed in the divinity, the Prophet says: You have known that the sending of a prophet is not repugnant to reason. I am the apostle of God sent to you. The sign of my veracity is that you know that God alone has the power to restore life to the dead and you know that God knows all our secrets as well as our public acts, what we conceal of our inner thoughts and what we display outwardly. Although I am merely an apostle of God sent to you, if I am speaking the truth, then, O Lord, transform this piece of wood into a coursing serpent. Then, when it was transformed as he had asked, since the assembled people knew of God, the Exalted, at that moment they also understood of necessity that the Lord intended, by effecting this transformation, to confirm his veracity, as in the example we cited for the visible world.

Their misrepresentations in regard to associated circumstances come to nothing of value. Those who were absent from the assembly just described certainly heard about what happened and thus shared with those present knowing about the announced mission, even though they did not experience the actual circumstances. In the same way, if the king had been isolated by himself in a compartment, behind a hanging curtain, and the person claiming to be his delegate said: If I am your delegate, shake the screen and lift the curtain, the king's doing that would constitute a confirmation, even though no one actually saw the king. Since the confirmation happens behind the enclosures, these conditional circumstances cease to be factors, the matter is settled and the truth is apparent. But in all cases, God is the One to whom we express our gratitude.

What we have cited is supported by the disagreement of the hypocrites and sceptics at the time of the Prophet. Some denied the divinity and, for this reason, were overcome by doubts in regard to the prophetic mission. Others believed that the Prophet was a sorcerer and held that what issued from him was an illusion. However, no person in any age who believes that the miracle originates as an act of God in conformity with the claim of a prophet believes once and, then subsequently, commences to doubt prophecy. It is testimony that this is a matter involving necessity and there is no room in it for doubts.

This is our doctrine in regard to proving the veracity of the Prophet by miracles. The Muʿtazilites can hardly call on this for their doctrine, since the meaning of what we have said specifies an intention to confirm veracity and it is difficult for the Muʿtazilites to affirm the existence of an intention in God. They reject an eternal will and preclude His being purposeful in and of Himself. In previous discussions, we clarified the falseness of His being purposeful in response to a contingent will. They thus have no way left to have it prove the intention to confirm the veracity of the declaration.

Chapter: [*That there is no proof of the veracity of the Prophet other than the miracle*]

Someone might ask: Is it possible to ascribe a proof for the Prophet's veracity to something other than the miracle? We reply: That is not possible, since what is presumed a proof of the Prophet's veracity must be either an ordinary fact or a rupturing of the habitual order. If it were a commonplace event, access to it would be the same for the pious and the profligate and it could not possibly constitute a proof. If it is a rupturing of the habitual order, it cannot constitute a proof unless it applies to the claim of a prophet, since all situations that involve the supernatural can happen spontaneously as an act of God, the Exalted. When there is no doubt as to its being applied to the claim of prophecy, it constitutes a miracle, pure and simple.

Chapter: [*The impossibility of God lying is a condition in the miracle's proof*]

Someone may observe at this point: If what you assert is granted concerning the miracle occupying the place of a verbal declaration of veracity, your purpose is not completely achieved, unless you provide a proof also of the impossibility of deceit and lying on the part of God, may He be sanctified. There is no way to prove this on the basis of tradition, since proofs taken from tradition have as their source the words of God, the Exalted. What cannot be proven to be valid and true of necessity does not continue to be a principle on the basis of tradition. One cannot derive an argument for it from consensus either, because reason cannot prove the validity of consensus. Its validity derives solely from the Book of God, the Exalted.

It is also not possible to base excepting God from lying on its being a defect for two reasons. One is that deceit, according to you, is determined arbitrarily and is not bad in and of itself. The second is that, were one to concede that it is a defect, the authority for rejecting defects is the proof supplied by tradition. We respond: In regard to the prophetic mission, its existence is proven in the present without this. Its being proven does not depend on reports about which one can say they are either true or false. It is as if the person sending someone had said: "I made him an apostle and I did it earlier." He does not say this to confirm an event that has passed.

It is the same as if someone were to say: I have given you my power of attorney and appointed you to look after my affairs. This power of attorney is equally valid whether on behalf of a truthful person or a liar. Basically the form of the power of attorney, even if it announces a fact, has as its purpose giving an order delegating affairs and appointing someone to conduct one's business. Truth and falseness do not enter into the issuing of the order. The sign of this is that, even if we charge the king with falsehood and deceit, the act which we stipulate of him confirms the veracity of the messenger and affirms his mission decisively and without any doubt. Affirming this point does not depend on denying deceit on the part of God, may He be sanctified and exalted. Understand it well!

However, although the prophetic mission is acknowledged, the veracity of the Prophet in regard to what he proclaims and transmits, the rules he makes law, the explanations he gives as to what is licit and illicit, is not proven, unless one has certainty that God, the Exalted, is exempt from deceit and lying. In transmitting what he conveys, the Prophet bases what he asserts as to his own truthfulness on God's confirmation of his veracity. What does not prove that God's confirming the veracity is necessarily valid and true does not prove the truthfulness of the Prophet in making his announcements. Confirming his truthfulness in the details of what he conveys is not the same as his having been appointed a messenger. The actuality of his appointment goes back to the proof of the order being given, but his veracity in reporting what he relates brings up the question of whether he himself is truthful or deceitful.

The scholar Abū Isḥāq [al-Isfarāyīnī], may God be pleased with him, in a book of his which is an introduction to the *Jāmiʿ*,[1] relied on a distinction the acceptance of which he urged. He said: The rules of law, in our view, do not go back to the attributes of these acts. Rather they go back only to the application of the eternal word. A thing is not obligatory in and of itself but one judges it to be obligatory because of the threat against abstaining from it or the promise of reward for having done it. The promise and the threat are communications. If they were not proven to be based on truth, no one would have confidence in them. If the matter is like this, one would have no notion of obligation, prohibition, recommendation to perform acts of obedience or warning against disobedience. The ultimate end of this leads to being unable to conceive a single order of God that one obeys, even though it is proven that He is a powerful and knowledgeable God, and despite not being able to perceive rationally of a divine being that one does not envision commanding and prohibiting. He said also, at the conclusion of this chapter: "If nothing in our book other than this meets with agreement, it would be a cause for joy."

---

1 The works of al-Isfarāyīnī have apparently not survived.

We have explained what we understand of the words of this illustrious master, may God approve of him. However, we do not believe that these arguments are sufficiently convincing. There is no means to decide the questions asked in regard to matters we have raised and there is no way to appeal to evident necessity. What is to be relied on to attain the objective behind this chapter is for us to state: We have explained clearly the course to follow to prove that the Creator, may He be sanctified, is knowing and purposeful. We have established previously, in a convincing fashion, the reality of spiritual speech. The person who knows something and who wants it is not precluded from proclaiming in himself what he knows and wants, consonant with the application of knowledge and will. Every quality to which the existent being is susceptible must exist in it, or the opposite of it must exist, if it has an opposite, as determined at the beginning of this theological handbook. Thus, if the Creator is not characterized as reporting truthfully, He must necessarily be qualified by its opposite. If He is qualified by its opposite, it is impossible to assume that truthfulness is inadvertent or heedless in regard to what we assumed was being reported. In that forgetting is contrary to reporting something, it is also contrary to knowing it and wanting it. Furthermore, if the contrary of the truthful proclamation is a proclamation that is false and deceitful and it comes out differently than proclaimed, having assumed such a qualification, it must be eternal and judged impossible of not being, since we previously proved that the speech is eternal.

Going down this route results in declaring it possible that what He knows by the application of knowledge the Creator cannot proclaim. And this is known to be false. We know with certainty that the knower of a thing, in so far as he knows it, cannot be characterized by a quality that precludes his having interior speech which applies to what he knows as he knows it. And this leads to maintaining the impossibility that, when he knows it, he can proclaim it inwardly. If asserting this impossibility is precluded in the visible world, and if those who reject what we have said relate it to denying intuitive evidence, it is necessary to generalize this to both the visible and invisible worlds.

Now it may be said: How were you able to insist on intuitive evidence in a matter of which the very principle is contested? Most of the theologians uphold the rejecting of interior speech. We respond: What the orthodox claim is that interior speech is undeniable. What is contested in our assertion is merely whether it is a speech or a belief or knowledge. As for the thoughts and ideas of the soul, what characterizes them is known and cannot be denied.

If they say: Given that interior speech exists, it is not impossible that someone knows that Zayd is in the house but nevertheless there circulates in his mind the thought that he is not in the house, we reply: This is an imaginary fantasy. The speech that circulates is a proclamation and it proclaims something that is neither complete nor positively affirmed. What verifies this is that someone who knows a thing and proclaims it as he knows it in a definitive manner has circulating in his soul the question which was posed to him. The conversation of the soul continuously reflects the truth as it was prior to any thought of this other presumption.

If what this question aimed to impose were actually true, its being joined with its contrary would be impossible. All persons who know something and who proclaim it as it really is would find of necessity in themselves the qualification of having proclaimed it, despite any presumption of theirs that they proclaimed it falsely. This is like someone knowing a thing as it really is despite the possibility of his believing that it is otherwise than it really is. A belief that is merely presumed to accompany certified knowledge is not an authentic belief.

What we have said makes it quite clear that to presume the possibility of a quality incompatible with the soul's conversing about what is known by knowledge and in conformity with the application of knowledge is an assertion of an impossibility that reason rejects. What corroborates what we say is the fact that someone who knows a thing, if thoughts of the falsity were not imposed on his heart, he would continue to have an inner truthful conversation about it, despite knowing about the assumption that he could impose on himself. But it is thus not a qualification contrary to a communication that is true.

This evaluation should suffice here. It demonstrates that the Creator is qualified by speech that applies to what is known in conformity to the knowledge applicable to that thing. If someone desires a more extensive explanation than this, let him consult the *Shāmil.*

Section
THE DOCTRINE ABOUT PROVING THE PROPHECY OF OUR PROPHET MUHAMMAD, GOD BLESS HIM AND KEEP HIM

Chapter: [*On abrogation*]

The foregoing discussion concerned the proof of the principle of prophecy in general and our purpose now is to provide a proof of the prophetic mission of our Prophet Muhammad, God bless him and keep him.

Two sorts of people reject prophecy. One of the two bases its doctrine on the inadmissibility of abrogation and the other on the controversies about the Prophet's signs and miracles. A sect of the Jews called the ʿĪsawiyya[1] uphold the prophecy of Muhammad, God bless him and keep him, but they regard his law as particular to the Arabs, to the exclusion of all other peoples.

As for those who reject abrogation, as is the case with most of the Jews, our objective in proving their doctrines false is best demonstrated by mentioning briefly and succinctly the exact nature of abrogation. The concept we approve is that abrogation is a pronouncement that institutes the cancellation of an established rule by replacing it with another pronouncement in such a way that, if the second did not exist, the abrogated rule would continue in force. For an abrogation really to exist, it must of necessity nullify a rule that had been established previously.

The Muʿtazilites maintain that abrogation does not nullify an established rule but rather makes specific the terminal point of a law's duration. Some of our own leading masters leaned in that direction as well. They held that abrogation specifies a period of time. They mean by it that, if those under obligation had been imposed upon by a law without qualifications, their being under imposition would appear to endure forever. But if and when it is abrogated, it becomes clear that its terms applied only for a specific time in the past.

This, in our view, denies abrogation and rejects its very principle. It limits abrogation to providing explanations of meanings in terms that one did not understand in the beginning or assigning it the function of making specific some general formulation. But it was not intended to make specific some general formulation. To the Muʿtazilites and to those leaning their way who are related to us, we counter with the following two objections based on the requirements of two principles.

We say to the Muʿtazilites: It is a principle of yours that the delay of the explanation beyond the advent of the commandment until a time it is needed is

---

1 The ʿĪsawiyya were a Jewish sect from the early Islamic period. They were followers of a certain Abū ʿĪsā al-Iṣfahānī. On them see the article by S. Pines, "al-ʿĪsāwiyya" in the *EI2*.

unacceptable. Thus, if abrogation were an explanation of the rule, it could not be delayed beyond the initial expression of the commandment, just as, in your view, the determination of specific factors in a general formulation, if it was originally devoid of restricting factors, cannot be delayed. They have no way to escape from this.

We say to our own associates: You know that we uphold the possibility of an imposed act of devotion being abrogated before the time for its execution has elapsed. It is impossible, if one maintains this, to hold that abrogation makes clear the termination of the time to perform an act of devotion, since it is impossible to suppose that acts of devotion are allotted a time period which is not sufficient for their performance. Moreover, Abraham, God bless him and keep him, was commanded, in our view and those of our associates, to slaughter his son initially, and only later was that order abrogated. What he was commanded to do was to slaughter his son, pure and simple. It was not a series of extended and repeated acts, such that the command might apply to one and the abrogation to another of them.

If the abrogation pertains to the commanded act in itself, it must in reality mean the cancellation of the command's application. Having made this clear, we will refute the Jews who reject abrogation. We say: Between the possible and the impossible, no intermediate degree is conceivable. The aspects of impossibility have been fully determined. Some things are impossible in and of themselves, such as the alteration of genus or the simultaneity of two opposites. But to command something prohibited is not impossible in and of itself. One can conceive of it; nothing makes it impossible. If it is not impossible in and of itself, ascribing that impossibility to another is also precluded, since its being possible does not change the reality of any of the divine attributes. The characteristic of the act is not an essential attribute of that act, as we determined earlier. In the presumption of abrogation, there is nothing requiring the alteration of either knowledge or will. One can proceed with this generally until it becomes clear that abrogation is neither impossible in and of itself, nor does it entail the impossibility of anything else.

They may ask: How do you rebut those who insist that it is impossible because it leads to attributing to God, the Exalted, a change of mind [*badā*] from which He is exempt. We reply: "Change of mind" [*al-badā*ʾ] is an expression for the acquisition of some knowledge that did not exist previously; the person who comes to comprehend that thing did not previously have knowledge of it. Thus one says, "It appeared [*badā*] to him." One also employs this term for someone who is intent on doing something but then subsequently regrets what he had been about to do. Neither of these senses of the term applies in abrogation. God's knowledge, may He be sanctified, applies to things known in the way they are. No new knowledge that did not exist previously comes to Him. Moreover, according to our principles, will is not a consideration in commanding since God, may He be sanctified and exalted, commands what He does not want and

He wants what He does not order. There is thus no way to assert that something new appeared [*badā*] to Him.

Those who deny abrogation also derive support from a fantasy that none can refute properly, except those extremely well versed in this subject matter. This consists of their saying: In respect to whatever God makes obligatory, He issues a proclamation of its obligatory status. If He forbids it and declares that it is forbidden, He converts the first proclamation into another creation that happens to be the opposite of what He had declared. And that is impossible.

What they cite here is a useless fantasy. According our doctrine, obligation does not derive from an attribute belonging to the obligatory thing. Instead, the meaning of a thing's being obligatory is that someone has said in reference to it: "Do it." If God, the Exalted, proclaims something obligatory, it means that He announces that He has commanded that it be done. If He forbids it, He declares that He has forbid it. Between the proclamation of the command to do it and the declaration forbidding it, there is no confirmation in one that is contradicted in the other. Both of the two declarations must be characterized as completely true.

These people imagined what they mentioned only because they believe that the obligatoriness is an attribute of the obligatory thing. They assume that the proclamation refers to it and the subsequent declaration is then contrary to that very thing in itself. This position is extremely difficult for them to defend in that they acknowledge the abrogation is the cancellation of an established rule and has as its purpose the elucidation of a previously established matter. Whoever grasps what we have just mentioned will easily perceive how to refute this question. Having proven the possibility of abrogation rationally, nothing further precludes it according to evidence of tradition.

However, a small group of Jews have appeared who were inspired by Ibn al-Rāwandī[2] to raise questions and to cause the common folk and the ordinary people who follow them to fall into error. They say: Abrogation is accepted by the Muslims. However, the Muslims maintain that their law will last until the end of mortal life. But, if they are asked for proof of this, they revert to their own Prophet's declaration to them of the perpetuity of his law. We say that Moses informed us of the perpetuity of his law and thus it is his which will be perpetuated since he is accepted as truthful by universal consensus. This argument of theirs is false for two reasons.

One is that, if what they report were true, it would be valid. But, if it were really true, no miracles would have appeared in connection with Jesus and Muḥammad, on both be peace. Once they did appear, however, they demonstrated the mendacity of the Jews. Should ever a miracle appear, according

2 Abuʾl-Ḥusayn Aḥmad b. al-Rāwandī was an enigmatic figure of the third/ninth century who is usually described as a heretic or a free-thinker. On him see the entry "Ibn al-Rāwandī" in the *EI2* and Sarah Stroumsa, *Free thinkers of Medieval Islam: Ibn al-Rāwandī, Abū Bakr al-Rāzī, and Their Impact on Islamic Thought* (Leiden: Brill, 1999).

to our law, at the hand of a pretender to prophecy, that would reveal our mendacity in regard to the perpetuity of our law. This first reason is obvious. If they now resort to the repudiation of the miracles of Jesus and Muḥammad, on whom be peace, any argument they bring forth to that end can be used against them in regard to the miracle of Moses, on whom be peace.

The second reason consists in our saying that, if what you said or intimated were correct, it would be more proper that the era for this to appear would be the era of the Prophet, God bless him and keep him. It is known that those of you who rejected the prophecy of Muḥammad, God bless and keep him, were not able to refute his prophecy and so altered the description of Muḥammad, God bless him and keep him, in the Torah. If there had been in it a formal, incontrovertible designation about the perpetuity of the law of Moses, on whom be peace, it would have been proclaimed and considered the strongest safeguard. But, since they did not invoke it in either the time of Jesus or the era of Muḥammad, on whom be peace, given that for them to have invoked it then would have aided their claims about their reports substantially, it becomes clear from this that it was an invention of those who inspired them. And God refuses but to perfect His light.[3]

This fulfils our purpose in regard to the subject of abrogation. Having just proven that the possibility of abrogation accords with the rules of reason, it is now time to speak about the miracle of the apostle.

Chapter: [*On the miracles of Muḥammad, God bless him and keep him*]

It is best for us to begin this chapter with what applies to the Qurʾān and to confirm that it constitutes a miracle. Our goals are most clearly reached here by reviewing our responses to a number of questions.

Someone may inquire: What is your proof that your Prophet divulged the Qurʾān? And what assures you that it was not forged after him? We reply: One cannot argue against the self-evident. We know necessarily that our Prophet, on whom be peace, used to teach the Qurʾān and to recite it. He expounded it to his Companions and his followers. Whatever is proven by multiple concurring reports is known with self-evident certainty. To reject this is tantamount to denying that Muḥammad, God bless him and keep him, was ever in this world. That would be like denying the nations, events and times of those in bygone eras. There is no sense in going on about this at length.

Now it maybe said: Even if his divulging it in his own era were conceded to you, what is your proof of his having issued his prophetic challenge through it and having caused the nations summoned to contest with him not being able to do so? We respond to this: This also is known with self-evident certainty. The

3 "They want to extinguish the light of God with their mouths; and God refuses but to perfect His light . . ." [Qurʾān 9:32].

apostle of God, God bless him and keep him, never stopped speaking about the Qurʾān, applying it as evidence, insisting that he alone was singled out by having the Book of God, the Exalted, revealed to him. Those who deny the claim of his having been chosen for it and his being connected by the Lord God's specifically designating him with His Book, have rejected something attested by multiple and concordant reports.

What confirms what we say is that we know with intuitive certainty that, if one of the Arabs had produced – for the sake of argument – another Qurʾān like it, that would reject as unacceptable the pretension to a claim of prophecy, discredit the person making the claim and lower his status. This cannot be denied. If he had not issued his prophetic challenge in conjunction with it, the matter would not have been as it was. But there is no concealing what we have said; verses of the Qurʾān proclaim clearly the prophetic challenge and the resulting incapacity of the Arabs. Among them are the following words of God: "Say: if men and the jinn joined together to produce the like of this Qurʾān, they could not produce its like, even if they backed one another" [17:88]. And there are other verses with the same meaning.

If someone says: It is not inconceivable to suppose divergences in these verses in their own right, since attaining the status of inimitability does not preclude assuming that they were themselves an invention, we reply: There is no verse of the Qurʾān whose transmission is not fully confirmed by multiple reports, since the reading of the later follows that of the preceding generations. The matter has been like this continuously; the younger generations transmit it from the older, going back without break in transmission to the reading of the Companions, may God be pleased with them. Nor did the number of readers in any given era decrease below the number that assures certainty. What further clarifies what we have just said is that, if we were to be able to doubt the origin of a given verse, this would extend to every verse and thereby invalidate the integrity of the transmission of the whole Qurʾān.

Someone may ask: What assures you that the Qurʾān was not contested and that what was contested in it was not subsequently hidden? We respond: This is absurd since, if it had happened like that, the matter would have been revealed and become well known. Circumstances so momentous as that could not be concealed over the course of time. Claiming what the questioner claims is tantamount to asserting that there was a caliph in charge of the Muslims prior to Abū Bakr, may God be pleased with him. And that is self-evidently known to be false.

What supports our contention is that the unbelievers, from the time of the apostle of God, God bless him and keep him, until our era, have expended the utmost effort they have been capable of to destroy our religion. If the contestation had been possible and not completely unrealizable, over the past centuries and eras, they would have used every trick to achieve it. If the contesting of it were to have once been concealed, another instance of it or like it would have taken its place.

Furthermore, if this question or one like it were posed by those who uphold prophetic missions, one can turn against them all they advance with respect to the miracles of their own prophet. Say thus to the Jews: What assures you that Moses, on whom be peace, did not have his signs contested and that subsequently the tribe of Israel agreed among themselves to eradicate any information about occurrence of the contestation?

Someone may ask: How would you rebut those who insist that the Arabs did not refrain from contesting the Qurʾān because of an inability but rather they did not undertake it only because they had almost no interest in doing so? We reply: This is a weak argument indeed and one that no person with the least education would offer in public. The discussions and conferences of the Arabs were lively and animated, and they were vehement about disputing the weakness or strength of poetry. From this we know of necessity that the Qurʾān, in their belief, was not so inferior to the poetry of a poet or a work in prose that they took so little notice of it as to refrain even from discussing it.

How could this be when the Apostle, on whom be peace, and his supporters, said: "If you can contest successfully even one *sūra* of the Qurʾān, we will accord you peace; we will abandon the struggle and submit willingly to you. But, if it turns out to be otherwise, we will light the fire of war, devote our power entirely to it, make ourselves masters of its art, and desist neither from killing men nor violating freed Arab women." How could an intelligent person think, after the word of Islam had appeared and the flags and banners of the Muslims were waving, that the unbelievers would prefer to face horrors that turn forelocks white and events that make the immovable vanish, rather than to contest a *sūra* simply out of disdain for them?

Thus the miracle, the prophetic challenge, and the inability of anyone to contest it are proven. This evaluation suffices to accomplish what we wanted. And God alone is the guide to the truth.

Chapter: [*On the various ways the Qurʾān is inimitable*]

If it is said: Explain to us in how, in what way, and to what degree the Qurʾān is inimitable, we respond: The doctrine approved by us is that the Qurʾān is inimitable because it combines eloquence with an elegance of form in an arrangement distinct from the ordinary speech of the Arabs. Hence the arrangement of words by itself does not yield the inimitability in it, nor does its eloquence alone.

The proof of this is for us to suppose simply that its eloquence is inimitable. This will not eliminate the following hypothetical challenge. Someone might say: If the Qurʾān were to be compared to the discourse of the Arabs, their prose, their grand poetry, and their poetry of short metres, the language of the masters of eloquence and rhetorical talents would not, in a manner that is clearly and decisively convincing, be judged inferior to the eloquence of the Qurʾān. On the other hand, if we claim that its inimitability resides solely in its form and an arrangement it has that differs from other modes of speech, one might direct against us examples of feeble utterances that resemble the order in Qurʾānic diction, such as in the shame speech of Musaylama, the impostor, when he said: "The elephant! What is the elephant? And how can one grasp what an elephant is with its small thin tail and long trunk?" Something like this is not inimitable but is merely the condoning of absurdities and vile utterances designed to shock the ears. The sum of what we have just said forces us to tie together the inimitability in its wondrous order and in its eloquence.

Someone may say: What sort of rhetorical eloquence does the Qurʾān contain and in what way does its order differ from ordinary modes of speech? We answer: With respect to rhetorical eloquence, this is quite evident and obvious. Eloquence consists in expressing an appropriate meaning with a noble, apt and clear phrase, indicating what is to be said without superfluous additions. That is eloquent speech and precise discourse. Moreover, eloquence in speaking is comprised of several types.

Of them all, one consists of a discourse that indicates a multiplicity of meanings in few expressions. There are innumerable examples of this type in the Qurʾān.

One such example is God's providing, in only part of a verse, a lesson in the stories of bygone peoples about the future outcome reserved for those who exaggerate and the punishments for those who wreak destruction. He, the Mighty and Glorious, says: "[Each We seized for his sin]; and of them, against some We sent a storm of stones, some were caught by a mighty cry, some We caused the earth to swallow and some We drowned; God would never harm them but they wronged themselves" [29:40].

The Lord also said, at the beginning of the story of Noah's ark, of its floating above the waves and the destruction of the unbelievers, of its coming to rest and standing stationary, and of the commandment directed at the earth and the heavens to desist, and all that in His saying: "So he said, 'Embark in it, in God's name is its course and its berthing'" on to His words, "And it was said, 'Away with those who do evil'" [11:41–44].

God also teaches about the dead, the grief of separation, the life everlasting and its rewards and punishments, the good fortune of those who succeed, and the misfortune of those who commit sins. He warns against the deceptions of this world and describes its insignificance in relationship to that abode of permanent life. All of this He provides in His statement: "Every soul will taste of death; and only on the day of resurrection you will be paid your wages" (to the end of the verse) [3:185].

Another type of eloquent speech consists in telling a story without losing the elements of eloquence. Most masters of eloquence use an elevated style when they compose amorous praises of a beloved. But, if they are giving an intimate account of internal states, they employ threadbare language and scrawny words. If they were to try to use eloquent speech, one will be unable to perceive in it what they want to say in such a case.

Note, however, the story of Joseph, God bless him and keep him, which, despite comprising diverse and complex elements, was put together in the most pleasing arrangement and with the most elegant language, well ordered throughout, nicely assembled, as if its verses stood one on the neck of the other. Moreover, stories cannot be devoid of ambiguity and redundancy, especially if the meanings are identical. But we have not imposed on ourselves in this handbook the task of draining an inexhaustible sea.

Among the most valid signs of the eloquence of the Qurʾān is its acknowledgment by the Arabs without exception, explicitly or implicitly. Some recognized it and declared so outright; others remained silent and did not speak about it. If there were in the Qurʾān the least inelegance, the ones with the most right to charge it with this weakness would have been the specialists in language.

If someone asks here: Is there in the Qurʾān any type of inimitability other than its arrangement and eloquence? We reply: Certainly, there are two other areas of its inimitability.

One is its relating of the stories about bygone peoples that are found to be in conformity to what exists in the other books that God revealed and yet the apostle of God, God bless him and keep him, was neither a scholar nor proficient at absorbing books. He was born among the Arabs and he had not undertaken trips abroad in which he could absorb knowledge and study literature. This is the truest of the signs of his veracity.

The Qurʾān, moreover, contains predictions that apply to future events and information about unseen matters, which might ordinarily come to pass once, perhaps, or twice. But when they follow in unerring succession, it constitutes a supernatural break in the habitual order. An example of secret matters in the Qurʾān is God's statement, "Say: if men and the jinn joined together . . ." (to the end of the verse) [17:88]; and His saying, "But if you do not – and certainly you will not . . ." [2:24]; and the Exalted saying, "You will enter the sacred mosque" [48:27]; His saying, "Alif, lām, mīm; the Roman Empire has been defeated" [30:2]; His saying, "God has promised you many spoils" [48:20] and others it would take too long to enumerate.

Chapter: [*The miraculous signs of the apostle, God bless him and keep him, other than the Qurʾān*]

Aside from the Qurʾān, the apostle, God bless him and keep him, has innumerable miracles, such as the splitting of the moon, causing the mute to speak, water springing from between the fingers, the stone that glorified God and making much food out of only a little.

The view we approve is that any one of these miracles by itself has not been proven by sufficiently numerous reports, but the aggregate of them provides decisive knowledge of his having been distinguished by extraordinary supernatural events. It is similar to the individual acts of generosity done by

Ḥātim,[4] which each by itself is not attested by sufficient reports but which together yield undeniable knowledge of his liberality. Like this are the reports about the courage of the Commander of the Faithful, ʿAlī, may God be pleased with him, and his bravery. With respect to the splitting of the moon, it is related by verses of the Book of God whose transmission is confirmed by multiple and concordant reports. This evaluation should be effective and sufficient for what we hope to accomplish here.

4 Ḥātim al-Ṭāʾī was an Arab poet of the sixth century who is known proverbially as the paragon of generosity and hospitality.

Section
The General Characteristics of the Prophets

[*Chapter*]: *The doctrine of the prophets' characteristics in general, the blessings of God be upon them all*

Understand that the best approach to the subject of this section is to start with the various meanings of the term "prophecy". Prophecy does not designate the individual being of a particular prophet, nor one of his accidental qualities. It is also false to ascribe it to his knowledge of his Lord, since that exists without the presumption of prophecy. It is likewise false to ascribe prophecy to the prophet's knowing that he is a prophet, since if what is known is indeterminate, knowledge cannot determine it. If a prophet knows that he has prophecy, what is his prophecy? This was the question after all.

Prophecy derives then from the declaration by God, the Exalted, to the one He selects, "You are my apostle", and this is the same as with its characteristics. They go back to the declaration of God. They are not attributes of human acts; the obligatory act does not have a quality by which it is in itself obligatory. Rather the act is declared so by the command "Do it", which makes it obligatory on account of this statement. This is the same as something said which does not acquire any quality in itself from having been uttered.

Chapter: [*On the impeccability of the prophets*]

If someone says: Explain to us the impeccability of the prophets and what necessitates that they have it, we respond: Their impeccability is required against those who would controvert the evidence of miracles. This is something we know rationally. The significance of the miracle is their veracity with respect to what they convey from God. It may be asked: Is it necessary that they be exempt from acts of disobedience? We answer: In regard to vile acts that imply defects and a diminution of faith, it is necessary by unanimous agreement of the community that the prophets be exempt from them.

But reason does not attest to this. Rather it bears witness to the necessity of impeccability only with regard to those who controvert the evidence provided by miracles. As for sins counted as being minor, according to the provisions we will explain later, reason does not deny them in prophets. In my view, there exists no decisive proof in tradition that either denies or affirms them, because decisive proofs exist only in the textual passages or in consensus and, since the scholars differ among themselves regarding the permissibility of attributing minor sins to the prophets, there is no consensus. And textual passages, on the basis of which principles are affirmed as decisively proven and which are not susceptible to interpretation, do not exist in this case.

If someone says: If the question is one of probability, whaṭ in your opinion is most probably true? We reply: Most probably, in our view, they are possible [on the part of prophets]. A number of stories about the prophets in the verses of the book of God attest to this. But God alone knows the truth.

If someone says: You have investigated every issue that concerns the prophetic missions that is appropriate to a handbook of theology but you have neglected to refute the ʿIsawiyya. We answer: We did that only because the explanation of the incoherence of their doctrine seemed clear. They accept Muḥammad's law but then declare it false. We, however, know of necessity that he asserted that he had been sent to men and the jinn and that he himself sent missionaries to the rulers of Persia and other foreign kings. Clearly, based on this, their doctrine falls apart. And it fills in a matter that should not be ignored in the subject of the prophetic missions.

Section
[The Doctrine Concerning Evidence from Tradition]

Understand, and may God, the Exalted, guide you rightly in this, that the principles of faith are divided into what can be perceived by reason which one is not permitted to presume that it can be perceived by tradition, what can be perceived on the basis of tradition but which cannot be assumed to be perceived by reason, and what one is allowed to perceive on the basis of both tradition and reason.

As for what cannot be perceived except by reason, all elements of faith depend originally on knowing the word of God, the Exalted, and on the necessity of its having the quality of being true. The evidence supplied by tradition is grounded in the speech of God. Thus, prior to the affirmation of the speech, what one must acknowledge cannot possibly be grasped through tradition.

As for what cannot be grasped except through tradition, it is the judgment that affirms the realization of what is possible according to reason. But, in regard to something not present to us, the rule that establishes its acceptability and makes its application necessary depends solely on tradition. One finds in these categories, in our view, all of the rules covering the imposed obligations and the situations they involve pertaining to determining the bad and the good, the obligatory and forbidden, the recommended and the permitted.

As for what may be perceived both by reason and tradition, it is that to which reason attests and is preceded by envisioning affirming the knowledge of the speech of God. This category can be perceived both by tradition and by reason. An example of this category is the affirmation of the possibility of seeing God, of God the Creator alone having the power to create and originate, and other things like these that fall under the definition just given. In regard to the existence of the vision of God, it is proven on the basis of a truthful promise and authentic statement.

Having established these preliminary points, it becomes incumbent next on every person who is attentive to religion, and who is confident in his ability to reason, to reflect on that to which the proofs supplied by tradition apply. If he finds that this is not impossible according to reason and yet also the proofs of tradition are decisive in their application – leaving no scope for doubting the affirmation of its basis or for interpretations of it – if this was how the matter proceeded, it must be taken as decisively established.

If, on the contrary, the proofs of tradition do not establish it in a conclusive manner, even though what it contains is not impossible in reason and its root principles are confirmed decisively, it remains susceptible to divergent interpretations and it cannot be taken as decisive. Nevertheless, even though it does not have definitive certainty, the pious ought to consider probable the existence of what is proven by the proofs of tradition. If, however, something contained in the law that has come to us is contrary to the judgments of reason, on the basis that the law is not contrary to reason, it should be rejected decisively. In this category there is no way to formulate a decisive rule on the basis of tradition and that should be obvious.

These are the preliminary points that concern the evidence of tradition. One should grasp them well. We will now set forth its topics one after the other, seeking the aid of God, and we will mention in chapters keyed to each topic what needs to be said about each one, God willing.

Section
On Time Limits

Time limits denote periods of time. Thus the term of something is its time and the term of a life is the time period associated with it and likewise the term of death. Time periods in the general sense frequently connote the movements of the celestial spheres, the passing of day into night and night into day.

Speaking more precisely, times are not specific to certain categories of beings, as, for example, would be the specificity of certain substances and sciences and the like. On the contrary, everything that occurs must coincide with a temporal act and the act that coincides with it initiates its time period in accord with the intention and the wishes of what determines that time period. Thus, if someone were to say: Zayd came when the sun rose, he has made the rising of the sun the time of his coming. If, however, he had said: The sun rose when Zayd came, he has made the coming of Zayd the time for the rising of the sun.

The principle behind fixing the time consists in determining a temporal action that is known and supposing that, in what he wants to assign to another, it is uncertain. The imagined uncertainty ceases by linking the mention of the second to the mention of the one that was known. Moreover, it is possible to determine as a time the coming into existence or renewal of some other thing, and it is possible for the time to be its extinction, if the coming or going of that thing is really known, as in the example of someone saying: That atom will move when it ceases to be black.

Some of the ancients maintained that all existent beings must necessarily have their own time. From this they decided that there were an infinite number of time periods without a beginning. They claimed that the Creator has always existed in endless time periods. But this is not acceptable and there is no meaning for time except the coinciding of something coming to be with a temporal act or the coincidence of a temporal act with another temporal act.

We have demonstrated clearly that God is eternal and we have shown the impossibility of there being contingent things that have no first term. These two premises require that what these people had said is false. If every existent being required its own time, times would require other times. Thus this doctrine leads back through an unbroken chain to an ignorance into which no person of intelligence would ever be forced.

The goal of this section was for us to acknowledge that every person murdered has met death at his proper term. This means that God already knew from eternity what would happen to the person who is eventually killed. Everything that God knows will come to pass will most certainly happen. Someone might ask: If one were to suppose that he was not killed, what would you say about his dying or continuing to live?

We would answer: Many of the Muʿtazilites hold that, if one assumes that he were not killed, he would continue to live for a certain period. It is the murderer who by that act cuts short his term. Others of them maintain that, if he were not killed, as supposed, he would die a natural death nevertheless at the time at which he was supposed to be killed. All this is a confused argument going nowhere.

The credible approach is to hold that the one about whom God knows that he will be killed will most certainly be killed. If someone were to suppose his not being killed and supposed also that it is known that he will not be killed, there cannot be with this supposition any certainty that his life will be extended or cut short by death at the same time in lieu of being killed. On the contrary, one is not precluded from presuming anything that is possible according to reason. One cannot say otherwise. Verses of the Book of God attest that every person who perishes completes his term. One of them is His saying: "When their term comes, they will not be able to delay it an hour or to advance it" [16:61].

Someone may ask: What is the meaning of God's saying: "Nor is an old man granted a long life or some part of it subtracted but it is in a book" [35:11]?

We reply: The intent of this verse involves two aspects of interpretation. One is that it means that the reduction in the life of an individual compares with other lives of the same kind or with the duration accorded others resembling it. It does not imply that the reduction of his life enters among what is known to God. How could this be allowed when it presumes a change in the knowledge of God, the Exalted? The second aspect is that the increase and decrease consist of effacing or affirming what is discovered on the pages taken from the angels. Some things on their pages may be confirmed in a general way although fixed within the knowledge of God as exactly what it was. The page is subsequently restored to conform to God's knowledge. The most authoritative commentators construe the following words of God to mean exactly that: "God blots out and He establishes whatsoever He will" [13:39].[1]

---

1 The line just prior to this verse reads, "Every term has a book" [13:38].

Section
On Subsistence

Subsistence applies to the thing that subsists as a beneficence applied to the thing that benefits from it. What we approve as the meaning of subsistence is that everything utilized by a person constitutes his subsistence and there is no difference between those he uses unjustly and those he uses justly.

Some of the Muʿtazilites hold that subsistence is what one possesses and the subsistence of all existing beings is what they possess. But one can raise against these people the objection that the Creator's property is His subsistence, given that He possesses it. They will find no way to defend against this.

Later Muʿtazilites added to the definition and said: The subsistence of the one who subsists consists in those possessions of his that he utilizes. These people thus guard themselves from having it understood to include the property of God, since they restrict the possessions to those actually utilized. The Lord God is beyond needing to use anything. But, despite this restriction, one can object that they are saying that God does not bestow subsistence on the animals, since, even though they put it to use, they would not be characterized as owning something. God, the Exalted, has said: "There is no beast on the earth whose subsistence is not provided by God" [11:6]. Thus, if what they say has proven false, nothing remains but to use subsistence in the sense of utilization without taking into consideration proprietorship.

Should they now say: This principle forces one to consider things extorted as sustenance for the extortionist, if and when he puts them to use. Moreover, there is no way to prevent him from having his sustenance and keep him from the subsistence God provided him or to direct at him reproach for it. But what they want to reject is evidence for our doctrine. Everyone who utilizes something is sustained by it.

Furthermore, subsistence is divided into the illicit and the licit. What they mention as a subject receiving sustenance who cannot be deprived of his subsistence is simply precluded and unacceptable. Quite obviously, in raising this objection, they contradict their own doctrine in which the power for faith is also the power for unbelief. The unbeliever is, therefore, according to them, aided by God, the Exalted, in his unbelief. Thus, if it is not inconceivable that the punisher who punishes someone for his unbelief is also the enabler who makes the unbelief possible, what we have said is likewise not inconceivable.

Moreover, what they admit leads to monstrosities that no person of true religion would accept. That is to say about someone who took nourishment all his life from forbidden foods and used his sustenance for illicit purposes in every way that he was not accorded subsistence by God and that God had never given him sustenance. This is an enormity no religious person would advocate.

Subsistence, according to us, is said of something one utilizes when its use is effective. This is the result of employing the term in its general sense. Of a person who possesses considerable means but does not put them to use, it should be said to him that God did not grant him what he hoards as subsistence. Thus it is not feasible to apply subsistence to the acquisition of goods pure and simple, as in ordinary speech.

This then goes back to saying that subsistence is the utilization of goods and, when one calls utilization subsistence, what one means by it is expenditure, since if we make utilization in and of itself subsistence, we exclude foods, drink, and provisions from being considered subsistence. That departs from the rules of language. The statements in this section and in what preceded it concern solely the expressions themselves and the controversy about them.

Section
On Prices

The prices of all goods accord with the dictates of God, the Exalted. They are established as the exchange values of things. The price depends on factors over which a human has no control, such as scarcity and abundance, the fluctuation of interest and need, the increase and lessening of demand. Factors in them to which human choice applies are likewise acts of God, the Exalted, since there is no Creator other than He.

The Muʿtazilites profess a doctrine that prices are set by human action. In what we have set out previously, in regard to the creation of deeds, there is already a convincing refutation of their notions.

Section

On Commanding the Good and Prohibiting the Reprehensible

Customarily, the theologians would take up this topic in legal theory and indeed it falls more properly in the domain of the experts in jurisprudence. Commanding the good and forbidding the reprehensible is obligatory in general by unanimous agreement. One need not pay attention to the doctrine of the Shīʿa that commanding the good and forbidding the reprehensible must await the appearance of the Imam. The Muslims were in agreement, prior to the spread of these people, on the admonition to command the good and forbid the reprehensible and to censure those who neglect to undertake to do it. We can perhaps impart here enough elucidation to rebut the declarations of the Imāmiyya,[1] if God so wills.

If what we have said is admitted as a principle, commanding the good is not specifically a duty of those appointed to govern but is rather incumbent on every Muslim individually. This rule was also established by the unanimous agreement of the community. In the earliest days and in the era that followed, persons other than those appointed to govern used to command those who governed to do good and to enjoin them from doing what is reprehensible and, moreover, the Muslims supported them and refrained from blaming them for being occupied with commanding the good without an explicit commission to do so.

We would add here that the rule in the law divides into what the élite and the masses have equal ability to grasp without needing special legal investigation and what requires the counsel of experts. As for what does not require special competence, those knowledgeable and those not knowledgeable can command, in that area, the good and forbid the reprehensible. For what can only be apprehended by the specialists in law, the common folk are not allowed to command and forbid in that area but rather command in it has been entrusted exclusively to persons with special legal competence.

No legal authority may interpose an obstacle or a suppression against the judgment of another legal authority on issues in which there is dispute, since every authority, in our view, is correct in regard to the positive applications of the law. Those who maintain that only one is correct cannot specify which one he is. Thus, in either doctrine, one legal authority is prevented from trying to suppress another.

Furthermore, if the person who takes upon himself the commanding of the good is not himself virtuous, his commanding of the good does not cease. What

1 The Imāmiyya are the main branch of the Shīʿa otherwise called the Twelvers (the Ithnā ʿashariyya).

is specifically imposed on him personally is a duty that is distinct from what he is required to command in others. One of the two duties does not necessarily apply to the other. Moreover, commanding the good is a duty of sufficiency. If in each district there is someone who can undertake it adequately by himself, the obligation on the rest is removed.

A part of commanding the good and forbidding the reprehensible is stopping the perpetrator of mortal sins from committing them, if such a person cannot be kept from doing them by verbal admonitions. All of the people are permitted to undertake to do this, if the matter does not end by provoking fighting and the use of weapons. If it were to go that far, it would be a matter for the ruler to handle and only he. If the person in charge at the time happens to be a tyrant and manifests his injustice and inequity and he will not listen to the advice to refrain from the evil he commits, those who have the power to invest and depose should act in concert to get rid of him, even if it requires armed struggle and the onset of open war.

Commanding the good does not require investigation, inspection or the use of spies and breaking into houses on the basis of suspicions. Instead, if you encounter someone doing a reprehensible thing, make an effort to change what that person is doing.

These are the rules concerning commanding the good and forbidding the reprehensible. There is no exception for any of them; from beginning to end, the law provides explicit details.

Section
On Resurrection

The objective of this section will be comprised in two chapters, one of which consists of proving the possibility of resurrection and the other in its actual occurrence.

As for the possibility of the resurrection, reason attests to it, as also does tradition, as we mentioned at the beginning of the section on the evidence of tradition. Everything brought into being that ceases to exist may be restored to existence, no matter whether it is an atom or an accident.

Some of our colleagues maintain that the accidents will not be restored and they base this on the idea that what returns to existence is restored for the sake of a qualifying property and, if the accident returned, it would need to have such a property. But this notion is not accepted as a principle by those most correct, since being restored is tantamount to the first creation and what is restored is not restored for the sake of a property.

The Muʿtazilites admit the restoration of the atoms when they have ceased to exist and they divide the accidents into those that persist and those that do not persist. They say: Those that do not persist, such as sounds and will, cannot be returned to existence. Every accident whose persisting is impossible is particular, according to them, to a specific moment that one cannot presume could be either earlier or later. As for those of the accidents that persist, they are separated into those within the power of humans and those not in their power. With regard to those within their power, a human cannot restore them to existence, nor is it correct, according to them, to ascribe their restoration to the Eternal Being. As for that to which the power of humans does not apply, namely those that persist, it is possible for them to be restored to existence.

If we were asked for the proof of the possibility of resurrection, we would produce it on the basis of textual passages of the Holy Book and the sense of its words. We relate the resurrection to the first creation, just as God Himself said in refuting the one who denied the resurrection: "That person says, 'Who shall restore life to the bones when they are decayed?' Say: 'He will restore them to life who created them the first time, for He knows about all creating'" [36:78–79].

To facilitate the development of the proof we might assume that of necessity the resurrection differs from the first creation. But, if we presume that it is like the first creation, reason then admits its possibility since that whose existence is admitted, because it is a characteristic of two alike things that they are equal in being necessary and possible, its like is also possible. However, this is a digression. The resurrection is the restoration of existence and what is restored to existence is the very thing that was created once before. How could a thing be presumed to differ from its own self? Proof based on the moments which are merely the coincident relationship that one of the existents bears to another has no effect. What one assumes to exist at one moment is not precluded from being presumed to exist in another.

This will not help the Muʿtazilites since they cut off the principle on which resurrection is based by precluding it in that thing of which the accidents do not endure. They state: We only preclude the resurrection of the thing whose accidents do not endure because, if it returns to life and it had an existence once before, it will have existed in two moments of time. If it were possible for it to exist in two moments separated by non-existence, it would be possible for it to exist in two consecutive moments. But what they have said here is simply an unsubstantiated assertion and they should be asked to integrate the two cases.

Moreover, if existence persists over two moments, the accident would be qualified as having endurance and, if the accident endures accordingly, its non-existence is impossible. But that is not the case since the accident exists in two moments between which it is non-existent. In each moment it comes into being anew rather than enduring. It is subject to the power, in our view, in both situations of creation and resurrection, even though what endures cannot be within that power. They are thus forced to admit the restoration of human powers. They will find no way to succeed in avoiding this, as we have already mentioned in discussing the creation of [human] acts. This then constitutes our coverage of the subject of the possibility of resurrection.

As for its actual occurrence, that is apprehended from the evidence supplied by tradition. Decisive evidence there attests to the reality of the assembly and the resurrection of people to be examined and judged, to be rewarded and punished. Someone may ask: Do the atoms disappear and then are restored or do they endure while their accompanying accidents cease to be and are subsequently restored to their original configuration? We respond: Both cases are possible in reason but tradition does not indicate a decisive proof that specifies either one or the other. It is not inconceivable that the bodies of humans come to resemble the bodies in the ground and are subsequently reconstituted as they had been once before, but we do not consider it impossible that only some part of the body disappears to be later reconstituted. God alone has knowledge of what will ultimately happen to them and what is their final end.

Section
On Various Characteristics of the Afterlife as Stipulated in Tradition

Among these there is the punishment of the grave and the interrogation by Munkar and Nakīr. The orthodox consider these proven since they are among the things possible according to reason. God has the power to revive a dead person and to order the two angels to question him about his Lord and his Prophet. All of this is possible according to reason and the evidence of tradition attests to it as well. Thus it must be accepted. Concordant reports confirm that the Prophet, God bless him and keep him, requested the Lord God to spare him the punishment of the grave. Relating each one of these reports concerning these matters would be burdensome. Moreover, prior to the appearance of the proponents of heretical innovations and sectarian tendencies, they had not ceased to be advertised by the righteous forefathers.

Among the passages of the Book of God that testify to these matters is His statement in the story of Pharoah and his family: "And there encompassed the people of Pharoah an evil punishment; the fire, to which they shall be exposed morning and evening" [40:45–46]. This text proclaims the reality of their being punished in the grave prior to assembling for the last judgment since it is God Himself who mentions it. And it is then that He says: "And on the day when the Hour has arrived, 'cast the people of Pharoah into that most terrible punishment'" [continuation of 40:46].

In order to deny the punishment of the grave, those who do invoke the arguments of the heretics and who disparage the law, say: We observe a dead person in the same state as when we buried him and we know of necessity that he is dead. If we left him in full light for a long time, he would remain just as we are accustomed to see him. Saying this reveals the speaker's lack of composure in faith and trust in certainty. That is tantamount to considering inconceivable the resurrection of decayed bones and the reconstitution of body parts that have been dispersed in the bellies of wild beasts or the gizzards of birds of prey, in far flung regions following the path of the winds and in other situations like these.

Furthermore, understand that the doctrine we approve is that the interrogation takes place in the parts known to God, such as the heart or another organ, and that God restores that part to life in order for the questioning to be addressed to it. This is entirely possible according to reason and is attested decisively by the evidence of tradition. The denial and exaggeration they mention are the same as the denials of those persons who rejected the Prophet's having seen angels even while he was sitting among them.

Chapter: [*On the soul and its significance*]

Someone may say: Explain the soul to us; what is its significance? There are different opinions about it. We answer: What is most probably true, in our view, is that the soul is a subtle body that is intermingled with the sensible body. God, the Exalted, ordinarily preserves life in the body for as long as the soul is intermingled with it. If and when the soul separates from it, in the normal course of things, death succeeds life.

Furthermore, the soul of the believer is raised to the sky and transported in the gullet of a bird to paradise, as likewise that of the unbeliever drops into the abyss, as warranted by the sacred traditions. Life is an accident by which the atoms are revived, as also when life is restored to it, the soul is revived by life. This then is our doctrine concerning the soul.

Chapter: On paradise and hellfire

Paradise and hellfire have both been created, given that reason does not regard this as impossible and verses of the book of God attest to it. Among them is His saying: ". . . and a paradise as large as the heavens and the earth reserved for the righteous" [3:133]. To reserve a thing is to announce that it exists and is actually real. God, the Exalted, also says: ". . . and indeed he saw him in another instance, by the Lote-tree of the far boundary, near which is the Garden of Refuge" [53:13–15]. Numerous concordant reports in the story of Adam, on whom be peace, confirm the existence of paradise and of Adam's entry into it, his having committed an error in it, his having been expelled from it, and finally promised that he would return to it. All of this is attested by decisive evidence as derived from verses the import of which was elaborated through the transmission of solid and trustworthy persons.

Certain factions of the Muʿtazilites deny the creation of paradise and hellfire. They insist there is no advantage in having created them prior to the time for reward and punishment, and they construe what the verses in the story of Adam, on whom be peace, proclaim as indicating a garden in this world only. But this makes a mockery of religion and deviates from the universal agreement of Muslims. Among the things they rail on about is to say that there is no advantage in the creation of paradise and hellfire at the present moment – a statement that is worthless. According to the principles of the orthodox, the acts of the Creator cannot be attributed to specific purposes. He does whatever He wishes and decides however He wants.

Furthermore, how can they refute those who say to them: God, the Exalted, knew that the creation of paradise and hellfire is a benefit to faith and the rules of reason? This is not far from what their theories allege about grace, and about the good and the best.

Chapter: On the Bridge (and the Balance, the Pool and the pages)

The Bridge [*al-ṣirāṭ*] is confirmed on the basis of declarations in the *ḥadīth*. It is a bridge extending over the inferno by which the first and the last arrive. When they arrive there, the angels are told: "Stop them to be questioned" [37:24].

The Balance [*al-mīzān*] truly exists. Likewise does the Pool [*al-ḥawḍ*] and the books in which the accounts of created beings are recorded. Reason regards none of these impossible and the evidence in tradition establishes everything we mention here with complete certainty.

If they want to raise doubts about the Bridge, they point out that, in the *ḥadīth* concerned with the Bridge, it is described as thinner than a hair and sharper than a sword. It would be impossible for people to enter onto a bridge of that description. They likewise deny the Balance and maintain that the reward and punishment apply to the deeds themselves and they are accidents which cannot be weighed.

In regard to what they say about the Bridge, it is obvious in its worthlessness, since there is nothing impossible in moving about in the air and walking on water. How could someone deny this whose religion obliges them to admit that a staff changed into a serpent, the seas parted and the dead were restored to the world of the living? As for what is weighed, it is comprised in the pages that record the deeds which the Lord God weighs according to the value of the wages merited by the deeds and what they have earned in the way of rewards and punishments. This account will suffice to show you the correct way to affirm matters in tradition.

Section

On Reward and Punishment, the Spoiling of Human Acts, and the Refutation of the Muʿtazilites, the Khawārij, and the Murjiʾa on the Promise and the Threat

Reward, according to the orthodox, is not a predetermined right, nor is the compensation decided in advance. It is rather a gift bestowed by God, the Exalted. Likewise, punishment is not obligatory but, when it occurs, it is an act of justice on the part of God. What God promises in the way of reward or threatens as punishments He proclaims out of justice and pledges in full truth. Everything that we already said to prove that there exists no obligation on God, the Exalted, applies here.

The Muʿtazilites maintain that the reward is obligatory on God, the Exalted, and likewise punishment is required for the commission of mortal sins that have not been repented. However, according to the majority of them, punishment does not carry the same degree of obligation as reward because the reward must be fulfilled, whereas, according to the Basrans and one faction of the Baghdādīs, punishment may be waived. However, the meaning of saying that it is deserved, in their view, is that it is good in that it occurs to someone who deserves it. If it were not so, it would not be good for the punishment to last for an eternity. This is in reality the doctrine they hold.

If we should grant them here the premise that reason determines what is bad and what is good, we may still impose on them, following the rules of their own principle, examples that they have no way to deal with. One is that, if a master were to provide provisions for his servant and keep him from wanting, and yet the servant did not fully serve him but instead held back in the major portion of his efforts, the servant deserves nothing from his master as compensation for services rendered by him. Similarly, with a person who is highly respected within his family, if he is generous with his son and provides all his needs, and the son honours him, respects him and seeks his approval and strives to earn it, therefore, that person is not owed in regard for his assistance any more than he has already obtained from the beneficence that has accrued to his credit.

If then this is the situation with a person who provides services to another like himself, a servant who tried to compare his own acts of service with God's bounteous generosity to him in any single instance would find the beneficence of God completely acquitted and fulfilled in regard to any of his own good deeds. The Lord God has the right to be worshipped; His favours to humans come without interruption. If the servant tried to count them, he could not. How could the servant, who is already immersed in the favours bestowed by God, be owed additional rewards for the small trifling deeds of his that are not already the result of God's overwhelming generosity?

Furthermore, the human's worshipping is an acknowledgment of the favours already received. Reason does not insist, in the habitual order of things, on the right of being recompensed in exchange for fulfilling an obligation that was itself already a compensation. If the servant were owed a compensation simply for acknowledging God's generosity, the Lord God is due a compensation for the rewards He has already allotted the servant. There is no escape from this.

Chapter: [*On eternal reward*]

One might say to the Muʿtazilites: If it is conceded to you that the reward is earned by right, how would you justify its eternal duration, given that the acts of obedience that issue from the person subject to the imposed obligation were of limited extent? Why are the compensations not likewise limited in extent?

They may say: It is like this only because reward is a benefit that is agreeable, free from anything that might cause apprehension, and undisturbed by premonitions of trouble. If a reward might possibly cease, in that he would know that it might come to an end, the rewarded person would not find it agreeable. We answer: Why did you not state that the reward must be at the highest degree of tranquillity and be exempt from all troubles? Is that not what you were asking about?

Moreover, the favours the servant must acknowledge with gratitude in this world are mixed with ordeals and anxieties and yet they are none the less truly favours. If it is not inconceivable for the favours mixed with adversity still to require being acknowledged with gratitude, it is not inconceivable in regard to rewards as well. The Lord God has, moreover, the power to make those rewarded oblivious to considerations of cessation or apprehensions of changes all the way to the end of the period assigned them. Hence what precludes rewards being established, as we have just stipulated, for a limited time?

Furthermore, we can ask here: If this is your doctrine in regard to rewards, what do you say about punishment? Are they set with time limitations? If the situation follows the customary pattern of the visible world, we know of necessity that a person who has committed a single sin which is presumed thereafter to continue with that person indefinitely, does not rightly merit a punishment for it that is itself everlasting and without end. Hence how could that be regarded as good on the part of the absolutely Most Merciful and Most Generous?

They may say: God consigns to hellfire only those about whom He knows that if He relents, they will return to doing what they were forbidden to do. We reply: This will not save you from our objections. It is our doctrine to hold that the punishment may be prolonged and that later God causes the death of those He knows that, if He were to relent, they would revert to acts they were forbidden or that He deprives them of their minds after the punishment is complete. This should suffice to achieve our purpose here.

An issue that may be put to them concerns their doctrine that no reward occurs in this life but rather that they are postponed until the end of the world and until the day of heavy judgment gives way to the day of resurrection. But it is not in conformity with the rules of reason, when fulfilling and acquitting it is possible, to delay the right of those who deserve it or to withhold it from the person who has earned it. For a person of means to deliberately delay acquitting a debt is counted as an injustice according to the founder of the law.

This observation is further supported by the fact that punishment fulfils a certain role in the life of this world since, according to the unanimous agreement of the community, the penalties inflicted on those who deserve them are for them a punishment. If it is not inconceivable that punishment fulfils this function, what precludes understanding certain favours as aspects of reward, even though they have that function in this world?

Chapter: [*On the spoiling of good deeds and the threat*]

The Khawārij[1] maintain that a person who commits a single sin and is not inspired to repent of it, spoils his good deeds and dies deserving to remain forever in painful torment. They go so far as to declare the person who commits even a single sin an unbeliever [*kāfir*]. The Ibāḍiyya[2] among them held that he is to be characterized as guilty of ingratitude [*kufr*], as derived from the ingratitude for a favour given rather than to ascribe to him unbelief which makes him guilty of polytheism [*shirk*]. The Azāriqa[3] among them maintain that the person who disobeys does not believe in God in the same way as those guilty of polytheism.

The Muʿtazilites agree with the Khawārij in upholding the meriting of eternal future punishment, as we will explain in detail later. They, however, separate from the Khawārij on two points. In the first place, they do not regard the perpetrator of a grave sin as an unbeliever, nor would they describe him as faithful. They insist that he occupies an intermediate position and they classify him as impious [*fāsiq*]. They depart in a second respect in holding that the eternal punishment is reserved exclusively for those who commit grave sins, whereas, for the Khawārij, all sins are grave sins. The Muʿtazilites, by contrast, divide sins into those that are venial and those that are grave, in accord with a distinction we will outline in a special chapter.

Our purpose now is to rebut the proponents of the threat and thus we say: Following your principle the threat of an everlasting punishment applies to someone who commits a single lapse and because of it the reward for acts of

---

1 The Khawārij or Khārijites were one of the earliest dissenting sects in Islam. Many theological issues first arose when they were raised by this group, among them the status of a sinning Muslim and the matter discussed in this chapter.

2 The Ibāḍiyya are one faction of the Khawārij.

3 The Azāriqa were another subgroup of the Khawārij.

obedience are spoiled. That, despite conceding your false principle, is impossible according to reason. The bases of reasoning and its precepts refer to situations in the visible world. We know very well that in regard to someone who serves another and expends his effort constantly to fulfil his obligation to him during a period of a hundred years and beyond but then commits a single infraction, no one would consider good despoiling him of credit for all his good actions on account of a single bad deed. If it were true that reward and punishment cancel each other, reward is no more appropriately reduced and spoiled than punishment annulled. The law demonstrates the obviation of bad by good deeds and the vitiating of a punishment is the more appropriate. God, the Exalted, has said: "For good deeds remove those that are bad" [11:114].

Moreover, acts of obedience are well established as to their actuality and in the validity of fulfilling them. If persisting in a grave sin were to annul the rewards for such acts, that would deny their own validity as is the case with apostasy and departing from the Sunna. In such cases the act that spoils the effect of good deeds constitutes itself a rejection of the validity of the acts of worship. Furthermore, according to them, reward is merited by acts of obedience because they are good acts and take place as such. That is just as true, despite having committed one grave sin, as it is true without it.

They may say: The perpetrator of a grave sin is an impious person and a deviator. It is contradictory to conjoin the reward with impiety. The reward heralds saintliness whereas impiety denies it. We respond: There is no disagreement that he qualifies as being obediently pious, that he knows God, that he is of solid faith, a true monotheist, and has all the other traits we ascribe to the saints. The contradiction lies only in conjoining signs of deviation and agreement in the same instance. But it is not inconceivable to oppose one thing and to be in agreement on another. Moreover, if there is no doubt as to the spoiling and annulling, why not annul the punishment and make the reward prevail, as, in fact, we have determined to be the case.

On occasion the proponents of the threat invoke the literal sense of some passages of the Holy Book. We will mention here the most obscure of them and provide some guidance as to the method to follow in discussing them. One they draw support from is God's statement: ". . . and if someone kills a believer intentionally, his recompense is hell to abide forever in it" [4:93]. This is, they suppose, the formal designation of the threat and the eternity of the punishment. The commentators have discussed this verse at length. It is, however, not our aim here to review all that they have said about it. Rather we cite only what will help settle the matter here.

Ibn ʿAbbās has said that the meaning of the verse, "and if someone kills a believer," is that the person considered killing him permissible and the wilfulness in reality can only issue from a person who regards it as permissible. As for those who believe that the killing is one of the most grave sins, they are satisfied with their own inclination in the matter and are restrained by what they believe. They do not proceed with the matter except with great fear and horror. The sign of this is that, when the Lord God spoke of revenge and the obligation to seek it, He did not associate it with the threat and eternal punishment and yet where, as here, He mentioned eternal punishment He did not specify the obligation to seek revenge. This is the best proof that the threat of eternal punishment applies to the unbelievers whose killing is permitted and on whom the ostensible rule is not relevant. The person who makes war against Muslims [the *ḥarbī*] is not subject to our laws and, if he is killed, the obligation to seek revenge does not apply in his case.

Moreover, the term used for eternal punishment [*al-khulūd*], although it literally indicates an eternal duration, is not explicitly so stated. One can express it and intend by it the prolongation of a period or an extreme length of time. It has that sense when, for example, one expresses a wish for a king to have an everlasting reign. The proponents of the threat believe that their doctrine is definitive but it is obvious that an issue that is subject to different understandings cannot yield certainty.

Furthermore, their reasoning may be opposed by invoking the following saying of God: "God will never forgive those who associate other gods with Him but He will forgive everything else of whomever He may wish" [4:48]. This is an explicit textual reference to the point under discussion. There is no avenue open for them to construe this verse to allow for contrition, for two reasons. One is that the acceptance of contrition is obligatory, according to them, and thus the forgiveness does not depend on God's being willing to forgive. The second is that God, the Exalted, makes a distinction between the polytheist and all others. Contrition in the case of polytheism has no effect and is cut off, even as contrition for acts of disobedience may annul the application of the penalties associated with them. There is much more room for additional discussions about the ostensible application of the texts but this should suffice.

Chapter: [A grave sin ruins the reward for acts of obedience according to the Muʿtazilites]

The general run of the Muʿtazilites maintain that a single grave sin spoils the reward for acts of obedience even if they are numerous. Al-Jubbāʾī and his son held that lapses only spoil the reward for these pious acts if they exceed them. If the pious acts are more, they overrule the evil acts and cancel their effect. Moreover, they did not consider the number of pious acts and sins but only took into account the magnitudes of the remuneration and the penalties. It might happen that a single grave sin carries a penalty that surpasses the remuneration attached to numerous pious acts. However, there is no way to ascertain their respective magnitudes but rather this is a matter that is known exclusively by God. They have made a muddled attempt to find an equal standard for good and bad acts but they have come up with no precise standard for it. The son of al-Jubbāʾī said: That cannot happen since those subject to the legal obligation have in front of them only paradise or hell. If the values of the good and bad actions were equivalent, their being equivalent would entail another, intermediate location.

All that they have mentioned here is confused and goes nowhere. There is, in regard to the cognizance of God, no grave sin whose penalty exceeds the remuneration for that acknowledgment. Things are known by their opposites. The remuneration for the cognizance of God is known by the penalty for its opposite. They ought to have admitted that sins are annulled by acknowledging God. If they do not do this, their hallucinations about some acts surpassing others and how a few of them cancel a multitude prove false. Moreover, it is not rationally inconceivable that a servant whose obedient acts are many, but who commits some errors, may be punished by his master for a time and only subsequently restored to his good graces, even though his errors were fewer [than his good deeds]. Thus everything they have mentioned is purely arbitrary and yields no positive result.

Furthermore, contrition is a repentance, as we will describe it later. A person who endeavours to spread corruption on earth his whole life and persists in committing sacrilege throughout his days will find that a single repentance for those acts cancels them, even if repenting causes him less trouble and pain [than his evil acts are worth]. Therefore, all they have said is false.

Chapter: On the difference between venial and grave sins

Someone might say: You left off mentioning the venial and grave sins earlier. Make clear now how to distinguish between the two types. We respond: The doctrine we approve is that all sins are grave since one cannot measure the value of the sins by taking into consideration the person who is the one disobeyed by committing it. A thing might be counted as a minor fault if ascribed to a person of equal rank which, if it were to involve a king, would become a grave error for which one could be executed. The Lord God is the most awesome sovereign one can disobey and the most deserving of reverent obedience. Any sin that carries with it opposition to God is momentously grave. But sins, however momentous they might be for reasons just explained, vary in their degree of importance. Some are more momentous than others. This is similar to our judgment that the prophets each have an excellence and an elevated rank but that some are superior to others. This is the doctrine that we find most acceptable.

Someone might point out that there are sins which do not diminish one's integrity and do not necessitate excluding one's testimony, whereas there are some that make one's testimony unacceptable. In arriving at the judgment pertaining to this world, you should distinguish then those that take away integrity from those that do not invalidate its function. We respond: That is not part of our present purpose. The discussion of recusing and validating witnesses falls in the domain of the jurist. However, to state the matter briefly, we hold that every offence that shows how little regard the perpetrator has for religion and for religious sentiments is a matter that diminishes integrity and any offence that does not indicate this but instead preserves the good repute of the person who does it is something that does not cancel legal integrity. This then is the best way to distinguish one of the two types from the other.

Chapter: [*On those who die while persevering in an act of disobedience*]

A believer who dies while still persevering in an act of disobedience cannot be consigned conclusively to the chastisement of hell. Instead his case is entrusted to his Lord God. If God punishes him, that is fair of him; if He refrains from inflicting punishment, that is due to His beneficence and mercy. This cannot be denied either in reason or in the law. This is the doctrine of the Baṣrans and some of the Baghdādīs. But many of the Baghdādī Muʿtazilites hold that a pardon is not possible. It is incumbent on God, the Exalted, to inflict on the unrepentant sinner an eternal punishment. Yet this doctrine of theirs is averse to the rules of reason. The goodness of forgiveness and overlooking the commission of sins is unconcealable. The law articulates it and urges it be done. If it is good for one of us to forgive, despite taking pleasure in exacting revenge and satisfying one's thirst for it, and despite exposing himself to the harm inherent in suppressing his anger, how much more appropriate and apt to consider good God's grant of pardon since He is exempt of all need and truly bears the attribute of complete self-sufficiency. But what they assert would nullify the beneficence of God and His mercy. They declare what He does in this world obligatory and they impose on Him the rules of punishment that are to apply in the future. Those who adhere to such doctrines are no longer attached to religion.

Chapter: [*On intercession*]

Having confirmed the possibility of forgiveness and shown that the testimony of the Holy Book and the Sunna attest to it, we will not mention it further since it is so well known. Subsumed under it, however, is the intercession of the prophets and the reduction of the penalties of sinners because of their intervention.

The doctrine of the orthodox is that intercession is true. Those who deny forgiveness, deny it also. Those who admit the possibility of pardon and forgiveness coming spontaneously from God do not preclude the possibility of intercession. However, some of them preclude it, despite upholding the possibility of pardon. But that is the ultimate in ignorance and no serious person would accept it.

Our procedure consists of demonstrating by methods alluded to earlier that a prophet's intercession is rationally possible. If we base the matter on the pure truth and do not follow their doctrine about the determination of good and bad, the Lord God does whatever He wishes. If we follow along with them and agree with their false beliefs, this doctrine reverts to the evidence supplied by the visible world. It would not be considered bad, in the view of intelligent people, for a king to intercede on behalf of one of his most loyal and devoted associates for a crime of his that deserves to be punished. No one would deny this except the pigheaded.

Once it is proven that there is the possibility of intercession rationally, a superabundance of traditions also have attested to it and those who desire to consult them can find them recorded in books. These traditions, moreover, affirm the intercession on behalf of people who have committed grave sins because the Prophet, God bless him and keep him, said: "My intercession is for the people of my community who have committed grave sins." He also said *a propos* of intercession, "Do not consider that it is for the God-fearing, rather it is for the sinners who are defiled", and he said, "I chose between intercession and entering half of my community into paradise. I chose intercession because it will do the most good." Muslims agreed, prior to the appearance of deviations, on asking of God, the Exalted, that He accord them the benefits of intercession. This wish was unanimously agreed upon in centuries past without protest.

If reason attests to its possibility and the evidence of tradition corroborates it, there remains subsequently no reason to deny it. In what we have just mentioned, there is the refutation of the group who maintain that intercession can raise but not reduce the status of those who are guilty of evil actions, since reports that have been transmitted attest to the application of intercession in the case of persons who are guilty of grave sins. Likewise, the requests for intercession have never stopped coming from both the God-fearing and those guilty of crimes, without any manifestation of disapproval against those who beseech God for the intercession of the Prophet on their behalf.

Section
On Names and Characteristics

Chapter: [*On the meaning of faith*]

Understand that the purpose of this chapter demands that we speak first about the real nature of faith. It is a subject of dispute among various doctrinal factions in Islam.

The Khawārij maintain that faith is an act of obedience and many of the Muʿtazilites are inclined to this opinion as well. But their doctrines differ about whether or not to designate the supererogatory acts as faith. The Partisans of *hadith* [*aṣḥāb al-ḥadīth*] hold that faith is cognizance in the heart, confession by the tongue, and acts performed by limbs and members. One of the ancients maintained that faith is cognizance in the heart and confessing to it. The Karrāmiyya believe that faith is the confession of the tongue and that alone. Despite inner thoughts of unbelief, if faith is professed outwardly, such person is a true believer, according to them, even though he deserves an eternal punishment in hellfire. But a person whose faith is kept secret and is never actually made public is not a believer, although he merits the eternal life of paradise.

The doctrine we approve is that the real nature of faith is true belief in God, the Exalted. A believer then is a person who truly has faith in God. Moreover, the profession of true belief, in reality, is an interior discourse but it does not exist except with knowledge. We have explained clearly that interior discourse is produced in conformity with belief. The proof that faith is the declaration of true belief is its lexical sense and Arabic root. This cannot be denied and thus there is no need to prove it. In the revelation we find, for example: "You will never have faith in us even though we are truthful" [12:17]. That means: "You will never believe us to be truthful."

Furthermore, the purpose of this chapter is to show that it is a doctrine of the orthodox to portray the impious person [*fāsiq*] as a believer. The proof on the basis of which he is termed a believer is lexical. He is, in reality, a person who truly believes. The sign of this in the law is that legal judgments that are addressed exclusively to the believers are directed to the impious all the same as they are directed, according to the unanimous agreement of the community, towards the pious. Thus the impious person is treated as a believer in respect to the legal rules that apply to him. He takes a share of the booty and he receives from it the same amount as a righteous person. He is protected. He is buried in the cemetery of the Muslims and prayed over. All of this proves conclusively that he is one of them. Moreover, once one admits that he acknowledges God, submits to and obeys Him, declares his faith in Him, it is reasonable to call him a believer. But, on the contrary, it is absurd to say of him: This man who acknowledges God does not believe in Him. The discussion in this chapter applies to the designations only. Its central purpose is the subject of the threat and eternal chastisement. However, we covered that topic in a convincing manner earlier.

The unanimous agreement of the scholars confirms what we have mentioned about prayer and the other acts of worship needing to be preceded by faith. If there were parts to faith, one could not say this. In order to demonstrate that one designates the acts of obedience as faith, one cites God's statement: "God will not cause your faith to be lost" [2:143]. They say that what is meant here, namely with the term "faith", are prayers made in the direction of Jerusalem. They might also adduce as proof the following saying that has been related from the Prophet, God bless him and keep him: "Faith is composed of more than ninety qualities of which the first is to profess that there is no god but God and the last is to remove from the road harmful things." We now say: As for faith in the verse which they have invoked, it may be taken as signifying a declaration of true belief and its intent is as follows: God will never cause you to lose your conviction about what your prophet made known to you when he instructed you to pray in the two different directions. As for the *ḥadīth*, it is an isolated one and is moreover susceptible to interpretation. The Arabs designate a thing by the name of another thing if it indicates that thing or when it is a part of it for some reason.

Chapter: [*The increase of faith and its diminution*]

Someone may ask: What is your doctrine concerning the increase of faith and its diminution? To that we reply: If we construe faith as the profession of true belief, one profession of faith is not superior to another, just as no knowledge is superior to another. Those who construe it as an act of obedience whether secret or open – a view towards which al-Qalānisī[1] inclined – may conceivably maintain that faith increases with each act of obedience and diminishes with acts of disobedience. This, however, is a view we do not accept.

If someone should object and say: Your principle obliges you to admit that the faith of a person engrossed in his own impiety is like that of the Prophet, God bless him and keep him, we respond: The Prophet, on whom be blessing and peace, surpasses his enemies by the constancy of his belief and God's making him immune to the deception of doubts and the convulsion of suspicions. True belief is an accident that does not endure but which is uninterrupted for the Prophet, may blessings and peace be upon him, whereas it exists for other people only at certain moments. For them it ceases in moments of indifference. The Prophet, on whom be blessing and peace, has several qualities of belief that do not exist for other people except on some occasions. Thus his faith is in that

1 Evidently this is Abu'l-ʿAbbās Aḥmad b. ʿAbd al-Raḥmān al-Qalānisī, who was a student and follower of Ibn Kullāb, along with Abuʾl-Ḥasan al-Ashʿarī.

sense greater. If faith were to be characterized as increasing and decreasing and were to mean what we have just mentioned, this would be correct. Understand accordingly!

Someone may say: It has been reported from your ancestors that faith is linked to the will of God. When someone used to be asked about his faith, he would answer that he is a believer, God willing. What is one to make of that? We reply: Faith existed at that moment conclusively and without doubt, but the faith that is the mark of success and a sign of salvation is a faith to come at the end. The early Muslims were thinking of that and they associated it with God's will, without implying any doubt about the faith they already possessed.

Section
On Repentance

The true lexical meaning of repentance is to return. Thus one says in Arabic *tāba*, *nāba* or *anāba* about someone who "comes back" or "returns". If one ascribes repentance to a human, it implies that he returns from committing sins to a state of regretting having done them, as we would define it in the idiom of the theologians. If repentance is ascribed to the acts of God, it signifies the restoration of His favour and beneficence to His servant.

If someone asks us to formulate a precise expression of the nature of repentance according to our usage, we respond as follows: Repentance is regret for an act of disobedience for the sake of the thing that made regretting it necessary. Moreover, repentance is always accompanied by qualities that are not a part of it in general and it is accompanied by qualities that occur in certain cases and not in others. As for those qualities that always accompany repentance, one of them is grief and sadness over previously having been responsible for infringing the rights of God since it is impossible to properly repent without this. Those who are happy and joyous over what they have escaped from have not truly repented of having done it. Another quality associated with it is the wish that what happened in the past had never occurred. Every person who truly repents of an act must have the quality of wishing that what happened in the past had not happened.

Among the qualities associated with repentance in only certain cases is the resolution to avoid reverting to that of which the obligated person repented. This does not apply in every situation since this resolution is valid only for someone who can still do what he did previously. A eunuch, for example, cannot validly make a resolution to give up committing adultery, nor can a mute resolve to abandon falsely defaming honourable women. But if repentance issues from a person who still has the ability to commit an act like those he regrets, there should be no doubt but that his repentance is accompanied by the resolution not to revert to them. It is an impossibility for him to be prepared to resume what, out of respect for God, he repented of having done previously.

Someone may ask: Why did you not claim that contrition is repentance? We answer: Because repentance is that in which contrition does not cease. The other factors may increase or vary. An example is something that exists once and disappears another time. The Apostle of God, God bless him and keep him, has said: "Repentance is contrition." This definition must be ours as well because it derives from a report from the prophet and is thus confirmed by evidence. Someone asks: Why is it not permitted to label abstaining from acts of disobedience repentance even without contrition? We respond: This is something the law regards as repugnant. An insolent person who tires of his insolence and takes up some acceptable practices but has not repented of past sins and has instead resolved to return to them would be said to be a person who has given up sin but not someone who is contrite for having done it.

This then is the true nature of contrition and its characteristics and also a mention of what must accompany it in general and in specific situations. Someone may ask: What does it mean when you say that contrition is repentance for the sake of something requiring it? We respond: This precision is indispensable because those who commit an evil act and repent of it because it causes them harm and depletes their strength are persons who have repented but are not contrite. Legal contrition applies exclusively to a person who repents of having omitted a duty owed to God.

Chapter: [*On the acceptance of contrition*]

It is not obligatory in reason for God to accept contrition. The Muʿtazilites all agree in declaring that accepting contrition is incumbent on God, high indeed is He above their words. A general proof that there is no obligation on God was given previously. Furthermore, if we refer to what happens in the visible world, nothing here confirms that contrition must necessarily be accepted. If a person commits a wrong against another, violates his honour, and is excessive in his enmity toward him, but then offers his excuses, the acceptance of his contrition is not obligatory according to the rules of reason. On the contrary the person who was violated and whose rights were usurped may forgive him if he wishes or refuse to do so. About what we have said here there is no doubt.

From the point of view of tradition what confirms this is the universal agreement of the community to beseech God to accept contrition and of humility towards Him in supplication out of the hope that it will be acceptable. If the acceptance of contrition were obligatory, there would be no meaning for the supplications or urgency in praying for it.

Someone may say: This is your doctrine in regard to reason and what it requires. What is your doctrine in regard to the acceptance of contrition with respect to tradition? Is the acceptance certain or not? We answer: It is not certain, in our view, but is rather to be hoped for and it is likely to happen. However, the probability of it is not definite. This matter is, moreover, susceptible to interpretation. Nevertheless, we are certain that there is no reason why it must be accepted, nor are we sure of its acceptance on the basis of either tradition or God's promise. Instead we believe only that it is probable and, when the conditions denoting the contrition are most abundant, the probability of it surpasses even this.

Chapter: [*The necessity of contrition*]

Contrition is obligatory for humans but reason does not indicate its being obligatory, since none of the legal regulations were established on the basis of reason. Instead the proof for it is the unanimous agreement of Muslims that it is necessary to avoid sins and to repent of those done previously.

Furthermore, contrition is divided into two sorts. One concerns what one owes to God exclusively and the other is what one owes to other human beings.

In regard to the contrition one owes to God exclusively, it may be satisfied without taking into consideration anything other than God. As for what is owed that involves the rights of other human beings, it is further divided. A part cannot be satisfied short of being acquitted of what is due other humans and another part applies without that. In respect to what is satisfied without that, it concerns all cases in which a person's repentance can be real without being acquitted of the obligation to satisfy the rights of the humans involved.

An example of this is a killing which requires retaliation but which may be validly repented of without the killer submitting himself to those who have the right to retaliate against him. If he repents, his contrition satisfies what is due to God and his refusal to submit to the reprisal that is due someone else is a new act of disobedience which does not invalidate the contrition. Of the latter, nevertheless, he ought to acquit himself and show contrition in regard to it as well. Often contrition that would apply to a case involving the rights of humans cannot be effective unless one satisfies what is owed them. Such would be the case in the usurpation of goods belonging to another. Repenting for it is not valid as long as the perpetrator is still involved in the usurpation. Do not therefore hold on to the diversity in individual cases but take heed instead of the repentance due God, the exalted, in the negative or the affirmative.

Chapter: [*On contrition for some sins but not others*]

Those who have committed several crimes or several sins may validly repent of some of them even while persisting in the others. Abū Hāshim and those who follow him hold that contrition is not valid unless one abstains from all sins. But this opinion of theirs is contrary to good sense and the requirements of received law. A person who has made any number of blunders or even committed horrendous acts may, in the normal way things work, validly disavow the greater part of them and be excused even while he persists in doing some of them.

The leading masters coined the following example for this situation. They said: A person who usurps goods belonging to another man, committing several crimes against him and contributing to the violation of his honour, and who, among the multitude of crimes he commits, breaks a pen of his, but then subsequently repays him for all the damage he did and submits to the other man's judgment and willingly obeys his orders, although he does not excuse himself of having broken the pen, his being excused of the horrendous acts of which he repented is nevertheless valid. That cannot be denied by any reasonable person.

What confirms our doctrine here is that there is a unanimous consensus of the community that, if an unbeliever converts to Islam and repents of his previous unbelief, his repentance is valid, even if he persists in committing a single sin. The doctrine of Abū Hāshim is that his repentance is not valid. Even if he has accepted Islam and submitted to its regulations, he is still responsible for his previous unbelief. This, however, breaches the universal agreement of Muslims. If those who support his doctrine maintain that contrition for the sin is required only because it is bad and that applies to all sins in general, repentance for an evil act is not valid while persisting in another evil act. Their argument, however, is false in ways that are too many to enumerate and which this handbook of theology need not include.

Nevertheless, one of them that is more readily proven false is his argument that the pious act is so constituted by its being good. Accordingly, it follows necessarily that a pious act cannot validly be pious if one shuns any other pious act. The matter, however, was not like that according to Abū Hāshim himself. Likewise the evil act is to be avoided because it is bad and it would follow therefore that one should not think of avoiding an evil act as long as one is committing another evil act and intending to persist in doing so. Thus what they say is false in every way. Furthermore, contrition is repentance and one may envision a repentance for one variety of sin even in the midst of an overwhelming passion for a sin of another kind.

Chapter: [*On the renewal of repentance*]

Whoever repents of an evil act and whose repentance is accompanied by contrition according to its proper conditions but who subsequently remembers that evil act should, according to the doctrine of the Qāḍī [Abū Bakr al-Baqillānī], may God be pleased with him, renew his repentance each time he recalls it. If he does not repent of it on each occasion, he will begin to take comfort in it or satisfaction and that brings him back into the original impiety, thereby nullifying his repentance.

This is what he says but I believe it demands some further consideration since it is not inconceivable that a person repent and that later he remember it and turn away without taking any pleasure or joy from it but also not repenting for it all over again. It is incontestable that he is not required to prolong his repentance and be troubled his whole life by memories of it. That is something we ask God to help us with.

Here if someone asks: What do you say about a servant who performs his acts of obedience but then later repents of having done them? We reply: It is inconceivable that a person who has acknowledged God, the Exalted, would repent of having obeyed Him. To repent of a matter that brought upon oneself some harm attached to it is not inconceivable. But this situation is the same as repenting a pious act simply because it is a pious act.

Our purpose in the preceding statements is to show that the Qāḍī, may God be merciful to him, made the renewal of repentance obligatory, as specified earlier. Subsequently, he said: If he does not renew the repentance, this is a new act of disobedience. However, the first contrition remains valid since nothing annuls a previous act of worship after it has been done. Then he added: It is necessary to renew the repentance for that evil act and it is also necessary to repent of not having repented at the moment we determined that it had become obligatory on him. This then is his doctrine.

For our part this is a matter needing to be discussed. Contrition is one of the acts of religious worship and it is not necessary for all discussions of it to be absolutely conclusive. Rather it is quite possible for the experts who examine this subject to fail to agree.

Chapter: [*Is the new found faith in an unbeliever contrition?*]

When an unbeliever comes to believe in God, his faith is not contrition for his former unbelief. Contrition exists only if he repents of his unbelief. If someone asks: What if he believes but does not repent of his unbelief? That, in our view, is simply impossible. Rather it is necessary for his new faith to be associated with repentance for unbelief. Afterward the responsibility for unbelief is diminished by the faith and the repentance, according to the unanimous consensus of the community. This point is indisputable. Every other matter connected with modes of contrition is susceptible to suppositions that are uncertain, as we have said.

Chapter: [*On the contrition of a person who reverts to sin*]

For someone who repents and his contrition is valid but then reverts to the sin, his past contrition remains valid. The purpose in mentioning this is to inform you that contrition is one of the acts of worship which can be determined as being either valid or useless. If the act was done in accord with the proper conditions for it, one cannot declare its validity null and void on the basis of what happens after it has passed. Nevertheless, those who revert to a sin must renew the contrition. This new contrition is, moreover, another act of worship and is other than the one we cited.

These then are the principles of contrition that we would mention, leaving out nothing that properly belongs in a handbook of doctrines.

Section
The Doctrine of the Imamate

The subject of the discussion in this section does not in itself concern a fundamental principle of belief. However the danger of falling into a serious error over it is too grave for someone to remain ignorant of the principle involved here. Two tendencies, both forbidden, occur in regard to this subject according to those who specialize in disputation. One is an inclination on the part of various groups to engage in partisanship and to transcend the limits of truth. The second consists of taking into account matters in which interpretations are possible but concerning which there is no way to achieve certainty. The Qāḍī and other masters of ours, may God be pleased with him and them, have written books that cover the subject of the imamate exhaustively and in which a reasonable person will be completely satisfied – a sure guide for those who want to reach the end and comprehend it fully.

Our purpose in this handbook is to proclaim the basic principles of the topic and, accordingly, we cite those that are certain. With the aid of God, we distinguish those that are subject to the interpretations of experts from those that are of conclusive certainty. This arrangement requires us first to offer some comments concerning the oral traditions and their relative values since they are the foundation on which the imamate was established.

Section
On the Various Categories of Reports in the Tradition

If someone makes the following request: State first exactly what a report is and then indicate the various categories into which reports fall, we respond: A report is information about something that may be qualified as being either true or false. This characteristic distinguishes it from all other forms of discourse and modes of speech, such as a command, a prohibition, a plea, an inquiry or the like. None of these are qualified as conveying either the truth or a falsehood.

Moreover, narrative reports can be subdivided. Some are known conclusively to be true; others are known with certainty to be false; and yet others have the possibility of being judged to be either true or false. For the report the truth of which is a certainty, the information it conveys accords with the thing known definitively, either on the basis of necessity or a decisive proof. An example would be information reported about the objects of sensations that concord exactly to what they are and information related about anything known self-evidently. One also reaches this standard in respect to information reported about something known by reasoning when what is reported conforms to the thing known. What is known with certainty to be false is a report about something where what is reported does not conform, on the basis of either necessity or reason, to the thing known. An example would be information about objects of sensations that is not in conformity with the characteristic functions of the senses, or a report asserting that the world is eternal despite the existence of conclusive proofs of its temporal contingency. The information that is ambiguously uncertain consists of what admits to the possibility of being judged either negatively or positively.

Next there is a further subdivision and it is this we want to look at here. One part does not result in knowledge about what is reported, and the other does provide knowledge about what is reported. What yields knowledge about what it reports is the information reported by multiple and concordant informants. If these conditions [the multiplicity of concordant informants] are met and, if they are fulfilled completely, the knowledge it conveys about what it reports achieves self-evident certainty. By this kind of information, for example, we know about distant lands that we have never actually seen and about events and earlier peoples that do not exist in our own time. By it a person is able to distinguish his mother from other women. To deny this kind of knowledge is to deny the evidence and to place in doubt everything that is known by primary intuition.

Furthermore, information reported by multiple and concordant informants is not necessarily knowledge of the thing about which it reports in and of itself but is instead only a means leading to knowledge of the thing reported in the ordinary and habitual way things work. There is, however, a reasonable possibility that

God will interrupt the habitual pattern and not create the knowledge of the thing reported about, even though multiple and concordant informants report it. Likewise it is possible, contrary to the habitual order, that He create knowledge that is necessarily certain on the basis of a solitary report. But the habitual order of things, in accordance with what we have just said, is constant.

If some deviator wanted to risk causing trouble at this point, he might say: If none of the informants, taken in isolation one by one, conveys knowledge and, if combining the information reported by another person to the first reported does not alter the character of that report, as a result, the information conveyed in a collection of reports cannot supply more than is contained in a single isolated report. But this objection they would raise is worthless, since we explained carefully that information reported by multiple and concordant informants does not of necessity supply knowledge of the thing reported on, but it yields knowledge only in the ordinary course of things if and when this habitual order continues to exist. And the habitual course of things only exists, as we have mentioned, when we have information reported by a number of concordant informants. For example, in the ordinary course of things, it would not be inconceivable for a single individual to stand up at a predesignated moment. But, if someone reported that a considerable number or a crowd of people so numerous they could not be counted stood up without being in collusion or having an obvious need to do so or another motive prompting them to stand up *en masse*, one would know that this report is false because it runs counter to the habitual order of things. It is tantamount to a report that says the mountains have turned into gold or something else like this.

Moreover, the report of multiple and concordant informants comes with certain conditions. One is that the informants have certain knowledge of what they report, such as when they report on something they know by the senses or is known *a priori* in a way other than by the senses. If they report on what they came to know by reasoning or deduction, their information is not necessarily certain knowledge. Those who report that the world is temporally contingent exceed the number required for multiple and concordant informants but their information is not necessarily certain on that basis. However, whereas informants whose numbers are many and who attest to the existence of a country we have never seen must be acknowledged of necessity as reporting truthfully, this does not concern matters we would attempt to establish by induction or reflection or disjunction or deduction. Rather we are explaining here how knowledge comes to exist about a thing reported on in the normal course of things. We have seen that the habitual order is constant, as we said, in what is reported on the basis of necessity but not in regard to what is reported as a result of reasoning. Thus we follow here the rule of the normal order of things in determining negation or affirmation.

The second condition for a report to be multiple and concordant is that it emanate from a group of persons whose number exceeds the level where one might customarily suspect collusion or where, if they were in collusion, their collusion would have been revealed over the course of time. We would not fix a specific minimum number of informants but we know that every number stipulated in the law for corroborating witnesses should be exceeded in the case of the number of informants. The maximum number for witnesses in the law is four. Therefore, we know conclusively that the information of four informants does not yield certain knowledge of the thing about which they report, since if it were to yield certain knowledge, the judge, when presented with the testimony of the witnesses, would necessarily have to acknowledge their veracity, but the matter is not like this.

Furthermore, it seems preferable to me not to consider knowledge to be comprised by the reporting of five also, since in regard to witnesses in the court of the judge, even if they sought out the testimony of a fifth or a sixth, it would not produce certain knowledge of what they reported. We cannot set a minimum limit for the number of informants, since the law, just as it specifies the number of witnesses, specifies accordingly only that the number be greater than for the witnesses.

If those who seek precision ask for an exact rule, let them suppose a case where there is a single report about an object of sensation, then two reports and so on increasing progressively in number. All the while he continues to be aware of doubts and uncertain probabilities until the moment when the matter finally reaches certain knowledge. When he attains a perception at that level, all doubt about it ceases and he obtains a number for the informants and can judge the minimum number for sufficient multiplicity. Thereafter, we apply what we have just mentioned about the truthful informants who report about what they know on the basis of necessity. If a similar number does not conform to that required for certain knowledge, it is due to the interspersing of a few liars who reduce the number below the minimum necessary for unimpeachable testimony. The scope of this discussion is, however, too broad for us to go into it at this point.

Moreover, if the informants relate what they have seen and what they know for certain without an intermediary, the situation is the same as that we have just indicated. If, on the other hand, they recount what they have heard from others and those others relate from yet others before them and the ages follow successively and the reports become multiple while still concordant, certain knowledge of the matter aimed at by the information provided does not result unless there is parity at both ends of the series of informants and all of their intermediaries. What this means is that those reporting on the matter at the earliest end of the series reach the number required for multiple testimony, and likewise for the informants reporting from them and so on until the information reaches us. If any of the conditions for multiple testimony should be unfulfilled at the beginning or at the end or in-between, one cannot obtain the knowledge that the report aimed to convey from the information reported.

It is not a condition of multiple testimony that all the informants be irreproachable, nor that they be believers, since if there were multiple reports given by unbelieving informants concerning their own country to the effect that their king had been slain, we can be sure that they are telling the truth. If they were to provide this information about the farthest reaches of their lands, we could be certain of their having reported the truth if and when the conditions for multiplicity of testimony are met. It is also not essential for the informants to be from different regions because, even if the inhabitants of a single town provide us information, provided that they constitute a quite numerous group, we can be sure they are telling the truth, even if they all reside in the same town. For the same reason, it is not required that the informants include persons from a variety of religious communities because, if the inhabitants of Baghdad were to drive out of their midst all the protected minorities and then report about an event that happened afterward, we could be certain of their veracity, even though all of them belong to the same religion. For the same reason, it is known also that the informants may be members of minorities who are under protection.

Our purpose in indicating that the conditions we have just mentioned need not be met is to refute the Jews who often insist that such conditions are required. They attempt thereby to belittle our affirmation of the miracles of our Prophet, God bless him and keep him. This fulfils our purpose with respect to the subject of the information in reports from multiple informants.

A report that does not attain the level required to obtain the status of multiple testimony does not provide certain knowledge in itself, unless there is associated with it something that necessitates its being regarded as true, such as a concurring rational proof or a corroborating miracle or a statement whose truth is corroborated by a miracle. It is the same when a nation accepts some information and agrees unanimously that it is true. We know accordingly that it is true. If what we have outlined is lacking or if the reported information is not from sufficiently numerous informants, it is called an isolated report in the idiom of the theologians, even if it was related by a group of people.

One of the things the imamate is based on is decisive knowledge of the validity of the consensus of the community but this is a matter we are not interested in pursuing here. We outlined, in a book entitled, *The Summary of the Principles of Law*,[1] a proof of the validity of the consensus. We should, nevertheless, strengthen this handbook by adding a decisive confirmation that the consensus is valid, following up on our intention to supply conclusive proofs for each and every point. Therefore we say here:

If the scholars of all the cities are in accord on a legal decision and have declared it certain, that judgment must be either merely probable without reaching certainty or it has reached certainty. If it has attained certainty on account of their mutual agreement, that is what we want here. If it is merely probable without a way to know it with certainty, it is impossible, in the ordinary course of things, for the scholars, by methods involving probability or preponderance,

---

1 *Kitāb al-talkhīṣ fī uṣūl al-fiqh.*

to consider it certain knowledge, even if they all agree to it without any group of them raising the slightest doubt or being disturbed with misgivings about it. But that would truly be an extraordinary event.

Someone may inquire: What if the scholars split into two factions, one permitting a thing as licit and the other forbidding it as illicit and yet each faction exceeds in number the amount required for multiple testimony and each is determined to follow its own beliefs? We reply: If the question allows for different opinions, then each of the factions should admit that their belief is merely probable. We are here discussing only the consensus of the scholars about the conclusiveness of something probable and that is something undoubtedly extraordinary.

If someone says: In the example you have just cited, you would make the consensus of the scholars a proof of their own veracity, we respond: The law imposes on us the obligation to base beliefs on the proofs of reason. Even though consensus leads to certain knowledge in the normal course of things which is usually constant, that it is susceptible to being interrupted is considered a rational possibility. Therefore, it is necessary, in fulfilling what is imposed on us, to search for rational proofs. Moreover, they are diverse and only a proficient expert comprehends how to apply them. Numerous sophistical and fanciful notions get in the way from which one cannot escape except by the grace of God. Conclusive proofs based on tradition have not proliferated in so many directions but are clear declarations with a fixed source and form that are conclusive and such certainty cannot be obtained otherwise. When therefore we find the scholars in agreement about the certainty of a matter, despite the certainty having been established in a unique manner, we are sure conclusively that they speak the truth.

My own opinion is that the consensus of the scholars of all nations in regard to their decisions follows the general rule we posed here for the requirements of certain knowledge in accord with the normal constancy of things. This is the best and most convincing solution. We will develop this concept more fully in the book called the *Shāmil,* God willing. We will then mention the various excellent methods used in obtaining consensus, if God, the Mighty and Glorious, so wills. This is now the place to look closely at the imamate.

Section
On the Denial of Succession to the Imamate by Designation and the Affirmation of Election

The Imāmiyya maintain that the Prophet, God bless him and keep him, designated ʿAlī, on whom be peace, to assume the imamate after himself and that the person who was actually invested took office unjustly by arrogating to himself the right of ʿAlī.

We demand of them the following: Do you have knowledge that the designation really existed or do you merely consider it to have been possible? If you know it as a fact, by what means did you attain it? Reason does not require the designation of a specific person. If they base the knowledge they claim to have on a transmitted report, it may be said to them: Reports comprise those that are multiple and concordant and those considered isolated. The designation you claim was not transmitted by multiple informants and an isolated report cannot yield knowledge that is certain. By which method then do you claim to have knowledge of the designation? The Imāmiyya agree, moreover, that isolated reports do not entail the necessity of the act, let alone yield knowledge that is certain.

If someone were arbitrarily to raise an objection here and claim that there exist multiple and concordant reports and therefore necessary knowledge of the designation in favour of ʿAlī, may God be pleased with him, that is simply an absurd contrivance of the kind that seems to be common with the Shīʿa. It is necessary to oppose them at once by countering their claim to designation with the decision in favour of Abū Bakr, may God be pleased with him. Moreover, there is no doubt that the community, with the exception of the Imāmiyya, determined that such a designation did not exist. Knowledge that is absolutely certain about the community's agreement that it did not exist would be obtainable from a less numerous multitude of persons even than those who do not share the opinion of the Imāmiyya on this issue. If one were allowed to reject the evidence about this, it would be possible for a group to deny the existence of Baghdad, Basra, farthest China and other places. That is so obviously clear it need not be explained.

If someone now says: You have furnished a decisive proof that precludes the Imāmiyya from claiming a designation. Do you, however, know for certain that there was no designation in favour of ʿAlī, on whom be peace, or do you have some doubt about it? We respond: If the Imāmiyya insist on an open designation in favour of ʿAlī, on whom be peace, given in the presence of the Prophet's Companions and an assembled throng of people, we know for certain that this claim is false. A matter of such overwhelming significance could not remain hidden during the normal course of things, as, for example, was the appointment by the apostle of God, God bless him and keep him, of Muʿādh to govern Yemen, likewise for Zayd and Usāma, the son of Zayd, whom he entrusted with governing and put them in command of the armies, and those he authorized to collect taxes. Similarly, the appointment by Abū Bakr of ʿUmar was quite obvious, as was ʿUmar's creation of a council of Companions to decide the next succession. If we were to consider it possible that such openly public matters could have been kept concealed, we cannot be sure that the Qurʾān itself was not opposed and then subsequently the fact that this opposition once existed was kept hidden. Every principle relative to the imamate which reverts to declaring the prophetic mission itself false is itself certainly to be rejected as false.

Thus what they would insist was a designation widely and publicly recognized and not merely alleged could not possibly have been kept secret and not spoken about incessantly, particularly in the era of the Companions of the Apostle of God, God bless him and keep him, and its proximity to the claimed designation. It would be known if there had been disagreement about the choice for the imamate on the Day of the Saqīfa.

If they insist, on the contrary, that the designation was concealed and not made public, we know for sure that there is no way to ascertain this fact, but accordingly that it is proven to be false because there exists unanimous agreement of the community against it and this consensus has a probative force that is decisive. On the basis of this, we avert the question of those who say: Although an isolated report does not guarantee knowledge that is certain, it may still impose the obligation of a practice. Hence you should follow the report we have related. We reply: What you related we cannot possibly accept. In our view, the most favourable status we can accord you is that of people who have fallen into error but most of you are merely unbelievers. How can you demand that we accept the information you report when we do not doubt that you will not accept our reports. Moreover, the unanimous agreement of the community ought more properly to be acted on and it supports a view quite opposite to what you claim in regard to the era of the Companions of the Apostle of God, God bless him and keep him.

Among the Imāmiyya there are some who shamelessly assert a claim that the designation was conclusive and was not a matter of interpretation. They hold strongly to isolated reports that are unsubstantiated. One report, as an example, is related of the Prophet, God bless him and keep him, that he said: "I am dearer to the believers than they themselves. Of whosoever I am the master, ʿAlī is his master." We respond: This is one of the isolated reports and, furthermore, it is unacknowledged because it may be construed in various ways, since "master" [*mawlā*] is an ambiguous term. It may mean "guardian" or it may mean "protector". The latter is the most obvious meaning for it but it might be understood also as "emancipator". The sense in the *ḥadīth* is, "of whosoever I am his protector, ʿAlī is his protector." The proof is that [the Prophet] did not assign that role [to ʿAlī] after his death but rather solely in regard to matters of the moment when it was uttered. But there is no doubt that ʿAlī was never in charge of affairs during the lifetime of the Prophet, God bless him and keep him. This *ḥadīth* has been the subject of considerable discussion by various people and most of it is mere verbiage. What we have just said, however, ought to be sufficiently convincing.

Frequently, also they invoke in this regard what was related from the Prophet, God bless him and keep him, that he said to ʿAlī: "You are to me what Aaron was to Moses." But there is no proof in this statement of their contention because it was said for a particular reason which is that, when the Prophet, God bless him and keep him, was preparing for the Tabūk raid, he delegated ʿAlī, may God be pleased with him, to look after Madina. However, it grieved ʿAlī to be separated from the Apostle of God, God bless him and keep him. Thereupon the Apostle said to him these words indicating that he occupied the place of Aaron relative to Moses in rank order as long as Moses should live, but Aaron was never in charge after the death of Moses, since he instead died in the desert before Moses.

Moreover, we can offer in opposition to what they have mentioned nearly equivalent reports that are designations in favour of Abū Bakr and ʿUmar, may God be pleased with them both. One of them is the Prophet's, God bless him and keep him, delegation of Abū Bakr to lead prayers. Thereafter he exclaimed: "God and the Muslims insisted on Abū Bakr." He repeated it three times. He said also: "Be led by those who come after me, Abū Bakr and ʿUmar." It is not our intention here to relate every one of these *ḥadīths* since you can find them in books.

At this point, having proven that designation did not exist, there remains only election. Its proof is the unanimous consensus of the community since it has been in effect over the course of several centuries and no objection has been raised to this principle by the scholars.

Section
On Election, Its Characteristics, and How the Imamate is to be Invested

Know that universal consensus is not required for investiture to the imamate but rather the imamate may be validly invested, even if the community does not agree on conferring it. What proves this is that, as soon as the imamate was conferred on Abū Bakr, he set about implementing the regulations governing the Muslims without waiting for the news to reach those of the Companions in far off territories. However, no one raised an objection and none suggested that he should have delayed. If consensus is not a condition for the investiture to the imamate, a number may not be fixed nor limit defined. Thus the applicable rule is that the imamate may be invested on the basis of a single competent person's conferring it.

One of our associates said that the investiture must take place in the presence of witnesses since, if this were not one of the conditions, we would have no assurance against someone claiming to have been invested with it in secret prior to making a public proclamation of it. The imamate is not less significant than a marriage for which a public proclamation is required. That, however, is not altogether decisive, in my opinion, since reason does not attest to it and it is not proven on the basis of a preemptory tradition.

Chapter: [*On investing the imamate in two individuals*]

Our associates agree on precluding the investing of two different individuals with the imamate at either end of the world. But, they add: If it should happen that two different persons were invested with the imamate, that would be analogous to the situation of two guardians contracting a marriage for the same woman to two different suitors without either being aware of the other's contract. The decision in the matter rests on the application of jurisprudence. My opinion on this issue is that investiture of two individuals with the imamate in a single locality within relatively restricted boundaries and limited provinces is not permitted and the investiture should be in accord with a consensus. But, when the distances are great and the two imams quite remote from each other, there is room to allow it, although this cannot be established conclusively.

Chapter: [*On deposing the imam*]

A person invested with the imamate on the basis of one person's investiture validly holds the imamate and it is not possible to depose him in the absence of new events or a change in the situation. This is universally agreed upon. If he should commit acts of impiety or inequity and cease, because of his impiety, to have the qualities commensurate with the imamate, he may divest himself without being deposed, provided his resigning and the possibility of deposing him has not been decided on and is not regarded as allowable. Correcting his behaviour is allowed also if a means can be found to accomplish that. All of this is, in our view, subject to the scrutiny of specialists. Understand it well!

An imam may voluntarily depose himself without cause also. What is related about the resignation of al-Ḥasan, on whom be peace, may be understood as due to his realization of his own personal inability, or one may attribute it to some other cause.

Chapter: On the qualifications for the imamate

A condition for the imamate is that the person be one of those who are legal experts in that he has no need to seek legal advice from others about events that arise. This is agreed upon by all. Another condition for the imamate as well is that the imam apply himself to the betterment and direction of public affairs. He should be capable of organizing armies and defending the frontiers and be endowed with perceptive discrimination in examining the activities of the Muslims, not being restrained by personal complaisance or natural weakness from imposing capital punishment or other chastisement on those who deserve these penalties. These things we have cited should be combined as qualifications in the person holding the office and this is stipulated by the unanimous agreement of the community.

One of its conditions, in the view of our associates, is that the imam be a member of the Quraysh, since the apostle of God, God bless him and keep him, said, "The imams should be from Quraysh", and he said also, "Put the Quraysh ahead of the people and do not put anyone ahead of them." There is, however, some disagreement among the people over this and I personally believe there is room to construe the matter in different ways. Only God knows the truth for sure.

That the imam must be free and Muslim cannot be doubted. No woman can be the imam by universal agreement even though there exists a disagreement about the permissibility of a woman serving as judge [*qāḍī*] in cases where her testimony is allowed.

Section

Our Doctrine Affirms the Imamate of Abū Bakr, ʿUmar, ʿUthmān, and ʿAlī, May God be Pleased with Them All

The imamate of Abū Bakr, may God be pleased with him, was established by the unanimous agreement of the Companions, since they all proclaimed their allegiance to him and submitted to his authority, even those to whom the Shīʿa trace their allegation of lying as well as the others. Thus Abū Dharr, ʿAmmār, Ṣuhayb and others of those whom one cannot reproach on the part of God arrayed themselves under his command without exception. ʿAlī, may God be pleased with him, submitted to him and followed his orders, diligently pursuing the raid against the Banū Ḥanīfa, and taking pleasure in a young girl captured in the booty taken from them.

The lies the Shīʿa tell in this matter concerning the petulance and resistance he manifested at the moment of pledging allegiance are outright falsehoods. It is true that he, may God be pleased with him, was not at the meeting at the Saqīfa and was then by himself, overcome with grief on account of the Apostle of God, God bless him and keep him. But subsequently he joined in what the rest of the people were doing and gave his allegiance to Abū Bakr in the midst of many witnesses.

If someone says: Prove that Abū Bakr fulfilled the conditions for the imamate, we respond: There are two avenues to follow in this regard. One is to be content with citing the unanimous agreement of the community to his imamate. If he were not fit for it, they would not have agreed on ascribing it to him. If we go into the details, and this constitutes the second method, we note that among the conditions for the imamate, according to certain groups, is that the imam be a member of the Quraysh. Abū Bakr, may God be pleased with him, came from the very heart of that tribe. Another of its conditions is knowledge and we know with all certainty that he was one of the most expert among the Companions and was their jurisconsult. No one protested when he undertook to indicate what is licit or illicit. As for piety we have absolute assurance of it during the time of the Prophet, God bless him and keep him, and it is known to have continued afterward since there existed no one of whom reliable information is available who was critical of him. The unanimous agreement of the Companions to his imamate, despite their propensity to examine carefully matters involving religion, is the most authentic proof of his piety. His piety, moreover, has been conveyed to us even more assuredly than the generosity of Ḥātim or the bravery of ʿAmr b. Maʿdīkarib[1]

---

1 ʿAmr b. Maʿdīkarib b. ʿAbdallāh al-Zubaydī (d. 21/641) was a famous Arab warrior-poet. See "ʿAmr b. Maʿdīkarib" in the *EI2*.

and others. Thus the matter is simply incontestable. As for his sagacity and proficiency, these are well attested by his actions and are amply demonstrated in the accounts of his life.

In regard to ʿUmar, ʿUthmān, and ʿAlī, may God be pleased with them, the method of confirming their imamates and proving that they each fulfilled the conditions for the imamate is like that for the imamate of Abū Bakr. All of the conclusive proofs in this matter depend on reports related by multiple and concordant informants and on the universal agreement of the community. Our aim now, however, is to be brief. If an intelligent person considers it carefully, what we have said should suffice to assure him that there is here as much as could possibly be required.

The appointment by Abū Bakr of ʿUmar, may God be pleased with them both, his having made him the heir designate, and ʿUmar's leaving the matter of further succession to a council without any one raising an objection to either act constitutes in itself a unanimous agreement of the community to the validity of doing the same in all later periods. One need not pay attention to those who maintain that no consensus obtained in regard to the imamate of ʿAlī, may God be pleased with him, since his imamate was not what was contested; the unrest that was stirred up arose over other matters.

Chapter: [*On the imamate of the less qualified and the relative superiority of the Companions*]

Someone may ask: Were some of the Companions superior to others or would you avoid considerations of superiority? We reply: The purpose in raising this issue aims at precluding the imamate of the less qualified. The majority of the Sunnī Muslims hold that the imamate should be reserved for the most qualified person of the time unless designating him leads to troubles and the outbreak of violent struggle. It is permissible thus to designate the less qualified person, if he is otherwise fit to occupy the imamate. But this question does not allow opinions that have conclusive certainty. Those who would preclude the imamate of the less qualified have nothing to hold on to except isolated reports that concern specific imamates other than the ones we are speaking about here. Such is the case with the Prophet's, God bless him and keep him, statement: "Take as your imam the one of you who has read the most." This statement and others like it do not lead to decisive certainty. How could they, given that, if a person of lesser qualifications were to conduct the prayers, his leading the prayers is still valid, even though the more appropriate person is avoided in so doing? This is our doctrine in regard to the imamate of the less qualified.

Furthermore, there exists, in our opinion, no conclusive proof of the superiority of some of the imams over the others, since reason does not attest to it and the reports that have been transmitted about their virtues are so disparate that apprehending the superior in this regard makes it impossible to preclude the imamate of the less qualified. Nevertheless, it is highly probable that Abū Bakr, may God be pleased with him, was the most excellent person of all after the apostle, God bless him and keep him. Next the most excellent of them was ʿUmar. Opinions vary in regard to ʿUthmān and ʿAlī. It has been related from ʿAlī, may God be pleased with him, that he said: "The best of the people after their prophet is Abū Bakr, then ʿUmar, and then after these two only God knows who is the best of them." These are his words which we reproduce here to avoid uncritical belief and to follow the plainest truth possible.

Chapter: [*On the unjust killing of ʿUthmān*]

The killing of ʿUthmān, may God be pleased with him, was unjust since he was the imam. The rules under which killing is required are firmly defined according to the scholars. Nothing comprised in them justified killing him. Moreover, those responsible for killing him were the riff-raff, hooligans, a mixed crowd from all over the place, an odd assortment of men of the lowest kind, such as al-Tujībī,[2] al-Ashtar al-Nakhaʿī,[3] and those vile men from Khuzāʿa. Even for a person whose killing is justified, it was not up to the like of these men to do it. Thus there can be no doubt but that he was killed unjustly.

Chapter: [*On the calumny of the Companions*]

The calumnies against the leading Companions have multiplied and the most monstrous of them are the accusations and lies of the Shīʿa. But a believer is under a firm obligation to acknowledge that the principal Companions derived from the Apostle of God, God bless him and keep him, an enviable position and superior rank. There was not one of them who was not made fortunate and blessed by him. Passages of the Holy Book bear witness to their irreproachability, and to the approval of them all as expressed in connection with the oath of al-Raḍwān. Related textual evidence also bestows high praise on both the Emigrants and the Helpers.

It is thus right that every true believer should associate them with the position they each held during the time of the Apostle, God bless him and keep him. If some failing is reported of them, let it be carefully scrutinized as to how and by whom it was transmitted. If it derives from a weak source, reject it; or if it appears firm but is based on an isolated report, it should not detract from what is already known on the basis of information supplied by multiple and concordant informants and is also corroborated by textual passages. Moreover, it is essential not to hold back the effort to explain all the information related, and

2 Kināna b. Bishr al-Tujībī (d. 38/658).

3 Mālik b. al-Ḥārith al-Nakhaʿī (d. 37 or 38/658) was a prominent supporter of ʿAlī. On him see "al-Ashtar" in the *EI2*.

no person of true faith can be sure that it does not exist. This then is the basic principle which thus allows us to forgo examining the details and speaking at length on this subject.

Chapter: [*On the rule regarding waging war against ʿAlī*]

ʿAlī b. Abī Ṭālib was the imam and was rightfully invested with it. Those who fought him were rebels. But the high regard they are owed obliges us to believe that they had the best of intentions, even if they were mistaken. ʿĀʾisha, may God be pleased with her, intended by going to Basra to calm the rebellion and put out the fires of conflict just as the blaze threatened to get out of control. And what happened thereafter happened.

None of the Companions was immune to error but God accorded them an excess of His bounty and generosity. How could immunity to error be a condition of any given human when it is not a condition of the imamate? One need not pay attention to the claims of those among the Imāmiyya who assert that immunity to error is a condition of the imamate since reason allows no such stipulation. Every attempt they make to affirm the impeccability of the imam obliges them to uphold the impeccability of all his governors, judges and tax collectors.

Here then, may God grant you His mercy and improve your spirits, are the conclusive proofs that support our religious beliefs. The novice will be content with only a little in it and the advanced student will conceive through it a yearning to read the most celebrated works. The task is thus completed with the assistance of God and His support. Praise God whom we thank for His generosity; may God bestow His blessings on Muḥammad, the seal of all the prophets and the imam of all the apostles of God, and on his family, the chaste ones, and on his most honoured Companions, and peace everlasting.

Here ends, thanks to God, the Exalted, the book of "Guidance to the Conclusive Proofs for the Principles of Belief", dictated by the leading master, the Pillar of Islam, Abu'l-Maʿālī ʿAbd al-Malik b. ʿAbdallāh b. Yūsuf al-Juwaynī, may God be pleased with him.

Translated by Paul E. Walker

Bibliography

Allard, Michel, *Le Problème des attributs divins dans la doctrine d'al-Aš^carī et de ses premiers grands disciples*. Beirut, 1965.

Anawati, Georges C., "Kalām", *Encyclopedia of Religion*, ed. Mircea Eliade. New York: Macmillan Publishing Co., 1987.

Al-Ashʿarī, Abu'l-Ḥasan, *Maqālāt al-islāmiyyīn*, ed. H. Ritter, Istanbul, 1929–30; *Risālat istiḥsān al-khawd fī ʿilm al-kalām*, ed. with English translation by Richard J. McCarthy in *The Theology of Al-Ashʿarī*. Beirut, 1953.

Boyle, J. A., ed., *The Cambridge History of Iran: vol. 5, The Saljuq and Mongol Periods*. Cambridge University Press, 1968.

Bulliet, Richard W., *The Patricians of Nishapur: A Study in Medieval Islamic Social History*. Cambridge: Harvard University Press, 1972.

EI2=*The Encyclopaedia of Islam*, New Edition. Leiden: Brill, 1960.

Esquer, G., "M. Dominique Luciani", *Revue Africaine* 73 (1932), pp. 161–81.

Frank, Richard M., *Beings and Their Attributes*. Albany: State University of New York Press, 1978.

—*Creation and the Cosmic System*. Heidelberg, 1992.

—*The Metaphysics of Created Being*. Istanbul, 1966.

Gardet, Louis and M. M. Anawati, *Introduction à la théologie musulmane: essai de théologie comparée*. Paris, 1948.

Gimaret, D., "Muʿtazila", *EI2*.

Hallaq, Wael B., *Law and Legal Theory in Classical and Medieval Islam*. Aldershot: Variorum, 1994.

Halm, Heinz, "Der Wesir Al-Kundurī und die Fitna von Nīšāpūr", *Die Welt des Orients* 6 (1970–71), pp. 205–33.

Ibn ʿAsākir, Abu'l-Qāsim ʿAlī b. al-Ḥasan, *Tabyīn kadhib al-muftarī fīmā nusiba ilā al-imām Abi'l-Ḥasan al-Ashʿarī*. Damascus, 1928.

Ibn al-Athīr, *al-Kāmil fi'l-taʾrīkh*, ed., Tornberg. Leiden, 1853–67. Beirut reprint, 1965–67.

Ibn Khaldūn, *Muqaddima*, ed. M. Quatremere. Paris, 1858. English translation, *The Muqaddimah: An Introduction to History*, by Franz Rosenthal, 3 vols. New York: Bollingen Foundation, 1958.

Ibn Khallikān, *Wafayāt al-aʿyān*, ed. Iḥsān ʿAbbās, Beirut, 1968. English translation M. De Slane, 4 vols, London, 1842–71.

Ibn Qudāma, *Taḥrīm al-naẓar fī kutab ahl al-kalām*. See Makdisi below.

Imām al-Ḥaramayn al-Juwaynī, *al-ʿAqīda al-niẓāmiyya*, ed. by Muḥammad al-Kautharī. Cairo, 1948.

—*al-Shāmil fī uṣūl al-dīn*, ed. by ʿAlī Sāmī al-Nashshār. Alexandria, 1969.

—*El-Irchad*, Arabic text edited with French translation by J. D. Luciani. Paris, 1938.

—*Kitāb al-irshād ilā qawāṭiʿ al-adilla fī uṣūl al-iʿtiqād*. Ed. by J. D. Luciani, Paris, 1938; by Muḥammad Yūsuf Mūsā and ʿAlī ʿAbd al-Munʿim ʿAbd al-Ḥamīd, Cairo, 1950; by Asad Tamīm, Beirut, 1985; and by Zakariyā ʿUmayrāt, Beirut, 1995.

—*Lumaʿ al-adilla fī qawāʾid ʿaqāʾid ahl al-sunna wa'l-jamāʿa*, ed. by Fawqiyya Husayn Maḥmūd, verified by Maḥmūd al-Khuḍayrī, Cairo, 1965.

McCarthy, Richard J., *The Theology of Al-Ashʿarī*. Beirut, 1953.

Makdisi, George, *Ibn Qudāmah's Censure of Speculative Theology*. London, 1962.

Nagel, Tilman, *Die Festung des Glaubens: Triumph und Scheitern des islamischen Rationalismus im 11. Jahrhundert*. Munich: Verlag C. H. Beck, 1988.

Stroumsa, Sarah, *Free thinkers of Medieval Islam: Ibn al-Rāwandī, Abū Bakr al-Rāzī, and Their Impact on Islamic Thought*. Leiden: Brill, 1999.

—"The Barāhima in Early kalam", *Jerusalem Studies in Arabic and Islam*, vol. 6, 1985.

al-Subkī, Tāj al-Dīn Abū Naṣr ʿAbd al-Wahhāb b. ʿAlī, *Ṭabaqāt al-shāfiʿiyya al-kubrā*, ed. by M. M. al-Ṭanāḥī and A. M al-Juluw. Cairo, 1967.

Vajda, G., "Comptes rendus [of *El-Irchad par Imam el-Haramein* by Luciani]", 1938. *Journal asiatique* 230 (1938) pp. 149–53.

Walker, Paul E., *Early Philosophical Shiism: The Ismaili Neoplatonism of Abū Yaʿqūb al-Sijistānī*. Cambridge: Cambridge University Press, 1993.

INDEX

A

Aaron 233
ʿAbd al-Ḥamīd, ʿAlī ʿAbd al-Munʿim xxxv
Abraham, and his son Ismail 107, 134–5, 185
abrogation [*naskh*] 134, 184–5
Abu'l-Hudhayl *see* al-ʿAllāf
Abū Bakr 188, 231–3, 234, 236–8
Abū Dharr 236
Abū Ḥanīfa xxii
Abū Lahab 125
Abū Sahl Muḥammad xxiii, xxv
accidents [*aʿrāḍ*] 11-16, 27–8, 34, 77, 93, 95, 112, 118, 119, 128, 204
Adam 86-7, 91, 207
al-ʿAdl [the Just], name of God 83
the afterlife [*al-ākhira*] 206
Ahriman 140, 150
aḥwāl = modes
ʿĀʾisha 176, 239
ʿajz = impotence or incapacity 167–72
al-Ākhir [the Last], name of God 86
al-Akhṭal 60
ālām = suffering
ʿAlī b. Abī Ṭālib 192, 231–3, 236–9
al-ʿAlīm [the Omniscient], name of God 82
al-ʿAllāf, Abu'l-Hudhayl 53
Allāh, name of God 80
Alp Arslan xxiv
ʿAmmār 236
al-amr biʾl-maʿrūf = commanding the good
ancient [*qadīm*] 20, 77
the Ancients 3, 197
the Anthropomorphists 24, 197
appropriation [*kasb*], also performance 118
al-ʿAqīda al-niẓāmiyya xxvi
ʿaql = intellect
al-Ashʿarī, Abu'l-Ḥasan ʿAlī b. Ismāʿīl xxi, xxii, xxviii, xxx, xxxiii, 8, 19, 51, 59, 67, 124
Ashʿarites xxiii, xxviii, xxix
al-Ashtar al-Nakhmī 238
asmāʾ = names
atoms [*jawhar, jawāhir*] 11–16, 19, 22, 24, 26, 27–8, 34, 47, 49, 56, 76, 77, 93, 94, 95, 112, 119, 128, 204
attributes [*ṣifa, ṣifāt*] 87–8, 91
  attributes of self 19–35, 45
  attributes, qualifying 19, 36–77
aʿwāḍ = compensation
al-Awwal [the First], name of God 86
āyā = prophetic sign
the Azāriqa 211
al-ʿAzīz [the Mighty], name of God 81

B

badā = change of mind
al-Badīʿ [the Originator], name of God 86
Baghdādī Muʿtazilites xxix, 37, 158, 161, 162, 209, 215
Baghdad xxi, xxiii, xxiv, 229, 231
al-Bāhilī, Abu'l-Ḥasan xxi
the Bahshamiyya 98
al-Bāʿith, [the Resurrector], name of God 85
the Bakriyya 150, 152
the Balance [*al-mīzān*] 208
al-Balkhī al-Kaʿbī, Abu'l-Qāsim xxix, xxx, 14, 21, 37, 39, 40, 42, 54, 55, 98, 143
al-Bāqillānī, *qāḍī* Abū Bakr xxix, 37, 76, 172, 223, 225
the Barāhima 144, 165, 169
al-Bāriʾ [the Creator], name of God 82

al-Barr, name of God 86
al-Baṣīr [the All-seeing], name of God 83
Basra 231, 239
Basran Muʿtazilites xxix, xxx, 14, 21, 37, 39, 40, 42, 54, 55, 117, 157, 158, 162, 163, 164, 209, 215
al-Basāsīrī xxiv
al-Bāṭin [the Latent], name of God 86
al-Bāṭiniyya 23
Bayhaq xxi
the Bridge [*al-ṣirāṭ*] 208
al-Bukhārī, Muḥammad b. Ismāʿīl, his "Book of Commentary on the Qurʾān" in *al-Ṣaḥīḥ* 90
al-Burhān fī uṣūl al-fiqh xxv
Bushtaniqān xx, xxv
Byzantines 29, 30

C
capacity [*istiṭāʿa*] 118–40
Chaghrī Beg xxiv
change of mind [*badāʾ*] 186
Christians xxxi, 28–30, 72
commanding the good [*al-amr bi'l-maʿrūf*] 202–3
commemoration [*dhikr*] 73
the Companions 188, 231, 232, 234, 236–9
compensation [*aʿwāḍ*] 141, 149, 152, 161
contingency 11–16
contrition [*tawba*] 154, 213, 220–4

D
Dawn [al-Falaq] 175–6
designation [*naṣṣ*] (of the imamate) 231–3
Determinists 118
Dharwān, well of 176
difference [*mukhālafa*] 21–4
doubt [*shakk*] 9
the Dualists 150, 152
al-Durra al-muḍiya fīmā waqaʿa fīhi al-khilāf bayna al-Shāfiʿiyya wa'l-Ḥanafiyya xxvi

E
election [*ikhtiyār*] (to the imamate) 231–5
the Emigrants [*al-Muhājirūn*] 116, 238
the Esotericists xxxi, 23
essence [*dhāt*] 19–20, 22–3
eternity [*qadam, qadīm*] 17, 20, 34, 45
existence [*wujūd*] 19–20

F
faith [*īmān*] 107, 217–19
fallacy [*shubha*] 5
al-Fārābī xxvii
al-Farāhidī, Khalīl b. Aḥmad 81
fāsiq = impious
al-Fattāḥ [the Revealer], name of God 82
form [*ṣūra*] 14, 128
al-Furātī, Abu'l-Faḍl Aḥmad xxiii

G
Gabriel 74
al-Ghaffār [the Much Forgiving], name of God 82
al-Ghazzālī, Abū Ḥāmid Muḥammad xix, xx, xxxii
Ghiyāth al-umam fī iltiyāth al-ẓulam xxvi
the Ghulāt 150–1
God, the Maker 17–18
  as Creator 79–80
  attributes of 19–77
  His hands, eyes, face 86–91
  names of 78–86
  speech of 56–77
  vision of 92, 97–102
goodness and badness [*taḥsīn, taqbīḥ*] 141–56
the good and the best [*al-ṣalāḥ wa'l-aṣlaḥ*] 157–64
grace [*luṭf*] 132, 157, 158, 164
grace [*tawfīq*] 139–40

H
Ḥadīth 89–91
Ḥadīth, Partisans of 217
al-Ḥafīẓ [the Guardian], name of God 83
al-Ḥakam [the Judge], name of God 83
al-Ḥakīm [the Sage], name of God 84
al-Ḥalīm [the Magnanimous], name of God 83
al-Ḥamīd [the Highly Praised], name of God 85
Ḥanafīs xxii
Ḥanīfa, Banū 236
al-Ḥaqq [the Real], name of God 85
Hārūt and Mārūt 176
al-Ḥasan, son of ʿAlī 235
al-Ḥashwiyya 24, 71
al-Ḥasīb [the Reckoner], name of God 84

Ḥātim al-Ṭāʾī 191–2, 236
hayūlā = prime matter
al-Ḥayy [the Living]
the Helpers [*al-Anṣār*] 116, 238
the Hijaz xxiii, xxiv
al-Ḥusayn b. Muʿādh, cemetery of xxv
hypostases 28–30

I
al-Ibāḍiyya 211
Iblīs 86, 176
Ibn al-ʿAbbās, ʿAbdallāh 85
Ibn Abī Sulma, Zuhayr, the poet 139
Ibn Aʿṣam, Labīd, the Jew 176
Ibn Fūrak, Abū Bakr Muḥammad xxi
Ibn al-Jubbāʾī, Abū Hāshim ʿAbd al-Salām xxix, xxx, 21, 42, 59, 93, 98, 117, 213, 222–3
Ibn Karrām, Muḥammad 24
Ibn Khaldūn, ʿAbd al-Raḥmān, his *Muqaddima* xx
Ibn Kullāb, ʿAbdallāh b. Saʿīd 66
Ibn Maʿdīkarb, ʿAmr 236
Ibn al-Rāwandī, Abu'l-Ḥusayn Aḥmad 186
Ibn Rushd xxvii
Ibn Ṣafwān, Jahm xxii, 54, 55
Ibn al-Ṣalt, Ghiyāth b. Ghawth, *see* al-Akhṭal
Ibn Thābit, Ḥasan 69
Ibn Ukht ʿAbd al-Wāḥid, Bakr 150
Ibn ʿUmar 176
ignorance [*jahl*] 4, 9
iʿjāz = rendering incapable
ikhtiyār = election
ilāhiyyāt = metaphysics
Imām al-Ḥaramayn xix
Imām al-Muwaffaq xxiii
imamate 202, 225, 231–9
the Imāmīs, Imāmiyya 57, 202, 232, 239
īmān = faith
impeccability [*ʿiṣma*] 193–4
the impious [*fāsiq*] 211, 217
Incoherence of the Philosophers (*Tahāfut al-falāsifa*) xxxii
infinity, infinities 15–16
intellect [*ʿaql*] 8–9
intercession [*shafāʿa*] 215–16
interpretation, allegorical, [*taʾwīl*] 25–6, 88–91
the ʿĪsawiyya, a Jewish sect 184, 194
al-Isfarāyīnī, Abū Isḥāq Ibrāhīm xxi, 21, 172, 181
his introduction to the *Jāmiʿ* 181
al-Isfarāyīnī, Abu'l-Qāsim ʿAbd al-Jabbār al-Iskāf xxi
ʿiṣma = impeccability
the Ismāʿīlīs xxxi, 23
Ismail, son of Abraham *see* Abraham

J
al-Jabbār [the Omnipotent], name of God 81
Jahm *see* Ibn Ṣafwān
al-Jalīl [the Great], name of God 84
jawhar = atom(s)
Jerusalem 218
Jesus 87, 174, 186, 187
Jews 134, 184, 185, 189, 229
the jinn 175–6
Joseph 191
al-Jubbāʾī xxix, xxx, 42, 68, 73, 117, 213
justice [*taʿdīl*] 141–56
al-Juwaynī, Abu'l-Ḥasan ʿAlī xxi
al-Juwaynī, Abu'l-Maʿālī ʿAbd al-Malik b. Muḥammad xix
lectures of 44
al-Juwaynī, Abū Muḥammad ʿAbdallāh b. Yūsuf xxi

K
Kaʿba 87
al-Kaʿbī, *see* al-Balkhī
al-Kāfiya fi'l-jadal xxvi
kalām = theology
karāmāt = marvels
al-Karīm [the Generous], name of God 84
the Karrāmiyya xxxi, 24, 26, 27, 55, 57, 217
kasb = performance
al-Khabīr [the Knowing], name of God 83
al-Khāfiḍ and al-Rāfiʿ [the One who diminishes and the One who raises], names of God 83
Khalīl *see* al-Farāhidī
al-Khāliq [the Creator], name of God 82
Khārijites, Khawārij 57, 209, 211, 217
khatm = sealing
Khūzistān xxx
Khurasan xx, xxi, xxv, xxx
Khuzāʿa 238

knowledge [*ʿilm*] 4, 8–10, 50, 53
kufr = unbelief
al-Kundurī, ʿAmīd al-Mulk xxii, xxiii, xxiv

L
al-Laṭīf [the Kind], name of God 83
law [*sharīʿa*] 5, 26–7, 79, 131, 141, 145, 161, 166, 184, 186, 202
Lotus of Paradise 74
Luciani, J. Dominique xxxv
Lumaʿ al-adilla fī qawāʾid ʿaqāʾid ahl al-sunna wa'l-jamāʿa xxvi
luṭf = grace

M
Magians [Majūs] 140
al-Majīd [The Glorious], name of God 85
al-Mājid [the Noble], name of God 85
al-Malik [Sovereign], name of God 80
Mālikī *madhhab* in law xxii
Manīʿī Mosque xxv
marvels [*karamāt*] 172–6
Mary, mother of Jesus 174
Mecca and Madina xix, xxiv, 233
messiah 29, 30, 72
metaphysics [*ilāhiyyāt*] 129
miracle(s) [*muʿjiza, muʿjizāt*] 6–7, 44, 63–4, 68, 70, 99, 132, 141, 145, 167, 168, 169, 180–3, 193, 229
modes [*aḥwāl*] xxx, 29, 46–8, 49, 50, 51, 56, 61, 79, 98, 106, 111, 112, 118
modes or manners of being [*akwān*] 11, 14
Moses 30, 70–1, 74, 101, 102, 186, 187, 189, 233
  his mother 175
motion 11–14, 33, 34
Muʿādh 232
al-Muʾakhkhir [the One who retards], name of God 86
al-Mubdiʾ [the Initiator], name of God 85
al-Mudhill [the One who humbles], name of God 83
Mughīth al-khalq fī tarjīḥ al-qawl al-ḥaqq xxvi
Muhammad 138, 174, 186, 187
al-Muhaymin [the Supervisor], name of God 81
al-Muḥṣī [the Numberer], name of God 85
al-Muḥyī [the Revivifier], name of God 85
al-Muʿīd [the Returner], name of God 85
al-Muʿizz [the One who gives power], name of God 83
al-Mujīb [the Answerer], name of God 84
al muʿjiza = miracle
al-Muʾmin, name of God 81
al-Mumīt [the Bringer of death], name of God 85
Munkar and Nakīr 206
al-Muqaddim [the One who advances], name of God 86
al-Muqaddir [the Regulator], name of God 86
al-Muqīt [the Provisioner], name of God 83
al-Muqsiṭ [the Equitable], name of God 86
al-Muqtadir [the All-powerful], name of God 86
the Murjiʾa 209
al-Muṣawwir [the Creator], name of God 82
Musaylama 190
Mūsā, Muḥammad Yūsuf xxxv
al-Mutakabbir [the Overwhelmer], name of God 82
muʿtaqad, muʿtaqadāt 2, 57, 69, 91, 94, 123, 129, 156, 160, 165, 182, 191, 194, 223, 224, 225
the Muʿtazilites xxii, xxiii, xxviii, xxix, xxx, xxxi, xxxiv, 4, 6, 8, 14–15, 19, 21–2, 27, 32, 39, 41, 46, 48–9, 52–4, 57–9, 61, 63, 67, 76–8, 93–4, 97–8, 101–3, 106–7, 109, 111, 113, 116–17, 119–28, 130–1, 133–4, 136–9, 141–4, 152–6, 160–4, 172, 176, 178, 184, 198–9, 201, 204–5, 207, 209–11, 213, 215, 217, 221

N
al-Najjār, Abū ʿAbdallāh al-Ḥusayn 37, 39, 40, 41, 42, 73, 98
the Najjāriyya 62
names and naming [*asmāʾ, tasmiya*] 78
names of God 78–86
naskh = abrogation
naṣṣ = designation
nature [*ṭabīʿa*] 17
Nihāyat al-maṭlab fī dirāyat al-madhhab xxvi

Nishapur xx, xxi, xxii, xxiii, xxiv, xxv, xxviii
Niẓām al-Mulk xxiv
Niẓāmiyya *madrasas* xxiv
Noah's ark 87, 190
al-Nūr [the Light], name of God 86

O
obligation [*taklīf*] 123–5
One, oneness [*waḥdāniyya*] 31

P
paradise and hellfire 207
perception(s) [*idrākāt*] 93–6, 96–102
performance [*kasb*] 105
perpetuity 76–7
Persia 194
Pharoah 206
Philosophers (al-Falāsifa) xx, xxvii, xxxii, 127–8
polytheism [*shirk*] 211, 213
the Pool [*al-ḥawḍ*] 208
power [*qudra*] 118–28
prices [*asʿār*] 201
prime matter [*hayūlā*] 14, 128
principles [*uṣūl*] xxxii
proof(s) [*adilla*] 5, 43–5, 48, 105, 177
proofs, conclusive [*qawāṭiʿ al-adilla*] xxxii
prophecy [*nubuwwa*] 165–75, 177–83, 184–94, 214
the Prophet 2, 163, 166, 167, 175, 176, 177, 179, 184–9, 206, 216, 218, 229, 231, 233, 236–7
prophetic challenge [*taḥaddī*] 6, 167, 171, 173, 187
prophetic signs [*āyā*] 6, 168, 191–2
punishment [*ʿiqāb*] 209, 210, 213
punishment of the grave 206

Q
al-Qābid and al-Bāsit [the Gatherer and the Spreader], names of God 83
the Qadariyya 107, 140
the Qāḍī *see* al-Bāqillānī
qadīm = ancient
al-Qādir [the Powerful], name of God 86
al-Qahhār [the Subduer], name of God 82
al-Qalānisī, Abuʾl-ʿAbbās Aḥmad b. ʿAbd al-Raḥmān 218
qawāṭiʿ al-adilla = proofs, conclusive
al-Qawī [the Strong], name of God 85
al-Qayyūm [the Self-subsisting], name of God 85
al-Quddūs [the Most Holy], name of God 80
qudra = power
the Qurʾān 57, 68, 69, 70, 89, 187, 188, 189, 190, 232
Quraysh 138, 235
al-Qushayrī, Abu'l-Qāsim xxiii

R
al-Raḍwān, oath of 238
al-Raḥmān al-Raḥīm, names of God 80
al-Raqīb [the Overseer], name of God 84
al-Rashīd [the Leader], name of God 86
al-Razzāq [the Provider], name of God 82
reason and reasoning [*naẓar*] 3–7, 25, 43, 53–4, 55, 75, 86, 87, 109–11, 143, 144, 147–9, 165, 221, 230
recitation [*qirāʾa*] 72–3
reciting [*inshād*] 73
reincarnation [*tanāsukh*] 141, 150–1
Reincarnation, Proponents of 151–3
rendering incapable [*iʿjāz*] 167–72
repentance [*tawba*] 154, 220–4
resurrection [*iʿāda*] 204–5
revelation [*inzāl*] 74
reward [*thawāb*] 157, 161, 209, 210
rizq = subsistence

S
al-Ṣabūr [the Very Patient], name of God 86
saintly marvels [*karāmāt*] *see* marvels
al-Salām [the Sound], name of God 80
al-Ṣāliḥī, Abuʾl-Ḥusayn 14
salsabīl 160
al-Ṣamad [the Impenetrable], name of God 85
al-Samīʿ [the All-hearing], name of God 83
samʿiyyāt = traditions
Saqīfa 232, 236
satan(s) [*shayāṭīn, shayṭān*] 175–6
al-Ṣaymarī, ʿAbbād b. Sulaymān 151
sealing [*khatm*] 115–17
shafāʿa = intercession
Shāfiʿīs xxi, xxii, xxiv, xxv
al-Shahīd [the Witness], name of God 85

al-Shakūr [the Grateful], name of God 83
al-Shāmil fī uṣūl al-dīn xxvi, 158, 183, 230
shayāṭīn, pl. of *shayṭān* = satan(s)
the Shīʿa xxiii, 150, 202, 236–9
shirk = polytheism
shubha = fallacy
Sifāʾ al-ghalīl fī bayān mā waqaʿa fi'l-Tawra wa'l-Injīl min al-tabdīl. xxvi
ṣifāt maʿnawiyya = attributes, qualifying
ṣifāt nafsiyya = attributes of self
similarity [*mithl, mumaththal*] 21–4
sin [*dhanb, kabīra, ṣaghīra*] 150, 213–15
sorcery [*siḥr*] 165, 175–6
soul [*nafs, rūḥ*] 207
speech [*kalām*] xxxi, 27, 435, 57–75
the spoiling of acts [*iḥbāṭ al-aʿmāl*] 209
al-Subkī, Tāj al-Dīn Abu'l-Naṣr xxv
subsistence [*rizq*] 199–200
Ṣuhayb 236
suffering [*ālām*] 149–52
Sufyān al-Thawrī 25
Sulaymān 176
Summary of the Principles of Law, by al-Juwaynī 229
Sunna 212, 215
supposition [*ẓann*] 9
sūra = form

T
Tabūk 233
taḥaddī = prophetic challenge
taklīf = obligation
tanāsukh = reincarnation
tawba = contrition, repentance
tawfīq = grace
taʾwīl = interpretation
al-Tawwāb [the Merciful], name of God 86
theology [*kalām*] xxvii
the threat [*al-waʿīd*] 211–13
the Tigris 173
time [awqāt] 20
time limits [*ājāl*] 197–8
the Torah 187
tradition(s) [*al-samʿ, khabar, akhbār*] 43, 53–4, 57, 75, 79, 86, 107, 131, 141, 143, 180, 195–6, 205, 206, 221, 225, 226–30
Ṭughril Beg, Saljuq sultan xxii, xxiii, xxiv
al-Tujībī 238

U
ʿUmar 232, 233, 236–8
unbelief [*kufr*] 211
Usāma, the son of Zayd 232
uṣūl = principles
ʿUthmān 69, 236–8

W
al-Wadūd [the Very Loving], name of God 84
al-Wahhāb [the Giver], name of God 82
al-Wāḥid [the Unique], name of God 85
al-waʿīd = the threat
al-Wājid [the Opulent], name of God 85
al-Wakīl [the Trustee], name of God 85
al-Walī [the Protector], name of God 85
Waraqāt xxv
al-Wārith [the Survivor], name of God 85
al-Wāsiʿ [the All-comprising], name of God 84
the word [*logos*] 28

Y
Yaḥyā 86
Yazdān 140, 150
Yemen 232

Z
al-Ẓāhir [the Patient], name of God 86
al-Zajjāj, Abū Isḥāq 84
Zakariyāʾ 174
Zaqqūm 160
Zayd 232
the Zaydīs 57

Appendix

Corrections to the Arabic text of the Cairo edition [of Imam al-Haramayn al-Juwayni's Irshad]

The following corrections are all based on the edition of Luciani:

On p. 67, line 5, add after الصفات :
وشرعنا في نصب القواطع على علم بثبوت الصفات.

On p. 176, line 2, add after البنية :

لجاز حمل السهو والذهول والآلام ونحوها على انتفاض البنية.

On p. 222, line 13, read قادر in place of قارد

On p. 237, line 3, read لاجتمعت in place of لا اجتمعب

On p. 257, line 2, read والتجوير in place of والتجويز

line 9, read والاعواض in place of والاعراض

On p. 259, line 13, read بان in place of بل

On p. 270, line 10, read غرته in place of عزته

On p. 292, line 3, read الدعة in place of الدعوة

line 11, read النفل in place of العقل

Between pages 293 and 294 add:

[تعالى لا continuing تعالى بعبده فهو حتم عليه فينبغي ان تقضوا بأن الرب يستوجب على شيء من أعماله]

On p. 296, line 11, read منا يتضرر in place of منا لا يتضرر

On p. 307, line 12, add after فلا يتصور ايضا :
منهم العجز عنه فانه انما يعجز عما يقدر عليه وان كانت المعجزة من قبيل مقدورات البشر فلا يتصور ايضا

On p. 308, line 16, add after البشر :
ولكن الوجه في ذلك ان تقول القدرة على هذه الحركات معجزات وهي من فعل الله تعالى وليست من مقدورات البشر

On p. 319, line 16, add after النبوة :
ووقوع الكرامة دون ادعاء النبوة

On p. 343, line 2, read واستزلوا in place of واستذلوا
line 5, read فلتتأبد in place of فلتتأيد
line 12 read وأدمنًا in place of وأدمينا

On p. 349, line 12, read مختل in place of مخيلا

On p. 363, line 13, add after تقدير :
تغيير

line 15, add after تعالى :
بشريطة ثم تؤل الصحيفة في مآلها الى موجب علم الله تعالى

On p. 373, line 11, read الباقي in place of الباري

On p. 383, line 12, add after يجب :
أن يكون

line 15, add after النعم :
فاذا لم يعد ثبوت النعم مشوبة بالنقم

On p. 387, line 11, add after بطاعته :
عارفا

On p. 388, line 9, read التعمد in place of العمد
line 10, read فيجزئه in place of فيجرئه